PEANUT

John Cecil

AuthorHouse™ UK Ltd.
1663 Liberty Drive
Bloomington, IN 47403 USA
www.authorhouse.co.uk
Phone: 0800.197.4150

© 2013 by John Cecil. All rights reserved.

No part of this book may be reproduced, stored in a retrieval system, or transmitted by any means without the written permission of the author.

Published by AuthorHouse   05/24/2013

ISBN: 978-1-4685-7858-4 (sc)
ISBN: 978-1-4685-7859-1 (hc)
ISBN: 978-1-4685-7860-7 (e)

Any people depicted in stock imagery provided by Thinkstock are models, and such images are being used for illustrative purposes only.
Certain stock imagery © Thinkstock.

Because of the dynamic nature of the Internet, any web addresses or links contained in this book may have changed since publication and may no longer be valid. The views expressed in this work are solely those of the author and do not necessarily reflect the views of the publisher, and the publisher hereby disclaims any responsibility for them.

To Corena and Darren
And to my Sister, Christine.

In memory of my Mother,
Lilian Annie Orr (1925-2010)

In loving memory of my Dear Grandson,
Dylan John David Cecil.

Tragically taken from us on August 19th
2012 at Burnham on sea,
Aged 4

Shine bright like a Diamond.

Eternal Father, strong to save

Whose arm hath bound the restless wave.

Who bidd'st the mighty ocean deep

Its own appointed limits keep

Oh hear us when we cry to thee

For those in peril on the sea.

(William Whiting)

ACKNOWLEDGMENTS

Some information within this book sourced from "The Boatswain's Manual" by William A. Mcleod and revised by Captain A.G.W.Miller.

"School for Seamen—Gravesend" by Roy Derham MBE.

The National Sea Training School-trainee's handbook (1968).

Many thanks to Tom Quayle for the cover picture. It is of the "Anco Princess" Sister ship to the "Anco Empress" taken in the Mississippi (circa 1974).

A big thank you to Paul Cooper, Sean McNally, Luke Arnold, Kevin Meikle, Mark Severn, Rose Polson, Phil Fletcher, Paul Cooke and Phil Sharman for their encouragement and to my long suffering wife, Shirley, who has put up with me transporting myself back in time for months on end.

To anybody that may recognise themselves within the pages of this book; You have all been an inspiration in my life and without you this book could not have been written.

1

Let me quickly introduce myself. My name is John Derek Caswell. I am fifteen years of age and I live at the South end of the budding East Midlands Metropolis that is Kettering Town. Now Kettering is hardly a place you would chose to grow up in. It ranks very low indeed in the Country's list of 'interesting places to visit' and, apart from being a leading player in the Boot and Shoe Industry that the County of Northamptonshire is famed for, offers very little else to entice people to up sticks and take up residence in the area.

However, like everywhere else, once it has been stamped on your birth certificate and you commit yourself to education in the Borough that is it; hooked for life.

Situated as it is in the North of Northamptonshire most people only stumble upon it as a stop off point on the Midland Main Railway Line between London and more exotic locations such as Leicester, Nottingham, Derby and Sheffield. Here, in 1972, it boasts a population barely reaching the 50,000 mark and is fast being overtaken by Corby New Town to the North, who's Stewart and Lloyd's Steelworks are employing every waif and stray that has migrated down from Scotland and Wellingborough to the South, which is fast becoming London's latest over-spill.

It does, however, boast an aspiring football team, 'The Poppies', presently under the management of a journeyman central defender by the name of Ron Atkinson. Big Ron, 'The Tank', had been bought in mid-season eighteen months ago to arrest a slump that had seen the club relegated from the Southern League Premier Division.

He duly won the Championship and promotion back to the big time at the first attempt and the small town club that had once lured such legends as Tommy Lawton and Eddie Hapgood to Rockingham Road were now on the verge of taking up their rightful place in Division Four of the Football League.

Kettering is also the home of Weetabix Limited. Well, four miles to the South to be precise in a small town called Burton Latimer. As I live on Pytchley Road at the Southern End of Kettering the whiff of cooked wheat and malt can, especially on a dull, still, foggy morning, descend upon our part of the town quite nauseatingly as biscuits are churned out twenty four hours a day. One eventually becomes immune to the smell and some people actually quite like it but I have, at 15, already made a mental note that I would not even consider it as a future career path.

My Father had worked there, briefly, in the mid to late sixties as a Cooker Man. How he came to end up there I will never know. He had always been a Chef of some description at the George Hotel in the Market Place down the town. From as young as the age of five I can remember propping up the cycle shed with my golden lemonade outside The Vaults, the public house arm of the Hotel, or in the doorway of The Cherry Tree Pub across the road to the bus station, eagerly awaiting for him to consume his lunchtime ales and swift brandies before staggering out of the bar to catch the 407 or 408 bus to our end of town to go for his afternoon nap (generally four hours until it was time to go back to the hotel for his evening shift).

Many is the time I would have to call him back from down the road to the bus station as he had forgotten me. 'Sorry Son.' He would pathetically apologise, 'Nearly forgot you did I?'

I'm almost certain he did it on purpose.

There must have been one sozzled return to work too many for the Hotel's Management because all of a sudden there he was; working shifts at Weetabix.

The term Cooker Man is used fairly loosely as a job description as it merely involves filling a cooker up with pre-cleaned wheat and adding a pre-determined measure of salt, sugar, water and malt then battening down the cooker lid and cooking under steam pressure for twenty minutes before tipping the cooked mixture into a hopper which is then fed through a drier, milled into a flake, moulded into a biscuit and then baked in an oven. Hardly cordon bleu but nutritionally effective and unique none the less. I love the stuff mashed to a pulp with warm milk. My thinking is that he must have homed in on the word 'Cook' at the Employment Exchange and thought 'Yeah, I can do that.'

It didn't last long and for whatever reason, be it that the three—shift rotation pattern didn't fit in with his social life, or that he had just turned in plastered one afternoon shift and got the boot, but he was soon back slaving over a hot stove churning out meat and two veg. for the poor all-too-ill-to-argue at The Kettering General Hospital.

Kettering is also famous for its Wicksteed's Park. Opened in 1921 after a man from Leeds named Charles Wicksteed donated over 100 acres of land to a Village Trust to be made available to the Children of Kettering. A mighty fine gesture which has, over the years, developed into a superb attraction with a 32 acre boating lake and now attracting well over a million visitors through its gates from Easter through to early October.

I must have visited 'Wickies' practically every day this year. For one it is a short cut to my school, The Kettering Grammar School for Boys in Windmill Avenue, but most importantly it is a magnet for the birds. Not only from the nearby High School for Girls, but also from far and wide that arrive daily in coaches of all different shapes and sizes during the school summer holidays. It is the daily ritual for me and my fellow gigolo, Phil Brown, to turn up at the park during the holidays and hang around the coach parking area awaiting any talent which may alight and wander over in our direction.

Once two subjects are chosen we then follow them around the park all morning. With our expectancy rising with each giggle and wave enough encouragement is usually given to us by mid-day and we then leg it home, untangle our mop-top hair and, in my case, don my fading Wranglers and pink flowered shirt with matching cravat (and if it is a bit cold my cream and brown tank top). Phil returns equally dapper and then it is all about catching up with the two beauties again only to discover that in our absence two other smooth looking bastards have made off with our intended prey.

On the rare occasions that our tactics do work we will then dupe our subjects into a walk around the boating lake to lure them into the backwaters at the far end of the lake.

Now this is where my own achievements fall down slightly. Phil has always had a one hundred percent success rate in the backwaters but, at my tender age, I am already a chronic hay-fever sufferer and in amongst the highly pollinated field grasses and shrubbery of the backwaters my sinuses always go into overdrive. As if it isn't bad enough going into a sneezing fit just as a quick fumble is looking likely my on the spot cure will generally send many a girl screaming for her mate and any excuse for a quick getaway, thus also scuppering Phil's chances.

What I have to carry around with me is two capsules of anti histamine powder called Rynacrom. This isn't a problem but they have to be administered with what I can only describe as a rather large bulbous unit. I have to insert one capsule at a time into the unit's six-inch long chamber, depress to pierce the capsule, thrust up one nostril and then in almost the same movement squeeze the bulb to release the powder. After such an exhibition needless to say all negotiations fail and I am, once again, left to reflect that all of my successes generally come on rainy days.

The lake itself is always a good area of the park to pose in. It comprises a fleet of 30 rowing boats which, once you have established that both oars are required to enter the water simultaneously, is not beyond the bounds of even the most incompetent navigator to embark on a voyage to the other end of the lake and back in the allotted one hour and twenty minutes. One sound piece of advice, however, is to make sure that you don't lose an oar overboard. They are most useful for splashing out at other boats that draw close alongside and are a must if confronted by any of the lake's resident swans. Detailing a landing party ashore on either of the lake's three small islands to hoist female hosiery or someone's T shirt from a tree is met with severe resistance from these necky bastards and a good solid clout with an oar is, more often than not, the only way of making good your escape (providing of course your fellow boat companions have not already made off without you).

Both oars, not to mention great nerve and oarsmanship, are also required if you are to play 'Chicken' with the bows of the 'Mississippi Queen', the thirty foot paddle steamer which tramps the waters of the lake taking the visitors too idle to row a boat to the other side of the lake in a fraction of the time and in complete safety . . . well it hasn't sunk to date!

Also in this bottom area of the park is a child's boating lake which, unfortunately since the age of 12 and the near accidental scuttling of Phil's younger Sister Julie's paddle boat, we have been barred from.

There is also the death defying Water Chute ride. Launched from a tower some fifty foot in the air this boat shaped tub, which holds up to twenty four screaming passengers, careers down two rails at a rate of knots and smashes into the water sending a spray cascading over the boat and soaking everyone onboard. As if this dunking is not enough the tub then serenely travels through the water until it reaches the end of the hawser to which it is attached. The tightening of the rope then sends a signal back to the mechanism at the top of the tower, and once it has reached the end of its tether it jerks back at breakneck speed to pull the boat back onto the tracks and back to the top of the tower. The process is then repeated for those still not in a state of whiplash. The first aid hut receives a fair share of its customers from the water chute.

Before walking back up to the park's main focal point, the children's playground, there is a pet's corner, which is home to a couple of flea-bitten Goats, a Monkey, some Tortoises and a few Rabbits, which hardly enhances the appearance (or smell) of the area.

In close proximity though there is a nice area which comprises several aviaries with rare species of birds and an open area for a couple of Herons and Peacocks who's bloody wailing and mating calls are enough to wake me up in the mornings almost half a mile away.

The miniature railway train station is situated halfway between the lake and the playground from where 'King Arthur' and 'The Lady of the Lake' commence their fun packed twelve—minute journey around the lake. If you have enough money on you like 5p (a major rip-off as far as I'm concerned as it was only 9d before decimalisation), and are fortunate enough to be able to entice a young female onto the train with you the tunnel halfway through the ride and round the back of the lake is always a good indication as to your chances of success. The train's duration in the tunnel lasts only fifteen seconds at maximum so timing is of the essence and one either exits the tunnel with a huge satisfied smile (Phil) or with a clout around the ear (Me).

Behind the railway station and leading up to the banqueting pavilion, which also incorporates a band—stand where the local brass bands play on a Sunday afternoon, are the immaculately kept sunken gardens. They are not quite up to Babylon standards but as long as I am equipped with my Rynacrom I can generally rush past without any embarrassing consequences.

Then we are in to the playground, the parks golden oasis, this is the place to be. Not only does it have the new attraction of the bumper cars to go alongside the crazy golf and the pathetic four carriage roller coaster but all the swings and slides and various other pieces of rotting, rickety playground equipment are free but far more importantly highly dangerous. The best of times are most definitely to be had in the evenings when all the day trippers have gone home and we are left to our own devices to see how many swings we can wrap round the crossbars of the frames or how much fabric damage we can inflict on the wooden seats of the rocking horses.

The swings come in all shapes and sizes and once standing up on them to reinforce the swinging motion it is quite simple to jump off and kick the swing forward so that it wraps itself over the metal crossbar. The timing has to be nigh on perfect though. I have long since given up this practice after I slipped off one in 1970 on the final kick/thrust manoeuvre, landed flat on my back and the returning wooden seat (which had failed to double back over the crossbar), caught me squarely on the forehead.

Four monster swings sit at the entrance to the playground from the Barton Road End. These buggers are almost impossible to flip over as they are suspended from at least thirty-five feet of chain and, with the backdrop of the trees along the Barton Road, are completely undetectable in flight. At any given time during a sunny day these 24'x 10'x 2' planks of wood with a twelve stone cargo of uncaring youth on board can come hurtling down from the heavens straight into the back of 6 year old Sarah Louise who, whilst eagerly contemplating her award winning Wicksteed Park ice cream, has wandered unwittingly into its flight path. Another one for the first aid hut.

Three gigantic slides also stand proudly close by with their ladders forever full of expectant two second thrill seekers. One favourite trick of ours is to shimmy up the slide itself holding on to the sides for dear life. Then, once at the top sit on the ladder's handrails and with legs akimbo, slide down the handrails, much as you would do with a stair banister only with a greater degree of difficulty, and see how many heads you can clatter into on the way down.

Once all the day trippers have gone home we can always be found helpfully polishing up the slides to ensure tomorrow's brats fly straight off the end, landing with an almighty thud on their arses onto the concrete or prising small slivers of metal up out of the joints in the knowledge that they would either embed themselves into an infant tomorrow or at least shred their new petticoat.

Not that we are all heartless, of course. We will often pass parents on their way to the first aid hut with a bleeding, wailing child and sympathetically enquire:—'Baby slide? Dangerous bit of kit that.'

Also dotted around the play area are pieces of equipment known as 'Jazzes.' The name probably deriving from the fairground 'Waltz', this being the poor man's version. All this consists of is a ten foot long plank of wood with enough room to accommodate four brave passengers and two 'drivers' who can work up a head of steam either end pretty much as if standing up on a swing and working it up as high as possible. Once the Jazz has reached its full height and the terrified passengers are screaming their submissions it is possible, albeit mighty daring, for the drivers to give one last almighty thrust and jump off leaving those on board to crouch down as low as possible in a sometimes vain attempt to avoid being crushed in between their seat and the top crossbeam it is suspended from. A very flexible vertebra is always required for this ride and victims of the jazz can often be seen up to an hour later walking around like Quasimodo.

The 'Mushroom' is probably the most deceiving of all. Standing solitary and away from the slides and jazzes this is exactly as the name suggests. A six-foot high thick green post with a mushroom shaped lid on top painted red with cream spots a la Alice in Wonderland. But this thing packs a punch, as underneath the mushroom hood are six bars to hang on to. The idea is to trot round for a few seconds whilst it gathers speed and then lift your legs off the ground to gently float round until it sedately comes to a halt. The truth is that six of you can race round it building it up to a speed of up to 100 r.p.m. and, at a previously arranged silent count, leap away from it leaving one unsuspecting member fully prone and hanging on for dear life. It is then a straight choice: Either hang on and grin and bear it or let go and risk severe gravel rash if you are not fortunate enough to land in the strategically placed sand pit some twenty feet away.

Then there is the very peculiar-shaped Umbrella. About fifteen feet high this metal construction tapers outwards from the top until, about two feet from the ground, it ends with a circular wooden base enough to seat up to twelve people. It is a very odd sight as by human propulsion it lurches in and out and round and round, flinging the occasional 'first timer' onto the gravel. It has been recently re-commissioned since one glorious sunset twelve months ago when forty—three of us piled onto it and the poor thing gave way at the apex and bobbled helplessly towards the sandpit.

With the long, hot summer of 1972 now finally drawing to a close we can safely look back and conclude that Phil and I had achieved very little despite our best efforts during the eight—week school holiday. A couple of semi interested fourteen year old 'lasses' from Corby had hung around us for the past couple of weeks but seemed to lose interest when they discovered that we were not actually the trainee garage mechanics we had professed to be and that we would soon be going back to school, just like them.

It would be strange for me this time round as the three lads that I had grown up with on our row of houses along Pytchley Road had all left school in the summer, as they are a year older than me. Malc, who lives next door across the alley to me, is now going to Corby Technical College to become a Chef. I will miss not walking to school with him in the mornings. Bobby is in the throws of taking up an apprenticeship at a garage and Barry is working in some electrical shop down town, I couldn't even be sure where as I had hardly seen him over the past three months since he took his O levels.

This was the year, of course, when everything was expected of me. I had somehow scraped through to the Kettering Grammar School for Boys by virtue of passing my eleven plus which I'd taken at Highfield Road Primary School in 1968. This meant that I would have to sit the more difficult O level tests come next spring rather than the easier CSE's on offer at the secondary modern schools that make up the rest of the Kettering Borough Education System. My Sister, Catherine, had left Kettering High School for Girls three years previously with 9 O levels to her credit and I suppose my parents expected a similar return from me. I know a bit differently, however, as I have struggled to come to terms with some of the subjects of my curriculum in the previous year and already I have been dropped down to CSE level for French, Art and English Literature. Nothing short of a grade A pass in these subjects will guarantee me an O level standard pass. Unfortunately I cannot be afforded such luxuries in English Language, Maths, History, Scripture and Engineering Drawing or Biology and a bit of concentration will be required.

Sometime, during the upcoming term, we will be having a couple of hours 'career studies' when someone from the tax office will be coming to the school to tell us about how wonderful and fulfilling their daily chores are in the hopes that we will follow them into a long and prosperous future in some mundane job. No doubt they will bring all their leaflets with them and tell us all that we need are six O levels, stay on in the sixth form at school for a further two years, three A levels and then we can begin a five year apprenticeship with them. Yeah, right!

Still, I suppose it must be better than the morning and evening paper rounds that I currently possess. The prospect of getting up at six o'clock in the morning for another winter to deliver the 'Daily Mirror' and the newly established 'Daily Sun' to the stuck-up, ungrateful bleeders down Bryant Road does not augur too well. Especially as I am starting to become extremely suspicious of the male shop assistant who collates the various rounds for the paperboys.

I don't know what it is about David Denton, the twenty five-year-old odd job lad that has worked for Bob and Janet Bailey probably ever since he was my age. We call him Ten Ton Denton due to his rather plumpish persona but as I have got older he always seems rather too eager to involve me a bit more than is necessary in the marking up of the papers 'before any of the other lads get in for their round.'

He is always far too keen to show me the latest monthly edition of Health and Efficiency, a publication for people of a naturistic tendency, with its quite explicit photos of families prancing about with no clothes on that Mr Ward from Spinney Lane receives hand delivered by David himself in a plain brown paper bag.

'What do you think of this, John?' He enquired as I am still trying to come to terms with the fact that it is five past six in the morning and minus two outside of the unheated wooden hut we were in at the back of the shop. 'Got a big one, hasn't he?' He nodded and winked. 'Have you seen this weeks Reveille? You can almost see a nipple on page seven. Your Dad gets that doesn't he, John? Or is it Titbits? Plenty of bits but no tits, eh, John.'

I humoured him and tried to ignore the fact that he was getting ever closer to me and prayed that the other boys would turn in for their rounds pretty damn quickly.

'I'm thinking of packing my paper rounds in Dave.' I announced one morning as he was thumbing through an edition of 'People's Friend' (God only knows what he was expecting to find in there).

'Oh! Um it's not because of me is it John?'

'No!' I said defensively, 'I'm about to start my last year at school next week and I doubt very much that getting up at six o clock every morning will enhance my already limited span of attention during lessons. I may try and get myself a shelf stacking job down town on a Saturday.'

'No guarantees, boy. You'll miss the money if you pack your paper rounds in and there's no job for you down town.'

True. I did get 75p from my evening round, £1.15p from my morning and 50p for my Sunday round although the papers weighed a ton.

'I'd suggest you stayed on here and asked Bob about stacking the shelves here, but . . .'

'Yes Dave, I know. You do it!' I finished the sentence for him. 'I wouldn't pack it in without getting something else first anyway, it's just the mornings that are getting too much for me.'

He seemed to take the hint and left me alone after that but it has got me thinking. Maybe I was getting a bit too old for this paper boy lark. I had been traipsing the Bryant Road Beat for three years now and, hey; maybe I was getting a bit too mature for it now. I liked to think so.

And so the big day finally arrived. Monday September 6th 1972. The beginning of the final chapter in my education. Phil called round for me at eight twenty, all bleary-eyed having only been out of bed for ten minutes. Damn him. How I envied the two and a half hours extra sleep he had enjoyed.

Assembly followed registration and it was as if the summer holidays had never even existed. Our school year, roughly 120 pupils, the cream of the local talent from as far afield as Barton Seagrave, a village just over the bridge from Wicksteed Park, Geddington, Rothwell and Desborough, towns to the North and West of Kettering, was split into four different sections—P, Q, R and S—depending on potential.

Form P are the swats, the untouchables. Here are your budding rocket scientists and brain surgeons that are expected to pass 11 O levels with distinction, four A levels and then go on to university and achieve World domination by the age of 30. Bollocks, they squealed like pigs when confronted on their own in the playground, (although some of them do excel on the Rugby pitch).

Form Q are not quite so loathsome, spotty or intelligent as form P but all are expected to perform well come exam time and there are a good many prospective six formers in this group.

Form R is getting down towards the dregs, Phil is in this group and where there is a glimmer of hope for some that did not quite make it up to form Q category the boat certainly is not being pushed out to assist the members of this form to achieve the highest standard.

What can I say about form S? Personally I take great pride in being a member of this ragbag outfit. Considered the flotsam and jetsam of our year we are beyond redemption in the eyes of most of the Masters (and fellow pupils, it must be said). However we have built up a strange sort of camaraderie amongst ourselves and have vowed that we are going to prove all the doubters and knockers wrong and that we are going to achieve O level results the likes of which has never before been attained by an S form.

That was the theory. At least until our first double period of maths on that very first Monday morning back behind the desk. After four years at the school all of our strengths and weaknesses in the various subjects have long since been recognised, hence my inclusion in form S. I have to admit to being rather good at anything that could be written down, or anything that could be learnt from the pages of a book and then reproduced in my own words: i.e. English, Scripture and History. I had opted for English Literature as a CSE as it is far easier than the O level course and I am quietly confident I will pass with an A grade. English Language is just a breeze for me. I can confound my critics by surpassing even some of the P formers in this field, but my total inadequacies in the maths, physics, language and science departments have left me floundering. Ho hum, so I'll never get to discuss quantum physics with Charles de Gaulle. I'll survive.

My history teacher, Donald Baxter, is also my form Master and a generally all round good egg. He always gives the class encouragement where others wouldn't and as a consequence I always feel that I owe it to him to both behave and do well at history. The O level course is, after all, only about the British Social and Industrial Revolution between 1725 and 1925. It isn't that difficult, I even have a player in my Subbuteo Team called Isambard Kingdom Brunel and, as with scripture, we only have to remember names, dates and places and convert that into some kind of logic on paper. It is in such debacles as our French lessons that we tend to let the side down. It is blatantly obvious that nobody from form S is going to master any language be it French, German, Latin or Outer bloody Mongolian and it is almost as if the whole of the form has opted for CSE French.

We are never going to get a pass so let's have a hoot along the way and see how many Masters we can send packing with a nervous breakdown being the class philosophy.

It had worked quite successfully in the third year with poor Mr. Jones but Mr. Lindsay; 'Flo', was proving a harder nut to crack. Why 'Flo' I can only hazard a guess. Probably because he is a bit of an old woman and always nagging his pupils like Florrie Capp, the long suffering wife of the cartoon strip drop out Andy.

Nothing seemed to faze Flo, though it is not for the lack of trying. It is most humorous to watch his thin, ageing face contort with every French word he utters, and this is always mimicked when one of us has to stand in front of the class and recite a bit of French. The most exaggerated example being the French word for an armchair, which is a 'fauteuil', pronounced fort-eye. We purposely refer to our wooden desk seats as 'fauteuils' when engaging Flo in routine nonsensical French conversation. This winds him up a treat with the addition of bulging eyes and a red face to accompany his rage that we have once again misunderstood the meaning of the word.

We also use a catalogue of books to base our syllabus on. Nothing too strenuous or demanding. The sort of series of books that a four—year old in France was learning his Mother tongue from. The translation proves quite interesting, as English words are often thrown in to amuse ourselves.

The main character in the series of books is one Henri Lemoire. He leads a very dull and uninspired lifestyle and one only hopes, for his sake, that he is a pensioner. He gets up in the morning, has his breakfast, walks along the road to the bakery, has his dinner and, thankfully for all concerned, has an afternoon sleep in his armchair. He then has his supper and goes to bed. Occasionally he would bump in to his friend Bertrand who might happen to be walking his dog.

Most of this can be derived from the pictures but just out of sheer devilment we will occasionally twist it round so that Henry Lemon, as we have christened him, was running to the butchers and having an afternoon sleep in his 'er! Is it his bed, Sir?'

'It's his armchair, for goodness sake, lad, his fauteuil is his armchair.'

Book seven, which we have only just about managed to get to, tries to be clever and link a bit of German with the French by sending good old Henri off on holiday to a place on the Rhine called Winkelhaussen. A mistake when it came to Dave Jackson from Rothwell translating the passage into English.

'In the morning Henry Lemon got on to the train to go to the Wank House'.

Flo lost it and Jackson received a Saturday morning detention.

We were winning.

There are sound—proof booths that we are allowed to use occasionally to practice our French oration in. Headphones, as well as tape decks, we have the lot. The idea being to mimic some old French git in an attempt to improve our accent. Modern technology, unfortunately, allowed Flo to listen in on us though and Nick Judd and Myself were inclined from time to time to press the record button, make up silly noises, sometimes of a suggestive nature or more than likely just animalistic, and then swap booths to listen to what each other had produced.

It was whilst I was doubled up in hysterics listening to Nick singing 'Oh, them golden slippers' in an amazingly stupid high pitched voice like Bill Oddie on helium that Flo broke in.

'Caswell! Caswell! What on Earth is going on?'

'Err, I think the second year must have been in before us, Sir, and I've rewound the tape too far, Sir.'

Nick was in raptures as my excuses fell on deaf ears and I earned Myself a Saturday morning detention.

Biology lessons are always very interesting and well attended due to the fact that we have a female teacher. Of all the Masters in the school that could have been assigned to taking S form through their O level biology course they chose to give us the chemistry teacher's wife, June Salter.

We'd all flicked through our text—books. We all knew what was coming. It was just a matter of when, and indeed how. Each weekly class was attended religiously as we thought that this must be the day that she finally uttered the immortal words. Now Mrs. Salter was no looker by any stretch of the imagination but she is still female and has the undivided attention of a class of twenty, eagerly awaiting, fifteen—year old male students. She had been close on several occasions this particular morning and when it was eventually delivered to us for the first time it was slightly unexpected. But she had gone for it in style and there it was out in the open;

'The erect penis enters the vagina.'

A quick glance around the room caught everyone with their mouths wide open and eyes agog. She turned slightly red but nothing more. It was as if the entire weight of the World had been lifted from her shoulders and we gasped quite audibly as she proceeded with a torrent of vaginas, penises, sperms, orgasms and ejaculations.

Go on Mrs S.' a cry went up from the back of the room and I, like many others around me, could have burst into applause such was the style and confidence that she was now portraying. It was no doubt a defining moment in my education.

It helped me not a jot further on in the lesson as we were requested to draw and locate every functional part of the Common Housefly. The only parts of its anatomy I could pinpoint with any degree of accuracy were its bloody reproductive organs.

The school itself is quite strictly run. I suppose it still hankers for the good old days when there was little else to do other than go home of an evening and revise for your exams or read a book. Not an option any more. Far more interesting pass times nowadays such as Radio 1, going round Nick Judd's house to listen to the new 'Focus' album, play Subbutteo or just hanging around any street corner in any weather. Homework was just not fashionable any more.

The Headmaster of the school, 'Piggy' Stern, and his second in command Ivan Collier were enough to put the fear of God into any pubescent. Both were of the cape and mortarboard brigade unlike some of the more trendy Masters who even dared to turn in without a tie on the odd occasion. In assembly Ivan would slowly walk on to the school stage and quell the ongoing hullabaloo by crashing his fifty—year old ninety-six volume prayer book down onto the table with such force that it sounded like a shotgun going off. No matter that you knew it was coming the sheer volume of the crack made you stand bolt upright.

'All rise.'

Piggy would bounce in with his cape flowing behind him. Probably in his mid forties, bespectacled, and with a scowl permanently etched onto his face.

'Sit.'

No good morning school. No please be seated. No kiss my arse, just 'Sit.'

And we were expected to respect this shower. The only respect that Stern got was that we all respected 'the twig'. All this man had going for him was that he was lethal with his cane from two feet and if you were ever summoned to his office for a date with 'the twig' you knew what you had coming. This fate had befallen me once last year and I was not going to let it happen again. I was casually walking back to school through Wickies one lunchtime when all of a sudden I was passed by eight class mates running as if their lives depended on it and shouting 'run!'

I ran but, weighed down by my satchel, home made shepherd's pie and treacle tart with strawberry blancmange, was easily caught by a Wicksteed Park Groundsman and accused of uprooting various Calluna Vulgaris from the herbaceous borders of the sunken gardens. I tried to protest my innocence but decided to take the rap and 'the twig' as a consequence. An easier option than dropping my classmates in it and being pulped as an alternative on my way home later on in the afternoon.

It didn't take too long to settle in to the routine of school again. Nick Judd who, unlike me, had never previously owned a paper round had got himself a Friday evening and all day Saturday job in Tesco's in the town centre behind the delicatessen counter.

'Bloody hell, Nick! There aren't any more jobs going are there?'

The idea appealed greatly to me. Nick was earning a fiver for three hours Friday evening and eight till five thirty on Saturday. He asked and to my surprise landed me a job shelf stacking and helping out in the warehouse at the back unloading the goods inwards.

Tesco's is only a small high street shop struggling to compete with the many Co-Op and Spar outlets that the town has to offer plus the much larger Sainsbury's just up the road. It was a very friendly place though and after my interview with the shop manager, Graham Cairns, I immediately made up my mind that the days of the paper round were over. I did keep the Sunday round on for an extra month, I thought that the extra 75p would contribute to my ever growing record collection but I soon tired of it and acknowledged that as a fifteen year old, still at school, I could survive on £5 a week.

It wasn't as if my outgoings were all that great. I couldn't, for obvious reasons, now go and watch Kettering Town play at home on a Saturday afternoon any more and my Mum, bless her, would still subsidise the entrance fee anyway when we had an evening match.

I promised myself to put 50p a week by to purchase an album every six weeks or so, buy a single a week and the other £4 can go towards S form's invasion of The Windmill Club disco every Saturday night.

The Windmill is an affiliated working men's club in Edmund Street just at the town end of Windmill Avenue next to the 'Primecut' meat—processing factory. The occasional smell of Weetabix to the South of the town is incense in comparison to the stench of rotting carcasses that emanate from this place.

The Windmill has three large social areas; the bingo hall, the dance hall and the more sophisticated snooker lounge (strictly no females).

How we always manage to get ourselves signed into the place God only knows. Being an affiliated club it is open to members and their bona fide guests only. Under the strict guidelines of the Working Men's Club and Institute Union Ltd., only fully paid up members of the club are permitted to sign guests in and, as this was the Windmill, there were not too many fully paid up members about. Patrons of the snooker lounge would, as a rule, politely tell us to fuck off when approached about lending us their signature for the evening and thus vouching for our behaviour whilst on the premises. However enough members can generally be tapped up and although up to twenty of us could be hanging around outside at any one time we are usually all inside and installed at the bar by nine o'clock in the evening. That was the irony of it all. The union's hard line rules about who could and who could not enter the establishment soon went by the wayside on the realisation that a hundred or so fifteen year olds with a fiver each to burn on watered down vodka were waiting to get in.

Even better; as guests we are not even allowed to purchase drinks from the bar. Officially the members who have signed us in had to go to the bar for us! Good grief, you can't even get to the bar for school kids. It was great for the ego that we were passing for eighteen, or so we thought, but in reality of course everyone else just avoided the Windmill disco on a Saturday night like the plague for the very reason that it was crawling with acneyed, loathsome oiks from the town's schools. Unperturbed, however, we can stand around all night drinking Vodka and lime until violently sick, watching all the birds from the High School and the Rockingham Road School for Girls strutting their stuff to the latest Motown sounds. I just hoped upon hope that I could stay upright enough, yet pissed up enough, to pluck up the courage when the slow numbers came on to go over and ask any of them for a smooch. It doesn't help that I have two left feet in the dancing department and to this end my chances have already been dramatically reduced as I would never have the nerve to be up dancing earlier in the evening. Those that had, as a rule, would have the pick when it came to smooching time leaving me and the other non-dancers to make the best of the remainder.

'Ditn't see you dancin' earlier?' my catch inevitably inquires (Why do Kettering girls always say ditn't)?

'Oh, didn't you? Er I danced to that one by The San Remo strings.'
'What one's that then? Ditn't think I 'eard that one.'
'It's the instrumental . . . ., you know?'

Breaking off from the (half hearted) smooch I now give a two second demonstration of disco dancing with my hands waving frantically in the air, looking as if I know what I'm doing.

'Blimey, I'm sure I'd have seen someone dancin' like that.' She unenthusiastically replied.

The evening degenerates after that as the vodka and three pints of Double Diamond fuel the youthful testosterone levels and things start to get a tad boisterous. Someone inevitably pukes up over someone else's new Corduroys or smooches with a bit of stuff that someone else fancies. Whatever the excuse it will more often than not kick off around ten past eleven. A convenient enough occurrence for the bouncers to wade in, heavy handed, and throw the lot of us out with a couple of black eyes in to the bargain. Besides the bar had shut and thus any money we had left over will be spent on fish and chips from the Mill Road 'Chippy' just around the corner. Any scraps that do spill over into the street are soon dispersed as parents arrive to pick up those from further afield of Kettering.

I walk home alone. Most of my class—mates live in the area of the Windmill and I am almost a mile and a half away. Phil would never come with me on a Saturday night, he didn't have the luxury of a part time job to supplement his income and I generally stagger in around twelve thirty.

There is never an inquiry the following morning as to where I had been until such an hour (I'm quite convinced that my Father was comatose from his own alcohol consumption at that time of the morning anyway). Mum would have still been awake but was probably more concerned as to my Sister's whereabouts until three or four in the morning to worry about me.

It's strange how, when you become older, you start to realise what is and has been going on around you for all these years but never had the curiosity to find out why. My parents had never slept in the same bedroom from as long as I can care to remember. Mum and my Sister Cath, four years and ten months my senior, had the main bedroom whilst my Father the back bedroom and myself the rabbit hutch at the front of the house. At least I had a bit of privacy but the house itself was hardly a palace and you certainly didn't want to invite too many people round.

The kitchen consists of a gas cooker, (for which I am eternally grateful for during the winter months—I would pull up my chair and stick my feet in to the oven to keep warm), a stone sink, a table and chairs, a copper for doing the washing and a mangle.

Wash days are interesting to say the least. The copper is filled up with water and then lit. A bar of 'Fairy' domestic soap hurled in with the whites, boiled for an eternity and the whole lot occasionally agitated with a large wooden spoon. Upon transferring the scolding hot whites to the sink for their 'freeze rinse' the colours are then introduced and you then pray that with the soaring high temperatures that your clothes were being subjected to they do not disfigure beyond all recognition. The whole lot is then rinsed and passed through the mangle before being put outside on the line to dry.

'Does anyone want this water for a bath?' Mum would enquire.

'Don't think so!' would be the resounding response.

'O.k., I'll fill it up anyway for your Dad'.

How my Father must dread wash days. He knows that he will have the remaining water emptied from the copper into various buckets and bowls, carted upstairs and then tipped into the bath for him. He can only hope that none of the colours have run.

The living room fares little better. It has been painted in a hideous shade of purple and light blue. A legacy from one of my Sister's ex boyfriends who came round and painted it one afternoon and admitted to it looking 'cool, man.' Two threadbare settees take centre stage with two equally, but not in the slightest bit belonging to, moth bitten chairs by the open hearth. The coal fire is very seldom lit hence my tendency to prefer to cook my toes in the oven. The carpet is wafer thin but on the plus side holds my Subbuteo pitch superbly, making my house possibly the best venue for our games albeit the coldest.

We have a sideboard with a few ornaments on, anything of value being my Uncle Ted's who has since emigrated to Australia (so I have been lead to believe), and a massive drop leaf table that houses my Sister's 'touch it and you're dead' record player, record collection and spool to spool tape recorder.

Religiously on a Saturday evening Cath will always tape anything off the radio that John Peel is endorsing. Her record collection was already decidedly weird with LP's from Captain Beefheart, the Groundhogs and the Velvet Underground. The trick is that once she has set the mic. up next to the radio and pressed the record button to bounce down the stairs as loud as possible and shout, 'Mum . . . Where's my mauve and light green tank top?'

This draws the expected 'Shut up, you moron, I'm recording' response that was always intended thus ruining the finished, recorded, item even more.

I finally got a record player Myself for Christmas last year so I no longer needed to borrow her scabby player while she was at work and I could at least listen to a bit of David Bowie and Alice Cooper without having to put up with her obscure, wacky, way-out crap.

We have never owned a television set. 'They don't want a telly' my Father had always implied. Er, try asking us.

I am treated as an outcast. I cannot discuss Saturday's Match of the Day, what is going on in Crossroads or Thunderbirds, and I have absolutely no idea who Diana Rigg is. It hadn't really bothered me much in the past as I suppose we had not been the only ones without a telly before now, but colour television was becoming all the rage and we haven't even got a black and white one.

The debate became pretty serious in our household. I don't think Cath was particularly bothered as she was now almost twenty-one and had possibly accepted that there were never going to be any luxuries for her whilst still at home. However even she found it difficult not to agree with my point of view for once in her life. I could see no reason other than the fact that the license fee and rental fee for a set was going to come out of my Father's beer money. I even offered to contribute from my wages but my Mother was having none of it. I sulked for a couple of days but soon got over it. It did make me realise, however, where all the money in the family budget had gone down the years.

My Mother does a couple of hours cleaning in the mornings for well to do old ladies in Spinney Lane and Lewis Road nearby and I guess that is where the money came from to keep me reasonably well clothed all this time.

It all changed, however, on my sixteenth birthday eight days before Christmas 1972 and once again I have been 'honoured' to get my Birthday and Christmas presents all rolled into one (God how I envied people that had their birthdays in June or July). But this year I don't mind, I've got my television. I don't know what I'm supposed to do with it now though. Do I not let anyone else watch it?

'Get out of the living room, please. I'm watching MY telly.'

I couldn't really now, could I? But if this was the level that my Mother has had to go to in securing the services of a television set for the rest of the family then I was prepared to forego my presents this year. Possibly by way of a thank you I have even received a £5 Roadnights clothing voucher from Cath.

Reaching sixteen fully five months before I leave school is something that I thoroughly resent. I am old enough to leave now, however I know it makes more sense to stay on and see what I can in fact achieve, if anything.

The arrival of 1973 has been pretty bleak to put it mildly. I have been bored out of my skull during the festive two weeks school holiday. I have done absolutely no revision whatsoever for my May examinations, hadn't seen any football due to the adverse weather conditions, and had definitely not pulled any birds over the past few months. I tell a lie. Malc was going out with a girl he'd met at Corby Technical College and got her to bring a mate along so that we could go to the pictures as a foursome. It was kind of like my first ever blind date and we went along to the fleapit that is the Savoy Cinema in Russell Street, one of the many back streets off the town centre, to see 'A Clockwork Orange.'

	I seemed to be getting on all right and I even managed to put my arm around her shoulder on a couple of occasions when, during the interval, I got up to get the pair of us a 'Zoom' ice lolly and a 5p cone of popcorn and there three rows back is my bloody Sister and two of her mates. How sodding unlucky is that? I must have turned ten shades of pink and found myself giving a pathetic wave in her direction as she and her gorky mates fell about laughing uncontrollably. I spent the rest of the film trying to repel my newly acquired girlfriend's advances. Needless to say I have not seen her again.

	I did sit glued to the telly though, marvelling at Morecambe & Wise over the festive period. My Father, in an ever more pathetic attempt to impart a bit of humour into our relationship called me 'Goggle eyes' as he poked his head round the door before he went to bed, but I think he knew that his game was well and truly up and that relations between the two of us could only get progressively worse as I grew older.

	Cath had actually got herself a half-decent boy friend over the Christmas period. He'd turned up at the front door the other week with a bouquet of flowers and a box of Milk Tray for her. What a wimp! God only knows what the attraction is. Still, it takes all sorts I suppose.

Steve is quite an impressive character. He is a Cadet in the Merchant Navy with a company called Silver Line and after his next six month trip to sea was going to College in Newcastle for another six months. He was currently under negotiations with my Mum and Dad to take her up to Newcastle with him and hey, that's about as OK with me as any other idea I had ever heard before in my entire life. It is difficult to imagine that she has now been left school for almost five years herself and, quite understandably, pissed off with working at a bank and presumably pissed off with going out every Friday and Saturday night and letting her hair down. Most of her friends were now settled down with families and it seemed as if she wanted a bit of the same. Just a pity that a decent sort of chap like Steve had drawn the short straw.

Her twenty first birthday duly arrived late February 1973 and I have been given the distinction of being DJ for the evening in our living room for her party. At least all her horrible friends have brought plenty of Gin and Vodka round for our consumption. Mum made herself scarce in the kitchen for the evening and Dad just stuck his head round the door at eleven o'clock on his way to bed.

'Not watching telly, son? Hee! Hee!'

'Piss off!'

I was violently sick in the toilet about mid-night. Nobody actually aware, except Steve who was my supply line, that I was downing large volumes of vodka and orange whilst playing all my records that I knew Cath hated.

The subject of her moving to Newcastle with Steve next August was never discussed again. Cath was twenty-one now. She was going to do as she jolly well pleased. Steve went back to sea a couple of weeks later and my Mum and I felt as if we had been sentenced to purgatory for six months. Cath had long since given up even acknowledging Dad, so he was least affected. If she was unreasonable to live with before she was now downright impossible.

I just needed her constant nagging to revise for my O levels like I needed a hole in the head.

'How can I revise when I'm constantly getting nagged to revise? I'm going out'. I protested.

'You'll never get a decent job.' She sneered.

'Yeah, like I'm going to be a bank clerk.'

'What? What did you say?'

I suppose she did have a point to some extent. What kind of a job WAS I going to get? The career seminars that we had once every fortnight at school were very limited. By that I mean that if you were looking to get nine O levels and then go on to college for another couple of years then fine. The police had been to see us (not about the Wicksteed's Park incident, I hasten to add). Some geezer from a local solicitor had been down, a doctor for Christ sakes, and the inevitable visit from the Army Recruitment Office in town.

None of them seemed at all appealing and I know for a fact that many of my class-mates were already looking forward to becoming builders, or trainee plumbers and the likes. Stacking shelves at Tesco's over the past eight months has hardly endeared me to the retail trade either although Nick was doing quite well in the butchery department and thought he may be offered something in that line come the summer. 'Superb, Nick, All this great education and we can now teach you how to swing a meat cleaver around at Primecut!'

Malc was getting on well with his culinary skills at Corby Tech. and can now knock up a mean soufflé when he puts his mind to it but, with one supposed Chef in the family already, the idea just didn't appeal. I couldn't imagine being cooped up in a red—hot kitchen all day. No thanks.

Strangely enough though the thoughts of Steve being back at sea and having a whale of a time seemed to have struck a chord with me. Not that he was having a whale of a time, of course. He was, according to his many letters to Cath, in a state of manic depression, desperate to get off the ship to see her again and saving all his money whilst, at the same time, becoming a complete alcohol free recluse whenever the ship got in to port. I guessed differently.

I didn't share this feeling with anybody, least of all with my Sister or my Mother. Not with one of them in a state of love-sick depression already and the other trying to come to terms with the fact that she was shortly to lose a daughter anyway. I thought that maybe I would just bide my time and see what results I do manage to achieve. By then Steve should be back from this trip and I could take things from there.

With the long winter finally drawing to a close all of a sudden the Easter Holiday was upon us. The park always opened on Good Friday giving us a fore-taste of what to expect during the summer with all roads to the South of Kettering blocked with traffic trying to get into the park via Paradise Lane or from the Barton road entrance. It was time for some serious revision.

Or maybe not.

Apart from actually going in to school come late May through to mid June to sit the exams we were finished. We were on extended revision leave. This was it. My theory now being that surely if I didn't know it all by now I never would. Besides none of us had a clue as to what questions we were going to be asked in the O level papers and to prepare Myself totally for the maths examination I would need to sit through the entire syllabus again from day one and this time give a shit.

In the subjects that I could slightly relate to I felt that I had sufficient knowledge to be able to blag my way through most of them. I could see no reason to revise any English. I knew where all the comma's and full stops had to go and had a vivid enough imagination to be able to write about anything they decided to throw at me. I guessed that as long as I could remember the dates of the Toll-Puddle Martyrs and the consequence of their actions, plus other significant events during the British Social and Economical Revolution of the 19th century that I would be OK in my history examination (maybe a couple of days revision before the actual exam itself would suffice).

Scripture was a breeze. Based purely on the accounts of Matthew, Mark, Luke and John I need only sit down and refresh myself on their versions of events just prior to the exam.

I had already given up on French and Biology so it was hardly worth putting too much effort into these categories. I knew a bit about most of the areas that we may be asked questions on but I see no point in wasting the glorious weather when I already knew it would be in vain.

So there it is, revision sorted. Right let's get up that park.

I must admit to a very strange feeling when everyone else went back to school after the Easter break. It is as if I am cheating or something. Phil came round for me on the Monday morning at eleven o' clock and we strolled up to the park, but there was nobody there, completely empty, a couple of coaches of horrible kids on school outings but nothing to fire our enthusiasm. The thought did briefly cross our minds that maybe we should go home and revise a little but it was soon dismissed out of hand. Both of us were still unsure as to what career path we should follow so in the evenings we took to scanning the local job section of the Kettering Evening Telegraph. Looking primarily, I suppose, for anyone advertising for school leavers. We wrote to several asking for application forms but were a little dissuaded when they announced that they would like us to include our 'expected' O level results.

'Bloody hell' Phil lamented. 'How am I going to improve my job prospects by answering that honestly?'

I did put a few half-hearted feelers out and wrote to a couple of garages (not that I knew anything about cars), a couple of shoe factories and some shops but it all seemed to be in the sense of duty. There was nothing there that I really could see myself doing for the rest of my life. All of the encouraging replies that came back were telling me to contact them again once I had got my results through which I am pretty satisfied with. I can put that part of my future to sleep for the time being and ignore it for the next couple of months. I know it won't go away but it is one less thing to concern myself with at the moment.

One immediate hurdle to get over was the winning of the Southern League Premier Division for the mighty Red and Blacks of Kettering Town. I have missed a vast majority of the campaign back in the Premier Division due to my having to stack the shelves at Tesco's all day every Saturday but as luck would have it the deciding game at home to Barnet has fallen on a Tuesday evening.

Myself and Nick Judd, along with 4,500 other fervent 'Poppies' fans, took up our places in the Rockingham Road Ground behind the Cowper Street Goal and shouted ourselves completely hoarse as we ran out 2-0 winners. All of a sudden nothing else mattered. My impending exams, my future career, the fact that I had just kissed Nick (Yeuck).

We were the Champions!

We could go to Lancaster Gate and demand that they elect us into the Football League on the basis that we were the best team outside of the four divisions and could quite easily replace the deadwood that is Workington, Rochdale, Hartlepool and Crewe Alexander.

Ron Atkinson IS God!

The feel-good factor had definitely arrived in the town of Kettering. For the first time in my life I was beginning to take some pride in this wonderful town with its marvellous people. I had never had such feelings before except when the dunderheads of Corby occasionally came over to the park on a bank holiday in an attempt to wreck the place. It's our park, if you don't mind. If anybody's going to wreck it, we will.

The feeling of euphoria that surrounded that balmy Tuesday evening in April was soon replaced by the feeling of impending doom that accompanied the rapidly approaching Monday 19th May and our first exam, Maths! Did it have to be Maths? Could we not be broken in gently with the Scripture Examination or something? With the possible exception of the French Exam, Maths is always going to be my Achilles Heel. Oh, God, please don't subject me to this torture.

Phil called at half eight. The exam would run from nine until a quarter to twelve. The big moment has arrived. There was no going back now.

Shit!

It seemed strange to see Phil in his school uniform again, as indeed it felt slightly uncomfortable back in mine. They had been in mothballs since the Easter Holiday and my trousers were by now a good two inches too short for me given my Mother's quite understandable refusal to buy me another pair. For some strange reason I have opted to wear my 'House' tie for the occasion. House ties were optional once you had survived the first three years at the school and could be replaced by a more sombre black tie, which I always preferred as I hated the black and white stripes of my house, Kirby. Black may have been more appropriate for this occasion but I had felt that this small, subtle change to my attire might just affect my fortunes to the good.

Who was I kidding? A quick glance around the room at five to nine showed that I was not alone. Despite all the claims to the contrary this was not going to be 'a piece of piss.'

It was a stiflingly hot morning. We were in an end of the corridor classroom, which meant that two of the classroom's sides were predominantly window thus adding to our very own 'greenhouse' effect. My hay fever always kicked in with a vengeance at this time of the year and, despite all my precautions, I was conscious of the fact that I could, at any given moment in time and without warning, convulse into an embarrassing fit of sneezing. My eyes would stream and I would be continually sniffing on days like these. I had actually returned to wearing glasses on odd occasions and, although the glasses were of the thick black rimmed national health variety that I had had since I was twelve and definitely not 'cool', helped immensely on such heavily pollinated days.

The Master in charge of the exam for the day, whom we'd never had teach us before, handed out the papers at five to nine as we sat at the desks nervously tapping our pens or trying to engage ourselves in small talk and reassure ourselves that all would end well.

'You may begin.'

Our first printed instruction on the paper was to read all the questions thoroughly before attempting to answer any. I thought it best to ignore this instruction once I had read and been totally baffled by question number one. I made a half-hearted attempt at a few answers. The sly buggers had instructed us to show our workings out in the margins down the side of the answer paper so there was very little scope for having a wild guess and hoping for the best. I gazed hopelessly around the room searching for any kind of inspiration. Why was maths not simply about numbers? Why did x have to equal certain parts of y minus z?

Why could I not grasp any of this?

I had gone through the entire paper twice. I had a stab at a couple of the not so difficult questions and knew I could not possibly answer any better than I already had. I continued to gaze hopelessly around the room. It was ten fifteen. An hour and a half still to go.

'Howdit go, Caz?' Turner enquired afterwards.

'Fucking awful, I'd not even seen half of what they were bloody on about before.'

'You're joking, it wasn't that bad. Not as bad as I expected anyway.'

'Thanks for the confirmation, now I know it was just me that was shite.'

I trudged home through the park with Phil. He hadn't made too good a fist of it either so I suppose I was able to gain a crumb of comfort from his failings as well.

We didn't have too long to dwell on our poor maths performance, however, as it was English Literature (part one) on Wednesday Afternoon and they would be coming at us thick and fast for the next four weeks.

By the end of June it was all over. Twelve years of supposedly the best years of my life have drawn to a close culminating in the torture I have just endured over the past six weeks. If they were the best years of my life then boy am I in for a wretched time for the next 85. (I am immortal).

It was now an agonising wait until early August for the results to come through but I was none too optimistic. The intention never was to stay on at school to further my education which was probably just as well given my performance over the past few weeks.

It was probably about the right time to start looking for a job. There was no mileage in pursuing a career at Tesco's. I didn't fancy becoming a butcher or a professional shelf stacker and I definitely did not see myself as management material (and neither did anybody else, especially Tesco's current manager who could have guided me along that path had I been 'a bit more suitable', whatever he meant by that).

I decided that I would write off again to various local businesses asking them if they were taking on school leavers but this time I would be one step ahead and mention that I had just taken my O levels at the Grammar School and expected three passes of which maths and physics would not be one of them. It did, unsurprisingly, limit the number of positive replies I would receive. A firm of solicitors were the first to send me a 'thanks, but no thanks' reply although what use I ever thought I could possibly offer our judicial system I have absolutely no idea. It did make me realise, however, just how naïve I was being in the whole of the situation.

I told my Mother that I had written to over ten different firms but there was never any real discussion with my family as to what I intended to do.

'You'll have to get a job and not loaf about for the rest of the summer', was about as much encouragement as I got, and that came from my stressed out Sister.

'Yes, I'd worked that one out, thank you, but I've an idea that people don't just knock on your door and say, 'hello John, come and work for us. It doesn't matter that you didn't do too well in your exams, we'll still employ you.'

In all honesty I didn't have a clue where to turn for advice.

It didn't help that now that I had left school and the football season was over that I wasn't seeing any of my schoolmates any more. And if the truth be realised I probably was never going to see half of them ever again. It had only been a matter of a couple of weeks but I had already drifted away from Phil, probably my most consistent ally from school, who for all I knew had probably got a job already.

Malc offered little help as he was still at tech. Barry, from three doors up the road, had already passed his driving test having not long since turned seventeen and suggested training to be a motor mechanic.

'What I know about cars, mate, can be written on the back of a postage stamp.'

'Never mind, you'll get all the training you need and be sent to college. By the time you're twenty-one you'll be a fully fledged mechanic.' He enthused.

I had written to a couple of garages on my diverse list of potential employees and one had written back asking me to 'pop down' for a look around if I wanted to. A bit informal, I thought, but never mind; maybe I will give it a go.

I decided to visit the garage that had replied to my letter. It was only a ten minute walk away in the 'dip' in London Road, halfway between my house and the town. It was predominantly a used car showroom but had a small workshop round the back to M.O.T. test any cars that would pass through their books. Barry had recommended that I try them as it was where he'd acquired his four year old Hillman Avenger from.

I was no stranger to the showroom itself. For some inexplicable reason there was a barber's shop situated inside the lobby and I had been going there for a number of years once every nine months or so whether I needed my hair cut or not.

I tentatively walked into the showroom on a Tuesday afternoon when I guessed they would not be particularly busy and started to wander around the selection of used cars on offer. There was a fairly new Ford Mark Three Cortina and a nearly new Morris Marina at the fore of the display of cars purposely positioned, one would suspect, to catch the eye of any potential buyer before you encountered the rusty, battered Hillman Imp, Mark One Escort and Austin Mini that made up the 'cheep and cheerful' selection. A young lad was furiously polishing the Escort for all he was worth but from where I was standing any attempts to buff the car up so that he could see his face in it seemed futile bearing in mind the heap of rust above the wheel arches. I was already beginning to feel uncomfortable with the surroundings and I hoped at this point in time that if there was a job going in the garage then this lad had already got it.

I was about to turn on my heels when a middle-aged bloke, his tatty blue overalls covered in grease and oil, spotted me.

'Looking for a car, Son?' He enquired.

'Nice little Escort there for you, boy.'

I thought not.

'No, mate! I . . er! . . I don't drive.' I said, wishing I hadn't.

'I was wondering if you were taking on any apprentices this year, I've just left school and I'm looking to start work.'

'Oh, you are, are you?' He seemed to mock.

'Know anything about cars?' He continued.

I was hardly likely to tell him that I knew Jack shit so I replied;

'A little, my mate has a car and I've helped him on occasions' I lied.

'Is that so, Son? Let's have a little look at this beauty then.'

With that he leant into the Escort and flipped the bonnet up from inside.

I must admit to having visions of what his wife must look like if he was describing this rust bucket as 'a beauty.' I decidedly disliked the git already.

'Now then, Son, any idea what the Carburettor does?'

Shit, I could feel myself turning red.

'No Idea, Son? It supplies and mixes the fuel to the engine, Son. You are aware that a car has an engine aren't you, Son?'

I don't want to be here any more.

'Any idea what the letters B.V.R. stand for, Son?'

'British Volvo er something', I offered.

'No, Son, it's a Black Vinyl Roof, there are loads of them about, you must have seen them.'

'Do you know anything about points and plugs, Son?' He continued.

'What, electricity plugs?'

I could see him starting to stifle a laugh. The obnoxious little shit that had been buffing the car was now sat down inside it and paying full attention.

'No, Son. The points and plugs that help to fire the engine, you are aware that a car has an . . . . . .'

'Yes, yes it has an engine.' I interrupted.

'Do you know what the common firing order is for the pistons? There they are, Son . . . look, four of them.'

Blank.

'The firing order?' He repeated.

'Er, one-two-three-four, I suppose.' I reluctantly offered.

'Sorry, Son, try one-three-four-two'.

'If you heard a knocking or tapping coming from the engine what would you suspect, Son?'

'Probably that something had fallen off.' I replied, certain that I had got something right.

'You may be right there, but more likely than not your tappets may need resetting'.

Tappets?.. tapping?.... now he is taking the piss, I was convinced.

'What's this thing here at the front?' He asked, pointing to the radiator grill.

I knew this one, this is getting easier.

'It's the radiator.' I confidently announced.

'Well, hurrah for that, we've got one right.' Came the sarcastic reply.

'Now you know that to change the radiator the engine must have first cooled right down to reduce any chance of burning yourself, yes?'

This sounded logical so I saw no reason to doubt, and felt that at long last he was trying to offer some encouragement.

'Yes.' I agreed.

'OK, Son, then whereabouts in the Volkswagen Beetle do you think you would find the radiator?'

He was grinning again.

'Same place?' I guessed.

'Tell him, Boy'. He said to the buffer in the car.

'It hasn't got one, Dad, Beetles are air cooled.'

'Well done, son, anybody who knows anything about cars knows that.'

Bollocks, I felt about four inches tall.

'Have you any idea where the engine is in a Hillman Imp, Son.'

I sensed another trick but had no idea how to respond.

'It doesn't have an engine.' I feebly replied.

'Of course it's got a bloody engine, Son. All cars have engines, tell him, boy.'

'It's in the boot, Dad.'

'Of course it's in the boot, any idiot knows that.' He said, patting the little shit on the head like he'd just become 'Brain of Britain.'

'Look, Son.' He placed his grubby hand onto my shoulder, 'Take a bit of friendly advice. You don't know the first thing about cars do you?'

I couldn't argue.

'My lad here is only fourteen and has been coming here to the shop with me since he was seven. You need to have a love and a feel for the cars that you are working on. You can't just treat them as any old job.'

He had a point and, although still detesting him and his oily rag of a son with a passion for stringing me along, felt I should heed his words.

I cursed Barry for putting me up to the idea in the first place. I had known that I was not particularly interested in cars from the outset but I suppose I had to give it a try. Now I could never go back to the barbers in the garage for fear of bumping in to Father and bloody son again.

Barry laughed uncontrollably when I told him of my experience at the garage.

'Why didn't you tell me you were going, I could have at least talked a few basic things through with you first, instead of you going in blind and making a pig's ear of it for yourself.'

'Thanks a lot, mate, a bit bloody late now though.' I groaned.

I didn't tell anyone else that I'd been to a garage. It was still all too painful and I think I have learnt my lesson.

I was still at Tesco's in the High Street and had managed to secure an extra day (Thursdays) to cover the summer period. I do not intend to stay there for much longer whatever happens as I have already made it clear that my future lies elsewhere other than in baked beans and kitchen towels. Nick was still in the butchery department and had hinted that he may continue at school for a further two years if results went favourably for him. I was shocked. If anybody was on a par with me at school I felt it was Nick. He could possibly have endured a spot of peer pressure prior to his examinations and without my knowledge actually knuckled down and done quite well. I felt rather betrayed. It seemed as if all this talk of not bothering to revise and just take each exam as it comes was adhered to only by good old, stupid old me. Pals that had said they couldn't wait to see the back of school had in the end put their names down to continue in the sixth form if their results allowed. How could they?

It was, of course, not even an option open to me by now. I had made my intentions clear from the outset and there is no way I was going to renege now. No, I would keep on trying. I was not going to let one little setback at a poxy garage put me off. There's a job somewhere out there with my name on it. It's just a matter of finding it.

Kettering is predominantly a shoe trade town. Like Northampton and the surrounding areas for some reason fate had decreed that Northamptonshire would be awash with tanneries and the likes to become the throbbing centre of the countries boot and shoe making industry.

Half of Kettering's working population is employed in a shoe factory in some capacity or another, be it in management or on the shop floor. Almost every small back street in the North End of the town must have two or three factories ranging from the larger Timpsons, or the Dolcis and G.U.S. Footwear Corporations to the smaller family businesses such as Loake Brothers, Frank Wrights' and Allen and Caswells.

It was very easy to swap allegiances as well during your working life in the trade. Once you have become an experienced and reliable craftsman you can pick and chose the best paying company at the time to work for.

Most of the firms operate a piece—work scheme, which means the more shoes you can bash out in a week the more wages you will receive. It is very much a cut throat market in that one firm's order books could be full for the next couple of months whereby another firm was putting their labour onto a three day week due to a lack of orders. In three months time the roles were reversed as the company with falling orders would go out canvassing to win custom back from those heavily producing at the time and thus the labour would move around accordingly to satisfy each factories needs.

The job section in the local paper was always awash with companies advertising: 'Six experienced Clickers urgently required.' or 'Skilled Finishing Room Operators needed for immediate start.' Consequently Joe Bloggs, on a four day week down the road, would be hammering on the door at eight o' clock the next morning and as the company were so desperate for his services due to an order for 25,000 Brogues from France was not only guaranteed a start by a quarter past eight but could also haggle his own salary.

Once again I did not know if a job in a shoe factory would suit me. Certainly the money looked to be there, once fully qualified, but I somehow could not foresee myself stuck in a hot, sweaty factory all day.

'It's bloody hard work, Son.' My Father had commented in one of his very rare showings of interest.

'Never fancied it myself.' He dismissively remarked.

No, I thought. No nipping down to the pub for a swift six or seven—pint interlude and then going back to operate complex machinery.

'There are other areas in the trade, Dad. Management, Sales, Engineering.'

He shrugged his shoulders, 'Whatever.'

Thanks for the show of support.

I had written to a couple of the larger companies to no avail but had received a fairly encouraging reply from the Cohen Brother's, one of the smaller factories, in Wood Street. I had told them of my expected achievements at school and they had suggested that I call in for an informal meeting with their personnel department to see if I was suitable.

I was determined not to make the same mistake as with the garage and this time phoned them before I caught the bus to let them know I was coming down and to establish a contact.

I had even made the effort to look smart as I had put on my pastille green shirt with massive 'dog' collars and a decent pair of trousers (a pity my budget hadn't stretched to a smart pair of shoes considering my destination).

I met a Peter Hurst who, immediately impressed with my educational background, informed me that I was far too qualified to work on the factory floor.

'But I haven't even got my exam results yet, Sir.' I explained.

'With all due respect, Mr. Caswell, it's a bit rough and ready out there and I just feel you may be more suited to, how shall I put it, a more delicate a start to your working career.'

I wasn't quite sure what he meant.

'We tend to take on kids of your age who haven't been to the Grammar School or who's Fathers and their Fathers before them have been in the shoe trade.'

Bloody hell, I've only been left the Grammar School for a couple of months and already there's a stigma attached.

'If you like,' He continued, 'It's only Wednesday today, come in again tomorrow morning and we'll get one of the men on the floor to show you around a bit more on the factory floor and see how you feel then.'

'Okay, that's fine.' I accepted.

I got the impression that Mr. Hurst had at least been slightly more positive than the garage prat and decided to take him up on his offer.

I duly arrived back outside the factory at ten to eight the next morning and went straight to Mr. Hurst's office.

I stood outside and witnessed the rush to 'clock in' as the expressionless workforce took their positions at their various machines and lit their last fag, with one eye on the massive clock at the end of the room, in readiness to fire their machines into action dead on the stroke of eight.

'Ah, you've decided to come along.' Mr Hurst greeted me at five past eight. 'Sorry I'm a bit late.'

I noticed he was still wearing the same shirt and tie that he'd had on yesterday. I, for my part, had dressed down a bit with an old grey school shirt and a pair of dungies.

'I had a word with one of our gaffers after you left last night and he'll be along at half past eight to give you a bit of a guided tour once everything has settled down outside on the floor, we'll have a coffee while we're waiting.'

I was already starting to like Mr. Hurst.

'We've just received a large order from Germany for a range of men's shoes that we produce here on the site.' With that he proceeded to show me a quite impressive brochure of men's and ladies shoes that the sales team would take all over the continent to show potential customers.

'It's very much supply on demand in this industry.' He pointed out. 'But hopefully this contract and others that we have in the pipeline will keep us active for the foreseeable future.'

There was a knock on Mr. Hurst's office door and a scrawny looking man entered. He must have been about fifty with slick, greasy grey hair, the biggest pair of spectacles I have ever seen in my life, tatty jeans, light blue shirt, a grey work jacket and a red tie that looked decidedly out of place with the rest of his attire.

'Ah, come in Fred.' Mr. Hurst beckoned.

He already had.

He continued, 'Fred! This is John Caswell, who we spoke about last night. John! This is Fred Wilson, our closing room gaffer. He will show you all he knows . . . and then at twenty to nine . . . Ha! Ha!'

The two men shared the joke and Fred led me outside the office and onto the factory floor.

'Tosser, that bloke is.' Fred muttered immediately, referring to Mr. Hurst. 'Always in late every morning, doesn't have to clock in like the workers on the shop floor 'cause he's management'.

He aimed a tiny piece of spittle onto the floor and mumbled to himself. 'Tosser.'

I didn't argue, but because this was my first experience of people clocking in asked about the system.

'You're allowed three minutes grace.' Fred explained. 'If you haven't clocked in by three minutes past eight you lose half an hours pay. Same at lunchtime (twelve 'til one). That tosser will stroll back at quarter past one some days and nothing gets said because he works in the bloody office.'

I quickly detected a big resentment of the office management in his voice despite the fact that he, himself, was a foreman.

'Right then, Sir. What do you want to know?' Fred asked.

I suspected the 'Sir' to be slightly patronising.

It obviously was.

'Are you coming to work here on the floor or are you intending to become another tosser in the office?'

'Please, Fred. It's John.' I quickly pointed out. 'I don't know yet. I did write to the company explaining that I had just left Grammar School and they invited me along for a look around.'

'Grammar School, eh! Oh well, there's always a first.'

As we entered the first room I was quite taken aback by the smell of the leather. Not an unpleasant smell at all but very strong.

'OK, John, we'll try to follow the process through from start to finish . . . . . . and in here' he began, pointing through 360 degrees, 'the clicking room . . . we are preparing the 'Uppers'. The upper part of the shoe. The leather upper is cut to shape along with the soft leather or cloth inner shoe lining using one of these.'

He proceeds to snatch a rather lethal looking knife from a work colleague, who protests, and thrusts it in front of my face.

'It'll have your eye out if you're not careful.'

It very nearly did, I thought.

About four inches long, the knife ended with a very sharp hook, which could pattern the shoe with deadly precision. Not that Fred showed any of this skill as he cut a star shape out of the piece of leather his friend had just cut.

All of the Uppers' material came in skins and were cut out in this fashion and any wastage of leather was frowned upon.

Speed was also of the essence and considering that most of the workers were on 'piece work' (£1 per 200 cuts), borrowing a clicker's knife to demonstrate to some school kid was not met with too much approval.

'Leave it out, Fred; I'm not doing too good today as it is.' The unfortunate clicker argued.

'Tosser.' Fred muttered under his breath.

'Right then John, next we visit the closing room.'

Fred led the way to another area. I can only assume that the terminology 'room' came from much bigger factories, as this one seemed all very open-plan. It did, however, have a very strong smell of glue in this part of the room though.

'Christ, you could get pissed in here!' I joked to Fred.

Fred laughed. 'Yeah, not too advanced with the ventilation system in here, mate. OK in the summer with the windows open.'

'Right, as you can see, some sewing machines in here along with various other gadgets for closing the shoe. That is; joining the uppers and the linings together. Glued at first and then sewn. Pretty much the same is going on in the parallel benches over there only they are dealing with the soles of the shoes, a bit more complex bearing in mind that a rib is attached to the insole so that a welt can be sewn on to allow you to accommodate the heel of the shoe.'

He paused, took a deep breath and looked me in the eye.

'With me?'

I definitely was not. The effects of the glue coupled with the strong smell of the leather were combining with the 'this is a Riveter, this is a Sole Grading Machine, this is a Beeder' to send my tiny mind spinning.

Thankfully Fred took me outside so that he could have a crafty fag and I was able to clear my head a bit.

'Smoke, John?' He offered.

'No thanks, Fred. I don't.' I replied.

'Definitely a well educated lad, they're no good for you.' He advised.

'Not well educated, just wise after listening to my Father spluttering up his lungs every morning for all these years. I will never smoke.' I confidently replied.

Back inside we went to the 'Last' preparation room. This is where the uppers that have been collected from the closing room have stiffeners inserted into the backs and are moulded into shape and brought together with the bottom part of the shoe in readiness to become one in the shoe making room.

'I just can't believe that a single pair of shoes passes through so many pairs of hands.' I commented to Fred.

'And each one on piece work, John.' He replied. 'So if the clicker is having an off day and doesn't produce his quota of uppers, it has a snowball effect and the people in the prep. room don't have so many pairs pass through and so on and so on. It can get a bit bitchy, I'll tell you.'

I was getting along fine with Fred and it was no sleight on him that I was fast losing interest in my surroundings.

I accompanied him to the delicatessen just down the road in the lunch hour and he bought me a wonderful ham sarnie and a bottle of orange. A lot of the workers, a fair percentage of them on push—bikes, went home for lunch. Many lived locally anyway and I'm sure that if I were spending every day working in that stuffy, stinking environment I would also be seeking some home comforts after four hours.

'A penny for them?' Fred said as we sat in the factory's back yard.

'What are you thinking? You don't seem too sure.'

I told Fred about my garage experience and that if the truth were known I had absolutely no idea what I was going to do with myself job-wise.

'I don't think I want to be stuck in a factory, Fred. It's not that I'm not interested. I am enjoying Myself today but I think that the only thing I will leave here with is the knowledge that I don't want to work in a shoe factory.'

'I sensed that quite early on, mate, you don't want to become a tosser either though, do you?' He smiled.

'No, I don't.' I chuckled.

Fred managed to persuade me to go back with him for the afternoon, he was getting a good skive out of showing me around and the experience wouldn't do me any harm.

We went back after lunch and made for the making room. This is where the welt, sole and heel are put onto the shoe. The whole process passed by from one person to another in a flash as first the welt was sewn around the upper, passed on to the inseam trimmer who in turn passed it on to the welt beater. Through the tack machine to fix the seat board and shank and eventually on to the gang nailer which fixed the seat of the shoe to the insole. I think!

I was totally lost now, and Fred knew it.

The factory did actually have a second room and the surroundings were a little bit more pleasant in the finishing room.

At least you could actually see an end product in here and the distinct smell of wax and shoe polish was a bit better than the glue, although still slightly overpowering.

First the heel and sole edges are smoothed and trimmed with the completed shoe then waxed and polished to a glass shine. Any fine details to the shoe are then added by hand at this stage before the last is removed and the inside checked by hand to make sure there are no tacks or nails left protruding up through the insole.

'Is this part purposely overlooked when making school shoes?' I joked.

'Yes, probably' Fred acknowledged with a grin.

The shoes then pass through a strict final examination to make sure that the finished product measures up to the highest of standards and where the upper is cleaned and the laces inserted. The sole is then stamped and the pair of shoes wrapped in tissue, boxed and labelled ready for dispatch to the customer.

'And that', concluded Fred, 'as they say is that. It's getting on for half four now so I'll return you to the tosser. I'd like to say that we'll see you again sometime in the future but somehow I doubt it.'

'Thanks, Fred.' I genuinely replied. 'How does the saying go? I'll make my excuses and leave?'

It was a pity. I got the impression that Fred was very well liked on the factory floor by his colleagues and, if at all possible, today had taught me not to judge people by first impressions.

I returned to Mr. Hurst's office to collect my jacket.

'Well, John. Did Fred look after you OK?' He enquired. 'Fred's a good chap. Me and him get along just like that.' He crossed his fingers on one hand as if to imply blood brothers.

If only he knew.

'Yes, fine.' I replied. 'It's a bit hectic out there though, isn't it? And it is very uncomfortable.' I added trying to leave him in no doubt that I wasn't altogether impressed.

'Well, I did try to warn you. Still all the better to find out now isn't it? How would you feel about coming in to this side of the business, though?' He asked, inferring the office side. I mulled over how Fred saw 'this side of the business.' I had enjoyed Fred's company and had had a bit of banter with those on the shop floor so I didn't particularly relish the prospect of being perceived as 'one of the tossers in the office.'

'I would maybe need to think about it a bit.' I replied. 'I will need to wait for my results, surely, before committing myself.'

'Not necessarily John, I've been impressed with your honesty and the way you have presented yourself over the past two days. We can always find something for you if you are willing to learn.'

Good Lord, a compliment. I wasn't used to this.

'Thank you.' I must have seemed taken aback. 'I will see if anything else crops up but yes, I will bear your words in mind.'

'Good luck.' He wished, offering me his hand and then sending me on my way.

I have to say that I felt really pleased with myself on the bus home. I knew that I was not going to go back to Cohen's in any capacity whatsoever but having got along so well with Fred and having Mr. Hurst's words of encouragement ringing in my ears the future didn't seem so bleak after all.

I continued to plod along at Tesco's for the next four weeks until out of the blue I received a letter from a builder's merchant in Wellingborough, T.G.Lewis's. I had written to them way back in April before I had even taken my exams and forgotten all about them.

'Dear Mr. Caswell,' the letter began. 'Further to your enquiry of a vacancy for an office junior I am pleased to inform you that we do presently have such a position available.'

It had completely slipped my mind that I had written to these people, and it made me chuckle to Myself wondering what Fred at Cohen's would have thought at the sight of the words 'office junior.'

'If you are still interested in the position and would like to make an appointment for an interview please call this number and ask for Simon Lake, our transport manager.'

I did just that and arranged for an interview the following day at one thirty in the afternoon.

Getting to Wellingborough was not too difficult. The 407 bus stopped right outside my row of houses and, with only a short detour through the villages of Orlingbury, Little Harrowden and Great Harrowden, was pulling up in Church Street in the centre of Wellingborough some twenty—five minutes later. A round trip of just over nine miles.

The main yard and very small office block of T.G.Lewis Ltd. was a further ten minutes walk away in Station Road. I presented myself quite smartly once again with my old faithful green shirt but this time with a new pair of shoes. I had even spent the morning running a comb through my matted, curly locks but my Mother had needed to cut out some of the more stubborn tangles.

'You really must get yourself down to the garage for a haircut, Son.' My Mother had berated me.

'I can't go there again!' I retorted.

'Why ever not? You've always gone there, and besides, your hair is a mess.'

'I know, I know, I'll try the new Italian one in town at the weekend. I offered.

'Probably too late to help you in this interview by then, son.' She nagged. 'Are you going to wear a tie?'

It seemed pathetic but I only possessed my two school ties so I decided not to.

Once I had found my way to Station Road, this being my first solo jaunt to the wondrous town of Wellingborough, the yard itself rather took me by surprise.

I had actually walked past the tiny office building and across the entrance to the yard before I had realised I was there. It was not very well signed and I would have missed it completely had there not been a small hut on the other side of the entrance with a tiny notice board proclaiming 'T.G.Lewis (Builder's Merchants) Ltd.'

I walked up the three steps and opened the door into a six-foot square reception area with just enough room to accommodate a chair and stood at the glass hatch. There was a buzzer to press for attention but I felt it not necessary on this occasion as the two occupants of the office had lifted their heads in perfect synchronicity as I had opened the outside door and had already noticed me.

The first man sitting at the long desk, which spanned the width of the office, wheeled his chair over to the hatch and slid it open. He was probably in his early to mid thirties, mousy brown hair, with a safe short haircut, no particular style, and a patchy beard. Smartly dressed with a suit and tie.

'Good afternoon. I'm John Caswell.' I announced.

He offered his hand. 'Simon Lake.' He replied, and proceeded to give me the firmest handshake I had ever encountered in my entire life. 'Mr. Lewis is expecting you, so please come in. Oh! and this is our clerk David Heeley.'

He introduced me to the other bloke in the office, sat a good twenty feet away from where his chair originally was. Probably early twenties with thick, wiry black curly hair a bit like Noddy Holder with his fingers stuck in an electric socket.

I smiled as this time I received a very wimpish handshake and a nervous greeting. Fred would have had a field day with this one, I thought.

At the back of the office there was a single desk and chair and then a small corridor, which led to two more, smaller, separate offices with a large alcove which had a desk, chair and row upon row of files stacked up in no particular order on shelves above the desk.

A smart, smaller (about 5 foot 4 inches) gentleman then walked through the door and Simon introduced me to Mr. Thomas Lewis.

'Please, John, follow me and we'll talk in the Colonel's Office.'

Colonel's Office? Not in the army are we? I thought.

'Please sit down, John.' He beckoned as he eased himself gently into a large, leather seat behind the desk.

'My cousin and I run the business,' He began. 'Colonel Jack and I are both equal partners in the firm which was left to us by our Fathers who were brothers.'

Very nice I thought.

'We are a very small family business but have gained a very good reputation amongst local builders not only for our supply but also through our prices.' He continued.

'As well as being builder's merchants we are also stonemasons, which was Colonel Jack's Father's side of the business. We have tended to scale down that side of the business over the past couple of years as Colonel Jack is now approaching 60 and only comes into the office on three days a week, hence he is not here today.'

I was already beginning to like this warm and very friendly man.

'All we need at the moment is to add to the very small team that we have in the front office. You have already met Simon and Dave and with myself that is the team. So as you can deduce it is indeed a very small team.' He smiled.

'Simon is the transport manager and arranges the next day's tours of duties for our two lorries; we occasionally hire in a third if necessary. It is with Simon that we would mainly like you to become involved with initially although we will be looking at teaching you all aspects of the operation. How do you feel about that?' He concluded.

I must admit to feeling quite flattered by Mr. Lewis's tone and his explanation of what he was expecting. I assumed that others were applying for the position but he was conducting the interview as if a job offer to me was a formality.

'Yes, it sounds fine.' I found myself replying. 'I don't particularly know anything about the building trade though, I must admit.' I offered in complete honesty.

'That isn't a problem,' Replied Mr. Lewis, 'It is something that you will easily pick up and with your educational background that should not be too much of a difficulty. I won't be asking you to go out and build a wall, just to oversee the supply of materials to those who do want to build one.'

How eloquently put, I thought.

'Are there any other people who have put in for the job?' I asked.

'Oh, no there isn't, John. Sorry, please let me explain.' He continued.

'When we originally put the advert in the paper in April it was to look to get somebody in to help cover the summer holidays of Simon and David. Unfortunately when David took his holiday the poor lad that we took on just was not up to the task and he let us down two days in to Dave's holiday so we have been rather pushed. Instead of advertising again I remembered your letter at the time and realised that you must now have left school so I wrote to you.'

I nodded my understanding of the explanation.

'Would you like to give it a go?' He finally asked.

'Yes, Sir. Yes, I would.' I rather overly enthused.

'When can you start then, John?' He asked, standing up and shaking my hand.

'Will Monday be OK?' I asked with a broad, satisfied grin.

It was already fast approaching the end of June and I wanted to be installed somewhere by the school's summer holidays.

'Monday is fine. We look forward to seeing you at nine o' clock on Monday morning.'

As I left Mr. Lewis informed both Simon and David of my appointment for which they both nodded their approval and shook my hand again. I have never had my hand shook so many times in all of my life.

I walked back to Church Street to catch the bus back to Kettering feeling about ten feet tall. I had got my job. I didn't care that it was an office job. Mr. Lewis had been so kind and, I felt, genuine throughout my interview and I was going to make a good fist of it to repay his obvious faith in my potential.

My Mother was over the moon at the prospect of my starting work. I even received a complimentary grunt from Cath and a 'does that mean I won't have to give you any more pocket money' from my far from enthusiastic Father.

I completed the formalities of quitting as a shelf stacker at Tesco's the next day and I was offered the chance to work that weekend if I wanted to which I passed up on. I collected my wages from Mr Cairns on Friday morning and left with his good wishes ringing in my ears. We hadn't always seen eye to eye whilst I was there but I was always punctual and never missed a shift in all the time I was in his employ. I feel I may have just got under his skin a little in that I was never the most cultured of shelf stackers and was prone to dent the odd tin of tomato soup from time to time. However he had guaranteed me a reference should I require one in the future so I couldn't have been that bad.

I was up early the next Monday morning. My bus to Wellingborough passed the house at ten past eight which, barring delays, would get me into Wellingborough at twenty to nine at the very latest with only a ten-minute walk thereafter to ensure I would not be late. I knew I would be in for a battle for the bathroom with Cath at this time of day so decided on the early strategy to defuse any tension. I was in and out before she embarked on her mandatory half an hour's face attack. I was also acutely aware that she would not be around to hamper me for much longer. Steve was due home in four weeks time, mid-July, and due to start at college in Newcastle at the end of August. The plan was still very much that Cath would be accompanying him up to the Northeast and for that I remained eternally grateful. I was sure that I could live with her total domination of the bathroom for another eight weeks or so.

My Mum had treated me to a brand new shirt and tie set from 'Roadnights' the modern men's wear emporium of Kettering, and I had visited the 'Santos' Men's Barbers in Market Street to de-tangle and style my altogether much too long hair. I could now pass a comb through my locks without taking half my scalp with it but my trade mark centre parting remained and I still flatly refused to let him uncover my ears. I had had the length drastically reduced to shoulder length though.

My Father was also up at this time of the morning (he would catch the bus into town for an eight o' clock start at the hospital that I would get on for the return journey to Wellingborough).

'Making an effort, Son? If you'd have dolled yourself up like that at the interview you may have got the job.' He sniggered.

'I got the job, Dad.' I retorted.

'Oh, yes, so you did.'

I got the feeling that he resented the fact. He didn't wish me luck but that was no more than I had come to expect.

There was a slight drizzle as I waited for the bus, which annoyed me. I had not wanted to wear my old duffel coat if I could help it as I intended to buy myself a smart jacket with my first wage and I wanted desperately to look smart as I started work for the first time. The drizzle had turned into a downpour by the time I had reached Lewis's and I entered the office like a drowned rat.

'Morning, John. Raining is it?' Simon joked and immediately made me feel at ease.

'Here, let's get that coat off you.' He got up from his chair and helped me out of the sodden thing. Simon motioned back towards the tiny entrance I had just passed through.

'The door in the entry leads to the cloakroom come toilet; there are some clothes pegs there to hang your coat on. There is also a kettle for making the tea and coffee. A very important and integral part of your training today.' He smiled again. 'Put the kettle on, John.'

I hung my coat up to dry and returned to the office. It was ten to nine but still only Simon was in the office. A door around the back of the office block was unlocked and slammed shut.

'That'll be the girls.' Simon exclaimed.

I was introduced to the secretary, Jane Owens. Probably mid forties but all smiles and plenty of make up.

'And this is her assistant, Clare.' Simon continued.

My mouth must have hung open because Clare was a stunner. She could only have been about eighteen and I could feel myself turning beetroot. Clare went through to the cloakroom and started to brew up.

'What would you like, John?' She offered.

Wouldn't you like to know, I thought.

'Er, nothing for me thank you, I don't drink tea and I only ever have one cup of coffee a day which is usually first thing in the morning as soon as I get up.'

She brought me a glass of diluted orange anyway.

Dave then walked in right on the dot of nine. He had driven from Finedon where he lived and apparently always arrived at nine o' clock to the nanosecond.

'Bloody weather! Morning all.' He announced without looking at anybody in particular and plonked himself down at his desk.

Next to arrive at ten past nine was Mr. Lewis, although by now I already was aware that he was affectionately known as Mr. Thomas. The term being used, I guessed by the staff, because his partner and cousin had the title Colonel Jack so he was awarded the title 'Mr.'

Colonel Jack came into the office at ten. The aura that surrounded him quite plainly visible from the moment he entered the building. Stout, upright, grey bearded, spectacled and wearing a garish yellow and brown checked suit that only Colonel types can get away with. He was a tall man, a good six foot three with a very round and cheerful face and considering I had been told he was almost sixty looked remarkably fit and well toned.

'Good morning, Colonel.' Everyone called, comically, in unison.

'Good morning, ah! Is this the new recruit?' He bellowed fixing his gaze straight at me.

'Yes, Jack.' Replied Mr. Thomas. 'John Caswell.'

I shot up out of my seat like it was on fire. I needed no prompting.

'Welcome aboard, Son.' He shook my hand to the point of it being wrenched from my wrists and departed into his office.

At ten o'clock the final member of the office team breezed in and plonked himself down at the desk in the alcove with just a grunt as a greeting to us all.

'That is Cyril Munton', Simon informed me.

I was quite surprised as Cyril was well into his seventies.

'Cyril has worked for the company for years and is our one link to Colonel Jack's and Mr. Thomas's Fathers. He will constantly remind us of 'The good old days' and 'this wouldn't have happened if Mr. Thomas's Father was still alive etc. etc.'

I smiled as Simon continued. 'It is handy to keep him around the place as a lot of our customers have used us for years and having Cyril about helps maintain the continuity of things as far as our customers are concerned.'

We were introduced and I sat back to observe the rest of the hectic action for the remainder of the morning. A steady stream of small builders vans were turning up into the yard to pick up the odd 10 bags of cement here, the odd half a tonne of gravel there and the occasional concrete door lintel.

All the builders came to the hatch first to announce their requirements for which either Simon or Dave would fill in a numbered ticket with three copies and then direct them over to the small hut in the yard where three scruffy looking individuals loaded up their vans or lorries with the merchandise. I was taken over to the hut by Simon and introduced to the three lads who worked in there. Sam, the foreman, long, straight mousy hair and a blank stare, about 25. Tommy, probably the same age but with equally long greasy black hair, glasses and his head bowed so far down that to lift it took an enormous effort, and John Perkins, probably about 19 also with longish brown hair (about my length) but at least looked as if he had a bit more go in him than the other two, which I have to say wasn't particularly difficult.

I quite clearly knew very little about the building industry but was pleasantly surprised by how quickly I was able to pick things up. It amazed me at first as to how many different types of house brick there are from the obviously named 'Common' brick, which was by far the cheapest and used for most building purposes, especially council estates, to the more sophisticated 'Rustic' type and the effective 'Dapple' style patterned facing bricks. Obviously the more expensive the type of brick used for the purpose of the building the more expensive the finished said building.

Simon's role in the operation would be to take orders on the phone or in person from the various builders in the area and arrange day to day on site stock replenishment from our yard to the sites by means of our two small lorries.

Our main rivals for the trade were a much bigger company called Ellis and Everard's with whom we had no chance of competing. They had a fleet of around twenty lorries and were located on Wellingborough's much larger Finedon Road Industrial estate. Some of their lorries had ground breaking mechanical cranes on board and could load and unload 1,000 bricks within ten minutes. Whereas if one of our lorries were sent out to a site full to the gunwales with a similar amount of bricks poor Sam, Tommy and 'Perks' would have had to have spent the best part of a back breaking hour and a half humping the bricks on board by hand (and the process had to be repeated at the other end for off-loading the lorry).

All of this had to be taken into consideration by Simon when trying to arrange the itinerary of the two lorry drivers for the next day.

It was this part of the job that I quickly adapted to.

Orders were left haphazardly on scraps of paper on Simon's desk and at two o'clock precisely in the afternoon work began trying to decipher the scribble and collate it all into some sensible kind of order for the next morning. Just as Simon was putting the finishing touches to the rota at the third attempt on his typewriter (with the aid of a bottle of snowpache) Cyril's phone would ring and he could be heard promising one of his old builder chums two bags of cement for ten o'clock the next morning to a building site some twenty miles off the track that had been so painstakingly prepared and strategically worked out.

'I can't do it tomorrow, Cyril.' Simon would begin to explain as Cyril hung up, anticipating the request.

'But I've promised him now, Simon, that was Peter MaKay; can't you just fit it in?'

'Of course I can't just bloody fit it in, why didn't you check with me first before promising these things?'

'Okay, I'll have to phone him back. He won't be pleased.'

Cyril phones back.

'Hello, Peter, Cyril Munton from Lewis's again, I'm sorry but my transport will not be able to deliver to you at ten o' clock tomorrow morning. Sorry . . . . . Yes . . . . Yes . . . . . That's lovely Peter, thank you very much. Bye, now.'

'He said two o'clock would be fine, Simon.'

Simon dropped his head into his hands. He emerged quite red faced.

'I can't bloody do it at two o'clock, either Cyril, Oh for God's sake.' He shouted.

With that Simon ripped the freshly typed route plan from the typewriter, screwed it up and forcefully hurled it straight into the bin.

I looked at Dave who was doing his best to conceal a smirk.

'Nice shot, Simon.' Dave grinned.

'Thanks.' Simon looked up and sighed, before returning his head to his hands.

Ten minutes later Simon had plan D on the typewriter.

'Peter MaKay will be getting his cement at ten o'clock tomorrow morning, Cyril.' Simon announced with a touch of devilment.

'OK, thank you Simon.' Cyril sheepishly replied. I guessed he would wait until he was at home before phoning back to his builder with yet another change of plan.

With the exception of the occasional minor blip the entire operation went surprisingly smooth for most of the time. Colonel Jack's and Mr. Thomas' fingers were both firmly on the pulse at the helm and Simon was a more than competent aide to them both. Cyril did appear to have his uses although the two and a half days a week he would spend in the office did have a certain amount of 'nuisance' value attached to them.

Dave was the link from the main office to the two girls in the accounts and he spent most mornings chasing up unpaid bills.

It was quite comical, as Dave was by no means the most authoritative character one was ever going to meet. His fifth phone conversation of the week to a builder who still had an unsettled account to the tune of some two hundred pounds or more would take on the air of an invitation to bloody dinner.

'No, we still haven't received your cheque from last month and I may have to refer this to Mr. Thomas if it isn't paid soon, sorry.' He would threaten in his own, unique, monotonous drawl when I felt he should be ordering them to 'pay the fucking bill you tight arses or we wont be supplying you with any more bricks.'

I suppose tact plays an important role in the accounts side of things hence I was not allowed to interfere too much with Dave's side of the duties.

I was quite happy to organise the lorries, make the coffee from time to time, answer the phone and take the finished copies of the invoices from Dave's 'out' tray through to Jane and the lovely Clare.

I had stopped blushing by now every time I went through to their office but still hadn't plucked up the courage to say much more than 'Hi' to Clare.

'I think you might be in there, John.' Dave suggested when she made the teas and made me my 'special' orange drink. Imagine my horror when I learnt a few weeks later that Perkins from the yard had taken her to the pictures one night.

'He's a spotty, greasy oik covered from head to toe in bleedin' cement dust.' I argued in disgust.

'Ah, but he's probably got some hidden charisma that has so far eluded us, John.' Simon laughed.

I didn't know whether the bastards were winding me up or not but Sam, the yard foreman, was certainly in on the joke as he kept shaking his head and tutting whenever I went over to their hut.

'You should ask her out, John.' He encouraged one afternoon. 'Perks blew it the other week. Took her to the pictures and then went straight home when she wanted to go for a drink afterwards.'

I was still unsure and didn't say a word for a couple of days until, for some reason, I don't know what made me do it. I asked her. I was in the small cloakroom brewing up when she came in with a couple of dirty cups from her office. I closed the door.

'Er, Clare!' I began. 'I don't suppose you would like to come out for a drink with me on Friday night would you?'

Bloody hell, I've done it. I've asked her out.

I stood there for what seemed an eternity; I'd gone bright red. I knew—I could feel it.

Bloody hell she was gorgeous.

'Oh, John. That's sweet. I'm sorry but I don't think my boyfriend would approve.'

Boyfriend? Not bloody Perkins, I hoped.

'B.boyfriend, Clare? Oh. I didn't know.'

'He's in the army, John. I've been going out with him for three years now. Oh, I'm sorry. Don't worry, I wont tell anyone you asked.'

Phew! The bastards had stitched me up, I now realised.

'So you and Perkins didn't . . . ?' I began to ask.

'Perkins? What him in the yard? Do me a favour.' She scornfully protested.

I couldn't get out of there quick enough. What on Earth had possessed me to ask her out in the first place I will never know. Sure she was absolutely stunning but how had I ever thought that she would be remotely interested in a scrawny little geek like me that can't even keep his hair tidy and was only marginally better turned out than bloody Perkins.

Fortunately Clare did not embarrass me any further and as I had only really muttered a few pleasantries to her beforehand was able to continue likewise after the 'cloakroom' incident.

Dave did ask me a couple of weeks later, in front of Simon and Mr. Thomas, if I had 'Gone off the idea of taking Clare out.'

'No, Dave.' I countered. 'She's not really my type.'

'Just as well.' Piped up Mr. Thomas. 'Her boyfriend comes home on leave from the army at the weekend.' Dave and Simon just grinned to each other. I vowed not to be so gullible in the future.

It was now well in to August. I had been at Lewis's for just over two months and it was pure luxury to be able to have money to spend. It didn't exactly burn a hole in my pockets but £13.70p take home pay every Friday suited me very nicely indeed, thank you.

A Large blue envelope plopped through our front door one morning addressed to me. We knew what they were. My exam results.

'I'm not too bothered really.' I tried to offer as an excuse before I opened the envelope.

'I've got a job and it isn't reliant on the contents of this letter.'

'Come on, open it up.' huffed Cath, in pure anticipation of my failure.

It was late afternoon; the letter had been sitting on the kitchen table since half past nine.

'I've passed four.' I yelled in complete surprise.

They were the four that in all honesty I felt I had a chance in. English Language, Engineering Drawing, Scripture and History (grade C). The expected failures followed although I was disappointed to achieve a U in Maths (ungraded, I believe).

The next day's post bought my GCSE results with the expected passes of little use in Art and French but a Grade A pass in English Literature, which equated to an E grade success at O level standard, thus making an impressive return of five O level passes.

I was over the moon. My Mother was ecstatic. I had hoped for three but never expected five. It was also five more than several of my form S colleagues had achieved.

My future, at long last, was indeed beginning to look bright.

I was settled in my new job and I didn't have to work Saturday afternoons anymore, so I could now watch 'The Poppies' every home game.

We had found an excellent new Friday night venue for drinking at away from the annoying, childish school kids. We now went to the Kettering Town Rugby Football Club's Social Club, ironically right next door to the Grammar School.

And just to add the icing to the cake my Sister was about to move up to South Shields with Steve for six months (although rumour had it they would be back with us for four weeks at Christmas). Steve had been home for a month now and I had really grown to like him. In a strange sort of way it would be him that I would miss the most when they did eventually go 'Up North'.

I suppose never having an older or a kid brother adhered me a bit to him. The family hand of fate only lumbering me with an older Sister and I guess I found it fascinating to have someone around who could at least speak my own language.

Steve's last voyage to sea had been on a 'Geest' ship transporting bananas around the World and he had taken in, amongst others, The Bahamas and The Virgin Islands before going off to New Zealand. How I envied him that trip. My Grandfather, on my Mother's side, had emigrated to New Zealand years before and lived in Auckland. I still remained 'Pen-pals' with my Grandfather as I had done since I met him for the one and only time in 1964 when he stayed with us for two months. It still remained an ambition of mine to see him again.

I took Steve's tales of opening up the hatches and finding spiders as big as your fists peering out at you from amongst the bananas with a pinch of salt but hung on his every word that he spoke about concerning his 'runs ashore' and his boozy antics aboard ship (I think he was grateful to have someone to share these stories with as, according to Cath, he had led a monastic existence for the past six months).

'It's such a pity about your maths and physics results, John.' Steve had said to me. 'There are so many companies taking on Cadets, but you need those O levels to get in.'

I have to admit to being impressed with the idea. Had this conversation been taking place probably three months ago before I got the job at Lewis's I may even have been tempted.

'I don't need to be an Officer though Steve, surely?' I asked.

'Well, no. You could always try as a deck hand, although most people with your education would go as an Officer.' Steve replied.

'But most people with my education aren't shit at maths and physics.'

'Look'. He said. 'Before I go to South Shields I'll leave you the addresses of some shipping companies to write to if you want to.'

I nodded. I was quite interested I have to admit.

We had never had any such career seminars at school concerning the Merchant Navy and even if we had, before I met Steve, I doubt I would have been interested. Steve gave me the addresses of five shipping companies before he left. BP, Shell, Esso, Athel line and Stevenson Clarkes. The first four were tanker companies and Steve thought that these would be a better bet as all employed British Ratings (some other companies employed British Officers but with a Malaysian, Chinese or Philippine Crew).

I mentioned what Steve and I had discussed to Dave at work one day and that he had left me a list of companies to write to if I felt interested enough.

'My elder brother worked for BP for a couple of years.' He told me.

'What, you've never mentioned that to me before.' I exclaimed.

'You've never asked. I didn't know you were interested in joining the Merch.'

'I've never been interested before. I might be now.' I continued.

'What job did he do in the Navy? Why did he only do two years?'

'He went in the catering department as a galley boy at first and then went on to become a Steward. He came out because of his girlfriend. They got married and have got a couple of kids but he loved it while he was there. He's been all over the World, I bloody envy him I do. I couldn't do it.'

'Why not?' I questioned.

'Well, y'know I've been here eight years now.'

Bloody hell, I thought. You're only 24, man. Am I looking at myself in eight years time here?

Scary!

Doubts had definitely been put into my mind again. I kept harking back to the way Fred at Cohen's shoe factory had perceived office workers. I kept looking at Dave (and Simon for that matter), both safe and secure for life. No ambition, just plod on and organise tomorrow's transport and take the occasional bit of flack from Cyril until he's 130 years old.

My mind was made up for me in very strange circumstances at the end of September. I arrived home from work at half past five as usual to be met by my Mother sitting down at the kitchen table (nothing unusual in that).

'Sit down a minute, John. I've got something to tell you.'

Sounds serious I guessed.

'Your Father is going to leave home and move back to Bury St. Edmunds. We are going to get a divorce.' She announced quite matter of factly. As if she was just asking me if I wanted gravy with my dinner or not. No drama, no hysterics just a plain and simple statement.

'Oh!' I replied, not knowing particularly whether I was pleased or just relieved.

'Catherine has to all intense and purposes left home and you're more than capable of fending for yourself now that you have a job so I am going to get Myself a full time job to be able to afford to keep the house on.' She continued.

I fathomed that finding herself full time employment made my Dad surplus to requirements but in all fairness I had begun to realise a while ago just what she had had to endure during her quite obvious loveless marriage.

It became apparent that this had been simmering for a few weeks, months or more than likely years.

Whether or not Cath leaving had indeed fuelled my Mum's desire to break the chains or me leaving school and getting a job was a contributing factor I could not be sure. Probably a culmination of the two but it was quite plain to see that my Mother had no intention of growing old with my Father.

I should have felt a sense of remorse or possibly even guilt at the situation but I felt neither. I probably hadn't been the best of kids to have around the house at times but, hey, surely that should work both ways. Since taking me to stand outside the pub until the novelty wore off when I was about eight my Father had never done anything constructive with me. He had threatened to take me to see The Poppies on numerous occasions but never actually got round to it. Electing the paperboy who was four years my senior to take me to my first ever game in the 1964-65 season.

Mum and Cath had a regular twice monthly Saturday evening visit to the pictures. I had no such luxuries. If I was lucky I could walk down to the town on my own on a Saturday evening and get the 'Chronicle and Echo Sports Green 'un' newspaper for him whilst he slept off his lunchtime drinking session. Hardly the stuff to inspire strong male bonding.

He had got himself a job as a chef at the hospital in Bury St. Edmunds. He didn't even have the good grace to say a word to me about the situation until the evening before he was about to leave. And even then he chose a moment when I was all ready to go out and obviously running late.

'I suppose your Mother has told you what's going on has she, Son?' He asked with his head slightly bowed down.

'Yes, Dad, she has.'

'Well, keep in touch won't you son; I'll send you my address.'

He offered me his hand.

Was that it? I thought. Was that the only thing he was going to say to me? No explanation, no 'sorry it's turned out like this.'

Obviously that was it as he just stood there in my bedroom doorway looking slightly sorry for himself. I took his hand but pulled him towards me and embraced him.

'I do love you, son.' He said, quietly, patting my back.

I could feel myself starting to well up. If he had said those words to me before then they had been so long ago that I had forgotten them.

I left for Lewis's the next morning as usual and when I arrived home in the evening he had gone.

My Mother had my tea ready for me and we ate in total silence. She had quite visibly had a hefty burden removed from her shoulders and I felt very happy for her even if it would probably take me time to adjust to not having him around the house despite his paternal shortcomings.

I was feeling a little bit of sympathy for my Father at this moment in time but was not daft enough not to realise that the situation was very much of his own making. Mother spring-cleaned the house from top to bottom (in September) and within days all trace and smell of my Father had disappeared.

Cath was advised of his departure by letter and her single word response to the whole sorry episode was 'Good.'

I would like to think that if ever I have kids and left them when they were only 16 that they would feel just a little bit more compassion than both my Sister and me were showing at this very moment.

My Mother gave up her morning cleaning duties that had helped her to scrimp and scrape for pin money all those years and got herself a sewing machinist position at a lingerie factory at the other end of town. She didn't become extravagant overnight but she no longer worried about people knocking on the door for payment or of bills of the red variety dropping through the letterbox.

For the first time in my living memory she was happy.

I wrote to the shipping companies that Steve had given me. I wasn't quite sure what reception I would receive or either for that matter if it was definitely what I wanted. I guess I was still a bit mixed up with recent events at home, but I wrote none the less. BP, Esso and Shell all replied that they did not personally recruit ratings and that if I was looking to join the Merchant Navy should apply to the British Shipping Federation. Athel Line were slightly better in their response saying that if I was interested in joining their company as a Deck Hand I would need to undergo a fourteen week training course for Deck Boys at The National Sea Training School in Gravesend. If I did decide to enrol they would happily consider me once I had completed the course successfully.

Stevenson-Clarke didn't reply at all.

I kept the idea in mind for the time being. There was a lot to consider. For a start it would mean leaving home, a prospect not so bad in the present circumstances now that my Mum had gained her independence and, of course, fourteen weeks at a sea school literally meant going back to school. An idea I didn't fancy too strongly at all but something I knew I would have to endure if I was serious in my intentions.

I decided that I would mull things over for a bit longer. It's strange how you can have an absolutely brilliant idea one moment and then be just a little bit apprehensive once the chance to make the possibility become a reality presents itself.

I was starting to get on very well at Lewis's. Dave had become quite a good friend and I was working well with Simon. Mr Thomas and Colonel Jack were indeed excellent people to work for and it was fairly obvious why the small workforce remained totally loyal to them and to the company.

Despite Colonel Jack's quite overpowering and intimidating appearance of authority he treated all the members of his staff with respect and politeness. Even in the most obvious of foul moods when a customer or supplier had let him down he was never discourteous to us or made us the subject of his wrath. How I would have loved to have taken him in to meet the masters at my old Grammar School to give them a few lessons on how to win the respect of people.

Dave was also a keen football supporter, like myself, and followed Kettering's deadly rivals Northampton Town, aptly nicknamed 'The Cobblers.' Simon was not so keen on local football but confessed to liking to watch 'Match of the Day' on a Saturday night or England whenever their games appeared on the television.

With both the Poppies and the Cobblers having started their respective campaigns successfully the banter in the office generally revolved around matters football with the odd tonne of sand and cement thrown in occasionally.

Also looming on the horizon (October 17th, to be precise) was England's World Cup Qualifier at Wembley against Poland. This was much more Simon's cup of tea but a bit of a worry as well as England needed to win to stop the Poles qualifying at our expense.

'Shall we go?' Simon proposed one morning about a month before the game.

'What?' I laughed. 'It'll be sold out by now, surely.'

'I can get three tickets, no problem.' Simon assured Dave and me.

'I have my contacts. Do we want to go?'

'You're bloody right we want to go.' Piped up Dave.

Two days later Simon was true to his word and had us booked onto a 'Shelton-Osborne' coach with three seats high up in the Wembley South Stand opposite the twin towers.

The day could not come quick enough for me. I never in my wildest dreams ever imagined that I would get a chance to go to Wembley Stadium. It wasn't as if Kettering Town was ever going to grace the lush green playing surface in an F.A.Cup Final now, was it? Or Northampton Town for that matter.

The media hype before the game added to the sense of the occasion and the three of us must have been incredibly boring to those around us at work as we spoke of nothing else until the day arrived.

We all brought a change of clothes into work with us and at half past three Dave drove us to the coach pick up point and left his car in the nearby car park to drive us home on our return.

Simon had a holdall full of beer and sandwiches. I was most surprised considering how conservative Simon appeared at work. Dave only had the one can as he would be driving later on that evening but I helped Simon see the rest of the cans off as the coach became more and more rowdy as we headed down the M1 towards London.

I was most grateful of the service stop before we progressed into London however as I had just discovered that drinking beer and sitting on a coach unable to relieve oneself was not a very comfortable set of circumstances. It is just as well that we stopped when we did as the next two hours passed at snails pace as we approached Wembley. We finally arrived at 7.30, the scheduled kick off time, only to fortunately learn that the kick off had been delayed until eight o' clock due to the thousands of other fans in the same situation as ourselves. I.e. late!

It meant that we could soak up the atmosphere without having to rush too much and enjoy the awesome walk down Wembley way approaching the stadium. I had seen the pictures before and on the television on cup final day but to actually experience the sensation of being there was intoxicating to say the least.

We reached our seats just five minutes before the players came onto the pitch. I was numb with excitement. The noise as the players came out was deafening and the expectations of 100,000 people immense. It didn't matter that we went in at half time with the score goal less. The Polish goalkeeper Jan Tomaszewski could not possibly continue to defy the laws of gravity and pure, unadulterated, shit good luck to keep his goal intact for a further forty-five minutes and it would only be a matter of time before his defences were breached. Then, midway through the second half the unimaginable happened. Sloppy defending allowed the Poles to score in the goal right beneath us. The whole arena was stunned into silence.

Amazing. You could hear a pin drop. It was eerie.

A solitary voice to our left started a cry of England! England! and slowly but surely the whole crowd reacted until the volume was up to ear shattering again.

The whole turn of events only served to inspire their bloody goalkeeper to even greater heroics and although he was beaten once by an Allan Clarke penalty the Poles clung on to a fortunate draw and took their place in the 1974 finals in West Germany.

Amid the huge disappointment we left the ground wondering if we would ever see a goalkeeping display like that ever again. Somehow I doubted it. He just seemed to dive and the ball followed him. He saved with his feet, his hands, his arse, every bit of his bloody anatomy got in the way of the ball and the goal.

To compound our misery and to make matters even worse it took us a further two hours to get out of London, thanks mainly to people not being able to find the coach. Admittedly we found it more by luck than by judgement but what a nightmare it is trying to get in and out of this place. Still, I felt I should not complain. Dave didn't drop me off at home until ten to three in the morning but I had just had the experience of a lifetime and I would surely never get back to Wembley again with a full capacity of 100,000 people inside.

Needless to say I over slept the next day and was late into work but I was not alone.

Cath and Steve came home ten days before Christmas for a month and bought with them some staggering news.

They were to get married in early March the next year.

Steve was to finish his course in February and the plan was for Cath to then accompany him on his next trip to sea as Steve would have been promoted to Fourth Mate.

With the pair of them back around me for a few weeks the conversation predictably turned back to whether I was going to give it a go at sea Myself or not. Steve could not believe that I had dithered after receiving such a positive reply from Athel line.

'What on Earth are you waiting for, John?' He asked.

'I don't think this sea school recruits after you are about seventeen and a half and you're only two days away from your seventeenth birthday.'

Christ! I hadn't even considered that.

'To qualify as a deck boy I think part of the criteria is that you are actually a boy, John. You are a year away from being classed as a man, God help us all.' He pointed out.

It was definitely now or never. I felt that if I didn't make a positive move I would regret the whole thing for the rest of my life.

Did I really want to be stuck in Kettering for the rest of my life?

No.

Did I really want to be stuck in a Builder's Merchant's office and turn into Dave by the time I was twenty-four?

No.

Did I particularly fancy any of the alternatives? Shoe Trade, Weetabix, Steelworks at Corby?

No.

Did I really fancy listening to Cath and Steve coming home every six months and telling me about the wondrous places they have been to this voyage and what an absolute arse I had made of myself for passing up the opportunity to do likewise when it arose?

No.

Did I want to get away from this drudgery and see the World a little bit? You'd better believe it.

I sent off my application form to The National Sea Training School in Denton, Gravesend, Kent together with my proposal of work on completion of the course from Athel Line Ltd. I just prayed it didn't get lost in the Christmas post, but the deed was done. All I could do now was sit back and wait.

Dave was delighted that I had finally written but I hadn't told anyone else at Lewis's yet. I didn't want to count my chickens or build my own hopes up too much just to be let down with an almighty crash.

I sat back and enjoyed my Christmas.

I told my Mother what I had done and she seemed supportive.

'I'm not at all surprised.' She told me when I announced my move.

'I could see that Steve had made a huge impression on you, and if that's what you really want to do then who am I to stand in your way? I hope it works out for you.'

I hadn't foreseen any protest from her but it must have been a daunting prospect that I was about to up-roots as well. Just four months ago in August we were a (not so) happy family and here am I, at Christmas, providing the final twist in the break up of our home.

Things were going so well that I had even sort of got myself a girlfriend over the Christmas period. I had met Lorraine at the Rugby Club Disco that myself and Barry now frequented on a Saturday night. She had obviously taken a shine to me over the past couple of weekends although I was a bit slow to realise it. She was six months older than me and towered over my 5' 5' in her high heels.

She had long, straight shiny black hair and in all honesty was just a little bit podgy around the waist area (which is quite probably the reason why I had not paid much attention to her over the past couple of weeks—or if I had it was that I suspected she liked Barry, eleven months my senior and six inches taller and after all, he was the one with the car).

I'd had a slow dance with Lorraine the week previous and she was once again talking to Barry and me as the strains of 'Betcha by Golly Wow' by the Stylistics emanated from the turntables. This time the smooch got a bit more serious and lasted right the way through 'Nights in White Satin' by The Moody Blues (no mean feat either, It's a good five minutes long).

Now I don't know whether it was the effect of the double vodka and limes that I had been knocking back or whether it was the scent of Lorraine's perfume but something stirred and before I knew it I was locked into the most Earth shattering snog I had ever been involved in in my entire life.

'Hmmm, that was nice.' She sighed as Justin Hayward and the accompanying orchestra reached their glorious crescendo.

'Bloody hell, John.' Barry enthused as we drove to the Mill Road Chippy after kicking out time. 'I thought she was going to fucking eat you alive.'

'Tell me about it.' I replied, still catching my breath.

'D'yer fancy her then, John? Bit plump but, fucking hell, she nearly ate you alive, man.'

'I don't know. She's all right I suppose.' At least she seemed it whilst I was full of Double Diamond and Vodka.

It was a ritual that carried on for the next couple of weeks well into February until I started becoming a bit fed up with it. I felt terrible about it. I didn't fancy Lorraine at all at the beginning of the evening but always found myself getting reeled in around smooching time. I didn't see her any other time other than a Saturday night at the Rugby Club. I knew that she lived three miles away in Rothwell and that her mate Maureen's Dad always collected them at ten past eleven to take them home.

'Do you want me to tell her you want to dump her, John?' Barry had kindly offered on the way to the chippy. 'You can't keep her hanging on like this each week.'

'I know, I know.' I agreed. Besides I'm sure it was hampering Barry's chances of getting off.

Most other girls, I assumed, would have been giving us a wide berth at the end of the evening thinking to themselves; 'No good with them two, the scrawny short one always smooches with that fat, weird one.'

My chance came during the second week of February and I took it with open arms. I had told Lorraine that I had applied to join the Merchant Navy and my letter of acceptance duly arrived on the tenth.

'Dear Mr. Caswell, We are pleased to inform you that you have been accepted to attend The National Sea Training School as a deck hand trainee beginning on Monday May 29th 1974.'

Eureka! May 29th seemed a long way off but it was explained that the school only enrolled deck trainees at four weekly intervals and that demand for places was high.

They had gone on to mention that, because of my age, (I would be 17 years and five months old by the end of May), they had pushed my application through ahead of others.

'Fantastic!' Steve had shouted when He and Cath arrived home two days later. His course completed.

'Bloody hell, boy. I never thought you would go through with it.' Offered Dave at Lewis's. 'When will you tell Mr. Thomas?'

'I'll leave it until after my Sister's wedding, Dave. There's plenty of time.'

No point in telling him just yet in case he decides to get rid of me here and now, although I doubted he would, as I would need to save up some money.

Mum was genuinely overjoyed for me and stunned would be a good way to describe Barry's reaction although he knew I'd applied.

'You'll have to dump Lorraine now, John.' He had thoughtfully advised.

Unfortunately it wasn't that easy.

It was, in fact, an embarrassment. She balled her eyes out.

'We weren't exactly boyfriend / girlfriend, Lorraine were we?' I tried to explain as I broke protocol and approached her before the alcohol took effect.

'I thought we might be.' She wailed.

Oh, Christ. Bloody great, I thought. First girlfriend, never even particularly liked her and I'm struggling to dump her.

How could I without hurting her feelings?

'You knew I had applied to join the Merchant Navy, Lorraine. Well it's happening. It won't be fair on you if we did get together just for me to go off and leave you for six months at a time. Besides, you'd find somebody else while I was away'.

'No I wouldn't' she argued.

Shit. What do I try now?

I continued along the 'it won't be fair on you' path until I was blue in the face not realising that Lorraine was now on triple gins every time she went to the bar.

I had stayed relatively sober for the evening. I had wanted the deed done by ten to eleven and was not prepared to fall into her spell at smooching time. I needn't have worried. She had drunk herself into a stupor by then and had been violently sick down her dress a couple of times by the time her lift arrived to take her home.

'You bastard!' Her mate Maureen had spat at me as she helped her outside.

I did feel bad. But at the same time mightily relieved. I should never have let the situation go beyond the second week. I suppose I kind of liked the idea that someone actually liked me.

Cath and Steve's wedding was upon us before we knew it. The fact that the arrangements had been made rather quickly due to the timing of Steve's leave between College and voyage meant that they had opted to have the ceremony in the London Road Congregational Church rather than the more traditional Parish Church of St. Peter's and St. Paul's.

I woke on the morning of Saturday March 2nd with a hangover and to the sound of a distressed Bride-to-be, as there was a carpet of snow on the ground outside. I remembered that it had been bloody cold as I'd staggered home from the 'Leather Craftsman' pub on Kettering's Ise Lodge Estate the night before. Steve was being 'looked after' by his brother and best man, Tim, on the evening before the wedding and, of course, as Steve had been out on his stag night the week before there was no need for a return session on the eve of his wedding night now, was there?

Well, yes and no. We had planned a quiet evening in the pub just around the corner from Tim's house which had been met with muted approval and all was going well until a friend of Steve's from college showed up and the beer and stories began to flow.

My head ached but I knew I had to get over it pretty quickly. I had been awarded the honour of being one of the Ushers at the Church and with a distinct lack of volunteers to assist me Steve's mate, Mark, who had arrived last night had been drafted in as an eleventh hour assistant. I needed a clear head so I reached for the trusty Paracetamol.

I had really made an effort for the occasion and had bought Myself a cool, grey two piece suit with flared trousers, a spanking new white shirt and blue tie and I'd also pushed the boat right out with a pair of two-tone plastic grey and blue brogues.

Dapper or what?

How I now wished I had got a three-piece as I awoke to see the snow. I was going to bloody freeze.

Thankfully by the time I arrived at the church most of the snow had melted and we were now bathed in glorious sunshine, although it was accompanied with a force ten bloody gale. I felt happy for Cath. I had grown up a bit enough to realise that this was the one day in her life that she didn't want ruined. Had I been a couple of years younger then who knows but I felt quite proud in my duties as I enquired 'Bride or Groom?' to all who approached the inside of the church.

'The Bride, of course, you little shit.' One of Cath's closest friends of many years had politely informed me.

Cath duly arrived the obligatory eight and a half minutes late, which had allowed myself and Mark, Steve and Best Man, Tim, a welcome opportunity for another extra strong mint.

She actually looked quite nice, her dress was cream with an enormous train which the two bridesmaids struggled in vain to keep off the wet, slushy ground whilst at the same time battling against the wind to stop it lifting up and engulfing the whole bridal party. I couldn't resist a silent chuckle at her predicament.

My Father was not at the wedding, Cath choosing instead to elect the long-time boyfriend of one of her best friends to give her away. I am not too sure that he was invited or that he even knew of the event. I certainly hadn't told him in my one and only contact with him, just after Christmas, since he had left.

I caught my Mother wiping away a tear in a rare show of emotion as they exchanged their vows and the whole ceremony passed without a hitch.

The wind played havoc with the photographs afterwards which, fortunately, curtailed the proceedings and we all took the short walk down Church Walk to the George Hotel to join the happy couple in a slap up meal and disco.

I felt a little awkward I have to admit. It was never a family tradition to be waited on at a table especially in front of another hundred or so people, but the fare on offer was exceptional and I can only imagine that it must have improved considerably since my Father had worked in the kitchen here.

A lot of the guests were obviously Steve's family and although it was a bit of an embarrassment to be presented as 'my little brother' I humoured my Sister on this occasion.

Steve's Stepfather, Brent, was Canadian and had worked on tugboats out of Vancouver for a time so meeting him and talking to him was of great interest to me considering my impending venture to the Sea School.

'Just go for it and enjoy it, boy.' He bellowed at me above the thudding of the disco.

'You're only young once and if the opportunity has arisen to see the World, well then you cannot pass it by, son. Grasp it while you can.'

He was a small but stocky man and his enthusiasm came right up through his feet.

This was just the encouragement I needed and it was now easy to see how Steve had chosen the option of going to sea if he had received much of the same by way of stimulation from this man when he was my age.

'If you ever get to Vancouver or Bellingham in the States, where we also have a place, you be sure to give us a call and come and look us up.' He offered as he forcefully slapped me on the back once more.

'You know what, Brent. I might just hold you to that.' I replied, knowing that my chances of actually getting to Vancouver were minimal but you never know!

No sooner had the dust settled and the hangovers from the reception cured than Cath and Steve were on their way to join the 'Silver Eagle', a bulk ore carrier, in Rotterdam for their honeymoon voyage.

I enviously wished them well and knew now that my destiny lay in following suit.

The end of May could not come quick enough for me now that I had definitely set my sights.

Handing my notice in at Lewis's was nowhere near as traumatic as I had imagined it would be. If anything it was the complete opposite. I had decided to come clean with Mr. Thomas regarding my future intentions on the Monday back to work after the wedding. I could have left it longer as there was still some seven weeks to go before my start date at the sea school but I felt it only fair that should they want to advertise for another trainee they could do so whilst I worked out my notice (I should be so naive as to think that they would harbour thoughts of replacing me. After all, it wasn't as if I was that vital a cog in the well-oiled machine).

Far from being shocked or surprised by my announcement Mr. Thomas seemed to take it with an air of acceptance and with a little less dissatisfaction than I had wished for.

'I had a feeling that you may not last here, John.' He smiled at me.

'Oh?' I gestured inquisitively, wondering why.

'Not in a negative sense, John. I just had a sneaky suspicion that you have always had doubts about the work and that at times you have felt a little uncomfortable with office life, that's all.'

'Yes, Mr. Thomas.' I acknowledged, 'You're probably right, although I have certainly enjoyed my experience here. I would like to think that maybe if this opportunity to go to sea hadn't arisen for me that I may have been able to establish myself here.'

I cringed as I said it, knowing full well that I had no intentions of turning into a clone of Dave or Simon, but just hoping that I was saying the right things to earn myself the stay of execution I required until the end of May.

'I don't see a problem with you staying with us until you feel you want to leave, John.

Of course I'll have to confirm it with The Colonel but I'm sure we can put you to good use, maybe even send you out with the lorries to help build your muscles up for your life at sea.' Mr.Thomas chuckled.

I was grateful. The attitude was no less than I had expected from both Mr.Thomas and Colonel Jack, who was delighted by my announcement, having served abroad for many years in his army career. Although I was quick to point out that the Merchant Navy by no means had very strong military connections it mattered not to Colonel Jack.

'You're getting out and seeing the World, Lad.' He boisterously enthused.

'Too many youngsters these days are pampered and mollycoddled and just want to sit about in an office all day and do nothing.' He was not particularly having a go at Dave but I glanced across at him and gave him a wry smile all the same.

'You lucky bastard.' Dave later sneered across at me when there was only the three of us in the office. He was only joking (I think).

'I would have made you bloody leave now, bloody go out with the lorries for a bit to toughen you up, what a load of bollocks.'

I did not rise to the bait. Simon started to sing 'A life on the ocean wave' and then made a seriously feeble attempt to 'pipe' me aboard.

'How very pathetic of you both.' I tutted and shrugged my shoulders. As far as I was aware it was the first Simon had known about it, although judging by Mr.Thomas's initial reaction I doubted that Dave had refrained from spilling the beans to everyone before I had made it public knowledge.

'Seriously, though,' Simon began, 'Good luck to you. I don't know that it is something I would be able to do.' (I know it isn't, Simon!). 'I've heard there's a lot of nice boys in the navy though, so be careful, won't you!' He teased.

'Do me a favour Simon.' I tried my best to humour him.

The next few weeks did drag but, true to his word, Mr.Thomas did let me go out with the lorries to assist in the offloading of materials to the various building sites that we delivered to in the area. If I didn't know better I would almost accuse Simon of arranging the next day's itinerary to ensure that I had the most humping of bricks and bags of cement to the most inaccessible of building sites imaginable and then phoning the recipients of the goods beforehand to ensure that all the labourers on the site were conveniently up roofs or on tea breaks when we arrived with our delivery.

'Building your muscles up O.K. are we, John?' Dave had delightfully enquired as we got back to the yard, knackered, at half past four one afternoon.

'Fuck Off.' I gasped as I dropped onto my office chair.

'Oy! Don't get cement on the good furniture'. Simon joined in.

Roll on the end of May I thought. If there was ever anything I was not cut out to be it was a Builder's Merchants' lorry driver's mate.

I elected to leave on the Thursday beforehand. I had been at Lewis's for almost eleven months. Because Dave's brother had been to the sea school previously I had been forewarned that my mass of flowing locks (or tangles depending on how you viewed things) would have to go at some time or another.

'You don't want to be getting it done at Gravesend.' Dave had thoughtfully advised.

'They'll just shear the lot off and ask questions later, right down to the wood our kid got when he had his done at the school.'

I had decided that it was not a fate that I wanted to befall me so at lunchtime on my final day at Lewis's I went to the barbers in Cannon Street, just off Wellingborough town centre.

How the barber's eyes lit up when I went in and asked for a crew cut. He was about fifty, dressed in a huge white coat with pockets all over the place that accommodated a range of scissors, combs, brushes etc. etc. and with ominous, black, thick rimmed specs that marked him down as, at the very least, half blind.

'Are you sure you want a crew cut, lad?' He queried 'Most people come in here and ask for perms these days, you wouldn't even need one of them your hair is so curly as it is.'

'Can I just get this over with please. I'm joining the Merchant Navy on Monday. I have to go to a sea school in Gravesend for three months and they don't allow long hair.' And why the bloody hell do I need to explain this to you, I thought. Just cut the bloody thing.

Masses and masses of locks fell to the floor as this doddering old git of a barber snipped merrily away, oblivious to the fact that he was removing two years lovingly cultivated growth from my scalp.

I felt like crying.

'Oops! Little bit of a tangle there.' He seemed to be telling me off as he tugged for all he was worth at my head.

'It's hardly worth raking it if it's all coming off.' I argued.

'Well we do need to keep some of it there, don't we? To keep a little bit of style? Unless you do want it all shaved off? Sir?'

'Okay, okay, I'll leave you to it.' I conceded. 'I definitely do not want to be seen as a skinhead, certainly not in Gravesend and definitely not in Kettering.'

When he had finished I just stared into the mirror as he offered me the chance to check out the back.

'Oh, my God. My fucking ears.' I gulped.

'First time they've seen the light of day for a while, eh, Son?'

Will you please shut the fuck up I thought as I just gazed at the size of these monsters protruding from either side of my head. They were starting to glow and, not only that, I could feel myself starting to glow as well.

He was right. I hadn't had a short back and sides since I was at least ten almost seven years ago.

I felt acutely embarrassed and I was pleased that it was a complete stranger that was witnessing my initial reaction.

'You'll be surprised how quickly you'll get used to it, lad.' The barber sensibly advised. 'If you're going to be at sea school for three months then it will have to be done again before your time is up.

So the quicker you do get used to it the better.'

'Your right, of course.' I said. 'I know it sounds corny but it can't be stuck back on now, can it?'

He agreed. I thanked him and paid him, even leaving a tip.

I walked back to Lewis's feeling a lot lighter and strangely disorientated. Whereas I would occasionally flick my head to clear my eyes there was now no necessity but habit kept me doing it as I walked along the street. Anybody seeing me would believe I had a nervous twitch or something.

I walked back in to the office already used to my new look and with confidence.

Dave fell off his stool, clutching his stomach and gave out the most over-the-top laugh I have ever heard in my life. Simon was not so dramatic but went cherry red as he tried desperately not to follow Dave into such an obvious state of delirium.

Mr. Thomas's face was also contorted like a bulldog chewing a wasp as he tried to stifle his mirth.

I had the confirmation, as if I needed it.

I did, indeed, look a complete and utter twat.

Before I knew it the uproar emanating from the office had provoked Sam, Tommy and Perkins to come over from their hut and Jane and Clare out of their office to gawp at me like this was some kind of freak show. Even the reliably un-opinionated Cyril raised a smile from behind his mountain of ledgers but by now I think most people were more concerned for Dave's health as he had gone into a coughing fit and his face had turned purple.

'Well I think it looks very nice,' Jane said as the last gasps and giggles died down.

With everyone now in the main office Colonel Jack came out of his office holding a bottle of Smirnoff Red Label Vodka and a gift-wrapped parcel.

'Let's all settle down now.' He boomed.

Everybody settled.

'I would just like to say, John, on behalf of all of us present, that we will be sorry to see you go. Of course we wish you well and I hope that you will be able to keep us informed as to your progress once you eventually get to sea. We've had a little bit of a whip round and decided to get you a couple of things that will hopefully keep you warm on those long, dark, cold nights at sea. Not putting you off yet, am I?'

'No, not yet.' I answered, completely embarrassed even further by the attention.

'No doubt the vodka won't even see the weekend through, but hopefully this will be of use to you.'

With that Colonel Jack handed me the present and severely shook my hand.

'Oh, and by the way.' He added as an afterthought. 'Nice hair.'

Everyone applauded. 'Speech, Speech.'

I opened my present to reveal the thickest navy jumper I had ever seen. Obviously the real McCoy bought from somewhere like George Allen's Outdoor wear shop in the town.

'Cheers, folks.' I began. 'I think I'm gonna miss you people, who knows? I may even miss you once in a while, Dave.'

I could say very little else. I felt choked and I genuinely was going to miss them all, especially the honesty and integrity that had been displayed by both Mr. Thomas and Colonel Jack towards me.

I hoped that I would meet many more people like them in the future.

I left an hour early that afternoon. There seemed little point in me hanging around after the little impromptu farewell ceremony in the office and I think Mr. Thomas had sensed that I was a little overwhelmed by the occasion.

I had made two good friends in Dave and Simon and our day out at Wembley would, for certain, live long in my memory. I had even got a kiss off the gorgeous Clare. No tongues but boy did I melt.

I got home early, just as my Mother had arrived home from her work.

'Oh, John.' She smiled. 'Your hair looks so much better.' I got a hug. I didn't care that I was seventeen and a half. I got a reassuring hug and I was feeling pretty damned pleased with myself.

I decided not to go to the Rugby Club on Saturday night to bid my farewells. For one I didn't fancy bumping into Lorraine again. She still occasionally went there on a Saturday night and, despite my cold shoulder treatment and indifference to her, she still insisted on coming over to me towards the end of the evening.

Barry had reacted just slightly less over-dramatic than Dave at Lewis's had when confronted with my 'new' image. I tried pointing out that, although he was only just coming up to nineteen himself, he was actually starting to recede a little bit and that mine, given time, would all grow back again.

But it made little impact. He laughed until he cried . . . . . Arsehole!

If this was the type of reaction I was going to receive I thought I'd best keep a low profile and stay at home. Besides I would be gone on Monday morning and by Tuesday most people round here will be asking, 'Where's that long-haired little shit that lived at the bottom of the alley gone? What was his name?'

I had already written to my Father to tell him of my plans. Not that I felt I needed to but I suppose out of courtesy.

It was nice, on Saturday morning and right on cue, to receive a card from him wishing me 'Bon Voyage.' He approved for once although my explanation that I was going to a Sea School in Gravesend and not to actually join a ship just yet appeared to have got lost in the alcohol fuelled translation.

I had received a list of items from the sea school that I would need to take with me to Gravesend with my letter of acceptance and busied Myself on Saturday getting the last few items together for my small suitcase.

I didn't need to take a lot. Uniform and also casual uniform were to be issued on my arrival so it was basically a suitcase full of socks and underwear, my stock of which I had just replenished.

I prepared one change of clothes and took three pairs of pyjamas. I also packed my basic toiletries and optimistically included a razor in the hopes that I may miraculously start to sprout some facial hair whilst I was away.

Sunday was terrible. Malc came round from next door to wish me well and to revel in my unfortunate choice of hairstyle. I had no desire to see anybody else. Mum made me dinner and we ate in silence. It was my favourite. Roast beef, yorkie pud, boiled potatoes and cabbage followed by treacle pudding and raspberry blancmange.

'This isn't THE Last Supper, Mother.' I tried to joke. 'I will be coming back.'

'I know.' She smiled. 'I just wanted to send you off with a decent meal inside you.'

'I believe they feed us as well as put us up for the night.' I reassured her, but she just smiled back at me.

I spent the rest of the day kicking my heels and watching some crap on telly in the evening with my Mother and went to bed early. It must have been well past two o'clock in the morning before I finally got off to sleep, a mixture of excitement and nerves spinning round in my head and stopping me from nodding off. It was, after all, such a giant step for me to be taking.

We had never even had a family holiday as such before, so my experiences of being away from home for any length of time are quite limited. I vaguely remember boarding a train to Clacton when I was very young for a day out and Mum had taken me to Great Yarmouth on the coach a couple of years ago for the day.

I had gone to Govilon, in South Wales, for a week with the school when I was fourteen so I suppose that was as near as I can relate to what I was going to be confronted with in the morning.

Apart from occasionally going to Leicester on the train to see 'The Foxes' play at Filbert Street, twenty minutes up the main line, I could not even recall the last time I had been on a decent train journey.

Such is my sheltered life.

I need some sleep.

2

Mum woke me, as requested, at half past six the next morning. Despite the lateness of my dozing off I felt very fresh. Mum had asked if I wanted her to take the morning off work to come down to the train station with me but I had told her that she didn't need to. I was fully packed and ready by the time she caught the bus at a quarter to eight to go to work. The taxi to take me to the train station was not until a quarter to nine, to catch the nine o five to St. Pancras. I sat in the kitchen listening to Radio 1, alone, for the hour and took one last look at my familiar surroundings.

Although there was weekend 'leave' from the school I had made a conscientious decision that I would not even contemplate returning home for at least four weeks.

I went over my instructions for the day one last time. The school had sent me a one way ticket to Gravesend station via St. Pancras and Charring Cross. All new trainees were to report in at the school by two in the afternoon (1400 hrs. as the regimental instructions had informed us).

I maybe could have left it a bit later but I had to negotiate the London underground between the two stations and simply did not have a clue as to how to read the attached map of the system.

My taxi arrived on time and I stopped on the steps down to the main road and took one last, long, look back at the house and especially my bedroom window at the front. It was a gloriously hot, sunny morning and inevitably my hay fever began to kick in during the taxi ride down to the station.

'Hope I don't catch your cold.' My taxi driver ignorantly remarked trying to make small talk.

'It's hay fever actually.' I snapped.

'Going somewhere nice?' He tried again.

'No!'

End of conversation.

My train was only a couple of minutes late due to the obligatory maintenance work being carried out between Market Harborough and Desborough (as if I care why it's late), and I was in St. Pancras at just gone half past ten after marvelling at all the wondrous sights on the way down such as Wellingborough Station, Bedford Station, the Stewartby Brick Works, Luton Station and the delightfully black/grey brickwork introducing Kentish Town to name but a few.

Now to find Charring Cross.

I was relieved to find that it was not that far away but I did, however have to change underground lines. One consolation was that the maps on the underground walls were much easier to follow than the instructions I had been sent.

I managed to find my way to the Piccadilly Line (Southbound), which had appeared to be the easiest of several options, passing a Peter Sarstedt look-alike on the way down with an acoustic guitar bellowing out 'Where do you go to my lovely?' I had to stop and do a double take; no, surely it's not Peter Sarstedt?

My eyes were all over the place. People were just sat in corners with sleeping bags or blankets wrapped around them. I wanted to shout out to them, 'It's in the bloody eighties outside, what the hell are you doing huddled up down here.' I had never seen anything like it.

There were so many people rushing around, pushing, shoving, and running down moving escalators that were going as fast as they could downwards anyway. Total bedlam.

I got off my first train at Leicester Square and followed the signs to the Northern Line where Charring Cross was only one stop away.

Again people were still barging past and quite dangerously hurling themselves at the train doors as they were about to close. Why on Earth were these people in such a hurry?

It was quite amusing though. One largish suit managed to get halfway into the train before the doors bisected him and he let out a very loud 'Oooof!'

'Please mind the doors.' An automated voice rang out belatedly as the guy dropped, red faced, into his seat.

I waited for all of three minutes for the next train to arrive. The bloater had risked a puncture for the sake of three minutes.

I finally made it back into daylight, none the worse for my first experience of the London Underground and sat around until mid-day for the small three-carriage affair to lug me off to Gravesend.

What would have only been a twenty—minute journey on the Inter-City service that I had just come off took an hour and ten minutes stopping at what must have been every station along the way. I was glad, at this point in time, that I had opted to leave Kettering as early as I did.

I got into my taxi at a quarter past one. 'Sea School, son?' My driver immediately enquired.

Bloody hell, I thought. Was it that obvious? I suppose the haircut and the suitcase would have been a bit of a clue though.

'Yes please.'

'I've taken a few of you up there in the last couple of hours. Always get a few of you on induction day once a month.'

Good for you, I thought.

Just over five minutes later we had left the dreary, nondescript town behind and were heading towards what seemed to me to be a dead end with a distribution centre at the end of the road. A small, narrow, one-track lane then appeared off to our right with a huge white notice board proclaiming 'NATIONAL SEA TRAINING CENTRE' in six inch high deep blue lettering.

We slowly negotiated the pot holes and fencing to the right of us which kept us apart from the canal, marshland and train track, although I could not make out in which order such was the thickness of the marsh weeds, and pulled up at a barrier in front of a small gatehouse guarding the school grounds.

'Another one for you Guv'nor.' The taxi driver announced to the gate man.

He leaned out of his window, peered in at me and asked me my name. I was ticked off his list and the taxi driver was allowed to take me through to the school's car park.

'Best of luck, son.' My driver offered me and, knowing the drill only too well, pointed me in the direction of the reception area.

I stood and looked around me as he drove off. It didn't look that much different to my old Grammar School back in Kettering.

I picked up my suitcase and headed towards the reception area. Fourteen weeks I kept saying to myself. That's all it is, fourteen weeks, I am going to get through this.

I was determined.

I walked in through the main entrance and peered through two large double glass doors.

Already there were a lot of potential students sat down in what was obviously the assembly room. I was beckoned inside by a chap in uniform and once again went through the formality of giving my name and being ticked off another list.

I left my suitcase in the corner of the room where everyone else's was piled and sat nervously on the first available seat next to some lad who looked to be as equally ill at ease as I was feeling.

All eyes appeared to be on me but a second later the main doors swung open again as two more recruits walked in and my moment of embarrassment had passed.

The spotlight was now on somebody else.

This scenario carried on in silence for at least another twenty minutes. The silence was broken only once when one new recruit walked in with long, fairly greasy ginger hair.

A gasp went up around the room.

Either this guy was extremely silly or he hadn't been forewarned that he was about to have a date with the demon barber of Gravesend. His hair was halfway down his back. It did break the ice amongst the rest of us sitting and waiting for two o' clock to come round.

'He'll get fucking scalped.' The lad next to me whispered through a cupped hand.

'I know, I know.' I nervously chuckled back, 'Mine was not quite so long but very nearly up until last Thursday.'

It was just approaching two o'clock when the doors swung open again and in walked two tall, upstanding gentlemen in full navy uniform.

The Officer that had taken our names previously greeted them and all three walked up onto the stage in front of us.

We all seemed to freeze as they looked down at us.

'Quiet please.'

We already were!

'My name is Mr. John Arnem, I am one of the deck instructors here at the school and I would like to welcome you all to The National Sea Training School here in Denton in Gravesend. We are fully aware that you have had a long day travelling, some more than others, so I will try to make today's formalities as brief as possible.' He continued 'There are 90 of you students enrolling here today. 32 for deck training and 58 for catering. The first four weeks of your course will be your lifeboat training if you are a deck student, two weeks practical survival at sea if you are catering, and then you will divide up into your own groups with a further ten weeks training for deck and eight weeks for catering.'

Only ten weeks total for catering, I thought. No wonder they were opting for it at a ratio of two to one.

'After our brief introduction we would like you all to register into the school and then we will get you through to the dining room for some tea before all the other established students come down for theirs.'

I thought I sensed some trepidation in his voice, but I couldn't be sure.

'I would now like to introduce you to, on my right, Captain Spearing, who is the Captain Superintendent or in other words in charge of the whole school here, and to my left Mr Eric Duffy the Chief Steward.'

The Captain nodded to Mr. Arnem and began to address us.

'Thank you. Welcome to Gravesend Sea School. You have chosen to come here to learn not only about seamanship but also about the way of life at sea. It isn't like any other industry where you can get up in the morning, go to work, come home in the evening and forget about it until tomorrow morning. At sea your work is with you all the time.'

He paused to ensure that he had our full attention.

'You must be able to fit in with your surroundings. You must be able to go about your daily life in a safe and responsible manner. Not only towards yourselves but also with the safety and welfare of your fellow shipmates in mind.'

He paused again and surveyed the room. Content that we were all still listening he continued.

'Here at Gravesend we are looking to set you off on your adventure and yes, at the moment, you will see it as an adventure, with a good understanding of what is expected of you at sea and hopefully what you learn will stand you all in good stead for a long and safe sea going career.'

He looked around at all of us again, nodding his head approvingly.

'Good luck to you all.' He finished.

As Captain Spearing and the other guy (who did nothing during the course of events bar stand up scratching his arse) left the room, four others joined Mr. Arnem on the stage.

'Okay. Boys, settle down please.' Mr. Arnem pleaded.

'I'd like to split you all up in to deck and catering boys as quickly as possible, please. Deck boys over by the door and catering on the inside. Thank you.'

Two tables were set at the sides and we were made to form a rather random queue in front of them to sign our lives away to the sea school for the next fourteen weeks.

'You will all receive your handbook upon your registration.' Mr. Arnem was shouting to nobody in particular by now.

'And you should treat it as your bible. All your do's and don'ts are in there and we will discuss its contents and implications in full tomorrow during your induction.'

I signed on the dotted line and was assigned to room 27 in class 'U'.

I had a little chuckle to myself at the inappropriate letter of my class. Having been in form S at the Grammar school and considering that to be the lowest of the low, then U must be even lower!

I was also informed that I would be in the 'White' team. Whatever that meant.

We went through to the dining room and were treated to cheese and ham sarnies with a choice of tea or coffee. Just what was required after a solid day's travelling and my stomach was emitting all kinds of weird and wonderful noises even though the slices of bread were like doorsteps. I requested water and received an ice-cold stare from the catering student that was attending us as if I'd asked for a Czinzano and lemonade with a cherry on top.

'Only got tea or coffee.' The spotty geek replied.

'I'll help myself to a glass of water then, shall I?' I motioned at the tap behind him.

'Not allowed in there.'

'Then you'll have to do it for me won't you?'

He did. But very reluctantly and only half filling a small coffee cup with water at that.

'Thank you.' I sneered sarcastically.

Great. I've only been here five minutes and I've already had a run in with one of the kids that's going to be dishing up my grub.

I still hadn't really spoken to anyone except the lad I'd sat next to when I had initially got here and he had departed to the catering side of our group once we had been separated.

I found him again in the dining room and plonked my plate down beside him.

'Thought they might have saved us some dinner.' I began. 'I've already upset one of the Stewards.'

'I get the feeling they don't like us much.' My new found mate observed.

Within twenty minutes Mr. Arnem was back in the dining room.

'If you're all ready then boys, we'll take you to your rooms. Can room number 27 please follow me back to the assembly room to pick up your suitcases.'

I bid my friend farewell for the time being and wished him luck.

He waved in my general direction. The poor kid looked lost already.

We were led out of the assembly room and straight along the covered walkway immediately beneath the domestic block which ran in an L shaped block from the South and the West of the complex.

Mr. Arnem was leading us and stopped at the first set of double doors leading into the building.

'Room 27 is on the second floor, if you would like to follow me.' Mr. Arnem turned round and called out at us.

It was at this point that a shout rang out from the other side of the courtyard.

'Peanuts!'

A couple of us turned round to see what on Earth had prompted such a call.

Another shout rang out, this time more in excitement and wonderment, which echoed around the courtyard.

'PEANUTS!'

This time we all turned round. About six or seven other trainees were leaning out of what I assumed must have been a classroom window and gesticulating at us.

'You're never going home, Peanuts!' one of them proclaimed. I chuckled to myself as we walked through the doors and up the flight of stairs to room 27.

What a strange thing to be shouting at us. I wasn't exactly expecting to be welcomed with open arms but Peanuts? What was that all about?

We entered room 27. I was quite taken aback as to how big the dormitory was.

There were eight bunk beds and one single bed. There were separate lockers for each student and a curtain to slide across the bunk for privacy. There were two tables in the middle of the room, and the obligatory picture of The Queen and H.M.S. Falmouth cutting its way into harbour on the wall.

'Right lads; sit yourselves down on a bunk.' Mr Arnem began.

I was much too slow. By the time I had dropped my suitcase and checked left and right of me for a suitable location the entire set of top bunks had been claimed. I resigned myself to a bottom berth next to the door that we had just come in through.

Standing with Mr Arnem now and laying claim to the single bed was a student in full uniform.

'This is Richard Marker, lads. He will be your dormitory leading hand for the first six weeks of your stay with us.'

Richard gave us a nod and most of us nodded back and said 'hello' or 'hi' in acknowledgement.

'Marker is now eight weeks into his training so is familiar to the school rules and the whereabouts of most of the amenities available to you on the site. Any immediate questions you need answered; hopefully he will be able to assist you with.

At six o' clock this evening'....He tailed off as he glanced down at his watch, 'At six o, clock this evening, in just over an hour's time, the stores will be opened to allow you to collect your uniforms. The tannoy system will announce your room number and you will all be required to follow Marker down to the stores. You will need to know your shoe size, your collar size, chest size, your waist size and your inside leg measurement if you want to spend the next fourteen weeks in comfortable clothing.'

Judging by the look of Marker in his uniform I very much doubted that he was comfortable in his.

'As you have already been told the first four weeks of your training are for your lifeboat certificate and general health and safety at sea awareness courses. I will be your E.D.H. (Efficient Deck Hand) tutor after that. I would like to wish all of you good luck and I will see you in four weeks time.'

With that he gave Marker a nod and grinned.

'Look after them, Marker. They look terrified.'

Marker laughed as Mr Arnem left the room. I had no doubt whatsoever in my mind that most of us did indeed look terrified.

I sat on my bunk and looked around the room. The rest of the guys looked a decent enough bunch and on the cue of one of the lads opposite me we all dragged ourselves over to our suitcases which had been chucked into the middle of the room and began unpacking into our own lockers.

'The dorms are inspected each morning after breakfast at 0830.' Marker began to inform us.

A loud groan filled the room.

'Your kit, most of it that you will collect later this evening, is also inspected and that means that it must also be presented in a clean and tidy state in your lockers along with your bedding that must be folded up neatly and stowed away.'

'What? They inspect inside our lockers?' One of the lads chirped up. 'That's an invasion of privacy, surely.'

'Well, they do it.' Confirmed Marker.

'If it's kept tidy then there is nothing to worry about. It's not as if they go rooting through your possessions or anything . . .' Marker explained. '. . . and besides,' He continued, 'don't bank on getting too much privacy around here.'

I think I was already beginning to see what he was getting at.

With the seventeen of us moving around all of a sudden the dorm didn't seem as big as it had first looked. It was, at most, forty foot long and about twenty-five feet wide. At my end of the room next to the door to the stairs that we had originally came up I could look out onto the courtyard and across at the other accommodation block to my left, the assembly room and dining room to my right and the main classroom block immediately opposite. Out of the other windows at the far end of the room from my bunk the view was of the car park and of the small ditch, which was laughably known as the canal, and the railway line followed by the marsh.

'What time do the trains run 'til, Marker?' I asked.

'I think just gone mid-night is the last one. The first one in the morning is at five.'

'Fucking charming.' The lad in the bunk above me groaned.

There was another door at the far end of the room, which led to our small block of four toilets and a communal shower. Another double door after that separated our dorm and shower facilities from those of the next dorm.

'Who's in the dorm through there, Marker?' One of us enquired.

'Is it some of the lads that came today?'

'Er, No.' Marker hesitantly replied. 'They are from my class; they've been here eight weeks.

Don't worry though, they're a decent bunch.'

'There's a couple of you here that are going to have to visit the barber, 'Sweeney Todd', tomorrow, are you aware of that?' Marker asked.

Indeed most of us did realise although, I have to say, that a lot of us had made the effort and looked likely to be spared.

'Did you see the ginger freak with hair halfway down his back?' The lad in the bunk above me shouted to the rest of us.

We all laughed and said yes. Marker joined in the joke.

'He tends to go to town on anybody that joins looking like a rocker or like Noddy Holder.'

We all laughed again at the poor chaps impending misfortune.

It was very soon six o'clock and, as we had been told, the tannoy system burst into life instructing room 16 to proceed to the stores to collect their uniform.

It was quite a busy time around the perimeter of the courtyard with students wandering all over the place and as soon as the announcement came over the tannoy system all eyes seemed to focus on the bottom floor of the block immediately to our left (where the stores were situated according to Marker).

Within a minute we could see room 16 making their way to the stores complete with our friend the ginger greaser.

The howls of laughter from around the courtyard and the wolf whistles, I'm sure, could have been heard in downtown Gravesend.

'You won't have much of that mane left tomorrow, Peanut.' Somebody informed him at great volume.

I felt quite sorry for the lad. He did seem quite un-moved by the whole banter though and did not rise to any of the baiting. I just wished that he had had the sense to at least have had half of it chopped off before he had come down here.

It was our turn next to run the gauntlet to the stores.

'Let's get it over with, Marker.' We had unanimously decided as soon as our room number was called out.

There were some cat calls and some more pathetic cries of 'Peanuts!' aimed in our general direction but we seemed to have got away with it better than room 16 had thanks largely, no doubt, due to the fact that none in our midst had long, flowing, golden locks.

I had managed to remember all of my relevant sizes except my inside leg measurement, and I wasn't too keen on how the spotty kid assigned to tape measure duties went about finding out either.

'Oy, mind what you're doing with that, mate.' I protested.

'27 inch leg.' He shouted to his mate behind a pile of jeans and trousers. 'What size waist?'

'26!' I bellowed.

We staggered back to our dorm with the pile of kit. Quite a bit of kit at that, it has to be said.

'Try it all on now, lads.' Marker advised. 'At least the trousers, uniform jacket and shoes. You can take anything that doesn't fit at all back tomorrow morning only. After that you're lumbered.'

We had been issued with a black uniform jacket with trousers, two white shirts, a black tie and a pair of uniform shoes. I tried the lot on. The jacket was small in the arm but as they only came in small, medium or large it was not worth arguing the toss. A medium jacket, which I borrowed from a slightly larger lad than myself and tried on, swamped me although perfect in the arms.

Funnily enough the arms were too short on him when he wore his medium jacket and it appeared to be that no matter what size the jacket a major miscalculation in arm length must have occurred whence ordering the job lot of uniforms.

My trousers were also two inches too short. A 29-inch leg would have been my size but no doubt the little bastard with the tape measure had purposely set me up due to my lack of co-operation with him at measuring time. So no chance, I assumed, of going back and getting them changed in the morning either. I decided to content myself with the ill fitting uniform. I figured that I was going to look a complete and utter prat whilst wearing it anyway, along with everybody else, so what the hell.

Our number two's, or working uniform, consisted of two light blue cloth shirts, two pairs of cheap and nasty jeans, a navy blue pullover and a pair of brown, steel toe-capped, shoes. All in all it wasn't bad although the jeans, like my uniform trousers were at half—mast. I was going to be here for the duration of the summer and because of this we were not issued with 'donkey' jackets, which were only on issue for students between the winter months of September to April. I guess I can go through life without ever possessing one I thought.

'Lights out is at ten o'clock.' Marker began to inform us all as we tidied our lockers up and put all our kit away.

It was still only half past eight and Marker suggested that if we all put our uniforms on he could show us where the different games rooms, telly room, hobby room and 'tuck' shop were. Only half of us, myself included, took him up on his offer.

Once in uniform we weren't subjected to the amount of stick that we had earlier took even though it must have been fairly obvious, due to Marker's involvement with us, that we were 'peanuts'.

Having received the short guided tour we headed back to our dorm for half past nine. All of the students that have been on 'shore leave' as it was known had to be back on site by now and it was generally accepted that half past nine was the time to be getting ready for bed. Besides, the inhabitants of this particular dormitory were absolutely shattered by now and rest could not come quick enough for me.

'Lights out then, chaps.' Marker quietly instructed on the dot of ten and, although the curtains were drawn, you could sense the school plunging into darkness.

'I want me Mum,' a timid voice cried out in the darkness.

A snigger went round before the room fell silent.

It must have been for all of a full twenty seconds before someone on the other side of the room from me squeaked out a fart.

A couple of us chuckled before a steady stream of titters joined in.

'Dirty, fucking bastard.' The lad in the bunk above me shouted out.

'Who the fuck was that? Whoever it was had better check their skiddies in the morning.'

Now the whole room was laughing out loud.

'Sorry.' A voice piped up. 'Might be a gassy one.'

'I thought you lot would be tired after the day you'd all had.' Marker remarked from the comfort of his single bed.

'If sleep doesn't come naturally to us old Johnny fart pants over there will soon have us passing out.' The guy above me persisted. 'Come on, own up. Who are you?'

'When I first got here,' Marker began, 'we couldn't sleep on the first night so we all introduced ourselves at lights out. Y'know, name, where we came from, what football team we supported or music we like etc. etc.'

'Go on then, you start us off, Marker, Where are you from?' The guy above me encouraged.

'Okay, I'm Richard Marker. I'm nearly 17 and I'm from Birmingham. I support the City and I like Pink Floyd.'

'A blue nose, oh! No. A blue nose is going to be telling me to keep my room tidy. Aaaaaaaagh! I can't stand it.' A voice cried out from the dark.

'And you are?' Marker enquired.

'Mick Darnell, I'm 16, I'm from Sutton Coldfield and I'm Villa 'till I die. I recognised the Brummie accent earlier, Marker, but I was hoping you wouldn't be a blue nose. Honestly I was. But you are, you're a blue nose . . . help! Please tell me there's another Villa fan in the room.'

The room remained silent.

Then the bunk above me burst into life.

'Me name's Samuel Ferris. I'm from Burnley in Lancashire, I hate fucking football, I hate fucking Blackburn and I'm as hard as fucking nails.' He bellowed out in a well over-the-top put on Coronation Street type of Lancashire accent.

'Nobody, not even me Mutha dares to call me Samuel. It's Sam or Ferris to you lot.

I'm a bloody good mate to 'ave around but I make a lousy enemy. I love girls and I love tits and I love Northern Soul, clubbin' and dancin'.'

'What's Northern Soul?' a cockney voice asked.

'I just told you, for fuck's sake. It's clubbin' and dancin'.'

'A bit like ordinary soul, except Northern?'

'Yeah, that's it.' Ferris confirmed, oblivious to the piss-take in the question.

I certainly didn't have a clue what he was on about and neither did any of the others by the sound of it. I still marked him down as one not to get onto the wrong side of.

Silence again.

'Martin Teale. From Canterbury. Not that interested in football but if I have to show an allegiance it will have to be Arsenal. More so since Charlie George's goal in the cup final three years ago.'

A couple of boos rang round the room.

'Canterbury is only just down the road from here so, unlike most of you suckers, I will be going home each weekend.'

More boos rang out amidst the darkness.

'Stephen Kowlinski, I'm sixteen and from Wimbledon. I probably shouldn't be but I'm also a 'Gunner'. Oh! and I hate Tennis.'

'Nice name, anything Polish in there by chance?' Ferris asked.

'Yes, on my Father's side. He came over during the war but my Mother is English.' Kowlinski quite calmly replied.

'Anyway, Marker.' Kowlinski continued, 'what's the story behind all this Peanut carry on? Why are we getting 'Peanuts go home' shouted at us wherever we go?'

A few of us laughed at the absurdity of it.

'There are several stories behind it, actually.' Marker began as if an authority on the subject.

'The local people in Gravesend certainly call us it; maybe because once we've visited Sweeney Todd we have heads in the shape of a peanut. And be very wary of going ashore into Gravesend.'

'Going ashore? We're not even at sea.' I asked.

Marker sighed. 'It's just a bit of terminology we use. Anyway, they don't care for us much in Gravesend especially after a couple of lads from the school started knocking off some of the local girls a few months ago.'

'Yee-es! I'm up for some of that.' Ferris immediately announced.

'One theory is that we are known as 'Peanut heads' and if any of the scruffy, long haired youths of the town spot one of us, ahem, smartly dressed lads they shout out 'Peanuts' to their mates who then pursue the unfortunate individual and, if they catch him, generally give him a sound beating.'

'The bastards.' Someone commented.

'Yes, exactly. Which is why it is always best if you must go into Gravesend to at least go in a small group. Not that there's ever much need to go into town, but at least be warned.'

Marker paused for a moment and then continued.

'Another theory, and probably more likely, is that around the early fifties a peanut vendor used to sell 'Monkey Nuts' outside of the old sea school in the town. These became a firm favourite with the students of the time who were probably not fed as well as we are here today. Ha! Ha!' He mocked.

'The students would walk ashore leaving a trail of peanut shells on the floor for the local lads to follow, sort of like a paper chase. Once again, proving that the tradition dates back years the cry of 'Peanuts' would go up to alert his mates and the result would always be the same in that the poor student was chased around the streets of the town and subsequently battered if caught.'

'So why do the other students call us Peanuts, when they are in fact Peanuts themselves?' I logically asked.

'I suppose it's a way of getting used to the burden. They were called it when they first arrived and now it's your turn. Four weeks down the line, when you have completed your lifeboat course, and you will be calling the new students Peanuts yourselves.'

It was hard to disagree with that assumption.

Silence descended the darkness once more.

'I'm James McGuire from Glasgow and this bunk over here is a wee bit of Scotland because on top is Phil Laughlan who's also from Glasgow. We travelled down on the same train but didn't bump into each other until we got to Charring Cross and noticed that we both had similar short-ish hair, a suitcase and a one way ticket to Gravesend.'

'Pleased to meet you both.' A voice came out of the dark.

'Thanks very much', this must have been Laughlan replying because it was a different Scottish voice to the first.

'I'm Phil and I'm from Govan in Glasgow, Jimmy's from Clydebank and although I support Rangers and Jimmy's Celtic we're putting on a united front down here and besides we're expecting all you Sassenachs to be cheering Scotland on, with us, in the World Cup which is starting in just ten days time.'

'Bet you don't even beat Zaire.' Darnell's Brummie accent rang out.

'Well at least we qualified and didn't get stuffed already by Poland, and Wales ran you mighty close as well.' argued one of the Jocks.

'I was at Wembley for that Poland game. It was tragic.' I butted in.

The room fell silent again as everyone waited for me to introduce myself.

'John Caswell.' I began. 'I'm seventeen and a half and I'm from Kettering.'

'You're from where?' The darkness enquired.

'Kettering.' I began to explain. 'It's in Northamptonshire in the midlands seventy odd miles North of London. I also support the World famous Kettering Town F.C. and, of course, England although I suppose I will grudgingly be rooting for the Jocks in Germany.'

'Good man, good man.' The Jocks echoed.

'How is Kettering World famous?' a Scouse voice asked. 'I've never bloody heard of it. Which proper team do you support? Like Liverpool, or Villa or even Birmingham if you're from the Midlands.'

'Okay then, since you asked, if I have to nominate a league team it must be Leicester City as they're just up the main line from Kettering and I went through a spell a couple of seasons ago of watching Kettering at home one week and City the next.'

The two Birmingham boys and the Scouser groaned their disapproval.

'Oh, and if we're still interested I like Pink Floyd, Genesis, Caravan, Yes and my favourite album at the moment is Mike Oldfield's Tubular Bells.

'Tubular Bells is ok although I prefer Motown' another voice piped up from the darkness 'but I'm not going to argue because, like Caswell, I too was at Wembley for the England Poland game and I was also gutted. My name is Andrew Peters and I'm from Norwich. I do watch the 'Canaries' from time to time but they're crap whenever I go so I tend to stay away. There's always a load of trouble at the games and I just can't be bothered with it.'

'Why not, man? What's up with you?' My Lancastrian friend from the bunk above me butted in.

'I can't stand football but it's always worth hanging around outside Turf Moor on a Saturday afternoon in case anything kicks off. Some of my mates go and watch but most of us just wander around the town or go and get a Wimpy or something until a quarter to five when we all pile back to catch the fighting after the game.'

I was beginning to think that Mr. Ferris quite fancied himself and he was certainly beginning to dominate the proceedings at the moment.

'Ever got your head stoved in in the process?' I asked, knowing full well that our newly found hero wouldn't have.

'No, course not.' came the predictable answer although he quite unsuspectingly added; 'I'm too fast on my feet for them. Ex 100 meters school champion, me.' He disclosed with a chuckle.

I laughed with him at his reply but still felt he may become a little over powering.

Time will tell, I thought.

Meanwhile the room fell silent again.

'Paul Fisher, sixteen, from Liverpooool.' The scouse accent from earlier piped up.

'Love Liverpool, Love Shankley, Love the Kop, Love birds, Love the Beatles, hate Everton and hate anything to do with Everton.'

'What about Everton birds?'

'Hmmm! Tricky. Any bird with any sense supports Liverpool. I'd shag an Everton bird but I'd not discuss anything with her.'

More silence. 'Ryan Fielding from South Shields.' An even broader Northern accent announced. 'I've just turned seventeen and I've already worked in the shipyard for a few months with me Father before getting me place here at the school.'

'My brother in law has just been to college in South Shields.' I butted in.

'Aye, that's for Officers. I've had to come all the way down here, like, to train as a deck boy y'know. I'm not bright enough to be an Officer but I know all about ships and seamanship.'

Someone with a head start already, I said to myself.

'What kind of work in the shipyard?' Marker asked.

'Why, just jobbing around, y'know. They build ships up on the Tyne, y'know like and me old man's a Carpenter like, and works on the ships. Fittin' 'em oot and everything, y'know.'

I had a feeling we were going to hear quite a bit of 'y'know like.' over the next couple of months.

'No football then, Geordie?' Fisher demanded.

'Well, Newcastle's canny good, like.' Fielding observed. 'I've never been to a game, like but me older brother goes now and again. They just got to the cup final didn't they?'

'They sure did,' Fisher confirmed, 'and they lost 3-0 to the mighty Liverpooool. Liverpool, Liverpool, Liverpool . . .' Fisher burst into song, loud enough to wake the school.

'Hey, come on lads. Quieten it down a bit.' Marker pleaded. 'Who else hasn't spoken yet?'

'Me, I'm Steve Cooper from Leeds and I support the mighty, dirty Leeds. Don Revie should be the next England manager. He'll get us to the next World Cup Finals all right.'

'Yeah, by kicking lumps out of the opposition and cheating and diving all over the place. Dirty Leeds.' Fisher again shouted out.

'He's an excellent man manager, Scouse. I know Shankley's great but Revie has worked miracles at Leeds. Especially to keep us up at the top.'

Fisher reluctantly agreed.

'Anyway. I'm sixteen and like Status Quo.' Cooper then proceeded to burst into a rendition of 'Come on Sweet Caroline, you're my sweet Caroline.'

'Do you have to?' Marker groaned.

'I'm Pete Lancaster' a broad Southern accent announced after a brief silence. 'I'm from Taunton in Somerset and I can't stand bloody football. I cannot for the life of me imagine anything more ridiculous than twenty-two grown men charging around a playing field and for what? An hour and a half and at the end of the game not even having scored a goal between them.

And the result of today's game is nil nil. What is the point?'

'So what do you like then Pete?' somebody asked.

'I like a good walk in the countryside or a spot of fishing.' Pete replied.

A condescending laugh went round the room.

'Football's ridiculous? What does that make fishing?' Fisher was off again.

'Sit on a river bank from five in the morning for fourteen hours with a tin of maggots and a stale cheese and tomato sarnie for company. Lob a hook into the river and . . . er, sit and wait and wait and wait for what? A bite. Ye gads it's a bite. Oh no it's not it's an old wellie.'

The room laughed again.

Fisher continued 'So at the end of the day you go home, soaking wet, a sore arse from sitting on the bank all day and without any fish. I suppose that even if you were lucky enough to catch anything you would throw it back anyway, wouldn't you?'

Lancaster was quite unperturbed by Fisher's outburst.

'Yes, of course. That is the sport. At least we don't have to worry about getting beaten up walking to the river, unless the Chelsea firm are planning a trip to the River Tone in the near future. We do things quietly in Somerset. We enjoy our cricket. No nil nil draws in that and we enjoy our cider. I'm sure I could get you all drunk on two pints of 'Scrumpy' each.'

'I've heard that's lethal stuff.' One of the Jocks added.

'It most certainly is. I'm looking forward to being old enough to drink it legally and not have to hide a jug of it in my hamper along with my stale cheese and tomato sarnie for my fourteen hour stint on the river bank.'

'Anybody else?' Marker asked.

'Tony Furnell from Redcar. I'm sixteen. I don't like football either, but that doesn't mean that I'm fond of fishing. I like reggae and dance music but at the moment I'm bloody tired and just want to get to sleep, goodnight.'

'Goodnight.' We all seemed to bid in unison.

'I'm Mick Dempsey from Hull.' Another voice proclaimed.

'Shit team.' Fisher proclaimed, showing no signs of tiredness yet.

'I'm a rugby league man actually, Scouse. So you can call 'The Tigers' whatever you want.'

'Hull or Hull Kingston Rovers then?' Fisher asked.

'I'm a Rovers man if you must know.' Dempsey explained. 'And it's nothing like the friendly rivalry you Scousers enjoy, like half of your family being red and the other half blue, depending on which club is the most successful at the present moment in time.'

'Hey, now!' Fisher retorted, 'Don't be like that. How do you become one or the other in Hull, then?' Fisher grilled Dempsey.

'If you're from the West of the River Hull you're a scabby Hull supporter, but if you're fortunate enough to be born on the East-side of the river then you are a Rovers man. I know some people that even refuse to cross the river to the West side such is the animosity. And, before anyone asks, no! You definitely would not marry a bird from the West side if you're an Easterner. Not like you scousers inter breeding between Liverpool and Everton supporters. Just doesn't happen.'

'Still, it doesn't bother me,' He continued, "cuz I miss most weekend matches anyway as I've been going out on the trawlers at weekends for the past year or so.'

'No shit, have you?' someone asked.

'Yes, since I turned sixteen almost a year ago I've been going out, mainly just helping out in the galley if they're short, or just mending the nets on the quay side if there was nothing doing on board. I don't know if I would like to do it full time. Maybe I will in the future but I wanted to have a crack at it 'deep sea' first. I've seen plenty of bigger ships come up the Humber and they look a lot safer than some of the rust buckets I've seen head off into the North Sea. That's why I've come down here to get my ticket.'

'Fair play to you.' Someone commented before another silence.

'Anybody left to introduce themselves or are we all asleep now?' enquired Marker.

'I'm still Ferris from Burnley and I'm fucked.' Came a weary reply.

'Er! I'm Geoff Allen and I'm from Hounslow in Essex.'

Geoff's voice was quite deep but surprisingly without much of a Cockney twang. He sounded a little nervous and it was not a voice that I recognised as having spoken before during the last hour or so of introductions.

'Hi Geoff.' A tired reply came from somewhere in the room.

'I'm not a great football fan but have to support the Arsenal along with the rest of my family. I'm sixteen and like going to the cinema and watching films.'

There was no reply from around the room. It must have been getting mightily late I concluded.

'What's the time' somebody asked as if reading my mind.

'It's ten to twelve.' Marker informed those still awake. 'Anybody left?'

'Must be just Me.' a voice whispered out after a lengthy silence.

'I'm Gary Thompson and I'm from Barnet. I'll tell you about myself tomorrow if anyone's really bothered but if it's all the same to you all I'm getting my head down now.'

Nobody appeared to be that bothered and most were asleep now anyway. I had enjoyed the introductions. Most came over very friendly if one or two had seemed a little boisterous.

I felt much more at ease with my surroundings now than I had at lights out. It didn't take much longer for the excitement and events of the day to catch up with me and I was soon in a very deep sleep.

It only seemed about ten minutes later, but it was daylight outside and the tannoy in our room boomed into life.

'Wakey, Wakey, Rise and Shine.' It crackled at high volume.

'What the fuck was that?' Ferris asked from above me.

'Half six lads.' Marker confirmed as he leapt out of his bed. 'Hope you all slept well.

Right breakfast is at seven thirty, dormitory inspection at eight thirty and muster in the yard at ten to nine for kit inspection before the commencing of lessons which is at nine. All of this is in your handbook which, no doubt, none of you read last night.'

'Dormitory inspection? Kit inspection?' asked a horrified Fisher.

'I doubt your dorm will be inspected this morning as you've just arrived but generally you will have two choices. Either get up, shit, shave and get dressed then tidy the dorm before breakfast or; leave the cleaning and tidying up until after breakfast when you may only have twenty minutes or so to do it in.'

A groan and plenty of 'fuck sakes' went round the room.

'Friday morning is the big inspection. It's when Captain Spearing and any other top dignitaries that he cares to bring along with him come round and inspect. We have to get on our hands and knees and buff the floor up on a Friday morning. Or should I say you have to.' He chuckled.

The floor was not unlike that in a school's assembly room with a wooden tiled effect.

'Get away and shite.' Fisher scorned. 'On our hands and knees my arse.'

'We'll see.' concluded Marker.

With that I joined a few of the others at the wash basins, of which there were eight, to freshen up and clean my teeth.

We all seemed to be looking around at each other to try to put faces to the voices we had heard the night before. Ferris was at the sink next to me and smiled. He was a couple of inches taller than I was, quite skinny with a closely cropped mod style haircut.

'What did you say your name was?' He asked me.

'John, John Caswell.'

'That's right, from that place that nobody's heard of, right?'

'Right.' I replied without elaborating.

'I'm beginning to wonder if we've joined a school or a fucking prison. On our hands and knees buffing up the floor?' He asked as if seeking an assurance that his ears had not deceived him.

'Probably a cross between the two,' I remarked, 'It's only for fourteen weeks though so I suppose we'd better get used to it.'

'Yeah, your right. See you in a mo.' With that he went back into the dorm to be replaced at the sink by a fair-haired chap with a red face and spots but at least six-foot tall.

'Morning.' I greeted whilst still brushing my teeth allowing half of the toothpaste to dribble down my chin.

'Morning.' He responded quite shyly. Definitely Geoff Allen I deduced.

We all dressed in our number one's, on Marker's say so, for the beginning of the day.

'Most of the students have their lessons in their number ones so it makes sense to put them on for breakfast. Any that you do see in their number twos will probably be in the courtyard on the hatches for their first lesson.'

I had noticed the previous evening that to one side of the courtyard there was a mock up of a ship's hatch and a crane of some description at the back end of it.

We went down to breakfast at seven thirty on the dot. I still didn't feel that comfortable with my surroundings as we left the dorm as I still didn't know anybody too well just yet and I quietly followed Marker and the rest of the dorm down to the dining hall alongside, judging by his accent, Pete Lancaster the Ciderman from Somerset.

The queue for breakfast was massive but soon got down very quickly. I should think so as well considering the amount of trainee Stewards and kitchen staff that were actually in this place.

There was no choice but the breakfast itself, if you fancied the full works, looked quite good. Fried egg, sausage, baked beans and toast made from the same doorstep sized loaf as last night's sarnies by the looks of it.

I was quite hungry, and although never normally one for a big breakfast at home, I opted for a full house washed down with a bowl of cornflakes and a cup of vile looking coffee.

Our friend with the long ginger hair followed us in to the dining room and came over, with his dorm mates, to sit at our row of tables. They made up the rest of this month's intake of deck trainees and would therefore be our classmates for the duration. The jeering and wolf whistles continued as he sat down but he seemed unfazed.

'I know, I know. I've got an appointment at the hairdressing salon at eleven hundred hours this morning.' He began in a thick Scottish accent. 'Not sure yet whether to have it blow dried or permed.' He joked, flicking a couple of stray strands away from his eyes.

We laughed and ignored the now familiar and irritating cry of 'Peanuts' echoing all around us.

Breakfast over we all traipsed back to our dorm where, despite Marker's assurances to the contrary, there was a knock on our dormitory door at twenty to nine and an Officer on dorm inspection walked through.

'Morning Gentlemen.' The Officer greeted us. 'Just a quick word to remind you that your dorm does get inspected every morning, as your leading hand will have already told you. After parade would you all please go to the main assembly room for your school induction. Thank you.'

We debated in the next few minutes between ourselves that in future the best course of action every morning would be to clean the dorm after breakfast if we all made the effort to return to the dorm by ten past eight. Even the most unwilling of participants agreed.

At five minutes to nine the tannoy crackled into life again.

'Muster in the courtyard, all students muster in the courtyard.' The order rang out around the complex.

There was some symmetry to the muster, but not much. Marker attempted to get us to line up behind him and I observed other leading hands having similar difficulties in bringing their troops to order.

'Quiet please.' An Officer shouted.

I guessed there were around 400 students in the courtyard. All became silent and upstanding as a couple of other Officers, one sporting a couple of stripes on his arms, walked down the lines inspecting the students, pausing briefly to tuck a collar in here and brush a shoulder down there.

'Those shoes are filthy, Potts.' The Chief Officer said to a scruffy looking student.

'Put him on a charge.' He motioned to the second Officer who duly wrote Potts' name down.

As they strolled down our line I could feel myself becoming tense. I know it was only for show and I considered it a bit of a charade but all the same, despite my strict Grammar School upbringing, I had still never been subjected to such high levels of personal scrutiny before.

I was passed by with just a quick up and down glance for which I was grateful but the inspection party soon shuddered to a halt as they set their eyes on Dalgetty, our long haired ginger friend whom we had learnt at breakfast was from Inverness.

'I have a hair appointment at eleven o'clock.' Dalgetty explained with a smile to the Officer who definitely was not smiling.

'Make that five past nine, laddy.' The Officer scowled.

'Yes, Sir.' Dalgetty nervously replied.

It was all we could do to suppress our laughter at the seriousness of it all but, as the students disbursed to their various classrooms for the day's lessons and we made our way towards the assembly room, a hand was placed on Dalgetty's shoulders by the second Officer from the inspection and he was escorted to another part of the amenities block where I could only imagine 'Sweeny Todd' must have been waiting in anticipation sharpening his shears.

The 90 of us that had joined the school yesterday (minus Dalgetty for the time being) sat down again in the assembly room and were this time addressed by the Officer who had briefly entered our dorm to remind us of the days itinerary.

'Welcome, Gentlemen.' He began 'My name is Mr. Hoult and you will all be seeing a fair bit of me over the next couple of weeks as I will be taking you for your Lifeboat theory lessons.

Firstly, however, I would like to draw your attention to the School handbook that you received yesterday and that hopefully you will all have brought along with you this morning.'

There were several blank faces around the room but I had remembered mine.

'I will start by reiterating what is said in the introduction to the handbook by Captain Spearing and that is that the staff at the school are here to help you, as well as teach you, in any way they can. So if you have any problems, get them off your chest.'

He paused and looked around to make sure we were all paying attention before continuing.

'Obviously that means that although, yes, we do run a disciplined school here we do realise that you are all away from home, some of you possibly for the first time in your lives, and I want to stress to you that all the staff are approachable and will always be sympathetic to any of your needs.'

As Mr Hoult paused for breath the double doors to the assembly room opened and in, rather sheepishly, crept a very forlorn and somewhat embarrassed Dalgetty. A huge cheer went up around the room as he entered, smiling now but still red faced, as he made for his chair. He had been absolutely scalped. He had only been away from us for around ten minutes.

Mr Hoult had a grin as wide as his face. 'Okay, settle down, please.' He laughed.

'He isn't the only one with a hair appointment today, I'm sure, and all of you who were requested during inspection to visit the barber today should do so this morning between ten thirty and twelve.'

I hadn't realised. I must have escaped it, although I have to admit that my hair was a fair bit shorter than some in the room. Other students were nodding confirmation that they had been summoned.

'On the subject of hair.' Mr Hoult continued. 'The barber is only normally on the premises once a week on a Monday between six and eight in the evening, so if you are singled out for a re-style during Monday inspection you will lose your liberty for that evening in order to attend. Your liberty is something that we would like to hope you will all take seriously whilst you are at the school. It is your free time and your leisure time which, we feel, is the most valuable to you and it is the one thing that we insist we should take away from you if you continually flout the school's rules.'

He looked around the room nodding, as if to confirm that yes, that really is a fate worse than death for you.

'There are countless activities that we arrange and cater for in your spare time,' he continued, 'These include a library, a cinema which has two showings a week, a television room, a games room, a tuck shop and there are various hobby clubs such as model making and a photography club. You can even further your education by starting English correspondence courses if you wish. At weekends, for those students who do not proceed on weekend leave there are other organised activities such as cricket, football and tennis on the school's playing fields or gymnastics, five-a-side football and basketball are all arranged from time to time here in the assembly hall. Many other activities such as hiking, canoeing and camping expeditions are organised, especially at this time of the year, and the notice board is always kept up to date with the relevant details. So you see it's not that bad here after all.'

There were certainly some nods of approval from around the room.

'It can get very boring here at times, especially at the weekends if you do not go home, so I would encourage you all to try to get yourself involved in some of these activities. It also helps to build up your confidence and to get along with other people who you do not know. Something that will become very important to you once you do leave here and begin your life at sea. You are allowed local liberty, which means you can go in to Gravesend if you so desire. But there are strict rules for this which are outlined on page 18 of your handbook.'

We read the paragraph on leave and liberty as he recited.

'This is a privilege and not a right. Before you proceed 'ashore' you will be inspected by the Duty Officer who will then allow you ashore when he is satisfied that you are properly dressed in No.1 uniform. Whilst ashore you must remain correctly dressed at all times. You must not gather in groups of more than three and must not loiter with girls in the vicinity of the College or in the College or on the canal road. Remember to behave in such a manner as to be of a credit to yourselves and to the College.'

We all remembered Marker's sermon the previous night as to the dangers of going in to Gravesend and, in particular, the point about not being in groups of more than three caused a muttered discussion amongst us.

'Settle down again, please.' Mr Hoult interrupted.

'I'm sure you are well aware by that and by what you may have already heard that going in to Gravesend is not particularly advisable. Although the school is powerless to prevent you going in to town there really is no need and we do all we can to ensure that all your needs are met here within the confines of the ground. There has been trouble on and off in the town with sea school students from the year dot and I don't honestly believe that this situation is going to change during the few weeks that you are at the school. All I can advise is that if you feel you must go in to town please do not go alone and please do not try to provoke any of the locals that you come across. Along the canal road, that you would have come down yesterday and behind the West block you may have noticed a small building which is the 'Flying Angel' Club. Flying Angel Clubs are run world-wide by the 'Missions to Seamen' and we feel very honoured that a club has been provided for our use within the grounds of the school. A service is held in the chapel at ten thirty every Sunday morning and the Chaplain is available most evenings to any of the students who may wish to speak to him. The service provided by this organisation cannot be praised highly enough and if any of you feel that you cannot speak to the members of staff at the school with a problem then the Chaplain is always there for you.'

He paused for breath and scratched his arse.

'The club also offers a coffee room and tuck shop as well as a lounge area and a games room. You can even buy fish and chips in the canteen and every other Saturday night they hold a disco in the hall. Any students that are on duty watch or on a default (a charge) are not permitted to go to the Flying Angel Club as it is considered a part of your liberty.' He paused, giving his head a quick scratch.

'How do you get put on a charge?' Mr.Hoult asked to nobody in particular.

'Simple. You disobey the school rules or you commit an offence.

Offences are many fold but are blindingly obvious. Page 14 in your handbook outlines some of the more serious offences for which you run the risk of being expelled.'

The paragraph was then read to us for full effect.

'Damaging or misusing fire fighting appliances and equipment; Stealing; Possession and/or taking of drugs; Bullying; Defacing or damaging College property; Insolence to any member of staff.'

'All fairly obvious to you, I'm sure.' He surmised.

'Smoking is permitted but only BELOW the red line that you will see around the complex and which is situated at the foot of the stairs leading up to your dormitories. Offences that you will be put on a charge for range from carrying a knife, spike or offensive weapon or bringing alcohol onto the premises, which may still result in expulsion depending on the severity of the offence, to throwing litter, swearing, lounging around the College in a slovenly manner, chewing gum, gambling for gain, sitting or climbing on the courtyard rails etc. etc. All these minor offences will carry a charge which, again depending of the severity, could last from one day up to a couple of weeks where you will have your liberty taken away from you.'

He paused; gazing around the room to ensure that he still had our attention.

'Any questions?'

There weren't. I was beginning to think that Ferris might have been right in his assumption that we had entered a prison.

We studied our handbook which carried a full two pages of offences and minor offences for which our liberty could be in jeopardy from and it was difficult to imagine even the most angelic of us getting through the entire fourteen weeks with a clean slate.

'I like this one,' I remarked to Peters who was sitting next to me.

'You must not, number fourteen, make any alterations to your uniform.'

I flicked the bottom of my trousers.

'I already spent the best part of an hour last night picking at the stitching on the turn up of my uniform trousers to make them only an inch and a half short in the leg now.'

Peters laughed.

Tucked right at the bottom of the list of offences, almost as an afterthought, was a list of 'You musts.'

You must: Address staff in a proper manner; Be properly dressed at all times and wear the correct rig-of-the-day; Have a sensible haircut; Assist in keeping your dormitory clean and tidy, Fold and stow your bedding in the correct manner; Read and check the notice boards for 'daily routines' and orders.

No mention of receiving a prize or indeed extra liberty for conforming.

'Duty watch means a group of students that patrol the grounds during liberty periods ensuring that no defaulters leave the premises and that all the rules are abided to by all students in the various recreational areas. Check the notice board for details of when you are on duty watch. It is rotated by room number and teams; you will have each been allocated a team yesterday, Red, White or Blue.'

Ah, I remember now. I was in the white team.

'Duty watch will generally befall you once every two weeks and for one weekend during your time here.' Mr Hoult continued to explain.

'Okay, lads. It's approaching half past ten now so we'll stop for a break. Those of you who have been summoned to the barber should go to the administration block straight afterwards. I'm sure our friend here will be able to show you where to go.' He smiled gesticulating at Dalgetty.

'He's a fucking animal.' Dalgetty whispered so as not to be overheard and receive the intakes first charge for swearing.

'Sit, boy. Was all he said. He took my hair off in fucking sheets. The bastard. One minute and the lot was off. He never even offered me a mirror to check out the back.'

I couldn't help but laugh along with the rest of the group. About six others made their way to the barbers after break but none came back as severely cropped as Dalgetty. He was definitely made an example of.

With the formalities of the 'do nots' out of the way Mr Hoult proceeded, for the rest of the morning, to spell out our future for the next four weeks at least.

We received a timetable for both lifeboat theory and practical lessons for the duration of the course. Some of it I have to admit looked quite fun.

Everything seemed most varied. A film on safety at sea tomorrow morning, with basic survival lectures to follow. A mixture of lessons, pulling and coxing the school's longboat on the River Thames and practical inflatable life raft drill in the school's swimming pool (I was not too keen on this part being a bit of a lousy swimmer). I had taken swimming lessons at primary school and had a certificate of competency for managing to stay afloat from one length of the swimming pool to the other but Mark Spitz I was not!

'You will all need to attend the various safety awareness courses but only those who are continuing through to their E.D.H. Certificates will be required to sit their lifeboat examination. It is a distinct advantage for you lads nowadays that you can pass these examinations at the school and then progress through the ranks at sea based on your age and time served. Although it is not the end of the World and you will still be allowed to go to sea without these certificates there is no escaping the fact that with a bit of effort and application over the next fourteen weeks your life will be easier in the future.' Mr Hoult concluded.

Sound advice for sure I noted to myself.

It was just familiarisation. I had nowhere near the nautical background that a couple of my fellow dorm mates, notably Fielding and Dempsey, had but surely it couldn't be that difficult.

'After lunch, guys, and I've been particularly saving this treat up for you, we will be visiting both the school medical centre for your health check up and also the dentist for an exploratory dental check.' Mr. Hoult continued.

Yet another groan went round the room.

'Can't be as bad as the barbers.' Dalgetty suggested.

Lunch was taken from Mid-day until one o'clock and consisted of liver, which I had always detested, and onions with mashed potatoes, served in a splattering of thick, mud like gravy. It came with the statutory two rounds of thick bread and I was fast becoming accustomed to the fact that this may well be my prime means of sustenance over the coming weeks.

'I wasn't exactly expecting Lobster Thermadore,' Fisher commented turning his nose up at his dinner plate, 'but this is shite.'

Nobody argued with him but most of the group appeared resigned to what was before them and bravely scoffed the lot.

I couldn't.

'Is that gravy, or something that has been dredged up from the bed of the Thames?' I asked.

'Are these people really training to become ship's cooks?' Cooper bemoaned.

'Heaven help us.'

There was some form of bread and butter pudding with custard for afters that I managed to tackle but I wasn't impressed.

After lunch all 90 of us new recruits assembled outside the sick bay awaiting our medical and our visit to the dentist.

My name was called quite quickly to go into the dentist, as others were summoned to the Doctor.

I was told to sit in the chair and open wide.

The dentist, whom I casually glanced at in his white coat and amused Myself by thinking he was probably the barber as well, shoved my head unceremoniously back in the chair and began prodding at my fillings and gouging lumps out of them with what felt like a pitch-fork.

'Fine, fine, just relax lad.' He mumbled as he continued to rake at my gums.

He rattled off several numbers to his male assistant and within two minutes my check up was over.

Great, I thought. Not so bad after all.

'Okay, lad.' He concluded. 'I'll see you again tomorrow and we'll do a little work on those fillings. Nothing too bad in there.'

Shit. What would the psycho be like with a drill if he was prepared to inflict this much damage on my molars with just a bloody toothpick?

The medical that followed can only be best described as not quite what I was expecting. I had heard all the stories about army medicals where you stripped off and had your balls clutched and told to cough but never in a million years believed any of it.

'Behind the screen, please, and take your clothes off . . . . . Name?' The doctor ordered (well I can only assume he was the doctor, as he hadn't even lifted his head from the desk he was sitting at yet but he did have the bog standard white coat—and a stethoscope around his neck).

'Caswell.' I confirmed.

I came out from behind the screen. He still was not looking at me.

'Up on the scales, please.' He gestured towards the scales. He was looking at me now.

'All of your clothes off please, boy. That includes the underpants.'

Here we go, I thought. He'll be tickling my balls in a minute.

'Eight stone twelve.' He announced to me, completely ignoring the obvious unease I must have been displaying due to my nakedness.

He pointed me towards a height chart next to the scales.

'Let's check your height, boy.'

I stood, rigid and uncomfortably embarrassed, with my back firmly up against the wall.

'Five foot five inches. Good.'

He wrote it down.

Before I could move a muscle and in a move of lightening speed, catching me completely unawares, I felt his cold hand cupping my bollocks.

'Cough!' He ordered in a slightly raised tone.

I forced a pathetic excuse for a cough.

'That's good. Pop your underpants back on.'

It was over in a nano-second. I did not even have time to go red or to even contemplate smacking him one.

I reached for my underpants as quickly as I could almost falling over in my haste to cover myself back up.

'Sit down and put one leg over the other, please, and we'll test your reflexes.'

That done he then put the stethoscope to my torso and tapped my chest in a couple of places before asking me to read the bottom line of a chart a couple of feet away. I had purposely left my reading glasses at home and not even disclosed that I sometimes needed them for reading or watching television. I knew that I would not be allowed to join the deck department if I told them I needed glasses. I was sure I could blag my way through an eye test.

'H Y E X N T' I read slowly but with confidence.

'Okay, that's fine'. He then gave me a book with coloured numbers to check for colour blindness but that was also no problem.

He then checked my blood pressure and stuck a small light in my ears and up my nostrils. Unfortunately my sinuses lay dormant, how I would have loved to have covered him in mucus.

'Good, you're in fine shape boy. You could probably do with putting on a bit of weight whilst you're down here but other than that . . . Let's hope I don't have to see you again in the next fourteen weeks.'

I echoed his sentiments although it is more likely that I will be losing weight whilst I'm here rather than gaining it and I thought about advising him to warm his bloody hands up but thought better of it and just hurriedly got dressed and made good my escape.

There was only one topic of conversation back in the assembly room after we had all had our medicals.

'I was going to fuckin' twat him one.' Ferris announced.

'Grabbed me fuckin' balls, so he did.'

We were in hysterics. None of us were too pleased at the so-called inspection but Ferris seemed to have taken more exception than most.

'Did he squeeze them?' Jimmy McGuire asked.

'No, but it made me fuckin' eyes water, Jeezus!'

The final hour of our first full day consisted of a potted history of the school itself.

The concept of a unique sea training school for ratings was evolved towards the end of the First World War when over a million tons of shipping was lost during 1917. An old sailor's home on the river—front in Gravesend was empty and available and soon acquired by the Maritime Department of the Board of Trade. On September 18th 1918 it opened its doors to the first trainees and could take up to 150 boys at a time.

Although only a small school it was supplemented by a training vessel, *The Triton,* which was moored alongside on the nearby jetty and used as an extra training facility.

There were many other such training ships and establishments dotted around the country at the time but none specifically for deck boys and galley ratings such as at Gravesend.

In 1939 the premises were evacuated and the whole operation moved to a similar set up in Sharpness, the authorities deeming Gravesend most vulnerable to air attacks, where it remained until 1944.

A 2,000 ton former sailing ship, *The Vindicatrix,* was used for accommodation purposes and at the end of the war when Gravesend Sea School re-opened the Sharpness operation continued to run hand in hand such was the demand, yet again after war, for Merchant Navy ratings.

By the late fifties and early sixties and with both sites becoming outdated, not to mention the early post-war need for seafarers diminishing slightly, it became clear that new premises were required.

The 28 acre site on Denton marshes that the college we are now attending stands in was acquired and accepted its first students in January 1967. It signalled the end of the Sharpness operation but this new establishment would be able to cater for over 550 boys. Well above the amount the combined two locations could accommodate and assumedly at a much less overall cost.

'And to top it all off,' Mr. Hoult concluded, 'you will each receive £1 pocket money per week on a Friday. Now I can't say fairer than that, can I?'

Wow! A whole pound. I could see that dwindling in the tuck shop before the weekend was out.

I must admit that I hadn't brought much cash down with me to Gravesend. My train fare home, if I needed it for anything unforeseen, and about fifteen pounds, which is all I had left to my name, to see me through. So I suppose even a measly pound a week was a bit of an unexpected bonus.

'We're not going to get pissed on £1 a week are we?' Steve Cooper insisted as we sat down to our almost acceptable looking roast lamb, roast potatoes and carrots in the dining room at tea—time.

'It's almost a pound for a pint in some parts of London.' Thompson submitted to the conversation.

'What! A pound a pint! Fuck me, I think I'll pack up bloody drinking, and I've only just started.' Ferris spluttered. 'This pork's nice.'

'90p for a pint of lager last time I was up the West-End. I blame decimalisation.' Thompson weighed in; 'It's lamb.'

'You're jesting Thommo, lager's a poof's drink anyway. Still only 30p for a good old pint of Double Diamond up Burnley.' Ferris countered.

'20p for a double Vodka at the Rugby Club in Kettering,' I added to the proceedings.

'Yeah, but lager wouldn't have reached the outbacks yet, would it?' Cooper aimed at me.

'Thank God for that at a pound a pint.' I quickly retorted.

I hadn't noticed but in the few minutes that we had all been discussing the merits of a pound a week pocket money, and the luxuries we were going to be able to afford with it (sixteen packets of crisps, twelve packets of maltesers, or a pint up the West-end), I had eaten all of my dinner.

Rounded nicely off with apple pie and custard I walked back to the dorm with the rest of the lads feeling, for the first time since my arrival, a bit more relaxed and at long last not bloody hungry.

We were able to take a more leisurely tour of the complex on our second evening. We were still 'Peanuts,' I think we had all accepted that part of the bargain by now but already, after just 24 hours, didn't feel such outcasts anymore.

It still felt a bit strange in that nobody seemed quite sure who to tag along with. A couple of the quieter members of the dorm such as Geoff Allen, Pete Lancaster and Ryan Fielding had stayed fairly close together during the day or with Marker whenever we were in the dorm. The more obvious, boisterous ones such as Ferris, Fisher and the two Jocks had struck up an allegiance and I was caught in between the two stools.

Ferris had included me and looked out for Fisher and me for most of the day, most probably because I was his bunkmate (for want of a better phrase).

I, in turn, was probably a bit unsure of them. I thought Ferris was rather loud and a bit 'in-your-face' at times but I did find him to be very amusing company.

I ended up with them, along with Steve Cooper and Gary Thompson, exploring the telly room and the games room.

We had made a conscientious decision that we would stay in the grounds for this evening and check out the 'Flying Angel' tomorrow night.

'We'll have to check this notice board out and find out when the five-a-side footie's on,' Fisher declared.

'Most definitely,' I agreed. 'I played five-a-side with some school friends at the drill hall in Kettering in my last year at school. It's excellent.'

'Great stuff, we'll go for it. Sam? You up for it?'

'I can't play football, but I'll give it a go if I can kick someone.' Came the predictable response from Ferris.

'If Phil and Jimmy can find a couple more Jocks we can give them a pasting.' Ferris added.

Phil and Jimmy just fell about laughing and launched in to an equally absurd argument about how they were going to win the World Cup in June.

The Scotland debate continued until nine thirty when we all returned to our dormitory after a none too successful frame of snooker (we were all crap, we'd agreed).

Once again it was hard to settle at lights out. Even worse now that we had become a bit more acquainted with each other.

Anybody got any Irish jokes? Fisher asked.

'Did you hear about the Irishman that thought that Pontius Pilot worked for A.E.R.Lingus?'

It was hard to tell who had delivered the first crack in the darkness.

'Or the Irishman that thought that cunnilingus was a new airline?' Replied Ferris (I didn't understand that one).

'Did you hear about the worst ever Irish airline disaster?' Marker began.

'A two-seater light aircraft crashed into a cemetery and police recovered 285 bodies from the wreckage.'

'That is sick.' Steve Cooper joined in.

'What about Mick and Paddy?' He began. 'Mick and Paddy are coming over to England for the first time ever to work on a building site and before they come over on the ferry their mate Seamus tells them that the beer is not too good over in England. 'Make sure you drink in a Bass House when you get over there.' Is his advice to them. So they end up working in Liverpool and once they get their first pay packet it's straight off down to the pub. Remembering Seamus' advice they go in to the first pub and Mick asks, 'Is this a Bass House?'

'Sorry lads, Courage.' Was the reply.

'Oh well, never moind. We'll troiy somewhere else.'

Cooper apologises for the poor accent.

'Into the second pub and they ask again if this is a Bass House and get the same negative reply.'

Into the third pub.

'Is this a Bass house, Soir?'

'It certainly is, boys.' Came the reply, 'What'll you be having?'

'Two pints of Guinness, please.' Ordered Paddy.

By now everybody was trying to get in on the act and before we knew it the time had reached a quarter past eleven before Thompson delivered what was to be the final joke of a most entertaining session.

'The foreman of the building site asks Paddy to dig him a hole twelve foot deep, a hundred feet long and forty foot wide.

'By the end of today, please Paddy.'

'Oi can't do that in a day, it'll fockin' kill me, bejayzus.' Paddy argues.

'I'll give you a J.C.B.' the foreman replies.

'You can stick your fockin' medals up yer arse! I'm not killin' myself for no-one!'

With that the laughter died down and the dorm became silent. I would imagine that only a handful of us were still awake to have heard Thompson's last delivery.

'Shhh!, what was that?' Someone whispered in the darkness.

There was complete silence. I could hear nothing.

A couple of minutes later I heard a slight noise coming from our toilet block. Certainly nobody from our dorm was up and about.

'Shhh!' again someone whispered.

The door at the far end from me and leading to our washroom facilities suddenly burst open and before I knew it I could hear the sound of blows being rained down on my dorm-mates, more than likely with pillows or some other soft objects. Several Ooooofs and ooyahs were emitted from the far side of the room and I could feel my bunk shudder as Ferris leapt from the top bunk. The whole episode had so far been conducted in total silence.

'It's a fucking dorm raid! Get the bastards!' Ferris was shouting.

None of the infiltrators managed to get right through the dorm and over to my side of the room so I was left unscathed but Ferris and the two Scots, who were over that side of the room, managed to get a couple of punches in. The skirmish continued as the attackers made good their retreat back through the toilet block, with pillows flailing. About seven or eight of them in total but it was hard to tell in the darkness especially as a couple of our lot had given chase. It was over in a matter of less than a minute.

'Don't turn the lights on, for fuck's sake don't turn the lights on.' Marker barked in a frantic, hushed whisper.

'Bastards. Fuckin' Bastards'. Ferris fumed.

'Leave it, leave it.' Marker hissed. 'They've gone now. Anybody get hurt?'

'Did you know about this, Marker?' Fisher demanded. 'They're your fucking classmates.'

'No, I had no idea it would happen tonight. Sometimes the Peanuts do get raided, usually on the first night and when it didn't happen last night I thought that you had most probably escaped it. They certainly wouldn't have discussed it with me in class today anyway.'

'No, I suppose not.' Fisher conceded. 'Anybody get hurt?' He asked again.

Most of us were up now and scratching around in the dark re-making our bunks.

Some lockers had been tipped over as well in the melee. Several had obviously been attacked in their sleep.

'I took about ten blows. With a pillow, I think.' Geoff Allen admitted.

'I landed one good punch into the ribs of the bastard that was whacking me.' McGuire whispered across to Ferris.

'We'll get the bastards back.' Ferris announced and a fair few agreed.

'They'll be expecting that now.' Marker said. 'You're better off leaving it for now. They won't come back again.' He assured us.

It was midnight before we settled down again. The adrenaline was still pumping in Ferris as he kept tossing and fidgeting in the bunk above me muttering vengeance on the dorm next door.

At breakfast the next morning we informed Dalgetty and his mates from room 16 of the attack on us and warned them that they may receive a similar visit from a neighbouring dorm in the not too distant future.

The damage had been fairly minimal due to the fact that the assailants were only in the room for a minute at tops.

Nobody had been physically hurt but Ferris was still annoyed that Marker had not even warned us that the attack MAY occur and therefore we could have offered slightly better resistance.

Going to bed 'tooled up' I believe was the term Ferris and Fisher discussed with McGuire and Laughlan in case of future incidents.

Dorm and kit inspection passed that Wednesday morning and I was certain that by the weekend it would all be so old hat to us that it would not bother us in the slightest.

Our first lesson of the day was to be a Merchant Navy Board of Trade Film on safety at sea; a quite comical and over-the-top attempt to draw our attentions to the various hazards that we were likely to encounter during normal everyday life at sea.

The acting was superb.

Some imbecile waltzing around a ship's main deck in flip-flops, carrying three boxes piled so high as to impair his forward vision and smoking a cigarette.

Our friend is just about to step in to a patch of oil carelessly deposited on the deck when the ultra observant commentator announces. 'Surely an accident waiting to happen.'

You don't say.

With that he duly slips on the patch of oil with very little conviction. As he slips he throws the boxes, obviously filled with cotton wool, into the air in such a way that they land back down on top of his head once his fall is completed, only now they must contain tonne weights because once the camera pans back to him his head is covered in tomato ketchup.

Just what this guy is actually doing at sea in the first place then becomes a mystery to us all as he proceeds, later in the day I must assume, to throw his dog-end into another patch of oil and nearly send the ship up in flames, trip over a mooring rope whilst carrying more boxes, drop a tin of paint on his foot, and then chop half his hand off whilst attempting to cut a length of rope.

As the ambulance pulls away from the jetty to take him to the hospital to undergo major surgery on his severed limb the rest of the crew must have been heaving a huge sigh of relief.

'Don't become an accident waiting to happen and remember; safety first at all times.' The commentator instills upon us as the crackling soundtrack grinds to a thankful conclusion.

Now I appreciate that the point has to be hammered home to us but this was more farce than fact.

Still, if every time a potential hazard is averted at sea by remembering this unfortunate chap's antics in the film then it will have served its purpose.

At least that's what Mr. Hoult tried to persuade us, more than likely to justify the film's inclusion in our curriculum.

After the film I was summonsed back to the dentists. I had forgotten all about it after yesterdays exploratory 'prod' by the evil practitioner.

'Yes.' He enthused. 'You've had a few teeth out in the past haven't you, lad?'

I nodded my agreement at his astounding observation.

'And four fillings.' He gleefully added. 'What I am going to do is take those fillings out and replace them. Can't have you getting toothache in the middle of the Pacific now, can we?'

What? All four of them. Holy shit.

I then had to endure probably the worst forty-five minutes of my entire life. After several injections in my mouth all four fillings were systematically drilled out and replaced with God only knows what and I could feel that my mouth must have swollen to the size of Mick Jagger's eating a cricket ball.

It was impossible to rinse with any sort of co-ordination but I still had the presence of mind to use this as an excuse and purposely gobbed the horrible antiseptic solution over his shoes.

'Sorry.' I mumbled as best I could.

'I know it will be a bit painful for you now.' The dentist said.

Bloody understatement of the year!

'But it will soon wear off and you won't have any trouble now from those fillings for many a year to come.'

With that he gave me a signed note to say that I had received treatment and advised me to lay down for an hour or so and return to lessons in the afternoon but only if I felt able to.

I took him up on the advice to lie down on my bunk through the dinner hour but returned to the class for the afternoon period. I didn't exactly want to as I could hardly open my mouth but at the same time I didn't want to miss anything.

I needn't have particularly bothered as we received lectures in the afternoon just basically re-iterating the message that the film was trying to get across to us that morning.

We were treated to some much more authentic slides though of Galley staff with fingers chopped off and a rather gory looking leg that had been drenched in boiling fat.

The deck side of the group taking great delight in labelling the catering side 'stupid wankers' for allowing such accidents to happen until we saw a particularly graphic slide of a deck hand with half his leg hanging off where a mooring rope had parted and sliced straight through him.

The day had passed fairly quickly despite my obvious discomfort. Several others had been to the dentist but none seemed to have suffered as much as I had for the experience although I did hear of a couple of extractions which, fortunately, I had avoided.

I could only manage soup at tea—time, which I assumed was oxtail . . . hard to tell, with the usual two slices of bread.

I didn't accompany Ferris and the others to the Flying Angel that evening. I gathered from their reports on their return that it was just really an extension of the facilities we had on the site but with a chapel.

I chose to go to the telly room and to the library to choose something to read. Despite my success in my English exams at school I had never been a great reader. Perhaps, I thought, now would be a good time to start.

I went along with Kowinski, Mick Darnell and Andy Peters, all of whom seemed to be a little bit more on the quieter and refined side to the likes of Ferris, Fisher and the two Scots.

'Lights out' was a lot quieter on the third night after the excitement of the previous two. I could hear quite a bit of snoring from about fifteen minutes after being plunged into darkness but I still couldn't sleep. For one, although I still had a bit of pain in my mouth, I felt hungry enough to be able to eat anything that the Sea School Restaurant was able to throw at me (the rumblings coming from my stomach were drowning out some of the snores). Secondly: our itinerary for tomorrow was to include some survival techniques and advice in the school's training pool, not something I was looking forward to.

The training pool was situated on its own just off the main classroom block to the North of the site and in full view of the River Thames.

It was by no means the size of Kettering's swimming baths where I had tentatively learnt to keep my head above water but what it lacked in length in comparison it made up for in depth. Twenty foot deep at one end and four feet at the shallow end.

There were two diving boards at the deep end. The top one being at least twenty feet up in the air with the, presumably, baby board (and the one for cissy's) just over half the way up.

Personally I was a 'stick my toe in the water and gradually slide in' man myself but I feared that this may not be an option today.

We began the morning in the classroom after I had eaten a full breakfast due to the state of almost starvation that I had woken up in.

Today's subject and consequent practical course would be on 'abandoning ship' and inflatable life rafts.

All was well and good in the classroom and, once again, although the drill was fairly obvious, i.e. don't panic, go to your lifeboat stations, don your lifejacket, etc. etc. the actual thought of having to jump off the sinking ship into shark infested water filled none of us with immense joy.

The theory lasted until dinner time and covered all aspects of survival in a life raft from how to set off flares to how to catch and prepare to eat flying fish. I think I will stick to the digestive biscuits and barley sugar washed down with rainwater thank you.

The afternoon saw the fun begin and was to sort the men out from the wimps.

Unfortunately there was to be no hiding place. We changed in to our swimming trunks and gathered around the pool.

Inside the pool was a fully inflated life raft only it had been tipped on its side for the purpose of this particular exercise.

Our individual task was to jump off either of the diving boards, dependant on diving skills or just plain stupidity, and right the upturned craft.

Fortunately two lifeguards borrowed from the local swimming baths were on hand just in case of any unfortunate difficulties (I can only imagine that in the past there had been such incidents hence the necessity for their attendance).

The course tutor at least had the decency to throw himself off the diving board first and show us exactly what we were to do once in the water.

The overturned raft did have a couple of attached 'handles' that were specifically designed for situations when the raft was thrown into the sea from the stricken, fast sinking vessel and did not land upright.

The trick was to climb up onto the side of the overturned raft and with both feet firmly on the bottom of the raft and a tight grip on the handles throw yourself backwards pulling the raft down, thus upright, as you went.

With the raft now upright you were faced with one more dilemma; your actions in righting the raft have unfortunately left you underneath it, so as soon as you were submerged you are required to let go of the handles and swim out from underneath it, clamber aboard, and presumably wait to be rescued.

Before the first of us took our death defying plunge we were thankfully asked if there were any non-swimmers amongst us.

Out of the 90 of us that had started on Monday only four came forward as non-swimmers. All were from the catering contingent and all four of them were completely and utterly shitting themselves at what they had thought, up to now, they were going to have to do (as were several more of us too afraid to play the non-swimmer card).

I was not entirely happy with the prospect but I had worked out that if I adopted the 'baby board' strategy and landed on top of the raft rather than having to scamper up the side of it I should be okay.

The one thing that worried me was the being submerged and buried underneath the damn thing. I could never open my eyes under water. Some people can and it has always amazed me as to how they can manage it.

I worried that I would not be able to keep my bearings and emerge safely from underneath it but banked on the fact that the lifeguards would react if they saw me in difficulty.

There was no specific rota that we adopted but I let a good twenty or so go before me and I felt my stomach tighten even more as I watched each of those before me completing the task with different levels of success.

Some of the more accomplished swimmers were diving off the top board and landing yards from the raft, swimming up to it, climbing aboard and completing the task with annoying ease.

Others, with obvious deficiencies such as me, were making heavy weather of it and I could only cringe and feel sorry for them in the knowledge that I would not fare too much better.

All of a sudden it was me at the foot of the diving board ladder. I opted for the baby board and waited for what seemed an eternity as the two lifeguards tipped the raft back into its overturned position.

On their signal I took an almighty deep breath and prayed silently before gingerly leaping out into the abyss.

My idea almost paid off as I jumped outwards and towards the raft. It was just that little bit too far out for me to jump straight on to as planned but I managed to grab hold of a little piece of it to stop myself from sinking completely down to the bottom of the pool. I had already been ducked though as I pulled myself up on the raft and my eyes immediately began to sting. I managed to climb up the side and locate the handles. I took another deep breath as I rubbed my eyes and pulled for all I was worth. I couldn't have been doing enough thrusting with my legs as I managed to get the thing halfway over and all my strength disappeared. I could not get the purchase on it necessary to make it come over any further and I appeared to be in limbo just tugging away at the damn thing whilst almost laying down practically horizontal on top of the water.

I was just contemplating letting go and starting the manoeuvre again when, to my complete surprise, the lifeguards, who must have gone round the other side, gave the raft an almighty shove to send it toppling over me. Not being prepared for the sudden submergence I had not taken a deep enough breath to sustain myself for being under the raft. I let go of the raft, which was obviously righted by now and very much on top of me. I gulped and took in a lung full of water. My eyes instinctively opened but I only saw bubbles and the raft's orange hull.

I could then feel Myself being whisked up by one of the lifeguards and before I knew it my head was above water and I was swimming for all I was worth, my heart pounding and my eyes stinging unmercifully, towards the side of the pool.

I clambered out of the pool, with very little of my dignity still intact, and collapsed coughing and spluttering into a poolside chair.

Kowinski came over to me and slapped my back as I continued to struggle for air. I thanked him.

All the people from my dorm that had so far shown a very confident manner such as Ferris, Fisher, Steve Cooper, the two Jocks and Kowinski all excelled in the pool and completed their task with ease.

Apart from Ryan Fielding and Mick Dempsey, the rest of us only achieved minimal success and even my aborted attempt at clambering aboard the righted raft was surpassed by Andy Peters who thrashed about in the water for a most agonising thirty seconds before he was plucked to safety by the lifeguards.

Unfortunately for the likes of Fisher and Ferris the pool was not open for recreation purposes and later that evening they discussed plans to visit the local baths in town. I declined the offer for two reasons, the obvious being my limited prowess in the water and secondly I had absolutely no intentions of visiting downtown Gravesend for any reason whatsoever for the duration and told them so.

Friday soon arrived and unbelievably we have been here a week already. I have enjoyed the tuition that we had received during the week. What a difference it makes to be able to sit in a classroom and actually enjoy what is being taught.

Boy, I never thought I would hear myself say that. Perhaps life at school would not be so bad after all if only the curriculum could consist of, say, sex education, football, beer and wine making, photographing naked women and guaranteed ways to make a million pounds.

The week had solely been dedicated to health and safety at sea with just a brief short test at the end of the week that nobody but nobody could have failed to pass, well maybe our friend from the safety films might have!

'Q. What type of footwear should you use on deck?'

'A. Flip-flops, B. Plimsolls, C. Steel toe capped boots.'

Do me a favour.

We were to split into deck and catering groups next week as the catering boys would receive their tuition in galley safety and towards the end of the week we were to begin our lifeboat training.

Only Teale, who lived down the road in Canterbury, and Geoff Allen, from Hounslow, went home for the weekend. In all honesty I wondered if Geoff would return. He had struggled to make friends during the week and was oh so quiet and shy for a big lad. Still, he hadn't taken any of his clothes so I guessed he would come back on Sunday night.

The weekend was so boring. We were paid our £1 pocket money on the Friday evening before tea but after a couple of games of snooker in the Flying Angel Club, feeding the juke box, and treating Myself to a can of coke and a packet of crisps there wasn't much left of it by the time we returned to the dorm for lights out.

There was to be a disco in the Flying Angel Club on Saturday night but I wondered about the merits of attending if all I could now afford was a packet of wine gums. I had received a letter from my Mother on the Friday morning so I decided to reply to that on Saturday morning along with letters to Malc and Barry back home, Simon and Dave at Lewis's and just to confirm how drastic the situation had become even a line to my Sister, who by now must have been sunning herself in the Mediterranean somewhere.

There was no peace or privacy in the dorm to write my letters as most of the others were just moping about bored. Ferris, Fisher and the Jocks were, quite noisily, playing three-card brag for matchsticks so I upped tools and retired to the school library for a couple of hours.

I had taken my small transistor radio with me and listened to Alan Freeman's Saturday afternoon rock show until teatime. I would also be able to catch the top twenty on Sunday evening. It was just a matter of what I was going to be able to find myself to do for the remaining hours.

I decided to go along to the disco at the club after all in the evening, along with Ferris and a couple of the others, possibly against my better judgement. It felt weird. There was no difference in that it was dark, the music was blaring, there were disco lights on the ceiling and people were dancing (even going so far as to play 'one of these days' from Pink Floyd's 'Meddle' album, something unheard of at the Kettering Rugby Club).

It felt all the more weird in that I was sitting down in a comfy chair watching the proceedings in my bloody sea school uniform.

Oh yes, and there were no girls either.

Or alcohol.

At least I thought there was no alcohol.

Fisher came over to me and asked me if I had enough money for a can of orange. I had, just.

'Excellent.' He said. 'You and James go and get a can each and ask for four glasses as you're sharing it and we'll pep it up a little with some of this.'

With that Fisher produced, from his inside jacket pocket, a half-pint bottle of Smirnoff red label vodka, shielding it from any prying eyes.

'You little fucking beauty.' I exclaimed as my eyes nearly popped out of my head.

'Keep it quiet.' Fisher insisted. 'We'll get turfed out for sure if we're caught. Go and get the orange.'

We came back with the two cans of orange, poured out a couple of inches into the glasses and kept the remainder in the can for ourselves.

Fisher then, with military precision and with all of us covering him, discreetly poured equal measures of the vodka into the orange making sure that not a drop was spilled.

There was still over an hour of the disco left (it still finished at nine thirty—no extension to the opening hours despite the event) but nobody would question that it was taking so long to finish our drinks. It was common knowledge that very few of us had any money and would thus make a drink last ages.

It was pure nectar. Probably only just over a double shot as it had been shared out six ways but still enough to have the desired effect after a week without a drink. By nine thirty the six of us were in fine spirits and I could sense having a little bit of a glow on.

'How are you going to get rid of the bottle?' I asked Fisher as we walked back along the canal path.

'In case you hadn't noticed . . .' He replied. 'There's a fucking big river in our back garden.'

He pointed to the Thames but, with that, ran over to the fence that ran alongside the canal and threw the bottle into the canal.

Fortunately it was getting quite dark by now so the risk of being seen was minimal but I was still astounded that he had thrown the bottle so openly after being so discreet in the club.

Fisher must also have worked out that an empty bottle of vodka found floating in the canal would not raise too many eyebrows in amongst the bicycle tyres, supermarket trolley and half submerged three piece suite that already resided in this stretch of the water.

'Not a word when we get back.' Ferris ordered, obviously sharing my concern that we had broken one of the strictest rules in the book.

A few more jokes did the rounds at lights out but the effects of the vodka soon had us fast asleep.

I lay awake for a while contemplating what we had got up to earlier and, although admitting to enjoying the drink, wondered whether it was actually worth it bearing in mind the consequences of being caught.

If Saturday had been the most boring day of my entire life it was quickly overtaken by Sunday. I resisted the temptation of Sunday service back at the Flying Angel. I hadn't been to Church as such on a Sunday morning since I outgrew Sunday school at the age of about seven.

I decided, along with Andy Peters, Mick Dempsey and Tony Furnell, to instead suss out the laundry room.

It was surprisingly state of the art with eight large industrial washing machines and a couple of spin dryers.

It was stiflingly hot in the room, which was perhaps just as well as it ensured that the clothes dried in no time. With the amount of personnel on the site I guessed that it probably was not a good idea to leave any laundry hanging up in the drying room for collection at a later time. The four of us put our dungarees and shirts into one load and hand washed our underwear. Once the wash cycle had been completed and the gear passed through the spin dryer we then took it in turns to sit outside the room and guard the drying garments. A bit pathetic but we were not alone. Most people used this system as a safeguard against having their gear nicked. Although why anybody would want to steal regulation, cheap jeans or somebody else's skiddies is beyond me. Devilment I suppose.

The whole process from start to returning to the dorm with our dry, clean number twos had taken almost three hours.

I could think of better ways to spend a Sunday morning but none presented themselves so I resigned myself to making the space available in my none-too-overcrowded diary for further trips to the laundrette on the Sabbath.

Next Sunday would hopefully be slightly more entertaining as the World Cup opening ceremony was on in Germany, minus England of course.

We gave the dorm a bit of a tidy up on Sunday evening before lights out. There being no inspection on a Sunday morning the room had been allowed to fall into a state of some considerable untidiness over the weekend.

We had been a bit taken aback on Friday morning when the dorm inspection had been carried out by Captain Spearing himself, equipped with white gloves and torch looking in every single nook and cranny of the room whilst we stood to attention besides our open lockers.

Marker had warned us and we spent a good half an hour buffing the floor up on our hands and knees before the inspection. Most of us, myself included, had thought that Marker was taking the piss by explaining the intensity of the inspection but we soon discovered that he was not. Captain Spearing ran his fingers everywhere—along the window sills, above the doors (where his glove turned a neat shade of grey), on top of the lockers. His torch shone under the bunks, into our lockers and he spent a good five minutes finding umpteen faults with the cleanliness of our washroom facilities.

Poor Marker had to follow the inspection team around and was given a list as long as his arm of areas that 'needed attention' before next Friday's inspection otherwise the whole dorm would be put on a charge.

'Fucking charming!' Ferris had protested to Marker.

'We'll stick some razor blades over the fucking doors next Friday and see if his poncy white glove turns red instead of grey.'

'It's not that bad.' Marker explained.

'If we got all the items on the list cleaned and presentable for next week they would just find twenty more. It's just a game to them.

The only thing to do is to keep the place clean and grin and bear it.'

It was also obvious now, after the event, why Fisher got a bit of a sweat on when the torch had been shone into his locker. The vodka must have been stashed in there somewhere.

Geoff Allen did arrive back before lights out on Sunday but Martin Teale left it late and caught the early train back Monday morning from Canterbury arriving back on the grounds with just ten minutes to spare, weekend liberty expiring at 0845 Monday morning.

'You lucky bastard.' Steve Cooper, whom Teale had become quite friendly with, joked.

'I knew it would be touch and go.' Teale explained to us all. 'But now that I know I can make it back on the Monday morning I will do so in future. That means I'll only have to suffer in these bunks for four nights of the week.'

Bastard. I envied him and I think most of the others did as well.

Having mercifully survived the weekend, Monday morning of the second week bought with it the traditional rains and dampness of the wonderful British summer.

Who said that it was always sunny down South at this time of the year?

The courtyard was decidedly chilly for the morning inspection and the wind was fairly whipping up from the Thames just a few yards away from us.

We would, towards the end of the week, be out on the river brushing up on our rowing skills as part of our lifeboat training so I hoped that things would have improved by then.

Our second week's tuition introduced us to the lifeboats themselves and how they were maintained and, of course, how things worked aboard them should the unthinkable happen and you were cast adrift in one.

The catering contingent were to be included in the first three days of this week as even they needed to know the whereabouts on a ship that their own assigned lifeboat was situated (a ship's lifeboats are numbered starting with number one lifeboat being the forward most boat on the starboard side of a ship, the right hand side, and number two the forward most boat on the port side, left hand side of the vessel, and following thus should their be any more boats such as on a passenger ship).

We all agreed at first tea-break that morning, or 'smoko' as it was being nautically termed by now, that the women and children first philosophy would not apply to any of the ships that we were going to be abandoning in the future. In all honesty most of the deck trainees were now getting a bit fed up with having the catering crowd hanging on.

Because the classrooms could not accommodate all of us at the one time the groups were split in to two and as a consequence half of us were having the lesson it the morning that the others would be having in the afternoon and vice-versa.

There had already been some uneasy stand offs arising between the two groups (mainly at meal times with the criticism of the food and its preparation) and I felt that both Ferris and Fisher in particular would be in for some rather unpleasant meal time treats in the weeks ahead.

I personally won no friends amongst them when I commented that they would obviously much rather be peeling potatoes than rowing on the River Thames when several of them looked enviously over at us upon the realisation that they would not be partaking in that particular part of the lifeboat training.

Fortunately Thursday soon arrived and they departed to pursue their careers at sea either in the galley or cleaning toilets or whatever.

They were no great loss to the remaining 32 of us and if there was something that was strikingly noticeable about the school and it's occupants it was that there was a definite deck/catering divide in all aspects of life on the site.

I didn't mind at all. Despite probably being outnumbered by two to one the deck trainees seemed to be the most respected.

The deck trainees got to do all the interesting stuff such as rowing on the River Thames, operating the mock up of a ship's hatch and accompanying derricks in the courtyard and learning to wire and rope splice whilst the catering trainees got to prepare the dinner and learn how to wash up the dishes and clean the wine glasses that any ten year old could do with a minimal amount of difficulty.

I had maintained a reasonable friendship with the lad I had sat with on the first afternoon and hoped that should he ever serve me at the counter with my dinner he wouldn't grudgingly slop it onto my plate like the rest of his comrades-the only chance, I guess, they had of getting one over on us in the general scheme of things. There being no peanuts at the school at the moment (okay, we were still only into our second week but the initiations and being called peanuts had soon dissipated), any dorm raids now being carried out tended to be deck trainees going on a fifty second rampage through a neighbouring catering dorm.

Ferris and Fisher, and to his credit Geoff Allen who took the brunt of the beating during the attack on our dorm, had forgiven our assailants and taken it all as part of the initiation process. Since the raid the members of dorm 28 next door had been very helpful towards us in our first couple of weeks at the school, despite filling all our toilet bowls to the brim with Izal bog roll earlier this week.

We never heard them then either, the bastards.

The classroom lessons now became much more pleasant and more like that with which we had been used to at school. Rather than be talking to a wide audience, most of whom had little interest, our tutors could now concentrate on delivering the lessons to the 32 of us or to just 16 for the practical lessons.

We now had to focus our attentions on the lessons as well. For we knew that at the end of the courses we would be given tests that would determine whether or not we left the sea school with the desired lifeboat and E.D.H. tickets, which was, after all, our reason for being down here in the first place.

With this in mind I chose to distance myself slightly from the Ferris's and the Fisher's of our class. I didn't think for one moment that they weren't competent enough to pass the exams I just felt that they may have been a little bit of a distraction for me and my efforts.

Although I was enjoying my tuition and felt I was doing okay I still needed to realise that the whole subject was totally alien to me. A lot of the others in my dorm and from dorm 16 had at least had some nautical background in that they lived in a sea port or, like Fielding and Dempsey, had actually laboured on ships.

I chose to attach myself to Andy Peters and to Dempsey and Pete Lancaster as we were split into small groups of four.

I had begun to strike up a good friendship with Andy Peters. We had both made plans to watch as much of the World Cup together in the T.V. lounge over the coming weeks even agreeing to join forces with McGuire and Laughlan in support of the no hopers from North of the border.

Dempsey and Lancaster had palled up from the word go. They were a 'bunk' pairing and both reasonably level headed.

Friday morning of the second week and the weather had improved sufficiently enough for the first of our group to venture out onto the river.

Dorm 16 would be going out on the river in the two sessions today and we would have to frustratingly wait for our turn on Monday. The boat could only take 11 people at a time. 8 oarsmen (four either side), a coxswain, a tiller man, and 'Mad' Angus McGreggor our illustrious Captain.

The fact that this was a rowing boat bobbing up and down for several hundred yards and being propelled through the water by novices never once deterred Mad McGreggor from his insistence to being addressed as 'Captain.'

Dorm 28 had forewarned us of this character that was a cross between Captain Bird's-eye and Satan.

'He's an absolute, fucking loon.' We had been warned.

'A complete and utter nutcase.'

'Make sure you keep your oars in their crutches, for fucks sake.' One of dorm 28 had advised.

'We were out there in quite choppy waters one day and one of the lads' oars popped out of the crutch and he couldn't get it back in again. Obviously with four oars pulling one side and only three the other the boat began to turn. The coxswain gave a wrong order, telling one of the oarsmen on the already depleted rowing side to 'Ship oars' instead of the other side to balance things up, and Mad McGreggor lost it completely.

He leapt up out of his seat and tried to wrestle the oar from the lad to get it back in the crutch, all the time making the boat lurch from side to side even more so than it was already doing in the rough water.

'Let go of the fucking oar,' he roared at the top of his voice.

He let go all right. Straight into the River.'

'Oops!' I offered.

'Now look what you've fucking done.' He bellowed. 'You've lost a fucking oar.'

'We were in hysterics,' another lad, obviously on board at the time, continued.

'We circled this oar for a good fifteen minutes trying to retrieve it. Each time we got just that little bit closer and almost within touching distance then a wave would catch it and send it further away from us. We never did get it back.'

With these words ringing in our ears we were introduced in the classroom to Captain McGreggor.

The Captain Bird's-Eye reference was absolutely spot on. I could sense several others chuckling under their breath as this short, plump, grey bearded and red-faced man, well into his sixties I would have guessed, stood before us.

The broad Scottish accent, the thick, white woolly polo necked jumper and the wild staring eyes that he fixed upon us as he mapped out our impending voyage had us sniggering uncontrollably in our seats.

Without knowing any better it was not hard to imagine, from his description, that we were about to embark on a trip around Cape Horn on a narrow boat in a force twelve rather than stick eight oars into a flat calm river Thames and navigate ourselves to the jetty half a mile to the West of us in a small boat.

Dorm 16 went away with the Captain and we were left to learn a few rudimentaries of oarsmanship and await with bated breath for Dalgetty and the rest of the lads to come back at dinner time and tell us what he was really like.

'He's quite funny, actually,' the lads reported back at dinnertime.

'He swears like a trooper. All this bollocks about us not swearing and he's bellowing out: 'Get those fucking oars into the water, row you bastards, row. Pull; pull you fucking useless fannies, Pull.'

The second group went out in the afternoon and when they came back said that McGreggor had climbed out of the boat once they had got to the jetty and left them stranded there holding the boat alongside by the ladder for almost half an hour.

'Oh, yes. He often does that,' we were informed by another lad at teatime, 'He nips down the road to the pub.'

'You're joking,' Dalgetty gasped.

'I'm telling you. You can't see because the quayside is twenty foot above you as you're sat in the boat waiting for him. There's a pub only a hundred yards away.'

'You have to admire his style.' Ferris added.

We agreed and could only look forward to Monday and our turn.

Teale once again made his quick getaway on Friday evening, lucky sod, and the other three London boys, Gary Thompson, Kowinski and Geoff Allen shared his taxi to the station. None of the four were particularly boisterous but the dorm seemed remarkably empty with them away for a couple of nights. I think the fact that they were able to get home, as they were reasonably close, made the rest of us realise for an hour or so after they'd gone that we may be missing home ourselves just a tiny bit.

I could make it home, I suppose, at a push in just over three hours and the same could be said for Mick Darnell and Andy Peters who lived in Birmingham and Norwich but we would have to chance coming back on the Sunday evening and with the reliability of the trains as it was I wouldn't fancy missing lights out and roaming the streets of Gravesend in my sea school uniform at all hours of the night.

By the time Andy and I had finished our tea the opening ceremony to the World cup from Frankfurt was well under way. It fairly threw it down with rain and the pictures were none too brilliant.

The opening game that followed was a drab 0-0 draw between Brazil, the holders, and a stubborn Yugoslavia side who had put eleven men behind the ball in an attempt to combat the supposed flair from the Brazilians. Brazil were a pale shadow of the side that had beaten all comers, England included, to lift the title four years ago in Mexico. Pele, Gerson, Tostao and Carlos Alberto were all gone from that amazing side and only Rivelino (he of the famous 'banana' kick) and Jairzinho remained of anybody noteworthy.

Scotland were also in this group along with Zaire who clashed on the following afternoon and we took up our place in the telly lounge early on to see the Jocks run out easy 2-0 winners.

McGuire, Laughlan and Dalgetty along with several other of their countrymen had decked the lounge out in anything they could lay their hands on remotely Scottish and there was a good atmosphere as we watched. Peter Lorimer and Joe Jordan finally got the goals towards the end of the first half, but Andy and I both felt that a team that also included Kenny Dalglish, Billy Bremner and Dennis Law may regret not scoring a few more against such woeful opposition.

The Jock contingent, however, remained typically upbeat about the whole scenario believing that if they could get a result against the none too convincing Brazilians in their next game on Thursday evening they would beat Yugoslavia in their last game to progress through to the second stage.

The format of this year's tournament had been changed slightly in that after the first stage of round robin group matches the winners and runners up of the four groups then went into another two groups of four with the winners of those two groups contesting the final and the runners up doing battle for third and fourth place.

On Sunday we watched the impressive Dutch side beat the Uruguayan animals 2-0 and in the evening saw England's conquerors, Poland beat Argentina 3-2 in a superbly entertaining game.

It was quite a welcome distraction from the boredom of weekend life at the school for us football lovers. I certainly felt that I would be able to cope a lot better with the World Cup going on for the next few weeks.

Teale came back from Canterbury late Sunday evening just before the local liberty leave expiry time of 2145 (extended for a massive 15 minutes on Friday, Saturday and Sunday evenings). The lure of rowing on the Thames too great to risk a train delay in the morning.

Most of us had enjoyed a fairly eventful weekend. True, mine has been stuck in front of the telly but it was watching something that I could relate to.

Pete Lancaster, Ryan Fielding and, reluctantly, Mick Dempsey had joined the Angling Club and much to the consternation of Ferris had spent the day from before breakfast to late evening sat on a river bank some twenty miles outside of Gravesend in a futile attempt to land a couple of pounds of bream.

From the conversation at lights out I got the feeling that Dempsey would have preferred to have been trawling for cod in the North Sea rather than dangling a maggot off a stick but he had humoured the other two and gone along perhaps feeling that any excuse to escape for a day was well worth it, and who was I to disagree.

Ferris, Fisher, Steve Cooper and a couple of others from dorm 16 had gone down to the local swimming baths on Saturday afternoon. It did sound like quite a lot of trouble to go to.

The rules governing local liberty were strict in that you had to be wearing the full number one school uniform. However the swimming excuse did allow that you could take a personal towel with you in a carrier bag or duffel bag (which were inspected upon departure and again on arrival back at the school). The idea was to wear 'civvy' clothes under the uniform and shed the uniform as quickly as possible and shove it in the bags as soon as you were out of sight of the school grounds.

Unfortunately the local yobs had got wise to this over the years and would invariably hang around in small gangs along the Denton Road that led into town awaiting their chance to pounce as the transformation from peanut to human being was being performed.

Providing the number of peanuts was greater than that of the blood baying locals, which it was on this occasion, things generally passed event free apart from the odd icy stare. Ferris, by all accounts, did little to defuse any potential altercations with the local male population by insisting on chatting up every female in the pool and on several occasions swimming underneath them for a better view.

We had been warned to behave and keep a low profile whenever 'ashore' but the advice seemed to fall on stony ground where Ferris was concerned.

'They don't know we're from the school.' Ferris naively argued.

'Er, Is not the haircut a bit of a give-away? Not to mention the Lancashire accent?' I suggested.

Steve Cooper confirmed this by telling us what happened when they went into an off licence on the way back to the school.

All three had been served their fags when Fisher asked for a half-pint bottle of vodka. Taking one look at the three of them the shopkeeper asked, 'Are you boys from the Sea College?'

At the same time that both Steve and Fisher had exclaimed 'No!' with a convincing amount of shock and surprise that the question had even been asked, Ferris had smiled and said 'Yes.'

'Sorry boys. You can have your fags and copy of Penthouse, but no vodka. Okay?'

I found it quite amusing that Ferris had suffered a little bit of embarrassment and lifted my feet up to kick his mattress above me.

'Fuck off, the lot of you and leave me to have a wank in peace, will you.' Ferris hissed from his bunk.

I had noticed that he had pulled his curtains across his bunk and that a dim torchlight was shining from inside. His was obviously the Penthouse.

Monday morning parade was held in glorious sunshine. As we were to be on the river today we took the morning inspection in our number twos, much to everybody's approval.

We all donned our lifejackets at the end of the small path, which led from the back of the school and ran along the playing field, to the steps leading up to the riverbank. A few yards along the bank were more steps that led to the jetty where our rowing boat was secured.

With only ten of us allowed in the boat at one time six had to unfortunately be left behind but such was the short distance to row from jetty to jetty, just a few hundred yards along, all would get equal time in the boat during the course of the day, mad McGreggor had assured us.

The whole point of the exercise was to familiarise ourselves with what to do if your already unlucky day, having had to abandon ship and take to the lifeboats, was compounded by the engine breaking down and you had to guide the boat by human propulsion or by sail. A twenty-minute lecture, delivered on the riverbank before we even climbed aboard, by McGreggor was enough to convince most of us that this was going to be a piece of cake.

'The basic orders are,' McGreggor explained, 'Out oars meaning place your oars into the crutch; Give way starboard oars meaning row only on the starboard side to send the craft to the left or give way port oars to send the craft to the right: Give way together meaning send the craft in a, hopefully, straight line; Oars means to stop pulling and toss and boat oars means lifting your oars out of the water and bringing them back inside the boat.'

He paused and looked around at us all. 'Any questions?'

There wasn't. Just a slight snigger at the thought of tossing the oars.

'Right, I want eight good oarsmen, you, you, you, you, you, you, you and you.' He quickly pointed at eight of us, myself included.

'You, sonny.' He pointed at Dempsey 'And you, lad' pointing at Ferris, 'will be my coxswain and tillerman.'

We climbed tentatively aboard and took up our positions next to a crutch each. There were nine oars placed inside the boat. Four oars conveniently painted green for the starboard side oars and four red to denote the port sides. The ninth oar was painted white and was the steering oar should the rudder fall off!

The six who remained ashore cast the boat off and McGreggor gave us an almighty shove away from the jetty. We were adrift and at the mercy of the Thames (I had to admit to seeing Wicksteed park lake rougher than the Thames was today though).

The order to 'out oars' was soon given and as we headed north away from the jetty Mad McGreggor gave the order to 'Give way together.'

To say that it was unsynchronised would be a vast understatement but due, mainly, to the fact that there were four of us pulling either side the boat more or less went in a straight line, albeit lurching from one direction to another as we struggled to find any sort of rhythm.

Geoff Allen and Phil Laughlan clattered oars a couple of times opposite me on the port side of the boat causing McGreggor to flare up and bark 'Watch what the other fucking oarsmen are doing. Pull in fucking time . . . pull, pull, pull.'

At long last I had found something that I excelled at. My experiences on the boating lake back home had stood me in good stead and, as I was more than capable of rowing a boat using two oars, using only the one oar was a breeze. In fact the other three on my starboard side who were all sitting behind me, Kowinski, McGuire and Steve Cooper all seemed to have realised this and we got a fairly fluent motion going whilst those on the port side struggled.

The obvious outcome to this was that the boat began to turn inshore a bit sooner than McGreggor would have liked.

McGreggor ordered us to stop rowing and toss the oars, leaving them in their crutch but out of the water. He briefly explained that reversing the rowing motion and pushing the oars in the water the other way would stop the boat, known as backing the water. We gave it a try but with only limited success. Oars came flying out of the water nearly hitting others in the boat. Others didn't seem to be able to reverse the action and just carried on rowing.

McGreggor buried his head in his hands, turning scarlet as he did so.

'Fucking Hell! What are you fucking doing?' He screamed at us at the top of his voice.

'You pull to row and you push to stop the fucking thing. How difficult is that?'

People were standing on the river bank watching. I got the feeling that this was probably a regular occurrence and that some of the locals purposely walked along the riverbank on a Friday and a Monday morning purely for the entertainment.

'Out oars.' He calmly ordered as the boat came to a halt.

'Okay, the jetty is over on our port side that we are now going to attempt to head for.'

He had quickly regained his composure.

'I will guide you in this once and after that we will all take turns at operating the tiller and coxing the boat alongside.'

With the distinct lack of movement on the river the approach to the jetty was nice and smooth.

McGreggor gave the order to toss and boat the oars as we glided smoothly in after a couple of final thrusts from the starboard oars only. From there on in the tiller man took over, under McGreggor's instructions, and we manoeuvred alongside with consummate ease.

We placed our oars in the boat and McGreggor told us to keep hold of the ladder leading up the jetty whilst he nipped ashore for a minute.

He shimmied up the ladder and was gone.

We sat in silence for a couple of minutes as a small trough of water lapped up against the boat created by the wake of a passing ship on the river.

'It's too early for the pub.' Ferris whispered.

'Where's he gone?'

'Climb up the ladder and see what's up there, Ferris.' Steve Cooper urged.

Ferris climbed up the twenty odd rungs of the ladder and stuck his head up over the top.

'He's coming back.' He quickly announced as he scurried back down and jumped back into the boat.

'He must have just gone and got a paper. There are some shops just along a bit.'

'And a pub?' I asked.

'There might have been. I didn't get the chance to take it all in. I just saw him heading back.'

We fell silent again as McGreggor announced his return with a loud cough as he clambered back down the ladder.

We then spent the next three-quarters of an hour rowing a hundred yards or so away from the jetty and guiding the boat back alongside using a different tiller man each time.

Once in the swing of things it was fairly straightforward. I had no problem steering the boat back alongside and as the morning wore on McGreggor took more of a back seat and let us cox the boat backwards and forwards from the jetty ourselves.

By the time we left the town jetty to row back to the school for lunch McGregor had taken on a much more confident approach with us and whether it was his shock tactics initially or just that we had learnt very quickly everything seemed to slot in to place fairly rapidly and we rowed back quite stylishly.

The six that had remained ashore in the morning session took to the boat in the afternoon along with four more of us from the morning. McGregor had specifically selected me and Kowinski, on merit I liked to think, and two others to take to the water again.

A couple of the new rowers had the odd coming together of oars as we rowed back to the town jetty and were treated to some choice expletives from McGregor.

As expected, on our arrival back at the town jetty, McGregor scaled the ladders and disappeared again.

This time it was for much longer than it took to fetch a paper.

After a good seven minutes Fisher, who had replaced Ferris in the crew, guessed.

'That bastards at the pub.'

'He must be.' I agreed.

'I'd love to be able to row back and leave the mad bastard here to find his own way back to the college.' Fisher continued.

'Wonder if anybody has in the past.'

This conversation continued between us at lights out that evening.

We all agreed though that we had enjoyed the day. We would get another session next Monday, weather permitting, but McGregor would this time be assessing us on our capabilities as an oarsman, tiller man, and as a coxswain.

I personally felt that I had done extremely well especially as some had managed to clatter the bow of the boat quite heavily into the jetty, much to McGregor's frustration, on more than one occasion.

'I wouldn't fancy it in the winter much.' I observed. 'Imagine the fit McGregor would have if you're pulling for all your worth against a rough swell and the boat's just not responding.'

'Wonder if he nips off to the pub as well. I wouldn't want to be left hanging on to that jetty for dear life with the waves battering against the boat whilst he's playing fucking dominoes and supping ale in front of a roaring bloody fire.' Fisher added.

'I'd love to see him stranded there.'

The rest of the week in the classroom saw us dealing with the various components of the lifeboat and the art of actually sailing the craft.

This may have been delivered in Double Dutch to me. I ask you. What on Earth does this mean to me?

'A standing lug is the only sail used for lifeboats in the Merchant Navy. If the boat is over 25 feet long then a jib must also be carried.

These sails are made of the best quality duck and are fitted with reef cringles and reef points.'

What?

'The roping is sewn round the head, luff, tack, clew and up the after-leech as far as the reef cringles. The jib is only roped on the luff'.

Ahh! Well that explains it then!

I had to look around myself to make sure that I hadn't entered the Master Mariners course but was met with equally blank looks which acted as a kind of reassurance.

'Has anybody got a clue what a clew is?' I joked at lunchtime.

We were also introduced to the finer points of sailing the boat by means of 'tacking'.

That is sailing the boat in a zig-zag course, as it is impossible to sail directly into the wind (that bit I could just about relate to).

All In all it probably wasn't as bad as we were making it out to be. We had diagrams to study and as long as we could get an imprint in our minds as to the whereabouts of the various cringles within the set up we should be fine in the examination.

The good point, I felt, was that the examinations came at the end of the weeks whilst the subjects were still very much fresh in our minds.

Not like that of the O level examinations at school where you could be told one sequence of events eighteen months previously and then you're finding it popping up in front of you again, long since forgotten, in an exam that is going to affect you for the rest of your life.

Certainly I felt the need to keep revising my lifeboat handbook during the week and spent a couple of hours each evening in the library with Andy Peters and Pete Lancaster just brushing up and asking each other 'luff' related questions. The theory being that we could become experts in the subject by the time the exam rolled round and subsequently forget about it after then and hope that something may have stuck in the mind in the unlikely event of being cast adrift at some point in the future.

Thursday evening brought a little light relief from all things lifeboat as Scotland took on Brazil in the second game of their World Cup campaign. It ended in another drab 0-0 draw and I had to admit to being extremely disappointed with the Brazilians. Although Andy and I had sworn to pledge ourselves behind the Jocks we took no pleasure whatsoever in seeing the mighty Brazilians dragged down to gutter level by the unadventurous Scots. With the Yugoslav's ('they'll never score a goal in a million years' – quote Jimmy McGuire), smashing nine past Zaire at the same time things were starting to now look a bit bleak for Billy Bremner and his boys. Still. I couldn't argue with the upbeat Jock contingent in that they now only needed to beat Yugoslavia on Monday or, failing that, pray for the unlikely occurrence of Brazil not beating Zaire by more than the odd goal.

After a fairly uneventful weekend (I desperately had to visit the laundry on Sunday morning along with most of the other inhabitants of the school), we found ourselves back on the river on an equally glorious Monday morning to undertake our lifeboat handling assessment.

Dorm 16 had had their assessment on the Friday with only one person making a crucial error in judgement and he was to join us this afternoon for another attempt (I wondered how any of us would get a second chance if we failed).

With not so much tuition needed this time around (we had all hopefully remembered the basics from last week), dorm 16 had informed us that McGregor had taken his half hour sabbatical ashore during the morning session just after eleven o'clock.

I feared the worst on the morning trip as, along with me, alphabetical order had decreed that Ferris, Fisher and Cooper were amongst the crew onboard and had definitely been plotting something over the weekend for this morning's jaunt on the river.

We cast off from the sea school jetty shortly after nine o'clock. With much more confidence in our ability now McGregor took us a bit further out into the river before giving the instructions to head for the town jetty.

Once there we all took turns to guide the boat alongside whilst McGregor marked nice big ticks against our names for the various manoeuvring skills that we portrayed.

We had all taken our turn by eleven o'clock when McGregor announced what must have been music to Ferris's ears.

'We'll take a short rest now, boys. Before we head back to the school.'

McGregor, I thought, you are becoming all too predictable.

With that he leapt onto the ladder, climbed to the top and was gone, presumably for half an hour or as long as it took him to neck two pints of beer.

'Okay!' Fisher began after a couple of minutes to give McGregor the chance to get out of earshot.

'He's got fifteen minutes. If he hasn't come back we're letting go of the ladder and we'll row out a hundred yards or so into the river.'

'We can't leave him stranded here!' Kowinski sensibly argued.

'Don't worry, mate.' Cooper replied. 'We'll go just far enough out to put the shits up him once and for all. We're banking on the fact that as long as we get back alongside to take him back on board he won't dare report the incident as he shouldn't be leaving us unsupervised in the first place.'

'We're all competent enough to be able to manoeuvre this tub back alongside, aren't we?' Ferris added.

We agreed, reluctantly, and waited for fifteen minutes to expire.

'Right, fuck him. Geoff, let go of the ladder and push us off,' Fisher ordered Geoff Allen when it was obvious that McGregor was not on his way back.

Geoff was reluctant to let go, looking up the ladder in the hopes that we may hear McGregor's trademark cough to announce his imminent arrival back to the jetty.

'Let the fucking thing go, Geoff.' Ferris then barked at Allen and made to get up out of his seat to confront him.

Geoff let go and pushed us away from the jetty.

The last thing we wanted on the boat was confrontation and although there were only possibly four instigators to the plan we went along with it to keep the peace.

We levelled the boat out facing away from the jetty, Ferris on the tiller and Fisher giving the orders.

'Okay, give way together.' Fisher ordered.

'Fuck me; you've learnt something, Mr. Christian.' I joked, trying to break the tension.

A nervous laugh went round the crew as we rowed out just as far as we had gone earlier under McGregor before turning the boat to face along the river towards the school and bringing it to a halt.

We were still close enough to the jetty to be able to make ourselves heard and as half eleven approached, the time we reckoned McGregor would be ambling back, Fisher and Cooper began to shout from the boat.

'Help! Help!'

A figure came to the riverbank. It was an old boy walking his dog.

'Help!' Fisher cried again at him. 'Have you seen our captain, Mr.? We've come adrift from the jetty.'

With that he turned and he was gone.

We sat with bated breath and within a minute the man reappeared with our illustrious Captain.

'Help, Captain. Boy are we glad to see you.' Ferris shouted at him as, under Fisher's instructions, we thrashed a couple of oars in the water haphazardly although not enough to veer us away from our stationary position.

Although a good hundred yards away we could make out McGregor's rage.

'What the fucking hell are you doing out there?' He exploded.

'A speedboat went passed, Captain. Dead close it was Sir and we lost our grip of the ladder.' Ferris shouted back at him.

'Get that fucking boat back here now, you fucking idiots.' He screamed. 'Give way to fucking port, now.'

'Okay, Captain. Give way together was that?' Ferris bellowed back, cocking his hand to his ear, as if having difficulty hearing McGregor's barked orders (I can't imagine that anyone on the river at that time wouldn't have heard McGregor's orders). We gave way together, by now enjoying the charade, taking the boat further away from the jetty and sending McGregor even more ballistic.

'To port, you fucking imbeciles, give way to port. Toss the fucking starboard oars.' His contorted head shrieked at us.

In the confusion that we acted out we purposely clattered a couple more oars together, always in control of the situation of course, but he wasn't to know that.

We eventually brought the boat back round to face the jetty and with ease glided the thing back alongside. It had been fun while it lasted but we still had to face the music from a coughing and spluttering McGregor as he scurried back down the ladder.

'Very funny, arseholes, very, very funny.' He panted as he collapsed onto his seat, surprisingly, laughing.

We said very little but laughed with him. We knew that he knew that we had probably set the whole thing up and I thought then that this maybe wasn't the first time that such an incident had occurred.

A bit of mutual respect from both parties meant that such incidents never got reported back to the sea school.

McGregor spread his arms out over the side of the boat and let out an almighty sigh.

'Well, what are you waiting for?' He asked us all, looking around the boat. 'You don't fucking need me. Push the bloody boat off and let's get back to the school, eh!'

Strangely the incident wasn't shared when we got back to the school during dinner break.

I told my mate Andy Peters, who hadn't been in the boat at the time, later that evening and he did confess to McGregor being slightly subdued during the afternoon assessment.

Not surprisingly we all passed our lifeboat handling with flying colours. I doubted that very few could ever in fact fail, such was the simplicity of the basic manoeuvres but as we once again contemplated it may not be so easy in the winter months.

The day was rounded off back in the telly room as Scotland made their exit from the World cup more with a whimper than in a blaze of glory. They failed to beat Yugoslavia. In fact only drawing 1-1 by virtue of a last minute goal from Joe Jordan although the result was purely academic by then.

The useless, spineless, pathetic Jocks (McGuire's words, not mine) only had to beat the 'Slavs but when they went a goal behind midway through the second half and at the same time saw Brazil secure the necessary three goal margin against Zaire their efforts were all in vain. They were on the plane home having not lost a game and after holding the World champions to a draw.

My heart bled for them.

The next evening we were able to silence the Jocks even further as our conquerors, Poland, continued to impress and topped their group after beating Argentina, Italy and knocking seven past Haiti to gain a 100% record going into the second phase.

'That's what you need to do against the shite sides,' I advised McGuire and Laughlan, 'bang seven past them. At least England got knocked out by a decent side.'

They didn't appear to appreciate my point.

Our lifeboat theory tests came up on the Thursday and Friday of this, our fourth week, and as hoped the entire dorm and all of dorm 16 passed without too much trouble.

We could now concentrate on our E.D.H. training, which would take a further ten weeks. Six weeks between now and the school's three week summer holiday shutdown period and four weeks afterwards including our final examinations.

I had always planned to go home for the weekend at the end of my fourth week to break the monotony up a little and was pleased to share a taxi and catch a train at 5.15 into Charring Cross along with Geoff Allen and Steve Kowinski who had made returning home a weekly event.

The first thing we did on the train was to get out of the horrible number ones we were forced to wear ashore.

It wasn't until you left the site that you realised how decidedly un-cool and unfashionable the bloody uniform was.

I got back into Kettering at ten to nine and walked the short distance up Station Road to the bus station. As I was far too tired to go out that evening I had already decided to head straight for home.

I was happy just to see my Mother again. Although we had written to each other probably twice a week since I had left there was still no substitute for being in her company even if it was just sat in front of the telly and passing the odd comment. I could tell she was delighted to have me home again if only for a brief while, although she never actually said as much.

I visited the barbers again on Saturday morning and had enough lopped off, I hoped, to see me through the next six weeks. I had been fortunate enough so far to avoid the evil Sweeny Todd at Gravesend and wanted to keep it that way.

I went to the Rugby Club with Barry on Saturday evening but it didn't seem the same. It was as if I had moved on overnight.

I only dared have a couple of pints of lager and lime – I hadn't touched a drop of alcohol since sneaking that double vodka at the Flying Angel Club on my first weekend away.

Barry had picked up a girl, Vanessa, in the four weeks that I had been away thus confirming what I had always suspected that I had indeed been cramping his style whilst I was around.

Not to mind. She seemed a nice enough girl at first, superb figure, but at sixteen far too young for Barry I imagined, but who was I to tell him.

I was also relieved to see that my ex, Lorraine, had got her claws into another fellow and was pleased when she introduced me as a 'friend'. I had been a bit worried earlier in the evening when she had come over to me and confessed to thinking that my cropped hair looked gorgeous.

'We all look like this in Gravesend.' I pointed out to her. 'All with heads shaped like a peanut.' She laughed but of course the joke meant nothing to anybody here in Kettering.

I had to settle for walking home at eleven o' clock. Barry being far too preoccupied with the now, after a couple of pints, quite nauseating Vanessa.

I wondered, as I walked home, if it was down to the fact that my life had become quite monastic over the past four weeks but I simply had not enjoyed my night out tonight.

Barry had seemed quite disinterested in my tales of rowing on the River Thames and sneaking bottles of vodka into the club and having to scrub the dormitory floor etc. etc.

Was it me? Or was it that nobody was particularly bothered around here that I had actually got off my backside and was trying to do something with my life. Vanessa's voice had gone right through me. When Barry had first introduced me I thought she was an absolute cracker but as the night wore on all I could hear was this stupid, horrible high pitched shrill laugh coming from her and I could only imagine and hope that Barry was getting a good back seat grope out of the deal.

I popped next door to see Malc on Sunday morning. He had left college now and was actively seeking employment as a Chef. He figured that he too may have to leave home to find a suitable job and, after being away and in a different environment for only a matter of four weeks, I felt that I could only encourage him to do so.

'There really is fuck all round here' I had told him.

And, at long last, I had finally convinced myself of that fact as well.

I had dinner with my Mum and left for Gravesend mid-afternoon.

It would be another six weeks before I returned. Of that I was absolutely certain.

I got back into Gravesend at eight o'clock on the Sunday evening, changing back into my uniform in the train carriage's toilet (not an easy feat by any stretch of the imagination. It's difficult enough taking a piss).

God only knows what my fellow passengers must have thought. Here was this smart looking young man, quiet and polite, going about his business amongst other travellers and then without warning off he slopes to the toilets and conscientiously transforms himself into some pathetic looking geek with a stupid outfit that doesn't remotely fit. Or perhaps they had seen it so many times before that they just accepted it and looked on in pity.

As usual at lights out on a Sunday evening the events of the weekend were discussed. I took great delight in rubbing in the fact that I had been out on Saturday night. I didn't disclose that I had only had a couple of pints and was thoroughly bored with it all though Ferris, Fisher and Steve Cooper had once again been to the swimming baths on Saturday afternoon only this time Ferris had been slightly braver and actually had a small altercation with one or two of the town's mop-haired louts at the side of the pool. There had been an uneasy stand off, Cooper explained, after Ferris had been splashing a couple of local thirteen-year old girls.

'The twats gave me a right fucking glare.' Ferris laughed.

'Fucking grease-balls were contaminating the water.'

'They said they'd get you if you showed up at the pool again, Sam.' Cooper reflected.

'Whatever.' Ferris deliberated. 'They won't stop me going back.'

On that note we settled down to get a good nights sleep (I was shattered from the day's travelling), and look forward to a totally new phenomenon for us during the day tomorrow.

The arrival of new Peanuts!

We began the next stage of our course at the school on the Monday of the fifth week.

We were now to undergo ten weeks of intensive training to knock us into shape and make us all into Efficient Deck Hands.

During the morning lesson we were re-introduced to Mr. John Arnem, whom we'd met on our first couple of days at the school, and to Mr. Paul Macken and Mr. Roy Donovan who were to be our principal tutors for the duration.

All three had served their time at sea, Mr Arnhem and Mr. Macken being ex Officers and Mr. Donovan an ex Bosun.

We were also introduced to another 'old salt', in the McGregor mould, by the name of Captain John 'Jack' Jackson.

Captain Jackson would be taking us up onto the mock-up of a ship's bridge, which was situated above the main classroom block and overlooking the Thames, for our navigation and steering courses. The bridge was fully equipped with all the latest navigational equipment and a modern radar installation.

Jolly Jack, who we had quickly christened him, was well into his sixties and although wearing a hat which proclaimed 'Captain', as did McGregor, never in fact reached above the dizzy heights of second Officer during his sea going career.

Jolly Jack looked anything but as he scowled around the room explaining all that he expected of us by the time we had passed through his tuition.

Throughout the day a steady stream of Peanuts filtered through the gates and into the main assembly room. Only now could I appreciate the reasoning behind the school not letting the new arrivals mingle with the more established students upon their arrival.

I cringed when I remembered how I had felt only four weeks previously and vowed that I would never get involved with any of the shouting and balling at the expense of the newcomers that was largely expected of the rest of us.

Ferris on the other hand had a rather short memory and gleefully let the poor sods know that they were 'Never going home.'

The E.D.H. syllabus consisted of five main topics:—Ropework, i.e. bends and hitches and rope splicing and being introduced to the various different types of rope commonly used on board any vessel.

Wire splicing; Making an eye splice in various different sizes of wire; Derricks and hatches; Learning all the different types of blocks and tackles and taking practical tuition in the courtyard as well as the theory in the classroom; Navigation with Jolly Jack, which would include learning how to box the compass; How to steer a ship in a state of the art cubicle which had a ship's wheel and gyrocompass together with a ship's head cleverly homed in on a moving picture screen of an ocean with some rocks; How to use and decipher the various radar screens and a brief introduction as to how to use a sextant and various other bridge watch-keeping duties (polishing the brasswork being a favourite amongst defaulters). Also General Ship Knowledge (G.S.K), which covered just about every other aspect of ship board knowledge not covered in the previous four subjects.

The classes were small for the practical lessons, ropework, wirework, etc. with 16 to a lesson (we stayed in our dorm groups for the make up of the 16).

Considering there was a further group of 32 deck students four weeks ahead of us and also Marker's group on their final two weeks of examinations further ahead of them the whole schedule panned out fairly well.

There were also two other groups of tutors, Jackson apart, that saw their respective groups all the way through the course. I was particularly quite pleased with this arrangement as all three tutors assigned to us for the next ten weeks seemed very easy going and helpful.

At the end of the day it was also in their best interests to send as many pupils as possible out through the college gates and on to the British Shipping Federation with both their lifeboat and E.D.H. tickets in their back pockets.

It more than justified the existence of the school and also the nice little earner that these ex second Officers and Bosuns were all on in their semi-retirement.

I hung on every word I was taught during the first week of our E.D.H. course. Having passed the lifeboat ticket I was sure as hell going to make sure that I passed this as well.

Not all of it came easy to me though. I had nightmares with the wire splicing. I could whip the ends of the strands, once unravelled, in readiness for splicing and I could shape the eye and lock it in the vice but I could not come to terms with the sequence of the tucks in order to produce a safe and workable wire strop.

I was not alone but that was of little consolation to me when a pass in all five areas was needed for the certificate.

'You've a few weeks to learn yet.' Mr. Donovan, our wire and rope tutor, consoled to me as he threw another abortive attempt of mine and Andy Peters' into the waste bin.

My ropework was coming together nicely. Although never having been a Boy Scout placed me at a distinct disadvantage to some I was capable, at the end of the first week, to tie a bowline, a reef knot, a sheepshank and hundreds of granny knots not even invented yet but boy were they secure. The General Ship Knowledge seemed quite straightforward as well. We were generally taught all the features of the ship from the Christmas tree, (so called because it is the main mast, which houses most of the ship's navigation lights), to the poop deck and to the forecastle head.

The chain locker for the anchor cable, and how to read the various lengths of anchor cable that had been let out by their different markings to how to take the temperature of the sea. It was all there.

We each had a copy of our 'bible' the Boatswain's (Bosun's) manual. A crucial composition first published in 1944 and compiled by a Mr. William A. Mcleod especially for those such as ourselves only requiring the rudiments of seamanship knowledge. It had been through several re-editions and revisions since its inception, the latest being in 1972, and it was a Godsend.

I chose, along with several others perhaps a bit unsure of the subject, to spend a good hour even after the day's lessons studying the manual and found it worth its weight in gold.

The work in the courtyard on the derricks and hatches was fun. The blocks were all taken down daily by the classes and greased and re-reeved before being returned to their housing and used to open up the hatches. We all took turns operating the small electric winch at the foot of the Samson post which first raised the derrick's boom then, when shackled off in position, doubled up as a hoist to lift the hatches with a cargo runner wire. Hard hats were a must for the work in this area as the winch could be slightly temperamental (and the fact that Ferris had to be let loose on it at some point).

I also found the navigation classes interesting. Jolly Jack was a stern tutor. Very much like I had come across at the Grammar School with the difference being that if you actually did something right you had some praise offered towards you.

However, if things went wrong and you ended up putting the ship onto some rocks he turned into Mad McGregor.

Inside the steering simulator it is a bit like being at the fairground. As you stand at the wheel there is a small compass on the control panel in front of you. Jackson turns the whole contraption on by a button outside the cubicle and providing you keep the wheel steady the ship appears to be heading on a straight course as, on the screen in front of you, the horizon and the numerous objects on it slowly come closer towards you and pass you by on either side.

All well and good as you follow your plotted course, Jackson ordering you to change it by five degrees to starboard now and then, until you spot an iceberg dead ahead of you on the horizon (all the more strange considering you had only just passed a tropical island on your port side two minutes previous).

'Starboard ten' Jackson bellowed out.

I eased the wheel by ten degrees to starboard.

'Ten degrees starboard wheel on, Sir.' Came my correct response.

Nothing happened. The iceberg is now bearing down on me.

'Hard a starboard.' Jackson screamed.

I reacted instantly.

'Wheel hard a starboard, Sir.' I confirmed.

The iceberg on the screen vanished away to my left, as the ship's head appeared to be lurching to my right.

'Meet the helm.' Jackson barked out his next order.

Meeting the helm was not an easy order to carry out when the wheel is hard over to starboard and the compass is ticking over at ten degrees a second.

The order basically means to stop the ship going any further to starboard. To achieve this the starboard wheel has to be taken off and full port wheel applied to stop the vessel turning.

'Meet the helm.' I sharply replied, as instructed.

Not only do you have to stop the ship but you have to bring the ship's heading back to the exact course that it was on when the order was given.

Consequently as soon as the ship's head has stopped moving to starboard the port wheel has to be taken off and then the ship allowed to drift back slowly to port to return to the course that the head was on (if you were lucky and aware enough to catch it when the order was given).

'Helm met at 152 degrees, Sir.' I smugly confirmed shortly after with very little effort.

I was head and shoulders above the rest of the class at this little exercise and boy did I know it.

'That is exactly how you do it.' Jackson called to the rest of the class who had been peering into the booth from the side glass panels as I was performing my heroics.

'You jammy bastard.' Steve Cooper, who was struggling with the exercise, mouthed at me as I climbed out of the booth.

I shrugged my shoulders as if to signify that there was nothing to it but I knew that for all my talent in this particular field it would amount to nothing if I couldn't get to grips with my wire splicing.

The new peanuts had got off relatively lightly during their first week at the school. There had been no dorm raids that I knew of although having said that the new intake were housed several corridors away from our dorm.

On the Saturday evening Ferris, Fisher, Steve Cooper and Gary Thompson had ventured into our neighbouring dorm 28 armed with loaded water pistols that they had bought from the town earlier that day.

It was a daring raid executed after lights out and full retribution for their raid on us on our second night at the school.

Dorm 28, with Marker included, were to begin their final week at the school next week. By all accounts the time had gone quickly for them. With Marker leaving at the end of the week it meant that we would need to have a new leading hand in charge of the dorm.

The way things now worked was that of the 32 of us that started five weeks ago, at the end of the coming week, a leading hand from each dorm would be chosen and also a senior leading hand who would remain in charge of their existing dorm (the two appointed leading hands would then acquire a dorm of peanuts upon the next intake). It was very much a case of we've been here six weeks now we should know the drill and be able to conduct ourselves in the correct manner at all times according to the rules and regulations of the school.

Ferris, I'm absolutely certain, would remain a handful for whoever got the task of remaining in charge of our dorm.

The World Cup was still going on over the weekend although it seemed strange that there was still not going to be a knock out competition until the actual final itself.

Holland and the hosts Germany looked too strong at this stage for the likes of Brazil and Poland and so it proved by the end of this second round robin phase as they both topped their respective groups to set up a final showdown next Saturday afternoon. Not that I had much enthusiasm left for the competition. The Jocks had long since gone home and the whole competition smacked of conspiracy when the East Germans beat West Germany 1-0 in the first phase thus ensuring that West Germany would not meet Holland in the second group stage. It had pissed down for most of the tournament and the fact that there was no knock out rounds leading up to the final seemed to take that competitive edge out of the games.

During the day on the Sunday we had held our own five a side tournament in the gymnasium and the games between deck and catering had more passion about them than some of the World cup encounters, I can tell you.

I played in a 'white' team that consisted of Fisher and Gary Thompson in goal along with two members of dorm 16. We did well enough winning a couple of games but a poxy blue catering team knocked us out 4-2 in the semi finals much to our annoyance.

We were soundly beaten but at least refused to shake their hands and told them to 'piss off' at the end of the game.

The next week flew by. Whether it was due to the diversity of lessons we were having or just that the lessons were so interesting and, I had to admit, good fun I wasn't quite sure. I was certainly thoroughly enjoying them and was even beginning to make inroads into my wire splicing. It was the only aspect of the course that was still causing me concern.

Others were not so quick to grasp things which surprised me considering we all knew what we were going to have to learn whilst at the school.

Ferris generally struggled all round, as did Geoffrey Allen, Tony Furnell and my poor mate Andy, although I was doing all I could after lessons to encourage him.

Most of the others were doing reasonably well at most subjects but only Mick Dempsey and Ryan Fielding along with Steve Kowinski excelled at the wire splicing due to their previous experiences.

On the Thursday evening we said our farewells to Richard Marker. He had guided us through our first six weeks at the school fairly competently it must be said. He had passed his E.D.H. certificate along with 22 others out of his class of 32. A little bit disappointing I would have imagined for the school, who I'm sure would have liked a higher pass rate than somewhere around sixty percent.

Those that failed could sit the exam again after completing 18 months at sea and providing they were 18 years old but I personally felt that it must have been such a waste of time, the last 10 weeks, not to leave here without the certificate.

It made me strengthen my resolve to succeed.

That resolve was made even stronger the next afternoon when the announcements were made by Mr Arnem regarding the appointment of the leading hands from our group.

The two senior leading hands were announced first and it was no great surprise when Kowinski was given the position from our dormitory. He was by far the most level headed of the dorm and was doing well in all aspects of the course. A point not lost on the four tutors and also Marker, whom I believe had some input as well into the selection.

What I wasn't prepared for and took me completely by surprise was the announcement of my own name for the position of leading hand.

A rousing cheer went up around the classroom as I walked up to the front to collect my small rope lanyard, which would wrap around my uniform shoulder to signify my new status, from Mr. Arnem.

'Congratulations, Caz.' Mr Arnem said as he shook my hand.

'Thank you, Sir.' I delightedly replied, well aware that I was blushing profusely.

'Well done, mate.' Andy said as I sat back down next to him. 'You deserve it.'

I wasn't sure that I did. I thought a couple of others would have been in the frame ahead of me but then when I thought about it maybe there was only Kowinski ahead of me.

I certainly thought Martin Teale may have been in with a chance but then he went home every weekend and that would, in effect, leave a group of peanuts solely at the mercy of the Ferris's of the school over the weekend period.

I would also imagine that Jolly Jackson had a say as well and I knew that I was receiving rave comments from him not only for my steering ability but also by the fact that I could now box the compass with ease.

Kowinski immediately took charge of the dorm that evening as Marker had already departed to begin his sea going career and with his going we seemed to mature as a group. It was a bit of a milestone for us if you like.

I would have to wait two weeks to take my dorm of peanuts, presumably into dorm 28.

'And I'll be most aware of any fucking raids, Sam, so you needn't bother.' I immediately aimed at Ferris on our return to the dorm.

He picked up his empty water pistol from his bunk and jokingly fired it at me.

'As if I'd even dream of it.' He winked.

Andy and I spent a busy Saturday morning before the World Cup Final between West Germany and Holland. We'd caught up on our mountain of 'dhobi'-the seafarers slang word for laundry (although why I have absolutely no idea). I posted my usual Saturday letter to my Mother. I was receiving two from her a week without fail. One on a Tuesday and one on a Friday, bless her. She was even sending me the clippings from the Daily Sun with regard to the World Cup matches. I didn't have the heart to tell her that I had access to the daily newspapers through the school library.

I was grateful for any snippets of 'Poppies' news though, which she religiously cut out for me from the local Evening Telegraph.

We were just about to go through the door to the stairs and up to our dorm to get ready for tea when all hell broke loose.

Ferris came racing into the courtyard, closely followed by Steve Cooper, Fisher, Gary Thompson, four lads from dorm 16 and the two Jocks.

'Jimmy's been knifed.' Ferris shouted at us as they ran into the sick bay reception area.

They had told the watchkeeper on the gate at the entrance to the school grounds as they had ran back who had telephoned ahead and alerted the duty Officers.

Jim McGuire had been slashed down his right arm. The group had once again been to the swimming baths and I could only assume, at the time, that they had once again antagonised the local morons whilst there.

Jimmy's wound was quickly dealt with by the Officers, who were able to get into the sick bay to apply first aid, but severe enough for an ambulance to be called and for him to need twelve stitches at the local hospital.

Fisher and Thompson joined us in the telly room for the game half an hour later but we were all too interested in hearing their version of events ashore to be interested in the fact that Holland had scored before the Germans had even touched the ball.

'Was Ferris up to his usual tricks?' we asked Fisher.

'No, he was fine and strangely well behaved.' Fisher answered.

'There was no sign of any trouble at all until we got to the off licence on Denton Road.'

Just around the corner from the store was a side street that most of the returning students would use to put their uniforms back on over their T-shirt and jeans or whatever it was they were wearing.

'Ferris, Jimmy and Phil had gone into the shop to get their fags and the rest of us had slowly carried on around the corner and were walking towards the school.

According to Ferris a group of about ten of them went past, one of them thumped Jimmy in the stomach and nicked his fags as he was lighting one up. Jimmy tried to get the fags back and leapt on one of the tossers only to be hauled back by another one and thrown to the ground. As they ran off and Jimmy got up he felt a sharp pain in his arm and only then realised that he'd been slashed.'

'The Bastards.' We echoed as Holland continued to apply the pressure without making any telling inroads to increase their lead.

Ferris and Phil were already under interrogation at this very moment but no doubt worse was to follow as Captain Spearing, not to mention the police, were bound to become involved at some point.

Fisher cursed himself for leaving the three of them isolated in the shop. 'They didn't come past us otherwise we would have gone back to keep the numbers up. They could have been waiting for us to split up; there are loads of passageways between the houses to hide down behind the shop.' He lamented.

It was far more interesting than the football and even the Germans turning the game, undeservedly, on its head by going in at half time 2-1 up paled into insignificance as Jim returned to the school just after the start of the second half.

The police duly arrived after Germany had hung on to win the game and all ten of the party that had been ashore to the swimming baths were spoken to.

'Fucking charming.' Ferris later told us back in the dorm just before lights out and after the police had gone.

'Are you sure you didn't provoke them? Did you attack them first? Can you describe the youths?

Yeah, I can do that all right. About a dozen, fucking ugly long haired, greasy twats who haven't washed in weeks.'

'You've just described every Gravesend male between the age of twelve and thirty.' I observed.

'Exactly.' Said Ferris. 'How the fuck else are you supposed to describe them. We didn't even see them until they jumped on top of us.' He moaned.

'The cops aren't the slightest bit interested.' Jimmy weighed in. 'It's as if we've no right to go ashore in the first place and our mere presence is seen as provocation to them.'

'Unfortunately that does appear to be the case.' Kowinski added.

The three, Ferris, Jimmy and Phil were summonsed on Monday morning to a rather one sided hearing with Captain Spearing and a member of the local constabulary who had attended the school on the Saturday evening.

The upshot being that the police could not press charges as they had no idea who the felons were, a staggering piece of detective work considering they had not even attempted to find the culprits.

'Lots of local youths hang about the Denton road route to the school from time to time.' the most informative policeman had added.

'Well how about a bit of police presence from time to time to disperse the youths who are obviously milling around the school route for one purpose only.' Jimmy had argued.

'I'm sure the local police have enough on their plate without having to worry about the inhabitants of the sea school who should be able to conduct themselves in a responsible manner whilst on shore leave.' Captain Spearing had countered.

It was obvious to all three that there was to be no compromise from the Captain.

He obviously did not want to let on that things were out of his control to the local police and therefore thought that banning all local liberty for the next seven days would be seen as a commendable solution in the eyes of the police rather than the over-the-top knee jerk reaction that it actually was.

'So let's get this right,' Fisher began as we later attempted to make some sense of it all. 'The three of you get jumped coming out of the local shop by about twelve spunk trumpets. Jim has a go back and gets slashed down the arm in the process. We have the audacity to pull on local resources by requiring an ambulance and outpatient treatment at the hospital, so every single one of the students at the school gets their local liberty cancelled for seven days. Correct?'

'Hmmm! Sounds about right to me.' I confirmed.

'This place is a fucking joke.' Ferris added. 'And that Spearing is just a spineless arsehole too afraid of upsetting the natives. I reckon he must be one of those moronic, dodgy hand shake merchants.'

'Masonic, Sam. It's a Masonic handshake. Though moronic isn't a bad description.' I concluded.

The next seven days at the school were hardly a delight.

Despite the complete injustice of it all and despite the fact that only one or two, if any, pupils took advantage of local liberty during the weekdays Jim, Phil and Ferris were still frowned upon as being the reason why the privilege had been taken away from everyone.

The deck students mostly tended to sympathise and the group below us were only in their third week at the school so did not comment or let their thoughts be known.

Most of the vitriol aimed at the three came from the catering students but they soon backed off when threatened with castration, or worse.

If anything I felt that Captain Spearing had contributed towards invoking a problem which could so easily have been avoided.

The week soon passed. Thankfully weekend liberty was not affected and Teale and the regular absconders were able to go home as usual.

There would be no trip to the swimming baths this weekend but I think that by now we were all beginning to realise that this may not be such a bad thing after all.

'Surely word would be out locally concerning the incident.' Kowinski assumed at lights out on the Friday night. 'It may even have made the local papers. Perhaps it isn't that bad an idea to let the whole thing cool down for a couple of weeks.'

He had a point. We were now halfway through our fourteen weeks. I was acutely aware that next weekend would be my last in the dorm and I would move out to take charge of, presumably, dorm 28. I certainly felt that I didn't want any more adverse publicity heaped on my dorm and in all honesty could not wait to get away from the constant plotting of revenge that Ferris and the others were subjecting us to every lights out.

The whole sorry episode seemed to fill Ferris's day and I knew that it was drawing his attention away from the matter in hand, which was to pass his E.D.H. certificate.

Unfortunately he seemed to be dragging a few others down with him. Certainly Jimmy McGuire wasn't the same enthusiastic student that he was pre-incident and I was disappointed that Gary Thompson had allowed himself to be dragged into the debate although Fisher had not let any of it bother him and continued to do well in most of the subjects.

I dreaded the next weekend when a further sortie to the swimming baths was planned despite the attempts of Kowinski, myself and several of the others to talk them out of it.

'For Christ's sake.' Kowinski had argued. 'It's the summer holidays in three weeks time. Why not just sit tight and wait until you get home to go swimming.'

There was no reasoning with Ferris and he went to the baths the next weekend but only Steve Cooper and Gary Thompson went with him from our dorm plus a couple from dorm 16.

Fearing the worst it had been instructed that their bags were well and truly checked before they were allowed to stroll purposefully out through the school gates and up the canal path and into town. Ferris had threatened to go ashore armed with a knife but to his credit even Jimmy had talked long and hard to him in an attempt to dissuade him.

I spent the afternoon washing my gear in preparation to move lockers and indeed dorms the following day.

I had been assigned dorm 28.

It was almost in deathly silence that the group returned back from the swimming baths at five o'clock that evening. All in one piece but with Ferris sporting the most beautiful black eye.

'Don't say a fucking word.' Ferris immediately ordered as he plonked himself down on his bunk.

'You little beauty.' Fisher taunted. 'Did you get snorkelled in the eye, buddy?'

'Something like that.' Ferris muttered. 'Now can we just drop it.'

We did, although curiosity far got the better of us and we had to quiz Steve and Gary whilst he was out of the room.

'He got a dig in the pool.' Steve told us. 'I'm hoping it's done him a bit of good. He was messing with a couple of the local girls again and swam up to the side of the pool. As he did another of the girls standing at the side of the pool swung an almighty back heel at him and caught him full in the eye.'

'You're joking.' Jimmy laughed. 'You mean to tell me that after all his boasting about taking on half of Gravesend single handedly he's been floored by a bird? Classic, fucking classic.'

It brought a bit of light relief to the situation and I was just glad that there had been no all out war in the town that day. I must admit to also finding small pleasure in the fact that Ferris had been injured.

I wondered how he was going to explain it away to the teachers as there was bound to be questions asked.

That Sunday night was my last in the dorm. I had moved all of my stuff into my locker next door and was now looking forward to having my own bed and sixteen peanuts to look after.

'Not quite sure what night we'll raid you on, Caz!' Ferris began to warn me.

'Careful you don't get another black eye in the process.' Kowinski mocked at Ferris.

'Well I shall certainly be warning them that it may happen.' I said to Ferris through his mattress. 'I can remember you not liking it when we first got here, Sam, so I would like to think that you would show a little compassion towards the poor bastards who've got fourteen weeks of tedium ahead of them.'

It remained silent before I bravely added; 'Will you be recommending the talent at the local swimming baths to them?'

'Fuck off.' Ferris growled back at me.

The new group of peanuts duly arrived during the next day, Monday, the start of our ninth week.

I was to meet my new dorm members for the first time mid afternoon and be introduced to them as their leading hand as Marker had been introduced to us what now seemed such a long time ago.

They did their unpacking as I tried to answer as many questions about the school as I could for them.

'Why are we being called Peanuts?' Was the obvious first question to which I could now answer with a good air of conviction.

I went through the routine of showing them to the stores in the evening and endured all the cries of peanuts and wolf whistles alongside them with just as much embarrassment as they were feeling. I was not fond of having names shouted at me on my first evening at the school and felt ashamed now that people I had associated with over the last eight weeks still felt the necessity to continue the tradition.

'Behave yourselves.' I half-heartedly grinned at my own ex-dorm mates as I escorted the new starters down to the stores. 'You've got very short memories.'

'See you after lights out, Caz!' Ferris shouted.

I chose to ignore him, hoping that there would be no raid tonight.

I laughed to myself as they tried their uniforms on for the first time back at the dorm.

Nothing had changed in the eight weeks since we had been kitted out and it was now highly amusing to hear this crop of students referring to their newly acquired garb as 'cool' and 'hip' just as we had before.

I showed several of the new lads around the complex in the evening and some even braved it over to the Flying Angel Club. The lure obviously too much to be put off until such time as they had settled in properly.

At lights out I copied Marker's lead and suggested that everybody introduce themselves and, although this group had quite clearly talked amongst themselves much more than we had on our first day, I listened with interest as all the different accents piped up to announce themselves. It seemed so uncanny that there were three or four from the London area, a couple from the midlands, two or maybe even three Jocks and the obligatory scouser amongst the sixteen.

I deduced that the school must pre plan their intakes so as to strike a happy balance between class members. I.e. eight Scotts and eight English or, say, eight Geordies and eight Cockneys might just be a recipe for disaster.

I didn't detect a 'Ferris' amongst the group for which I felt eternally grateful. Most appeared very well mannered and much more positive than my original dorm had seemed on their first day at the school. Or maybe events of the past couple of weeks had just got the better of me a tad and I was subconsciously glad to be amongst a different group of people.

On their second day they had their induction to the school and the dreaded visit to the doctor/dentist/Sweeney Todd. Few escaped the demon barber this time around as I had warned them the previous evening (I was worried in case mine didn't last another three weeks before the summer holiday as I could feel it encroaching towards my collar). One poor lad had to undergo three teeth extractions the next day, he knew his teeth were bad but the dentist had trotted out the same excuse he had to me when giving me my four re-fillings at the time.

'We can't have you getting toothache in the middle of the Pacific Ocean now, can we.'

He had the extractions in the afternoon and I felt it my duty to sit with him and Mother him a little bit for an hour or so after tea.

Steve Cooper later on in the evening warned me of an impending 'pillow' attack that night now that my dorm had settled in. I pleaded with him not to due to the state of one of my dorm members. To my great surprise and eternal relief no raid took place that evening after lights out. It subsequently came on the Thursday evening but I had my new charges ready for it. Fortunately Paul Hook, who had suffered at the hands of the butcher the day before, was furthest away from the door which dorm 27 would appear through and as only six partook in the raid:—Steve Cooper, Fisher, Thompson, Jim, Phil and their self appointed leader Ferris they were quite easily overpowered and repelled by a very enthusiastic counter attack.

Once again it was all over in a matter of seconds. The urge to cheer as our assailants fled was overwhelming but I managed to suppress their joy thus ensuring that they didn't waken the whole school and took great pride in the fact that we had defended our territory.

I was not too popular in class the next day but by now I couldn't care less. I was only a few weeks away from never having to see Ferris again, hopefully in my entire life.

'You fucking turncoat, Caswell' He sneered at me the next day, the first time he had never referred to me as Caz.

'We'll be ready for any further attempts in the future as well, Samuel.' I goaded back. Steve Cooper and Fisher had reacted differently and congratulated me on our strategy. I got the feeling that they, too, had just about had enough of Ferris. We were now entering a critical point in our time here and the last thing anybody wanted now was needless distraction from the task in hand.

It didn't help that Ferris was beginning to look the most likely candidate to fail his E.D.H. certificate, his disinterest at times being painful to watch. We'd had our fun and games along the way and we were now only five weeks away from completing our course.

More crucially in two weeks time we would leave the school for our three weeks summer holiday period. I was not too sure that this was a good time to be having a break of such a long period of time.

I was certainly on a roll with my wire splicing. I did not fancy losing the momentum I had built up just to forget it all by being out of practice and then have to sit the exam more or less as soon as I returned.

It wasn't as if I had a vice in a garage at home that I could practice my wire splicing on whilst I was away from the school like some of the others had, or indeed was going to actually spend the summer holiday on a trawler as was Mick Dempsey to gain further experience. I would be taking my Bosun's Manual home with me to spend an hour or so a day studying with during the three weeks.

It seemed totally absurd that, after a lifetime at school wishing the time away until the summer holidays; here I was not wanting this one to occur.

The students four weeks our senior left the school just one week before the holiday. Perfect timing.

We were now so near and yet so far.

My new-found protégés, meanwhile, were going from strength to strength and continued to amaze me with their enthusiasm and drive.

If ever I needed an incentive to ensure that I passed my exams then they were it. After all, I had always looked upon Marker as being one of the most likely to pass his exams from his group so these must have thought the same of me.

There were no shenanigans with them when they went rowing on the Thames with McGregor. I had told them of his tendency to 'desert' the boat for the occasional half an hour and related our experiences to them but they seemed neither bothered nor impressed.

I almost found myself wishing at times that I had been part of their group. They all seemed to get on well together and worked for each other as a team, unlike my lot who, Andy Peters and probably Mick Dempsey and Pete Lancaster apart, I had drifted much further away from since leaving the dorm (Ferris now hardly spoke, but I could live with that).

There was little any of us could do about the situation of the summer holiday so we more or less resigned ourselves to the fact, towards the end of the week, that instead of passing out through the school in three weeks time we would in fact be returning for our final stint.

I felt quite envious that some of the lads were actually going on holiday. Martin Teale was, believe it or not, going abroad somewhere in Spain with his family although what the attraction was in going to these places escaped me. From what little I had seen on the television it was just a pile of concrete slabs being erected one on top of the other with no thought for comfort or sanitation whatsoever. You might just as well spend a fortnight on a building site.

Ryan Fielding, Mick Dempsey and Fisher were all hoping to get some practical experience over the three weeks be it on board a vessel or just 'jobbing around' on the quay side at their hometown ports.

I was NOT going to apply for a job on Wicksteed Park Lake even though the much sought after position of standing at the bottom of the 'water chute' track and gently prodding the tub back onto its tracks with a six foot pole did appeal.

My Mother had instead kindly negotiated three weeks of shelf stacking for me with Bob and Janet Bailey at the Bryant Road stores where I had previously worked as a paper boy.

Mothers, don't you just love them!

They had agreed to pay me 23p an hour for a maximum of twenty—five hours a week, unfortunately spread over six days, and as I was absolutely broke due to my sea school and Flying Angel Club tuck-shop habits had very little choice but to accept.

I did not tell any of my colleagues at Gravesend this.

I was, despite this thrilling news, very much looking forward to going home and seeing my Mum and a few of my old mates.

I would make a point of going over to Wellingborough to see everyone at Lewis's and despite not enjoying myself at the Rugby Club last time around was looking forward to having a pint. It had been seven weeks since I had last touched a drop, after all!

That Friday morning dorm and kit inspection was the most rigorous I had seen in my eleven weeks at the school. The threat of being kept behind whilst watching all the others leave even inspired dorm 27 to a little bit of spit and polish in the cause.

I had no such problems with my crew. From the outset they had maintained the highest level of cleanliness throughout the dorm due, in no small part I may add, to the fact that I mucked in and helped them. Something that Marker never did with us.

The exodus from the school had to be staggered as it was quite clear that Gravesend train station could not cope with the amount of bodies that would be piling onto it's platforms throughout the day all demanding one way tickets to remote and unheard of destinations such as . . . er Kettering.

In the interest of fairness dorms 16 and 27 were allowed to leave at nine o'clock along with the longest serving catering students (how gutting that was last weekend to see the catering crew that had started at the same time as us go off and, for all we know, be onboard their first ship by now). We were taken to the station in a fleet of buses, laid on for the departure, and I could well imagine that a huge, collective sigh of relief rang around Gravesend as we bade our farewells.

'Fuck Off, Peanuts. Don't bother coming back.'

Charming, I thought, as the well wishes of the local youths that had gathered at the station transpired to us. Had we the choice, I would gladly have informed them, we would certainly not be rushing back.

The rush to get into the toilets to discard the uniform was comical as the train pulled away from the station. I chose to leave mine on until I boarded my train to Kettering at St. Pancras although I received some fairly strange looks on the underground network.

I got back home mid-afternoon, tossed my case unceremoniously onto the floor in the hallway, threw myself onto the moth bitten settee and sprawled out with relief at being back on familiar territory. I promptly heard an almighty 'doinggg' sound and leapt back up as I felt a broken spring up my arse.

Welcome home, John. Nothing's changed!

Knackered or not I made my way down town that evening for a pint or four in 'The Peacock'. In fact four lager and limes, after the last seven alcohol free weeks, was enough to send my head spinning and I was on the bus back home by ten fifteen in the evening.

Mum had stayed up for me and made me a cheese sarnie for my supper. I slurred the events of the last few weeks to her as she informed me that I must go round to Bailey's shop in Bryant Road over the weekend to finalise my summer employment. I felt it was the least I could do to see it through as my Mum would be severely subsidising my three-week stay at home.

Malc from next door came round to see me on the Saturday morning. Aware of the fact that I was to be around for the next three weeks he had done what all excellent friends should do in the case of having a mate turn up at a loose end. He'd arranged a blind date for me up Wickie's park that afternoon.

'Cheers Mate!' I groaned remembering previous disasters that he had arranged for me.

'No, this is different mate,' he explained. 'There's this gorgeous sixteen year old bit of stuff that works at the Tudor Gate Hotel in Finedon as a part time waitress.'

My ears pricked up. Malc was now in full time work as a second chef at the hotel.

'I've been sort of knocking her off for a couple of weeks now and she's coming over to the park this afternoon with a mate to see us.'

'Us?' I enquired.

'Yes, Us! I've told her that I'd got a mate in the Merchant Navy and I think the thought of the uniform may have clinched it for you.'

'Ha!' I laughed out loud. 'I'm hardly in the Navy yet and the uniform trousers only need turning up once to make them into shorts'.

I went along anyway. We met Katie and Jackie by the train station at one in the afternoon and my face must have been a picture.

Malc's waitress, Katie, was a little under five feet tall but gorgeous looking with short dark hair. Her mate, Jackie, was about six inches taller and in her heels a good four inches taller than me, long blonde hair and with an hourglass figure that simply took my breath away.

'Hiya, Babes' Malc greeted Kate with a kiss and a quick fondle of the buttocks.

'Meet John and I'll presume this is the lovely Jackie.' He wasted no time in the introductions. Jackie smiled at me and I tried to make small talk as we proceeded down towards the boating lake.

For the first time in my life I actually had something remotely interesting to say about myself and was able to continue a conversation beyond a couple of grunts before resorting to the weather prospects for the rest of the week.

Jackie seemed suitably impressed as I told her of some of the scrapes we had been in at Gravesend and of Mad McGreggor and his antics whilst we were under his command.

I was glad I could keep the conversation going as Malc and Katie had disappeared around the back of the train tunnel around the back of the lake for a good twenty minutes and had left the two of us to amuse ourselves.

Jackie had just turned 16 but was staying on in the sixth form at a school in Wellingborough.

We continued on a slow circumnavigation of the lake just indulging in small talk whilst waiting, sometimes embarrassingly, for Malc and Katie to stop for a quick smooch and a grope.

Malc caught the bus back to Finedon with the girls at four in the afternoon as he was working at the hotel that evening. I got a little peck on the cheek from Jackie at the bus stop opposite the park before they left and I really hoped that I would see her again.

On my way back home from the bus stop I popped in to see Bob Bailey. He wanted me to stack the shelves and perform odd jobs around the shop from 8 a.m. until 1230 Monday to Friday and for just a couple of hours on a Saturday morning to suit myself and make the hours up to twenty five.

I would only have to put up with dodgy Dave Denton for the first week as he was going to check out the nudist beach at Brighton or something for

Peanut

the other two weeks and he would show me all I needed to know before he left (like I didn't know how to stack shelves in a corner shop).

Thankfully Barry had now ditched the nauseating Vanessa and I went down to the Peacock in his Ford Cortina with him on the Saturday evening. He too had tired of the Rugby Club disco and found a better craic down the town with its host of pubs in fairly close proximity and especially the Peacock which had a football table as well as a dance floor.

Malc came round to see me the next morning with the piece of information I had been hoping for. Jackie's phone number.

I had seemingly made a good impression of myself and phoned her that afternoon and she arranged to come back over to the park on Wednesday afternoon.

I duly turned up at Baileys at five to eight on Monday morning. Barry and Malc could hardly contain their mirth at the prospects of me being trained by 'Ten-ton' Denton and as Monday was Malc's day off he had promised to look me up during the morning to see how I was coping.

Bugger me if the first thing I had to do was to walk two poxy paper rounds as two of the paper boys were on holiday and nobody else would do an extra round. Usually Dave would do the round in his clapped out Capri but no, not while there's some mug on 23p a bloody hour that can do it. I felt such a twat and my saving grace was that neither round was anywhere near my estate.

I got back to the shop at half past bloody nine to a lecture by Dave on how to stack cans so that the labels face outwards and how to put cabbages in the vegetable rack and that I must keep my hands off the magazines on the top shelf (presumably until he had had the chance to thumb through them himself).

The hardest and most technical piece of equipment I was to be let loose on was to be the price sticker gun.

There was a price list in the small store cupboard to the rear of the shop and I could check the price of each commodity before programming the gun to print the correct price before applying the sticker to said can. Rocket science it was not!

'Do you think you can manage that?' My rotund trainer sneered at me.

I humoured him instead of taking up the more attractive option of thumping him in his smug, fat face.

Both Bob and Janet Bailey were nice people though and I felt that as they had been kind enough to offer me the small job that I would resist the temptation to tell them where to shove their price gun and their lardy errand boy along with it. He would be out of the way by the weekend and I still had Wednesday afternoon to look forward to.

It absolutely bucketed it down with rain on the Wednesday and I felt sure that Jackie would change her mind and not bother coming over to the park. Finedon was, after all, a good five miles away but to my surprise she turned up and in between dodging the showers I was able to walk her back to my house (on her insistence).

I was dreading it.

It seemed really strange when I saw her again. It's weird that having only seen her for a couple of hours a few days ago that your mind tends to forget what that person looks like exactly. I could remember that I thought she had looked absolutely stunning but seeing her again completely sent my knees to jelly. In truth I couldn't believe my luck.

I felt bad that I was embarrassed by my house and garden but amused Jackie by trotting out my departed Father's classic comment to Malc's Dad once in that all the gardens look the same when covered in snow.

Our grass was now at least four feet high and I suppose I will have to take a scythe to it during the next couple of weeks.

My bedroom had no wallpaper as such but was covered in football pictures taken from 'Goal' magazine but at least it had my record player and I could play Jackie my favourite Genesis tracks from 'Nursery Cryme' which I think confused her a little.

I brought us both a glass of Corona cherryade up to the bedroom and, after setting them down on my bedside table, bravely slipped my arm around her shoulders. Jackie responded and before I knew it I was locked in the sweetest kiss I had ever had in my entire life.

This was pure heaven.

We spent the next hour sitting on my bed watching the cars go by out of my bedroom window as the rain lashed down listening to my diverse collection of singles ranging from Black Sabbath to the Stylistics, occasionally locking arms and smooching for several minutes at a time. What else were we supposed to do?

'We must get going back to the park soon.' She broke off.

I agreed. My Mum got home from work around half four and heaven forbid she should find that I'd had a girl in my bedroom (although why I should think like that I have no idea).

We walked back to the park arm in arm and I have to confess to floating on air.

Peanut

As we kissed goodbye at the bus stop she promised to come over again with Katie on Saturday afternoon. I couldn't wait.

I stayed in for the rest of the week until Saturday came trying to keep Myself familiar with my Bosun's Manual but I couldn't get Jackie out of my mind. I was determined not to forget this time how fantastic she looked between now and Saturday afternoon and I'm afraid that trying to concentrate on remembering how many fathoms of anchor cable there were between each studded shackle was proving a little difficult.

Malc sensed I was smitten but on Saturday when we met up again both Jackie and me agreed just to enjoy the next couple of weeks but not get too serious. It just about summed up my luck. Having spent the last three or four years wondering if I was ever going to attract Myself a girlfriend, Lorraine excepted, here I was at the one time in my life that I definitely did not want to become attached, with the most beautiful bird I was ever likely to be with now or ever in the future.

The next week at the shop was a doddle without Dave around. Bob Bailey became a bit tetchy however as he had to get up at six o'clock to do the papers in Dave's absence but I just stayed out of his way and if no shelves needed stacking had the presence of mind to pick up the mop and bucket before he could allocate me any more strenuous, mundane shop related duties. God knows how much Dave was on but he had it bloody easy here.

On the following Wednesday it was my turn to go over to see Jackie in Finedon. I had only ever passed through the small town, if you could call it a town a couple of times before. You approached the place from the direction of Kettering down a steep hill until coming to a crossroad at the bottom of the hill, where the bus stopped. Back up the hill and you were out of the town and heading towards Irthlingborough, Rushden and Higham Ferrers. To the right of the cross-roads were a few shops, a Working Men's Club, a playing field and the way out to Wellingborough, and to the left of the cross-roads a two minute walk to Jackie's house on a small estate and you were in the countryside.

Despite my hay fever I accompanied Jackie through the fields at the back of her house and as we lay down under the sun with hardly a care in the world she put her arms around me, kissed me and smiled.

'You go back to Gravesend soon, don't you?' She pondered as a small bead of sweat trickling down her forehead.

'I'm going to miss you.'

'Thanks for reminding me, Jack.'

What a bloody dampener.

'I can write to you, you know.' I offered trying to sound as if the thought of going back wasn't upsetting me a great deal.

'That'll be nice.' She replied.

We both lay there in complete silence for what seemed an age but was probably only two minutes. I felt the chances of us ever having too serious a relationship slipping away there and then.

I liked Jackie such a lot that it hurt, but I knew I had to face up to the reality that even after my last three weeks back at Gravesend the chances were that I would be whisked away to sea very quickly after that and I had to maintain that ambition above everything else.

Fuck.

The rest of the three weeks flew by. I continued to see Jackie on the two remaining Saturdays and the next Wednesday but there were no dramatics on the final Saturday afternoon when I saw her onto her bus for the last time.

We promised to write to each other and I even said that if I could afford 20p out of my pound pocket money I would phone her once a week.

I felt gutted at going back to Gravesend.

I did my best not to show it but decided, probably against my better judgement, to go down the town with Barry on that Saturday night and get absolutely hammered.

I had a lie-in the next morning until ten o'clock nursing a sore head but that was it. No more drinking and total concentration for the next three weeks.

I slipped quietly out of Kettering mid afternoon to ensure my arrival back at Gravesend for early evening. I have to admit feeling rather sorry for myself.

I tried to put the events of the last three weeks behind me as I settled back into the routine at college. Certainly if the next three weeks passed as quick as the last three had then I would be out of here in no time.

I listened that night to Dorm 28 talking amongst themselves as to what they had got up to during the holiday but chose not to contribute. I did not wish to tempt fate by disclosing that I had been going out with a gorgeous blonde and certainly had no intention of revealing that I had spent my time as a part time shelf stacker and sometime paper boy.

I had come back to Gravesend with only a couple of pounds to my name and only a minimum amount of personal effects due to the briefness of the time I had left at the school.

I couldn't wait until Wednesday to phone Jackie as I had arranged and instead phoned her on Monday evening. She seemed genuinely pleased to hear from me and I was glad that I had chosen to phone to put my mind at rest a little bit.

I could now settle back and focus on the task in hand and after this first week back the examinations would come at us thick and fast.

I had, despite the obvious distractions, kept on top of my practical seamanship theory whilst on holiday but the wire splicing was, as I expected, a bit rusty.

I had until the middle of next week to prepare and if it meant Myself and a couple of the others that were still a bit unsure going back into the classroom for extra practice in the evenings then so be it. There was very little else to get carried away with in our spare time and even Ferris had admitted that it was time to knuckle down even though I felt he had personally left it too late.

Indeed the wire splicing examination was to be our first the next Wednesday and although dreading it I thought it would be good to get it out of the way first. I certainly felt that if I could come through this stage of the examination then I would be almost home and dry.

We were split into teams of two, which I hadn't expected, and had to produce a wire eye splice between the two of us in the allotted two and a half hours.

My partner for the exam was Andy Peters. I was slightly disappointed with the selection despite Andy being probably my best mate out of the entire group his wire splicing skills were pretty much the same as mine. But then again as I looked around the room the pairings seemed to make sense. Kowinski and Ryan Fielding, by far the most accomplished at wire splicing amongst us had been paired together as had Ferris and Tony Furnell, by far the worst. The rest of us seemed pretty equally inept at the task and therefore all pairings should be fairly assessed without one dragging the other back (in theory).

We were marked at various stages throughout the examination and in accordance with how far through the splice we were. The first being once the wire was opened out and gripped in the vice and the six strands 'whipped' to prevent fraying whilst performing the splice. This achieved and marked by the examiner we could then proceed to initiate the first set of tucks, left handed, to make the locking splice. And here is where the fun starts.

No matter that we had already performed around fifty eye splices previously, admittedly with various levels of success, remembering the correct procedure was still mighty baffling to most of us.

'Right,' Andy began as he stepped back from our, so far, not too bad looking a creation. 'This is strand Number 1.' I nodded as Andy picked up the strand on the extreme right of the six.

'Through here.' I motioned to the nearest strand in the wire and rammed my marline spike into the wire opening it up in preparation to accept the first tuck.

We breathed a huge sigh of relief at the ease in which it fell into place and took another step back to admire our handiwork.

'One down, five to go.' I whispered as I picked up strand number 2.

With number 2 strand tucked the trick now was to locate strand number six and tuck it through the same place that number two was only in the opposite direction. That completed the all important locking tuck and with only three strands now remaining it was not too difficult to complete the first round of tucks.

We stood back and awaited the assessor to come and inspect our masterpiece. It looked a bit bulky to me and the expression on the face of the examiner as he looked around it and prodded and pulled at it confirmed this. We were confident that all the tucks were in the right place however but it still took what seemed an age for him to tell us to continue with the next round of tucks. This was no problem as it was now a simple task of going over one and under one and then chiselling three strands off and continuing up with the remaining three to taper off the completed splice.

The whole issue is then battered into shape (not particularly possible with our specimen) and then parcelled using a piece of burlap and marline rope. The parcelling covered a multitude of sins and despite our effort probably only having a safe working load of just over two pounds the end result looked quite acceptable and must have been as Andy and I both gained a pass albeit with the lowest pass mark possible.

Six of our group of 32 failed, Geoffrey Allen and Mick Darnell being the surprise failures from dorm 27. The other four failures coming from dorm 16. Ferris had miraculously passed his wire splicing.

It was a pity, as these six now already knew that they would not be leaving Gravesend with their E.D.H. certificates. However the incentive was still there to do well in all the other categories as, if wire splicing was to be their only downfall, then they would only need to re-sit the wire splicing section of the exam at a later date when, hopefully, they would have gained some invaluable on board experience.

Our next examination was on the Friday up on the bridge where I had no problem passing the steering test and all other aspects navigational.

True, it was only basic stuff but some of our group were still amazingly baffled by the compass. Surely if South is opposite to North then you don't need to be Einstein to work out that the opposite of South East by South is North West by North. Or do you? I found it totally obvious.

Thankfully nobody failed in the navigational section but several came perilously close to failure and were given one or two chances to correct their mistakes.

I felt at the end of the week that it had been a job well done. We had our ropework exam to come on Monday. General Seamanship Knowledge would be on Tuesday plus Thursday morning with our derricks and hatches and cargo handling sandwiched in between on Wednesday.

I couldn't believe that after all this time we were now facing our final week at the school.

I received a letter from Jackie on the Friday and she had sent me a 50p piece sellotaped to the letter so that I could phone her. I was on the phone to her for nearly half an hour on the Saturday morning and immediately my spirits were lifted as she seemed really enthusiastic about my results so far.

I told her that I was missing her like mad and I was pleasantly chuffed that she had said, likewise, that she was missing me. Maybe there could be something in this for us after all, I hoped.

I visited the laundry for the last time that weekend and now took great delight in rubbing in to my dorm the fact of all the things that I would never have to do in my life again.

'My last Flying Angel Club disco tonight.' I cried to the unimpressed, whom I think were tiring a little at my gloating.

I did lie in bed that night and let my mind wander as to what the future may have in store for me. The next couple of weeks were going to be hectic, that was for sure. I had been in touch with Athel line over the holiday period and reminded them that I was about to complete my course at Gravesend and they had told me to report to the Prescott Street pool in London on Friday to register Myself as a Merchant Seaman. It all seemed to be getting so close now and what had been such a distant dream not even twelve months ago was so near to becoming a reality.

My last Monday morning inspection came and went without incident. I had made sure that I had paid a visit to the barbers whilst on holiday in Kettering so, with my escape today from being summoned to the barber (I never did once get to visit him in my time here), I could now start to grow my hair back in earnest.

It was now time for our knots and splices examination.

We were tested on our ability to be able to tie a number of commonly used knots on board ship. I had no idea as to how to tie any kind of knot other than the one to tie my shoe laces prior to my coming to the school but I found that it was pretty much like riding a bike. Once you had mastered the art of a certain knot it was very difficult to forget. We were each given several lengths of rope and had to both tie the knot plus write down on a piece of paper the circumstances in which the knot would be utilised in everyday shipboard usage.

The reef knot, a nice easy one to begin with which was used to join two pieces of rope of equal size together. The single and double sheet bend which was used to tie two pieces of rope of unequal size together. The bowline and running bowline, timber hitch, clove hitch, sheepshank, rolling hitch and figure of eight were all required to be demonstrated as well as a couple of basic rope splices. An eye splice (a darn sight easier with rope than with wire considering the rope had only three strands instead of the wire's six), and a back splice used for tidying up an end of rope that had been cut. As well as these we had to make a 'monkey's fist,' which was a large heavy knot made at the end of a heaving line, sometimes enhanced with a large bolt in the middle of it for more carrying power (a heaving line is used to throw ashore to the quayside and then attached to the ship's mooring ropes in the ship's docking process).

We also had to demonstrate that we were capable of pulling ourselves up and securing ourselves on both a Bosun's chair and on a stage (the best way to describe a stage is that it is a two-man Bosun's chair).

Both crude pieces of equipment are used on board for painting or accessing otherwise unreachable areas of the ship.

A rope is passed through a block for the rigging of a Bosun's chair and for the purposes of this exercise each individual had to haul themselves six feet into the air on a plank of wood attached to one end of the rope just big enough to fit the average arse into. Once six feet in the air both parts of the rope needed to be securely gripped to stop yourself from hurtling the six feet back to the ground. Then the lowering hitch has to be performed, and it is not an easy task to accomplish. Whilst still gripping the two parts of the rope firmly in your left hand above the chair to keep you in your lofted position you then have to pull the bite of the hauling part of the rope towards you, pass it over your head, allow enough slack to drop beneath your feet and then pass your feet and legs through the bite and back up over your body. This accomplished the slack then had to be picked up via your other hand (a quick switch over from left hand keeping you aloft to right hand was required at this point in time). The slack now picked up a hitch appeared before your very eyes which took the weight of yourself and the chair and you were able to relax.

You could now lower yourself in complete safety by working the slack of the rope through the hitch and allowing your weight to aid your descent.

Not too bad an exercise when only six feet above terra firma but it was pointed out that Bosun's chair and likewise stage work are generally carried out from about forty foot aloft on board ship.

The stage is a plank of wood about six to eight feet long with cross-horns at either end to attach a rope to for rigging. Two people at a time, one at either end of the stage, demonstrated their prowess at rigging and tying themselves off on the stage for the purposes of the examination.

My partner this time was Martin Teale and after we had both attached the rope correctly to our ends of the stage proceeded to pull ourselves up the required six feet in preparation to tie ourselves off. Again, as with the Bosun's chair, this required gripping the two parts of the rope but instead of having to perform a mid-air dance with yourself this time the rope just needed passing round the end of the stage itself three times and backed up with a half hitch around one of the horns to prevent the turns sliding off.

One point to remember was that the turns on the stage have to be made from opposite approaches. I.e. one person has to start his three turns from the inside of the rig and the other from the outside otherwise the stage will tilt. Not such a disaster from six feet up but a potential fatal error from forty feet.

Ferris and Phil Laughlan failed to remember this and the error was to cost them their E.D.H. certificate.

The examiner twice had asked them if they were sure that everything was all right before a slight movement on the stage from Ferris sent the rig tipping over slightly once they had let go. It was the safety aspect of the mistake that was paramount in the examiner's decision to fail the two of them. Although both had reacted quickly to prevent the stage tipping they had both been aware that something was likely to go wrong (as we all were throughout the exam). Had it been for real and forty feet up in the air, the examiner explained later, the other person on the stage may not have been so aware and could have fallen off the stage.

I felt a bit sorry for Ferris. He had clearly put a lot of effort in over the past couple of weeks in an attempt to chase what I had believed was a lost cause for himself but he had, at the end of the day, contributed a lot to his own downfall by not taking the whole course seriously enough at the start of the proceedings and I always suspected that he would slip up at some time during the course of the examinations.

Phil was none too pleased either although he had not realised the mistake at the time. It was a painful lesson for us all to learn and probably the realisation that this job did have some dangers linked to it was driven home to us at the expense of their misfortune.

Tuesday morning and afternoon we had two two-hour examinations in the classroom on General Ship Knowledge. It basically meant knowing the Bosun's manual off by heart. We had several diagrams placed in front of us concerning the various areas and cross sections of ships and we had to identify marked parts such as ballast tanks, bilges, strum boxes, bulkheads, beams, cleats, davits and so on and so on.

The strange thing was that although I was now familiar with them by name and location I had very little idea as to their significance on board a ship never having actually been on board one yet.

A lot of the terminology seamed alien to most of us and some caused a bit of a giggle such as the term 'old man' for a horizontal roller on a pedestal which permits mooring ropes to be led to a winch or a windlass from an awkward angle. Why 'old man'? Why not 'mooring rope lead?'

'Dhobie' for laundry, a 'Rosie' for a waste paper basket, the 'glory hole' for the Steward's quarters and we would have to wait until our first trip to sea to find out where the 'golden rivet' was. Fortunately we were not asked to pin point it in the examination. We were all fairly comfortable with this aspect of the course and I would find it very difficult to believe that many students failed this part of the exam.

In the afternoon we were tested much the same way only in the theory of a ship's derrick's and hatches systems. We were subjected to the Macgregor steel hatch cover system for which we had a small version of in the courtyard together with a small derrick for our practical work the following morning.

We each took turns in topping and lowering the derrick and opening the hatches in four groups of eight, swapping duties between winch driver, guy operator and co-ordinator, chain stopper operator and hatch cover operator.

With the amount of practice we had received over the weeks, once again, the tasks were performed well and with military precision.

By Thursday lunchtime it was all over.

Only eight of the class had failed the exams. Four from dorm 16 and Ferris, Laughlan, Geoff Allen and Mick Darnell from our dorm.

The rest of us breathed a huge sigh of relief and I personally couldn't believe that the fourteen weeks were at long last finally over.

In the afternoon we drifted back to our respective dorms for one final tidy up. Nothing too strenuous. We had long since worked out that in the two weeks that the dorm would lie empty contracted cleaners would be in to blitz the room in preparation for another intake of Peanuts.

As I was only next door I quickly packed what little possessions I had brought back to the school with me after the summer holidays and went back into dorm 27 and plonked myself down on my old bunk underneath Ferris.

'Sorry you didn't pass it, Sam.' I genuinely consoled to him, kicking his backside up through the mattress as I had done so many times whilst in the dorm.

'Cheer, Caz.' He replied swooping over the side of the bunk and aiming a playful swipe in my direction.

'Well done to you. Hope you get a good ship.'

He jumped down and offered me his hand. I was pleased that we could leave on good terms despite not seeing eye to eye for the latter stages of our time here.

Tomorrow morning we would all be issued with our discharge books and Seamen's cards and we would be on our way.

I hardly slept a wink that night. It didn't help that ten minutes after lights out four (although it felt like fourteen) of my dorm decided to attack me with pillows and throw cups of water over me as a leaving present.

Friday morning on September the twentieth 1974 and at long last I was in possession of my Department of Trade and Industry seaman's discharge book. My number being UK016422. Already stamped inside was confirmation of my attendance at Gravesend Sea School and the necessary stamps for the successful completion of Lifeboat and E.D.H. courses.

We were now free to leave but far from this being the end of a chapter in my life it is very much the beginning. Once again a bus was laid on to take us to the train station but this time I have to admit that I let Myself down and joined in with Ferris and Fisher and the rest of the bus as we slowly rolled out of the College grounds one last time. The top sections of the bus windows were pushed open and we just let them all have it at the top of our voices.

'Hey! Peanuts!! You're NEVER going fucking home . . . . YAHHOOOOO!'

We were all to report to the various shipping 'pools' around the country to register ourselves available for employment at the earliest opportunity.

Shipping 'pools' are basically just another name for an employment exchange only exclusively for Merchant Navy Ratings. Run by the British Shipping Federation they supply the huge demand of the British Merchant fleet with an able bodied workforce from their 'pool' of labour up and down the country.

All major ports throughout the United Kingdom, such as Liverpool, South Shields, Edinburgh and even Birmingham had their own pools to meet the constant demands of the various shipping companies of which there were many. The pool that I was assigned to was right in the heart of the docklands area of East London in Prescot Street.

Having bid our farewells on the train journey from Gravesend back to Charring Cross to the rest of our dorm mates and to those from dorm 16 four of us, myself, Steve Kowlinski, Gary Thompson and Geoff Allen all made our way straight to Prescot Street to register.

Fortunately Kowinski and Geoff both knew roughly where they were going and we followed them onto the underground from Charring Cross to Aldgate East Station.

The walk from the station to the Prescot Street pool could have only been just over ten minutes but I don't think I have ever felt so intimidated in all my life.

For one I had never seen so many coloured people in all my life as I encountered on the walk down Leman Street. Small cafes, turf accountants, laundrettes and taxi companies lined our route and I swear that they were all owned by different nationalities. There was a Greek restaurant next door to a Chinese takeaway next door to an Indian newsagent across the road from a Turkish kebab shop.

I gazed around in amazement and disbelief. Hopefully Kettering will never get like this I thought to myself.

'Is it just me, or is everyone staring at us?' I asked Kowinski.

It probably didn't help that we had not changed out of our Sea School uniforms. Mr Arnem had advised us to turn up at the pool looking smart and respectable. I was beginning to regret that we had taken his advice, as we must have looked odd even in these surroundings.

Prescot Street was off to the right of Leman Street just after a Large Metropolitan Police building (I could well imagine the need for it around here), and just before the railway bridge where Leman Street became Dock Street which led, unsurprisingly, to the Docks.

The Red Merchant Navy Ensign flew proudly from the mast outside a building halfway down the street and on our left as we turned in to Prescot Street so there was no danger of us getting lost from now on.

As the four of us walked into the main lobby of the building I could sense all eyes upon us. It had to be the bloody stupid uniforms.

'Good day to you, young sirs!' A red faced Irishman walked over to us holding his hand out to greet us.

His breath stank of stale beer and whisky as he offered each of us a handshake. I begrudgingly accepted as his equally scruffy and smelly mates laughed behind his back.

'Welcome aboard. Jeeze, you're all looking very smart. Can I take your bags for you, young sir?' He patronisingly continued.

'Er, No we're fine thank you. We've just come to register ourselves on the pool.' Kowinski diplomatically explained.

'Jeeze, I know that laddy.' He laughed and coughed at the same time. His face getting even redder as he spluttered.

'Here, let me take you over to the window to get yuzz fixed up, OK?'

We accepted his offer. I felt that the Paddy's had had their bit of fun as we walked in through the door and were now being helpful.

All around the central lobby there were desks and partitions and doors leading to different offices and along the whole of one wall was a bank of windows just like a large Post Office. Behind these screens and windows were several blackboards with the names of twenty or thirty ships on them advertising their immediate labour requirements.

Four A.B's, a Second Cook, three Stewards required for the *Esso Aberdeen* sailing from Purfleet on Monday.

A Bosun, two A.B's, two Deck Boys, two Donkey Greasers and two Stewards required for the *BritishRenown*.

'Brand new supertanker that bastard.' Our Irish friend informed us. 'You don't want to be on that fecking thing, miles and miles out of port those things go. No chance of going ashore on them things.'

'Get yourself a nice cargo ship, lads. Plenty of time to get up the road and see the sights. Ha! Ha!' He spluttered again at his own statement.

The four of us made our way to one desk and officially registered ourselves as British Merchant Seamen.

Then another desk to join the National Union of Seamen and then over to another window for the pick of the finest of what the Merchant Navy Establishment could offer us.

'OK then boys, what have we got to offer you?' The bloke in the tie behind the window said to us turning his head around to the ever-growing list of ships on the blackboard behind him.

I was dumbfounded at the whole operation. It just seemed as if you could walk in with your discharge book, go up to any window, scratch your chin as if deep in contemplation and say to the guy behind the window.

'Hmmm! Let me see now, A.B. on the *Humbergate*, think I'll give that one a go.'

I'm sure it must be a little more rigorous than that but that was certainly the impression I got.

'Any of you chaps had any correspondence through a shipping company before you went to sea school?' We were asked.

'Yes, I did.' I admitted and produced my letter from Athel Line that I had received during the holidays in reply to my reminder that I was nearing the end of my course at Gravesend.

With that he proceeded to pick up his desk phone and call up the personnel department of Athel Line who were based in Mark Lane not too far from where we were at the moment.

After only two minutes on the phone he came back to the window and looked directly at me.

Congratulations, Mr Caswell. You can join the *Anco Empress* in Liverpool on Wednesday.'

'Wednesday?' I repeated almost in terror. 'Yes, fine.' I added. 'Why Liverpool? I thought you just covered the London area here.' I assumed.

'Far from it.' I was told. 'We recruit from all over and if we feel someone is more suitable to a different type of ship it doesn't matter which area we recruit from.'

'Now then, even better news is that the ship will require two deck boys for the voyage. Anybody else fancy it? I must point out that the *Anco Empress* is a chemical tanker despite the fact that it is Molasses that it is bringing in to Liverpool next week.'

Geoff Allen hardly gave it any time for thought. 'I'll join it as well.' He immediately volunteered.

'Fine then. All you need to do now is to go round to Athel Line's offices in Mark Lane.

They will sort you out with a medical and I will wish you both the very best of luck.'

That's it? As simple as that? I couldn't believe it.

We shook hands with Kowinski and Thompson, wishing them all the best and waved to our Irish friends on the way out.

'What ship did you get?' They enquired.

I wasn't too encouraged by the face they pulled when I told them of the Anco Empress, I have to admit.

It was probably about the same distance, time-wise, from the pool to Mark Lane as it would have been walking back to Aldgate East underground station and hopping on board the one stop to Tower Hill. Geoff sort of knew his way around and we were very soon looking up at the office block at numbers 24/25 Mark Lane which housed the Athel Line offices on the fourth floor with the P. & O. offices taking up the first three. It was still only two o'clock in the afternoon and my head was still spinning from how quickly events had taken a turn so far today.

Geoff and I sat in the reception area awaiting the Personnel Manager. I was still lugging my small kitbag around with me and, despite my shirt being all creased up inside, decided that I would nip into the toilets and change out of this poxy uniform while we waited.

We were soon summonsed into the office by a very tall, slim man about twenty-six and immaculately dressed.

'My name is John Lawson and I am one of the Personnel Officers for Athel Line.' He said as he shook both our hands.

He then went on to explain the number of ships (twelve) that were in the small parcel chemical tanker fleet that Athel Line owned and manned and explained that they were in fact a subsidiary of P. & O. shipping, hence the location of the office in this building.

'Tours of duty tend to be from between five to six months depending on the location of the ship and availability of relief staff.' He continued.

'Most voyages tend to start in or around the United Kingdom and end up back again within that period of time. The *Empress*, which you will be joining on Wednesday, is scheduled to go to the East Coast of America, New York and Houston and then down to the coast of Brazil.'

I looked at Geoff. His eyes were already wide open. 'Brazil!' I mouthed at him.

We would both need a quick medical examination but it was nothing as stringent as we had already been subjected to at the sea school. Just a quick confirmation that our vaccinations were in order and that we were basically in sound shape. This would be carried out by a P. & O. doctor in the building whilst we were here this afternoon.

Our starting wage was to be £96 per month for a basic 40-hour week with overtime readily available at time and a half, double time on a Sunday. It was made quite clear though that we would be expected to work at all times required and that the demands put on us would be quite severe. This was nothing less than we had been led to believe at sea school anyway and both Geoff and I accepted this fact there and then.

'Good.' Mr Lawson finished. 'It is very hard work but I'm sure that at the same time you will both enjoy yourselves. I will be coming up to Liverpool on Wednesday Myself to ensure that the change over of personnel on board runs smoothly so I will have a chat with you both then.'

With that he wrote out two train tickets for both Myself and Geoff, one way, to Liverpool, Lime Street station to use next Wednesday and offered his hand again as he told us to go home and enjoy a couple of days rest.

I left Geoff on the platform at Tower Hill. He only had a short journey on the district line to Chiswick Park to make before getting a bus to Hounslow.

'See you Wednesday then, Geoff.'

'Yep, I can't believe it. America and Brazil here we come.' He replied quite nervously.

I waved at him from my underground carriage as the train pulled out of the station to make my way back to St. Pancras and couldn't help but shake my head and smile to Myself as I looked at him still in his sea school uniform. What absolute pratts we looked in that ill fitting get up. Geoff seemed not to care one bit though as he waved vigorously back at me.

The circle line train took me straight to St. Pancras but I just failed to make the 4.20 to Kettering. I had an hour to wait until the next train, the bloody commuter train, standing room only. I was starving by now so went into the buffet restaurant on the station and had an extortionately priced sausage roll and a coke.

America . . . Brazil . . . . I just sat there in a World of my own, alone with my thoughts and expectations.

Mum was overjoyed with the news that I gave to her when I got home later that evening. It wasn't too late for a quick wash and to run up to Barry's to also share my good fortune with him.

'This calls for a celebration down the Peacock indeed.' He smiled.

Indeed it did.

Malc had arranged for Jackie and Katie to come over to the park on the Saturday afternoon, not knowing that I was only going to be home for a couple of days before I went away again only this time for good. (Well, a few months at least).

The meeting with Jackie was rather subdued. I felt a bit uneasy and I sensed that she felt the same. With it now being late September the weather had taken a turn for the worse from the glorious August days that we had shared only just over a month ago and we sat huddled in the redundant train station with a gale howling through the platform.

'Will you write to me?' I tentatively asked.

'Yes, of course I will.' She responded. Half-heartedly, I felt.

I felt so annoyed with myself. I was in no position to embark on a full time relationship and I felt she sensed it.

Whether she felt the same or disappointed or indeed was just seeing this as an excuse to find a way out of our friendship I guess I will never know.

We dragged ourselves in almost silence back through the playground and sat uncomfortably in the bicycle shed for half an hour. Occasionally I attempted to put my arm around her shoulder and ran my hand through her fine blond hair but gained very little in the way of an enthusiastic response.

'Good luck.' She finally wished me as we waited for the bus to take her back to Finedon a while later. 'I hope you find what you're looking for.'

What she meant by that I haven't a clue. I wasn't even sure what it was that I was looking for.

I dossed about at home on the Sunday doing absolutely nothing while my Mother washed all my clothes that I would be taking up to Liverpool with me. We had finally caught up with the modern world in our household and actually possessed the luxury of a twin tub washing machine instead of the old copper and mangle.

Mum had also knitted me a couple of thick pullovers which, although I protested I would not need in Brazil, she still insisted on me taking for our arrival back in the UK around January/February time. Perhaps some sound advice.

It was ironic that Cath and Steve were only two weeks away from coming home themselves from their first trip to sea together. I would miss seeing them and wondered how many times in the future our paths would be destined to just miss each other. I could have done with a few tips from Steve as to what I would need to take to sea with me.

Mum, bless her, for all her good intentions would have had me taking countless packets of biscuits, twenty boxes of washing powder and enough toothpaste to sink the damn thing. In the end I did manage to fill one rather large suitcase and my small kitbag that I had used for the last three weeks at Gravesend.

Ahh! Gravesend. Already a lifetime away although I was all too aware of the fact that whereas I had worked my way to the top of the pecking order in my fourteen weeks at Gravesend I was now, once again, very much on the bottom rung of the ladder once I joined my first ship.

And very much a Peanut once more.

The Monday and the Tuesday were very weird days. As if I was in limbo and I suppose to all intents and purposes I was.

I decided to catch a bus over to Wellingborough on Monday morning as they had a George Allen's menswear shop that catered more for the 'outdoor' wear than any shop in Kettering.

I bought a couple of good pairs of working jeans to go with my now thinning sea school pairs and a couple of work shirts. I didn't need jumpers due to my Mother's handicraft supplementing the two from sea school and the one that had been presented to me by the staff of Lewis's.

As I was in Wellingborough I took a quick stroll down to the yard to see Dave and Simon and the rest of the workforce. It surprised me none to learn that I had not been replaced and contrary to my claims that I must have been irreplaceable Mr Thomas confirmed that they would be looking to bring in another trainee in the new year when trade picks up again after the usual winter slackness.

Dave continued to wind me up now that the time to actually join my first ship was about to be realised.

'Watch out for all those nice boys.' He advised. 'And never bend over in the shower to pick the soap up.'

Simon and Mr Thomas joined in with a chorus of cautionary sighs but I just laughed pathetically at him.

'I'm sure it's not a bit like that at all.' I protested, unsure as to whether it was them I was trying to convince or myself.

It was good to see them all again and to receive their encouragement as well as getting another peck on the cheeks from Clare although I was still wondering if I did indeed have any future with Jackie.

I had told Dave, in the strictest of confidence, about Jackie and that I wondered if she would write to me or not.

'You won't hear from her, mate.' Simon declared with some degree of authority after Dave had immediately blabbed that I had a girlfriend. 'She won't write, they never do.'

Thanks, I thought. Who needs enemies?

I managed to convince both Barry and Malc that it would be a good idea to go down to the Peacock on Monday evening for a final drink together.

Barry still had reservations as to what I was about to do with my life. Malc was a bit more optimistic and encouraging, failing to see what future, if any, Kettering could possibly offer any of us.

'You're only selling tellies in a shop in the High street, Barry.' Malc observed. 'Is that what you're going to be doing for the rest of your life?'

It appeared so.

Malc intended to further his apprenticeship and reputation as a second chef at the hotel in Finedon he was presently at but made no secret of the fact that he felt he was destined for higher things and was setting his sights on being a top chef in London or somewhere similar.

'Nothing wrong with a bit of ambition and a desire to see the World.' He had argued in my favour.

Barry felt that if it all went wrong I would find it very hard to get a trade other than be confined to factory life and the tedium that it consequently brought. I suppose at the end of the day, like all true friends, he only had my best interests at heart but of course it was all too late by now to change anything.

On Wednesday morning I would be off to Liverpool, nothing anybody could do or say was going to alter that fact.

For the rest of the evening both Barry and Malc continued to ply me with double vodkas, neither of them drinking much as they had to be up for work the next morning.

I had a stinking headache the next morning but glad of the fact that I had arranged the farewell bash last night so that I could leave tomorrow with a clear head.

3

Once again, as I had done four months previously when leaving for Gravesend, I refused my Mother's offer to come down to the train station to see me off on the Wednesday morning. I chose, as before, to sit alone with my thoughts for half an hour after she had gone to work and before my taxi arrived to take me to the station.

I will be catching the 0925 train to Leicester and connecting to Nuneaton before catching my final train to Liverpool. Hopefully arriving at Lime Street station just before one in the afternoon.

I had made the train journey to Leicester countless times before in recent years to follow 'The Foxes' home matches but never with a suitcase that weighed an absolute tonne before.

I had to catch the train on the other side of the station and this meant lugging the suitcase down two flights of stairs and dragging it along the subway, which ran underneath the railway tracks.

That was the easy bit!

Making the ascent back up to the platform on the other side proved a bit more difficult but I received a bit of assistance from a passing passenger who unexpectedly gave my suitcase an almighty shove from behind as he came up the stairs almost knocking me forwards in the process.

This time, as the train pulled slowly out of the station, I really did start to feel a bit nervous and felt a slight lump come to my throat. To my right hand side I was leaving behind the town that I had grown to love. The view of my beloved 'Poppies' football ground with it's distinctive floodlight pylons bearing the letter 'K' in high powered light bulbs and state of the art grandstand came and went and very soon we were out in the countryside and hurtling our way through Desborough and Market Harborough towards Leicester.

Bloody typically, once at Leicester station, I had to cross over the railway track for my Nuneaton connection and then bugger me if I didn't have to do the same again at Nuneaton for my connection to Liverpool. If ever there was an Olympic event for suitcase humping I was well on the way to qualifying with distinction. I was getting the training.

At least once settled into my seat on the Inter City Service to Liverpool I could relax and watch the unfamiliar countryside pass me by. The journey took me out through Staffordshire and onwards and upwards towards Crewe, which I had heard of due to its railway history and the fact that for some inexplicable reason they had a football team called Alexander.

Why? Nobody is called Manchester David, or Birmingham Simon! Why Crewe Alexander? Isn't it strange the thoughts that pass through your mind when bored on a train. It also occurred to me that here I was, at 17, travelling through the North Midlands and beyond passing places that I had never seen before in my entire life.

I had travelled a bit with the Poppies but due to our Southern league base had only ever travelled mainly South with them. The furthest North being Burton upon Trent. I was about to travel the World and I had seen practically nothing of my own country North of Nottingham.

I arrived at Liverpool's Lime Street Station right on time at a quarter to one. Probably the first time ever that I had not been delayed at some stage or another by good old British Rail.

I plonked my suitcase onto a trolley, much to the annoyance of a porter that had made a beeline for me after seeing me struggle off the train with it. I needed all the money that my Mum had given me; I wasn't going to waste it on tipping any scouse porters.

I followed the signs out of the station to the taxi rank and within five minutes was making the final leg of my journey to Canada Dock number 27.

It had only been a matter of days since I had left Fisher at Gravesend but as soon as the taxi driver opened his mouth I realised that yes, they do all speak like that up here.

I reached the dock where the *Anco Empress* was berthed within ten minutes.

Along the whole of the dock road ran a massive brick wall which meant that only the superstructure and the masts of the various ships could be visible from the road and this was the first sight that I gained of what was to be my home for the next five months.

There was a gateman at the barrier leading into the dock but I think he must have just took one look at my suitcase and realised that I was joining the ship as he just waved me through.

I turned the corner and had to step back in amazement as I looked up at this giant orange monster.

Looking up at the stern of the vessel, well out of the water due to its state of half emptiness the massive bulk was so much more than I had expected to see.

Although only just over four years old the hull was full of rust that was cleverly disguised by the fact that it was all painted orange. Even the proud name of ANCO EMPRESS with the name LIVERPOOL underneath had been strangely covered in fresh orange paint as I took in the sight in front of me.

The whole dockside reeked of fermenting treacle.

I made my way tentatively past the portholes in the ship's side, continuing to stare up at the massive accommodation block which then dropped away onto the main deck, trying to avoid all the pipes and hoses that were strewn across the quayside intent on tripping me up as I made my way to the accommodation ladder.

The ladder was fairly steep and I figured that I was not going to make it all the way up with both my suitcase and my kitbag. I decided to leave my suitcase on the jetty for the first run up the ladder.

The ladder itself certainly looked sturdy enough, made of aluminium and, at a guess, weighing an absolute ton, but the angle of ascent that it was presently at plus the feeble looking iron stanchions and manropes gave me cause for concern.

I made it to the top and plonked my kitbag down and was spotted by a young deck worker as I made my way back down for my suitcase.

'Need a hand?' He shouted.

He didn't wait for a reply but followed me back down the ladder and grabbed the suitcase from me and gingerly made his way back up the North face of Everest puffing and panting.

'Fuck me, what you got in here? A new anchor cable?'

I laughed as I jumped down on to the main deck after him.

'Cheers, mate. I've been lugging that about all day.'

'I'm Ray Newton.' He smiled at me offering his filthy hand. Ray was about six feet tall, slim, well tanned and with immaculate short curly, well groomed, light brown hair 'I'm on watch at the moment; most of the others are across the road at the pub.'

He gestured back from where I had just come through the gate.

'John Caswell.' I replied. 'This is my first trip.'

'I gathered that by the haircut.' Ray replied as he carried my suitcase along the deck to the accommodation block for me.

'This is only my second trip. I'm a J.O.S. on here; I joined three weeks ago in Durban.'

'Durban?' I enthused. 'Is that where you picked this treacle up from?'

Ray laughed. 'Does whiff a bit doesn't it. Yes we picked up the full cargo of Molasses from there and came straight back here with it.'

We made our way in through an accommodation door on the starboard side of the ship at poop deck level and into what looked like a bar.

'This is the crew bar.' Ray announced. 'Through there is the crew messroom.' He pointed to two rows of tables, each with twelve stools affixed to the deck, six either side.

'The galley is through there as well, but if you just plonk yourself on a chair for a minute I'll try and find the Bosun.'

'Boas!!!!' He screamed at the top of his voice as he went back out through the door we had entered and along a corridor where there were a row of cabins.

I took a look around as I sat in the bar on my own. It was quite poky. Certainly not much bigger than my Father's old bedroom in Kettering which was the biggest bedroom in our house. An upholstered bench seat skirted around the two short sides and the long outboard side of the room around three small fixed tables opposite a small bar which I noticed had a fridge behind it and a small hand pump with a 'Watney's' Red Barrel logo on it for keg beer.

I heard a door slam and two seconds later a guy in Chef's clothing rushed past me.

'Alright chap?'

He smiled at me and disappeared through the bar before I had time to reply.

Ray then emerged back through the door that the chef had just hurtled through. This time with a very serious looking, small thick set man in a boiler suit behind him.

'Boas, this is one of our new deck boys, John.'

I stood up and offered my hand, which he took hold of with a vice like grip and shook vigorously.

'Ron Skellern.' He snapped at me in one of the thickest West Country accents I had ever heard.

'You can call me Boas.' He turned to Ray and smiled.

'I'll leave you to it then, shall I Boas?' Ray replied.

'Aye, fuck off.' The Bosun replied with another smirk.

I laughed, sensing the non-seriousness of the conversation.

'We're expecting four boys today.' He began. 'Two deck boys and two engine room boys. Luckily you are the first to arrive, what's your name again?'

'John.'

'Luckily you are the first to arrive, John, so you get choice of cabins. There are two single cabins available and one double. Do you know the other deck boy that's joining?'

'Yes, Geoff Allen. I was at sea school with him.'

'Would you want to particularly spend the next five months with him in the same cabin?' He asked.

'Err, not particularly.' I replied.

'Thought not, OK son follow me.'

We descended the stairs from the crew bar and came out into a corridor with twelve doors along the outside.

'Right, son. You and the other boy have got these end two cabins, they're smaller than the rest as they run along the ship's stern but it's better than sharing.'

I nodded an agreement and chose the cabin next to the end, which was slightly larger than the end cabin that was to be reserved for Geoff.

'I'll leave you to it and see you at eight o'clock in the morning for turn too. Don't get drunk ashore.' He barked.

I thanked him and he went back up the stairs in the direction of the crew bar.

I plonked my suitcase on the bunk. Compared to the vision I had in my mind of the accommodation I was expecting on board this was quite luxurious.

Looking into the cabin from the doorway on my right I had a sizeable built in wardrobe. Then my single bunk, a chair and an upholstered day bed stretching the seven-foot length across the bottom of the cabin.

To my left a sink and toiletry cabinet, a desk with three drawers and a bookshelf above that. The floor was of a shiny grey vinyl, which I imagined could be very cold first thing in the morning, but all in all I had no complaints.

I unpacked a few things and thought of waiting for Geoff to arrive but decided to be nosy and do a bit of investigating as I couldn't be sure when he would turn up.

I found the shower and toilet block on the inboard side of our alleyway. I had heard a monotonous humming from the ship's generators in my cabin but the noise magnified ten fold as I opened up the door to the shower room.

There was an old industrial washing machine in the room opposite the three shower cubicles similar to that used at a public laundrette and to the ones that we had used at sea school as well as a large sink.

'Ah. You've found the showers then!' I looked round and saw Ray in the doorway with just a towel wrapped around him.

'What cabin are you in?'

I told him and quickly turned my head away as he whipped his towel off and turned the shower on.

'The Bosun's knocked me off early seeing as there's hardly anybody left on board. I'm going to have a quick shower and then I'm going over to the pub with the second cook. You coming?'

'The pub will be shut by now, won't it?' I asked, as it was now just gone three in the afternoon.

Ray let out a loud laugh. 'Ha! You're in Liverpool by the docks now, mate, not . . . . where are you from?'

'Kettering.'

'Not Kettering. The 'Dominion' across the road will be open all day.'

'I was going to wait for Geoff, and I haven't got much money on me.' I argued.

'Don't worry about that,' He shouted as he climbed into the shower.

'I'll see you all right for a few pints. Like the bronzy?' He shouted as he lathered himself under the shower, making no attempt to conceal himself by pulling the curtain across.

'Er, impressive.' I said desperately trying not to look at him.

Ray started singing as loud as he could and I gathered already that he was definitely a bit of a poser.

He turned the shower off after a further minute and wrapped his towel back round him. 'I'll see you upstairs in the bar in five minutes time, Yeah?'

I nodded.

'Make sure you lock your cabin door and keep the key either on you or hide it somewhere.' He advised.

I made my way back up to the bar where the second cook, the guy I had briefly seen dashing through a few minutes ago, was sitting.

'Hello again.' I said, 'I'm John.'

'Mel.' He smiled offering his hand.

His accent was also quite broad but pretty much East Anglian, I thought. Probably mid thirties in age, slim but quite tall with a Teddy boy style brylcreemed back hairstyle. He seemed friendly enough to me.

'Is this your first trip?' He asked.

I nodded the confirmation he was expecting.

'You'll be all right, especially after a couple of beers.' He smiled.

Ray came back into the bar and we left immediately as he beckoned us furiously.

'Cam on, you two.' He urged.

It was quite a struggle to negotiate all the pipes that were lying on the deck and the pools of spilt Molasses that had stuck like glue to the deck. A main deck wire spring was also in place to assist in keeping the ship alongside and this had to be vaulted before reaching the accommodation ladder.

The ladder was much easier going down than coming up although I perished at the thought of having to scale it with a few beers inside me later on.

'How long will the ship be here?' I asked Ray as we made our way back to the dock gate.

'We should leave around Friday breakfast time for Rotterdam.' He replied.

Mel confirmed that he had finished work for the day as we hurried towards the dock gate and that the cook that was leaving the ship was staying on to prepare the meal onboard for that evening.

'Most of the crew that are leaving have gone home now.' He explained. 'And most of them that are joining are either coming on board tomorrow as they're local or are already in The Dominion,' the pub we were heading for and that was in our sights as we crossed the dock road.

The Dominion looked massive from the outside and I could hear the noise coming from inside well before Mel pushed the door open to let out a plume of smoke that was hovering around the exit just waiting for it's chance to escape.

We fought our way to the bar. The place was absolutely jam packed and throbbing.

The juke box was thumping out George McCrae's 'rock your baby' and, hang on a minute . . . ., there were three girls with very little on dancing on the tables.

Bloody hell, what had I walked into? Just eight hours ago I was sat all alone in my kitchen in Kettering after saying my farewells to my Mother. I was now in a totally different World.

'What you having, John?' Ray screamed at me from the bar.

I stuck to lager and lime. I knew I could handle a few of them as Mel went straight on to the Vodkas.

The smoke in the place was almost overpowering as we made our way over to a couple of tables where about fourteen other lads in various stages of drunkenness were seated. They must have been from the ship, as they all seemed to recognise Mel and Ray. I just sat down without an introduction and decided to soak up the atmosphere.

A loud cheer went up around the room as one of the dancing girls on the tables removed her bra, swung it around her head and threw it over towards the bar area whilst everybody joined in the chorus of Chuck Berry's 'my ding-a-ling', closely followed by the removal of the two other girl's bras.

I had to pinch myself to reassure myself that this was happening.

Another pint of lager and lime was plonked in front of me before I had finished the one I was on by somebody that I did not know as all three girls came together on one table, still topless, and at the end of 'Take me home, country roads' sung by the entire bar whipped off their pants in unison and flung them into the crowd.

My eyes must have popped out of their sockets. A huge round of applause went round the bar accompanied with wolf whistles and cheers as the three girls legged it to the ladies toilets.

'Fucking hell, we just made that in time, didn't we?' Ray screamed across the table at me.

I responded with a positive thumbs up.

No sooner was I half way through my second pint than another was set in front of me by the burly chap, who I now knew as Bob, sitting next to me.

'Cheers, Bob.' I shouted. 'I haven't got enough money to buy you one back.' I apologised.

'Keep your money in your pocket, Lar.' Bob replied in a thick scouse accent.

'Are you off the Anco Empress?' I asked him.

'Yeah, I've just joined today as an AB, brought my gear up this morning. I was going to go back home but . . . well, you know how it is.' He shrugged his shoulders and looked around the bar as if to say 'how can you resist this for a lunchtime session.'

Bob must have been around twenty-four, built like a brick shithouse with a mass of blonde curly hair and rosy cheeks. He came across as great entertainment as the afternoon wore on.

It had not taken me long to get a bit of a glow on. I was used to dispatching six or seven pints of lager over an evening session at home but not within two hours. So by the time six o'clock arrived I was grateful when Ray said he was heading back to the ship to get his head down as he was due back on watch at midnight tonight.

I was also aware that I had had very little to eat so far today apart from a British Rail sarnie on the way up before Crewe so I approved Ray's plan to call into the chippy across the road from the dock on our way back.

I had to make one last desperate visit to the toilets before we headed back. My last visit about an hour ago had been yet another eye opener. Down a flight of dimly lit stairs, the walls covered in dark puke green paint and even smokier than the bar was, I had bravely pushed open the doors to find two young, scruffy lads sitting on toilets in two separate cubicles, fully clothed, smoking something the likes of which I had never smelt before.

'Wanna spliff, man?' One of the lads had looked up at me with hollow eyes and asked, pushing the 'cigarette' at me.

'Hey, got any skins on yer?' The other asked.

I quickly took my leak at the trough, which made the smell of the weed they were smoking even more gut wrenching, and dashed back up to the bar telling them that I didn't smoke.

I somehow didn't think they were from the ship. They certainly weren't from the two tables that I had been joining in with and I was glad when I had seen them stumble out of the bar some twenty minutes later.

My head swam as we entered the freshness of the late September evening from the suppressive atmosphere of the Dominion but the sausage and chips soon started to soak up the alcohol and by the time we reached the bottom of the accommodation ladder I felt much better and confident that I could scale it without too much difficulty.

There was still nobody about as I walked through the crew bar with Ray but as we got to the bottom of the stairs I noticed that the cabin door that Geoff had been allocated was open.

'Geoffrey!' I shouted as I barged through his door and plonked myself onto his bunk.

'Watcha, Caz!' He seemed delighted to see me.

Ray stood in the doorway grinning and I introduced them.

'Right, I'm off to bed now so keep the noise down.' Ray requested. 'Remember when you're in the accommodation block that there will nearly always be a watchkeeper off duty and asleep down below so it always pays to try and keep it quiet down here.'

'OK, mate. See you tomorrow.'

I closed Geoff's door and told him what we had been up to over at the Dominion whilst he continued to unpack his case.

I got the feeling that Geoff was rather pleased that he had arrived later than I had and that he had missed the afternoon's entertainment.

After I had been back to my cabin for ten minutes to finish off my own unpacking that I had cut short earlier Geoff and I went back up to the crew Messroom to try and get Geoff a cup of coffee.

The Bosun was propping up the crew bar on his own with a big mug of tea as we came through the door from the stairs.

'Aha! My two boys.' He growled. 'What can I do for you?'

'Er, I'd like a coffee.' Geoff whimpered.

The Bosun took us through to the galley hatch area and showed us where all the 'night pantry' facilities were; The tea, the coffee, hot water geyser, toaster, bread, biscuits and small fridge with a plate of cold meat, butter, cheese and milk inside.

'Are there any cold drinks, Boas?' I asked, trying to make out that I was less intimidated by him than Geoff obviously was. Or maybe the beer was making me brave.

'There's coke in the fridge, son, behind the bar. Five pence a can.'

I took one and asked if I could pay for it tomorrow.

'Don't forget.' The Bosun sighed.

'I wasn't expecting to find a bar on board the ship.' I commented as I poured my coke into a half-pint glass and sat with Geoff opposite the Bosun who continued to prop up the bar.

'I don't like them.' He scowled. 'More trouble than they're bloody well worth and if you're not careful things can get out of hand. I'll be running this bar and if there's any trouble or drunkenness on watch because of it I'll close the damn thing.'

I was in no doubt that he meant what he was saying.

'What time do we start work tomorrow, Boas?' Geoff asked.

'You'll be called at seven o'clock for breakfast at half past. We then start at eight o'clock. We've a busy day tomorrow. We've got to paint the ship's name in on the bow and the stern (ahh, so that's why the name was covered in orange paint when I noticed it earlier today), and we've stores to take on board including beer for this bloody bar. So I suggest you lads get an early night tonight and be raring to go in the morning.'

We both nodded our heads. The Bosun seemed quite an uncompromising bloke and I didn't feel like arguing with him. He did, however, seem quite happy to carry on talking to us for the next half an hour before we decided, at half past eight, to turn in. In that time we discovered that the Bosun was 56 years old and from Bristol. He had never married, still lived with his ageing Mother and had been at sea since he was 14. He too had just joined the ship this morning but it was his third trip on an Anco tanker so knew more or less what to expect.

'Once we leave here we will be going across to Rotterdam. It will be a week before we are able to load another cargo though as we will have to clean all the tanks first and this Molasses can be a bastard. All the tanks have heating coils to heat certain cargoes in transportation and with the Molasses it tends to burn itself onto the coils and we have to scrape the damn stuff off by hand. It all depends if the coils have been kept at the right temperature or not on our way up from Durban.'

Geoff and I nodded although neither of us had a remote clue as to what he was talking about.

The Bosun asked us our shoe size before we went to bed and said that he would get us shoes and boiler suits each before we started work tomorrow morning.

I said goodnight to Geoff, had a quick strip wash in my sink, decided to lock my cabin door and never heard another thing after my head hit the pillow until there was a loud banging at my door with somebody trying to get in at seven o'clock the next morning.

'Rise and shine, seven o'clock.' A thick Irish accent shouted through my door.

'Okay, okay.' I called and sat bolt upright in my bunk.

Oooooh, my head! Where the fuck am I?

I sank my head into my hands. I remember. I've got to go to work, haven't I.

It was only five past seven so I thought that the best possible way to quickly rid myself of my hangover would be a quick cold shower. I scurried down the alleyway with just my towel wrapped round me and dived under the cold water. I popped two paracetamols once back in my cabin, which my Mum had thoughtfully advised that I take with me, dressed in my sea school (half-mast) jeans and number two working shirt and knocked on Geoff's door.

He was ready and by twenty five past seven we had both made ourselves a cup of coffee and were sitting at a table eagerly awaiting our breakfast.

The Bosun was also in the Messroom along with three other men, all in their fifties, in white boilersuits.

The galley hatch opened noisily up from the inside and myself and Geoff made it there first. A scruffy, unshaved and totally hung-over thirtyish year old lad with uncombed shoulder length hair growled at us in a rough scouse accent.

'Breakfast?'

'Yes, please.' Both Geoff and I answered in unison.

Mel was in the galley along with the cook, who I assumed should have left the ship by now, and two other bodies one of which must have been the galley boy as he was wearing a sea school catering jacket. I didn't recognise him from Gravesend though.

The Steward that had served us returned with our plates brimming with fried egg, bacon, sausage, black pudding (which I loathed) and fried bread.

'Fucking hell, is there any left for the rest of us, Arthur, Eh?' One of the chaps that had been sitting with the Bosun asked as Geoff and I made our way back to our table.

'They won't be able to move if they down that fucking lot, eh?' He continued to tell everyone that was entering the Messroom at the top of his voice.

'Get it down you lads.' He urged as he returned to the table with two boiled eggs and a round of bread and butter. 'It's all part of your wages, eh?'

His name was Tony Hunt, the donkeyman, in charge of the engine room crew of four donkey greasers and two engine room boys and probably the loudest and broadest of all the scousers that I had so far encountered.

The two engine room boys, Dan Harvey and Keith Charlery, both came and sat with Geoff and me to eat their breakfast.

The Messroom was fast filling up now and there were far too many people about for me to even guess who they were or what they did on the ship. There did seem to me to be quite a lot more older crewmembers on board than I was expecting though.

At eight o'clock the Bosun and Tony stood up from their chairs and Tony was the first to speak.

'Okay, engine room crowd. Follow me and we'll have a chat down below.' With that Dan and Keith got up along with three other mid-fifty year old blokes and a younger lad possibly around mid twenties with brown curly hair halfway down his back which he proceeded to collect and gather up into a ponytail as he went out.

The Bosun, and indeed Geoff and I looked around the room at what was remaining.

Bob, who I had met in the Dominion yesterday, was sat near me as were a couple of other older guys that had been in the pub with us. There were two coloured AB's, Guyanese so I was told, Desmond Best and Wayvell Elliott and they were asked by the Bosun to paint the ship's name on the bows along with Willie Smith, the other J.O.S. who was to tend them.

'Er, and take this young man along with you as well, Willie.' The Bosun said pointing at Geoff.

'I've got you both your working boots and boilersuits.' The Bosun growled and threw the lot at me and Geoff. The rest of the group laughed.

'Who else have I got?' The Bosun enquired, looking around the room.

'Bertie Wills.' A plump cheerful looking mid forties chap piped up with his hand raised.

'I fucking know I've got you again, Bertie.' The Bosun smiled.

'Okay, Bertie, you and . . . er what's your name?' He pointed at a very thin, gaunt man that had sat silently from the minute he had entered the Messroom without taking any breakfast other than a large mug of tea. About fifty, I pondered, as I waited for him to answer.

'John McClean.'

Where you from, John?' The Bosun asked.

'Stornoway, Mr.Bosun.' Came a very straight reply.

'Okay, John. You and Bertie paint the name on the stern, please and Mr.Kelly will you tend them please? And take the other boy with you.' He pointed at me.

'Aye, Aye, Boas.' Mr.Kelly, probably the most ancient of all the old fogies that were on board the vessel, replied to the Bosun.

'Let's try and get these names painted this morning eh, as we've got stores arriving this afternoon, Okay?'

'Aye Aye, Boas, come on lad let's go and have a look at the job.' Mr Kelly led me by the arm.

There were still four AB's left in the Messroom as we made our way out. Bob (I'd now discovered his last name to be Dewhurst), a thick set very broad forty year old Londoner called Brian Haynes, Mr. Kelly's mate from Belfast John Powell who stood about five foot nothing and looked tragically on his last legs, and probably was after the state I had left him in in the Dominion yesterday evening, and another, thankfully younger, ginger bearded Irishman, George McVie who had been on the 4-8 watch and had been the voice that roused me from my slumber this morning.

George would be assisting the rest of them prepare the stores derricks for this afternoon's stores delivery and had been told by the Bosun to call Ray up for overtime at nine o'clock to assist.

The remainder of the deck crew were made up of a ship's Carpenter, Mick Avery who was forty one and from Worcester and two Geordie pumpmen, Sidney Moon who was 48 and Ronnie Short a year his senior.

Mr. Kelly and Willie waited for Geoff and me to thread our shoelaces and put our boiler suits on in the small decontamination area at the after end of the Messroom by the wooden door leading out to the poop deck.

My shoes, size nines, were a perfect fit and felt especially comfortable. The boiler suit however, despite being a small size, engulfed me. Geoff's medium was a better fit on him but then he was a good six inches taller than I was.

'Let's go for'ad and get some paint off the Bosun.' Mr Kelly instructed as Bertie and John prepared to lower their stage over the stern to access the ship's name they were about to paint.

Geoff and I stepped out and followed Mr. Kelly and Willie along the 'flying bridge', a raised walkway above the maindeck running from aft to forward along the length of the ship from poop deck to Forecastle (fo'c'stle) head.

The maindeck, in contrast to the hull, was painted in a dowdy battleship grey colour with all the superstructures raised from the deck being white. It did not look too impressive with all the streaks of rust running along the maindeck or from the various mushroom ventilation shafts or the Samson posts.

The Bosun was waiting for us in the paint store, situated beneath the fo'c'stle head and leading off from the rope store and accessed through an aft facing storm door on the ship's foremast. He poured Mr.Kelly and Myself a small pot of gloss white paint each and gave us two brand new two inch paint brushes which we took back to the poop deck for Bertie and John to use 'over the side' as Mr. Kelly had so eloquently put it.

As we strolled back along the flying bridge Mr.Kelly explained to me roughly a bit about the lay out of the maindeck (although he had never been on an Anco tanker himself before he had been on several others and the basics were the same).

'There are three pumprooms on here by the looks of it.' He began. Indeed there were three square superstructures at different places along the flying bridge.

'All the steam driven cargo pumps are in these rooms, John.' He continued, 'And they pump the cargo through the ship and out through the manifolds in the middle of the deck here.'

Situated halfway along the length of the maindeck was a 'spaghetti junction' style concoction of pipes leading to either side of the ship, merging from all three pumprooms to form the manifold.

'The shore hoses are connected to the manifold to discharge the cargo as you can see.'

He pointed to the three thick black hoses connected to the port-side manifold.

The banging and clattering of the pipes and the subsequent jerking movements of the shoreside hoses in time with the noise of the pumps confirming that, indeed, the cargo was being discharged.

The two main deck derricks were situated immediately after the manifolds, one either side, with their booms lying across the manifold area itself. The port derrick was raised at the moment but the starboard one was still down.

'We use the derricks to lift the shore hoses on board, John.' Mr.Kelly continued.

I stressed to him that I was familiar with them from sea school.

'The small lids you see dotted around the main deck are tank lids for dropping the tank cleaning 'Butterworth' machines and hoses down. The bigger lids are for us to gain access to the tanks once they have been cleaned.'

'The Bosun said last night that we may have to scrape the coils.' I added. 'How many tanks are there?' I asked.

Mr.Kelly was not too sure but he thought about thirty plus.

'The difference between this type of tanker and the others that I have been on,' He added, 'Is that this is a 'parcel' tanker as opposed to an oil tanker which means that so many different types of cargo be it chemicals or oils can be carried at any one time.

The trick is to be able to discharge them separately and not mix any of them in the process.'

'Dangerous!' I winced.

'Potentially, yes.' Mr.Kelly replied. 'You're sitting on a bomb basically.'

'Thank you.' I replied and made a mental note not to mention this to my Mother.

Bertie and John were waiting for us with their stage rigged over the side by the time we arrived with their paint and climbed over the stern railings and onto the already secured platform on our return.

We waited for them to lower themselves down to the level they required to meet the ship's name before lowering them their paint down on the end of a heaving line.

The name was surprisingly large close up and the job would need to be done in two shifts with ANCO EM and, below that, LIVER being painted in in the first instance and the stage then moved along and re-boarded to complete the PRESS and POOL part of the title afterwards.

The first part of the job was completed by 10 o'clock conveniently for all four of us to take our half-hour 'smoko' smoke break. All of the crew descended on the Messroom for this break to get a cup of tea or coffee and for the smokers amongst us to chain smoke their way through the half hour and generally discuss the day's events.

The second the minute hand clicked on to ten thirty the Bosun shot out of his seat.

'C'mon then lads, lets be having you.' He barked.

Several of the older lads tutted and cursed under their breath.

'We've got a right fucking task master here.' Mr.Kelly's mate John Powell groaned.

'Och! He's not that bad, Paddy!' Mr Kelly retorted.

'He's a fucking slave driver.' the very tired and hungover Paddy replied.

I'd had my smoko with Geoff, Willie and Ray. We had a laugh remembering the events of yesterday afternoon in the Dominion but it seemed unlikely that it would be repeated this afternoon or evening due to the imminent arrival of the ship's stores.

These duly arrived at one o'clock after Bert and John had finished their painting and we had gorged ourselves on a wondrous home made steak and mushroom pie, mashed potatoes, peas and gravy for lunch.

'Have you still got room for that lot after that bloody great big breakfast, eh?' Tony Hunt had shouted at Geoff and me. 'Don't forget there's dinner at five o'clock tonight, eh! Boys. Save some room for that, won't you? Jesus I've never seen anybody eat so much . . . get it down you, eh!'

I humoured him mainly because everyone else, especially the engine room staff, were laughing with him and besides . . . fuck him, I was starving.

At half past one Geoff and Myself, along with Danny and Keith the engine room boys and two of the AB's, Bob Dewhurst and Brian Haynes were detailed to go through the galley and down to the fridge flat to help man handle the catering stores.

The catering staff were all down here as well including the Chief Steward and the new Cook who had finally arrived this morning. The old cook was still on board to help us with the stores and for the next six hours we formed a 'daisy chain' from the closed engine room hatch that each pallet of stores was dropped onto from the stores derricks that the rest of the deck crew were operating, to their various fridge locations.

There was a massive meat freezer room, a fish freezer room, a vegetable room, a dry stores room and a 'cool' room where the cans of beer and soft drinks were kept.

600 cases of 'Tennent's' lager alone were lowered down in six different pallet loads. Fortunately a case dropped whilst being passed from one of the Stewards to the next along the chain and the Chief Steward ordered that it be

opened there and then. So in between unloading one pallet and the arrival of the next we were able to get in a few slurps.

The catering staff all seemed very friendly and jovial, although I wondered if this was always the case when a new crowd joined a ship and everybody was getting to know everybody else. Certainly the taking on of a full supply of four or five month stores went a long way towards bonding the members of the crew.

The new cook had Geoff and me in stitches, describing all the different cuts of meat and various types of vegetables with sexual innuendoes and making the old, outrageously camp Steward, James Crawley from Cowdenbeath, blush with acute embarrassment especially when a box of cucumbers passed through the chain.

Howard David, the cook, was a local lad from Liverpool only about 26, and about my height, 5'5' but fairly stocky with a mass of blond hair.

His sidekick and second chef, Mel, I was already getting on well with after yesterday in the Dominion and the Messman, Arthur, and the other Steward, Simon Parker along with the 2nd Steward, Paul Lake from Edinburgh had all sailed together at some stage in their careers before and seemed to get on well.

The galley boy was Alan Lewin who was also on his first trip to sea. He had been to Gravesend but had been left there for two months already before he could get a ship.

Although he had been there for our first six weeks I could not remember him although he thought he had a slight recollection of Geoff with his blond hair.

We stopped for dinner at half past five but despite Tony's encouragements I could not manage any of the roast pork that was on offer and contented myself with vegetable soup and a roll.

The last pallet of stores was finally stowed at eight o' clock that evening and I couldn't wait to get under the shower.

My limbs ached and as the cook had put it 'You'll have muscles on your muscles by the time today's out.' I didn't doubt it.

As the rest of the deck crowd plonked themselves down in the Messroom 'Paddy' Powell asked in a weary Irish plea, 'Are you going to be opening the bar tonight, Boas?'

To which came the stern reply, 'No, I'm not opening the fucking bar tonight just so that you can get pissed, Paddy.'

Paddy looked up at the Bosun like a little lost boy.

'I can't open the fucking thing even if I wanted to as all the beer is locked away until we leave port.

You'll just have to go over the road again, Paddy.'

'Might just do that.' Paddy replied under his breath.

I went down to my cabin with Geoff and Willie shortly afterwards. I had no intention of going back across to the Dominion again tonight but some of the others did.

I knew I wouldn't be able to go to sleep yet though as, despite being totally knackered from the day's work, I didn't want to miss anything that might be going on.

I wanted to get to know all these people that were to be my 'ship mates' for the next five months.

I was so excited. This is exactly why I had taken this decision almost a year ago now to come to sea.

I was here. I had arrived.

I was knackered but I was loving every minute of my new-found life. I quickly showered and knocked on Geoff's door to see if he was coming up to the bar for a coke. He didn't fancy it and said he may be up later to get a cup of tea.

I went back up to the bar and found the Bosun propping up the bar, as he had yesterday evening, with a large mug of tea.

The Carpenter and Day-shift Pumpman, Ronnie, were in the bar with the Bosun as well as James, the well queer Steward, and a couple of the older donkey greasers.

I felt as if I had stumbled into an old folk's convention but I was quite happy just to sit down and take in what they all had to say for themselves.

'That cheeky paddy bastard only wanted to know if I was opening the bar up tonight.' The Bosun was complaining to the others.

It seemed as if paddy was not alone, however.

'When will you be opening it, Boas?' David 'Dixie' Dean one of the greasers asked.

'We should be leaving here at mid-day tomorrow, all being well.' The Bosun sighed, 'We'll open up tomorrow night if we can but I'm having strict bar hours. Seven o'clock until ten thirty in the evenings and twelve 'til one thirty at lunch times.'

Nobody argued. We had taken on board thirty barrels of Watney's beer, which was stored in the swimming pool for the time being.

'It should work out about 8p a pint.' the Bosun declared.

'We have a swimming pool?' I piped up.

Apparently we did, behind the ship's funnel and about eight-foot square by six feet deep.

'But full of Watney's Red barrel at the moment.' The Bosun laughed.

I stayed up until about ten o'clock but I could feel my eyes getting heavier and heavier as the evening wore on. I said my goodnights, slipped quietly down the stairs to my cabin and climbed gratefully in to my bunk, shattered.

Tomorrow we would leave Liverpool and head out into the Irish Sea and down through the English Channel and across to Rotterdam, tank cleaning on our way and possibly anchoring off Rotterdam to prepare the ship for its next cargo for somewhere in America, the orders weren't quite finalised yet.

'Morning, John. It's seven o'clock. Sailing at ten. Cargo's finished now and the hoses are going ashore at eight.'

'Thanks, George.' I yawned.

I had not locked my cabin door last night and George was able to come in and turn my light on for me to encourage me out of my deep sleep.

I heard George continue knocking the doors down the alleyway with the same wake-up call.

My muscles did indeed ache from yesterday's humping but I decided that another good hearty breakfast should stand me in good stead for whatever lay ahead today. I grimaced my way through Tony's morning onslaught of my breakfast contents. No doubt this was to be a regular ritual so I decided that far from spoil his fun I would just go along with it.

'Part of the wages, Tone.' I told him. 'Said so yourself.'

'Aye, I did that, lad but you'll have worked your way through four months of fucking eggs in no time if you keep this rate up, lad.' He persisted.

'I know why your Mum's sent you to sea, lad, eh? Couldn't afford to feed you. Ha! Ha!'

He was humoured again by his engine room colleagues, which just made him worse.

At eight o'clock on the dot the Bosun rose from his chair, looked around and ordered, 'Cargo hoses to go ashore, eh! Let's go and have a look.'

'Fucking slave driver.' Paddy Powell, obviously the worse for wear after another night at the Dominion, groaned.

I laughed as I once again tagged on to Mr. Kelly and made my way onto the maindeck with the rest of the lads to help send the hoses back ashore using our derrick. The ship was high out of the water now in it's fully discharged state and we would be filling some of the tanks with ballast as we made our way South through the Irish Sea. The weather forecast was good.

Myself and Mr. Kelly operated the inboard guys of the derrick whilst Willie drove the winch, all under the command of the Bosun and the Chief Mate, Frank Pellew, a stocky black-bearded Irishman.

Immediately the last of the hoses were sent ashore the derrick boom was dropped and stowed. We then mucked in with the Pumpman and the Chief Mate to move extremely heavy flexible hoses around the deck in preparation for tank cleaning once clear of the mainland.

'Don't think the fish will mind a bit of sugar in their diet.' The Mate had joked.

We took an early smoko at nine thirty as we waited for the order to haul the accommodation ladder onboard and prepare to depart.

Once again I began to feel quite excited.

It was no mean feat bringing the accommodation ladder back on board. It now hung precariously almost vertically straight up and down on the ship's side and pity any poor bugger that had to carry anything on board up it now.

The Pilot had boarded by means of a Pilot Ladder rigged on the starboard side of the ship, a more conventional way of boarding for him rather than run the risk of scaling the dodgy rig that Ray and Bertie had now descended to remove the stanchions and manropes. Both crawled back up the ladder on all fours and once back on the ship the ladder was hauled back up the ship's side by hand until two bodies were able to pull down on the two remaining guide ropes from onboard and balance it on the ship's handrails. It was then just a matter of hauling it inboard and twelve people, six either side, lifting it up and shoving it unceremoniously on top of the port manifold.

'We'll stow it properly later.' The Bosun barked. 'Let go to stations For' and Aft now.'

I had been detailed to go forward with Mr.Kelly and Ray for my mooring station and Geoff was sent aft with Willie.

It was quite a simple operation and I encountered nothing that I wasn't prepared for from my many lessons on mooring and letting go the ship from sea school.

Once we had made fast the tug that was to assist in pulling us off the jetty we singled our ropes up to one spring and one headrope for'ad. Ray and the other AB's on the fo'c'stle head with me operated the winches and ran the ropes around the various fairleads and 'old men' to the drum ends of the windlasses and I was left to coil down the incoming slack behind me.

With us now singled up to one head rope and one spring the over enthusiastic tug began to try to pull us off the jetty before the order was received to let the two remaining ropes go. When that order was received it was with great bravery that Bob flicked the ropes off the bits as they jumped a good three feet into the air as the slack was fed out.

The Bosun aimed a few choice words at the tug's crew, which basically translated that if they didn't stop pulling he was going to personally ram something rather unsavoury and ill fitting up their arses.

Once enough slack had been let out both ropes were let go from the jetty and dropped into the water. We then recovered the ropes as quickly as possible as the ship began to swing out into the dock.

Coming out of the dock we swung a hard right into the River Mersey and slowly made our way past the cathedrals and out past the New Brighton headland and out into the Irish Sea.

After we had let go of our forward tug the Bosun detailed Myself and Ray down below and into the rope stores as the mooring ropes were sent down to us for stowing at a great rate of knots from above.

'Just pile them anyway and anyhow as they come down, John.' The Bosun had instructed.

'Aye, Aye, Boas.' I replied, not having much choice in the matter as the ropes came down so quickly they almost buried me.

The new plan now for the ship was to sail 200 miles off shore and into the Atlantic Ocean to perform our tank cleaning and then return to Rotterdam to pick up our next cargo of Toluene and Caustic Soda for Montreal in Canada, Peekskill on the Hudson River North of New York and Bayport, Texas, in the Gulf of Mexico.

By the early evening when knocking off time came round all the ropes were stored and all movable items on deck securely lashed down in case of any bad weather.

Everything was prepared to commence the tank cleaning around mid-day tomorrow when we would be clear of the Irish coast. We had long since left Holyhead behind and were now heading well down into Cardigan Bay.

'Will the bar be opening tonight, Boas?' Paddy Powell almost apologetically asked the Bosun as we tucked in to a fantastic Roast Beef dinner at half five in the evening.

'I suppose we might open it, aye.' The Bosun replied with a wry smile.

'But you won't be having any ale, Paddy. The watches will be doubled up until at least the morning and as you're second man on the twelve to four watch you'd better get your fucking head down this evening.'

Paddy's bottom lip looked as if it was going to droop into his dinner.

'Fucking Bastard.' He muttered as he stabbed a roast potato.

I was just about to go for a shower fifteen minutes later, after I had given my Bread and Butter pudding and custard time to settle down, when Tony Hunt and Bill Griggs walked into the Messroom from the poop deck.

Bill was quite excited and announced in his slow Manchester drawl; 'Great big helicopter out there, circling round the ship.'

'They might be dropping the mail to us in a minute, do you think, Bill?' Mr. Kelly added.

Tony then turned to me and Danny, one of the engine room boys.

'Could be the mail, eh? Do you want to go out onto the poop deck and see if they drop anything for us, Danny boy?'

I had no idea as to whether they were telling us the truth or not.

Danny shot out of his chair and made his way to the poop deck through the Messroom and I followed him.

Sure enough a helicopter was circling quite low around us but it had the words 'Coast Guard' written down the side of it and was probably checking that we were not polluting the Irish Sea (we weren't. Not yet anyway).

'I think it's a wind up, Danny.'

'Bollocks, I was looking forward to getting a letter from my girlfriend.' He cursed dejectedly.

'You've only been away from home for two days.' I tried to reason.

Danny laughed. Of course it was a wind up.

We spent the next ten minutes leaning on the handrail letting the cold sea breeze and occasional spray cool us down and discussing our various love lives.

Danny was absolutely besotted with his girlfriend, Sue, who at 19 was three years older than he was. I told him about Jackie but didn't get too carried away as I still wondered if I would hear from her at all although I did plan to write to her over the course of the next couple of days.

We trooped back into the Messroom as darkness descended and particularly as I was shivering by now. It had turned mightily cold outside and I only had a small work shirt on under my boiler suit.

We received a cheer and a round of applause from Tony and Bill and the catering staff who were now eating their own dinner, having made sure that the rest of the ship's complement were suitably stuffed, and had presumably been let in on the little wheeze to fool the gullible first trippers.

'No mail, lads. Eh?' Tony shouted about ten times louder than necessary but to laughs from his audience.

'Yes, there was actually.' I began, as Danny said 'No' at the same time.

'They dropped the sack of mail but missed the poop deck. It's probably about three miles behind us now.'

Tony seemed to like my reply and laughed annoyingly louder.

I had my shower and knocked on Geoff's door to see if he was coming up to the bar for a can of beer. I explained that the Bosun had said that he had got some stock from the Chief Steward but even though it was only eight o'clock Geoff had already elected to have an early night and was about to go to bed.

I walked down to the forward end of our alleyway and knocked on the cabin door that Danny and Keith were sharing. Thankfully they agreed to come up to the bar with me.

'How fucking old are you three?' The Bosun, who rather than propping up the bar with his mug of tea was now perched on a stool behind it guarding the fridge, scowled at us.

'I'll be 18 in about ten weeks.' I replied. Poor Danny and Keith had no such answer; they were both only 16.

After what seemed an eternity, as I was convinced the Bosun was not going to allow us a beer, he smiled.

'It's 12p a can and it's reasonably strong stuff so no getting drunk, OK?'

'OK, cheers Boas. Are you having one?'

I offered him 50p and he sat three cans down in front of us.

'I don't drink anymore on board ship, son. I've seen too much trouble.'

I thanked him and we took our cans of Tennants beer and sat with the engine room crowd and George Mcvie, the only member of the deck crowd in the bar until Mr. Kelly and Paddy walked in.

'Two cans, please. Boas!' Mr Kelly asked.

'Are they both for you, Kelly? He's not having a fucking beer he's on watch at midnight.' He pointed at little Paddy Powell who was by now quite visibly shaking through the lack of alcohol.

Kelly said they were both for him and poured one can and then a small bit of the second one into a pint glass. Paddy shuffled off into the Messroom to make a cup of tea, Mumbling as he went.

'Get your fucking head down.' The Bosun shouted after him, lowering his voice to add 'fucking Irish pisshead.'

'Fuck you.' Paddy barely audibly replied.

The rest of the evening passed so quickly. The catering lads came up to the bar with the exception of Alan, the galley boy, and James who stuck his head round but didn't stay when the Bosun explained to him he hadn't been able to get hold of any gin yet.

'Ok, dear.' James had sighed at the Bosun before mincing through the bar to the Messroom to make a cup of tea.

I couldn't stop laughing, along with Danny and Keith, at him.

'He's only a retired Queen,' Paul the Second Steward informed us.

'Did you see the fucking wig on him?' Tony shouted at the top of his voice. James must have heard him, as there was only a three-quarters pulled curtain separating the two areas to keep the bright lights of the Messroom out of the bar.

'He's got two of them,' Howard, the cook, explained, 'A work wig and one for socialising in.'

Now that he mentioned it his hair did look a little bit longer and a bit more 'ginger' as opposed to grey this evening. I thought it was the light.

He waltzed back through the bar a couple of minutes later going to great lengths to make sure he didn't spill any of his tea onto the deck and trying to counter the slight rocking motion of the ship that I had noticed steadily building up over the last half an hour or so.

'Will you let me know when you can get a bottle of gin, please dear?' He asked the Bosun on the way past.

The Bosun gave him a wink and James tutted.

'Goodnight, Jimmy.' Tony bellowed.

"Night dear.'

James disappeared out through the bar door. I looked at Tony, Tony looked at Mel, the Bosun was smirking and then the whole bar just collapsed into laughter.

'Fucking fruitier than a grocer's shop.' Tony shouted.

'He likes young boys as well so you three had better watch yourselves.' He remarked to me, Keith and Danny.

The Bosun then caught sight of an insect crawling up the bulkhead just over his left shoulder. He flicked a hand at it and stamped on it as it fell to the floor.

'Fucking jaspers.' He scoffed.

'Galley's full of them, Boas.' Howard the cook commented.

'Jaspers?' I asked.

'Fucking cockroaches.' Mel added. 'They'd supposedly survive a nuclear war, the little bastards.'

'I've never seen one before.' I admitted.

'Don't worry, you'll be sick of the sight of them by the time you get off here.' The cook added.

'Here, come with me.' he beckoned, 'there's loads in the galley.'

With that he got up and I followed him through to the galley where he picked up a small cardboard trap, about six inches long, with six or seven of the horrible little things squirming about with their antenna's going nineteen to the dozen and quite clearly in considerable discomfort.

'Just a little bit of sweet smelling poison that attracts them. They stay up here around the galley area in the colder climates but they'll soon start to creep all around the accommodation block as we get down into the tropics and the cabins warm up.

He strategically placed the trap back on the galley floor at the junction of the bulkhead and pointed to five more traps dotted around the galley.

'They can't be the most intelligent of creatures.' He added. 'Despite the fact that there are half a dozen of them in the trap already either dead or dying there'll be at least double that amount in there by tomorrow morning. They wander about at night as they don't like the light.'

I laughed and asked whether or not it really was poison in the traps and not just glue as the Cockroaches seemed pretty well stuck in the trap to me.

We returned to the bar and continued to discuss the creatures. Apparently the ship was fumigated in dry dock six months ago but all that does is kill a good percentage of the 'roaches on the surface but the bigger ones retreat and carry on breeding in the most inaccessible parts of the accommodation block.

'I would imagine that there are hundreds of fully grown adult ones lurking around somewhere up to two and a half inches long.' Mel guessed.

I shuddered.

'They don't need to expose themselves as the little ones get their food for them and take it back to them, a bit like ants.'

'Maybe,' I suggested, 'If they didn't make the poison so sticky the smaller cockroaches would carry that back to the nest or whatever it's called and feed the adults with it.'

'Good suggestion.' Tony nodded. 'Anyway, John are you sure you're not a relation to the jasper family?'

'He fucking certainly eats more than a jasper.' Howard butted in.

'Is that what your initials JC stand for, John? Jasper Cockroach!' The Bosun asked.

The rest of the bar seemed highly amused. It wasn't my fault that I was enjoying the food on board so much.

The Bosun called 'last orders' at dead on half past ten.

I couldn't believe the evening had passed so quickly.

Mr Kelly tried to get two cans of beer at half past but the Bosun would only allow him one and made him pour it whilst he was still there rather than take it down to his cabin.

'No cabin drinking on board this ship, Kelly.' He firmly snapped. 'It'll do that fucking matey boy of yours a bit of good to have a couple of days off the beer.'

Mr Kelly didn't acknowledge him but returned to his seat with his drink.

I went to bed soon afterwards. I was totally shattered. What with lugging those hoses around on deck all afternoon and a few beers to follow in the evening I was ready for sleep.

I got the feeling as I lay in bed that I was in for a good first trip.

I was starting to get to know all the different people now and beginning to enjoy their company. Tony was by far and away the loudest but also the most humorous of them all and although the Bosun was overpoweringly strict I felt he had his reasonable side as well.

I was beginning to realise just how tough a job his must be in keeping a crew of this size under control.

George's Irish tones were once again ringing in my ears no sooner than it seemed that my head had just hit the pillow.

'Morning, Jasper Caswell! It's seven o'clock.'

I rubbed my eyes wondering, briefly, what he was on about.

Then it came back to me, the cockroach conversation last night.

It didn't get any better at the breakfast hatch later on either.

'Eh, Chef! There's a cockroach at the hatch wanting a full breakfast.' Boomed Tony to everyone's delight.

'We'll have to sprinkle some poison on it, that'll get rid of it.' Howard replied.

'No good,' I countered, 'We can survive a nuclear holocaust . . . allegedly.'

I joined in the banter over the breakfast table. No point in resisting, I thought. Besides it was all good humoured and I liked to think it was helping me get myself respected with the other members of the crew.

Geoff was being very quiet and keeping himself to himself and I wondered if he may find himself getting left behind a little as the trip progressed as a result of his possible shyness. Even at this early stage he was not being included in conversations be they work related or otherwise and I felt he should be opening up a little.

I'd have a word later today, I thought.

The plan for the morning was to rig twelve tank cleaning machines into four different tanks in preparation for the tank cleaning programme which was to begin after mid-day despite the fact that we were nowhere near to being 200 miles off the coast of Southern Ireland yet.

The programme could begin providing we transferred all our dirty water into ballast 'slop' tanks until such time as we could adopt the much preferred method: A spool rigged from the manifold leading directly over the ship's side for depositing the waste gunge directly into the Atlantic Ocean.

The cleaning of the tanks itself was quite a simple process. The lugging about of the pure brass 'Butterworth' tank cleaning machines and their accompanying ninety feet of stout rubber hose, amongst all the obstacles that the main deck can offer up, not so. The Butterworth machine itself is roughly eighteen inches long but weighs an absolute ton. It is coupled to one end of the hose which, in turn, is coupled at the other end to a high-pressured Butterworth line which runs underneath the flying bridge. The water is blasted through the line by means of a Butterworth pump in the engine room and the water can be heated (if desired) to a temperature of between 150 and 180 degrees Fahrenheit by means of a Butterworth heater situated in the top of the after pumproom.

The machines are first lowered down through the main tank lid, a raised oval shaped section of about three feet above deck level to allow access to the ladder down into the tank itself, and through various Butterworth plates dotted around the maindeck purely for the purpose of introducing the cleaning machines into the tanks.

The tanks are washed at three levels. At first the machines are rigged into the tank at a ten-foot depth and roped off at any convenient nearby strong point to maintain the depth for the first hour or for however long the tank is to be washed for.

The hoses are then lowered to twenty feet for another hour and then to thirty-five feet for the final hour of the wash.

Once under high pressure the Butterworth machines will rotate horizontally whilst the three pronged jet-ends that the water shoots out from will rotate at the same time in a vertical plane thus, theoretically, reaching and blasting clean all areas of the tank.

With the watches having been 'singled up' at eight o'clock there seemed to be hundreds of us preparing to go out onto the maindeck to start rigging for the wash programme, for which the Bosun had knowledge of and a list of the order they were to be cleaned in but for some reason was keeping it a closely guarded secret from the rest of us.

It was murky and grey outside and although not raining the sea mist and slight spray deemed it necessary for us to don our wellies, oilskins and sou'wester for the trip out onto the maindeck.

As the ship only possessed twelve Butterworth machines we were limited as to how far ahead we could rig but we set about passing the Butterworth hoses off the top of the after pumproom and down onto the maindeck whilst Mr. Kelly was detailed by the Bosun to the stores to fetch the Butterworth connections and the Butterworth spanners.

'Butterworth fucking this, Butterworth fucking that.' Paddy Powell muttered to me with a smirk as we pulled on the ninety-foot lengths of hose.

I had to smile. The poor bloke had been a good forty eight hours without a beer now and he looked absolutely shocking. He seemed lost in his set of oilskins, which were miles too big for him, as indeed I must have done in my set.

I watched, along with Geoff, as the more experienced hands connected all the fittings together and lowered the machines to the required depth before tying them off and responded immediately to any request to 'pull a bit of slack through' or 'pass me that spanner' that came my way from them.

By ten o'clock smoko the job was ready.

The whole programme would last at least two days and would be continual round the clock.

The Bosun asked at smoko for volunteers to work the night shift: Seven in the evening until seven in the morning. Bob Dewhurst would be in charge of the shift along with Sid, the Pumpman and both Des and Wayvell, the Guyanese E.D.H's along with Brian Haynes volunteered.

'Okay, we need one more volunteer.' The Bosun asked.

'Paddy?'

Paddy looked mortified.

'Oh! Boas,' He whimpered. 'Sure I'm not too keen on doing the night shift.' He protested.

'Okay, Paddy. You join up with Bob and the lads at seven this evening then. You've just done two nights on the 12 to 4 watch so it shouldn't take you too much time to adjust.'

Paddy was speechless. Except for a disbelieving 'Bastard!' muttered under his breath.

I thought the poor bloke was going to break down and cry. He could see his potential drinking session in the bar this evening disappearing in front of his very eyes.

'I don't think much to this fucking Bosun, John.' Mr. Kelly confided in me as we jobbed around tidying up the deck before lunch prior to the tank cleaning.

'He seems Okay to me.' I admitted. 'A bit strict I suppose'

'A bit!' Mr.Kelly exclaimed. 'Poor John needs a beer and he's going out of his way to make sure he doesn't get one. He's a bully if you ask me.'

I couldn't agree. I was in no position to want to take sides in any potential arguments and told Mr.Kelly so.

Any fears of unrest were soon settled at lunchtime anyway as the Bosun opened the bar up between twelve and half past one.

I had an idea that Paddy had not been expecting it and his face was a picture as he poured his cans of Tennants into a pint glass, particularly as the Bosun had turned the tables and this time refused Mr.Kelly a beer.

'You're tank cleaning this afternoon, Kelly.' He barked. 'You can have your beer tonight.'

Paddy was still perched at the bar when we turned to again at one o'clock in the afternoon. He hadn't moved and had refused any offers of food from Arthur the Messman preferring to just sit and constantly sup ale.

'The cook's locking the bar up at half past one, Paddy.' The Bosun warned him on our way back out on deck. 'Make sure you get yourself to bed.'

'Aye! Aye! Thank you Mr. Bosun, Sir,' Paddy sarcastically slurred.

The tank washing on number nine centre tank, one of the biggest on the ship with a capacity to hold over 3,000 tonnes of cargo, had begun at mid-day and our first task at one o'clock was to lower the four machines down to twenty feet. This was achieved easily by slackening off the rope around the hose and feeding the slack through until the painted twenty-foot marker reached the Butterworth lid.

I did two of the drops with Mr.Kelly whilst Geoff did the other two with the Bosun. Albert Wills and John McLean went forward to drop the machines on number four starboard tank that was also washing at the same time.

Ray, who I hadn't seen much of since the first day due to his being on the 12 to 4 watch, had also joined us on deck.

Although the morning mist had disappeared and the sun was beginning to shine through, occasional spray from the choppy sea had forced me to decide to keep my oilskins on for the afternoon. Ray had been much braver and had elected to work in just his boiler suit, a move he regretted as a huge wall of spray engulfed him on the next set of drops sending him scurrying to the safety of beneath the flying bridge and leaving Albert to complete the task much to the amusement of myself and the Bosun watching from the sanctuary of the flying bridge.

We took an early afternoon smoko in preparation for the tanks finishing their wash before the fun started in moving the machines and hoses to the next tanks on the Bosun's master tank cleaning plan.

Once the tanks had completed their three hours worth of wash time two other tanks previously rigged were started up and the others shut off.

To say that the task of pulling the machines out of the tanks was backbreaking would be an understatement.

Ray, John and Albert seemed to have it down to a fine art though and Geoff didn't do too badly, as he was decidedly larger in size than I was. Still, I gave it a go but the combination of the weight I was attempting to pull out of the tank coupled with the red hot heat coming from the hose meant that I had to take two breathers along the way.

I received a generous round of applause from the rest of the lads and the Bosun, who was keeping well out of the way on the flying bridge, as I finally pulled the Butterworth machine out onto the deck and very nearly collapsed with exhaustion.

'Right, let's get these machines moved in to number 11 port tank ready for the night shift.' The Bosun ordered as he made his way onto the maindeck armed with his Butterworth spanners.

With the next set of tanks rigged we could relax for a couple of hours with just the drops to perform on the machines on the hour but as they would finish at six o'clock another round of humping was due in the final hour of our shift.

I was knackered again by the time we had finished for the day and just sat in my cabin on my daybed for half an hour, still in my dirty boiler suit, trying to catch my breath.

Geoff was already getting a shower as I went into the washroom, hung my towel up, and turned on the shower next to him.

'Coming up for a beer later on, Geoff?' I shouted through his shower curtain.

Geoff's head popped out from behind the curtain, shampoo racing down his face as he rubbed his eyes frantically to see who was shouting at him.

'I think I just might. I could murder one.' He replied.

I was surprised. I was about to have a word with him that he should try and get to know some of the other crew members a bit more but didn't need to now.

We went up to the bar at eight o'clock. The Bosun had already unlocked the fridge at seven as he passed through the bar on his way to his cabin, which was on the same deck.

The engine room and catering staff were eagerly awaiting to commence their evening session by then.

It was mine and Geoff's intention to only stay for an hour but, as last night had, the evening just flew by and before we knew it the Bosun was calling last orders.

'Come on, Jasper.' He barked at me. 'Get yourself away to fucking bed. You've got twelve hours tank cleaning ahead of you tomorrow.'

I groaned at the prospect but Geoff and I quickly finished our cans, neither of us at all sure yet whether the Bosun was being serious or not, but not wanting to upset him enough to find out.

I was out like a light again as soon as my head hit the pillow but this time I was suddenly awoken by a loud rapping on the door and Mr.Kelly barging into my room and turning the lights on.

'Quick, Jasper. The Bosun wants you to help us on deck.'

I rubbed my eyes. I didn't have a clue what he was on about.

'What!'

'The Bosun wants us to go on deck and lash some bottles down; it's going to get rough during the night.'

I didn't for one minute twig that we already had a night shift on deck that could quite easily perform the task that Mr.Kelly was getting so excited about.

'I'll see you in the Messroom in five minutes.' He said as he closed my cabin door and hurried away.

I looked at my watch. It was half past midnight. I stumbled round my cabin and put on my jeans, shirt, thick jumper as it was the middle of the night and, I suspected, cold and wet outside, my boiler suit on top of all that and collected my oilskins from my locker in the washroom area before making my way up to meet Mr.Kelly in the Messroom.

The bar was deserted as I sleepily opened the door at the top of the stairs but as I opened the curtain leading to the Messroom, Mr. Kelly and the rest of the night shift let out an almighty cheer to greet me.

'Mel is in the galley cooking the night shift supper and we wondered if you wanted some, Lar.' Bob Dewhurst laughed.

'I told them you'd be upset if you missed out, eh!' Tony Hunt butted in from the corner of the room.

Neither he nor Mr Kelly had gone to bed yet and by the looks of it had only just finished the beers they had got at last orders.

Mel came out of the galley with two big plates of bacon, eggs, sausage, chips, tomatoes and fried bread for Bob and Paddy. Des and Wayvell were already tucking into theirs.

'What's up, Jasper?' Mel called to me. 'Did the smell of the food wake you up? Do you want a supper?'

I was beginning to wake up now and, not wishing to disappoint anyone, agreed to a mega fry-up.

Mr.Kelly and Tony watched in disbelief as I scoffed the lot, thanked Mel, washed my plate and said goodnight to the lads on nights before promptly going back down to my cabin.

The next day was equally as tiring with the continual lugging about of the machines and hoses on the deck from tank to tank. The end of the hose being dragged inevitably catching and jamming up on every conceivable pipe or deck fitting that we had to manoeuvre our way around.

The only bright spot of the day being the stand up argument in the Messroom just after breakfast between the Bosun and Paddy when the Bosun refused to let him have two cans of beer to take to his cabin for a night-cap.

Paddy got round it by going to bed and setting his alarm for a quarter to twelve and coming up to the bar for a lunchtime session (something I presume he already had planned regardless as to whether the Bosun gave him a couple of cans or not at seven in the morning).

By early afternoon the next day all the tank cleaning had finished and we were to make our way through the English Channel and on up to Rotterdam, or Vlaardingen as our noon position sheet on the Messroom notice board was telling us.

There was still plenty of work to do to bring the tanks up to scratch and in a pristine enough condition to accept the new cargo that we were to take on board and this was carried out during our two days heading back towards Rotterdam and our two days at anchor awaiting our berth.

Neither cargo required the tanks to be absolutely spotless, but the less trace of Molasses remaining in the tanks the better the chances of the inspectors passing the holds fit to carry the liquids at the first time of asking.

The Toluene, bound for Montreal and Peekskill, was just a solution made from petroleum and coal tar used as a solvent and in dyes and, worryingly, in explosives. This made up three-quarters of our cargo. The rest was of Caustic Soda, neat liquid Sodium Hydroxide, used in various detergents and soaps as well as in the manufacture of paper and aluminium and bound for Bayport in the Houston area of Texas.

The remaining water at the bottom of the tanks that the pumps could not remove after their Butterworth machine wash had to be removed manually either by scooping up into a bucket or by an ingenious contraption called an 'Educter.'

An Educter consisted of two small hoses being lowered down the tank with a small machine attached which, when high pressure water was sent through it created a vacuum thus allowing a smaller hose to be attached as a suction hose to suck up all the remaining water without the need to manually pull twenty or thirty full buckets of water the thirty five feet out of the tank.

Once the water had been baled out one way or another it was just a matter of wiping the bottom of the tanks dry, sometimes just with mops but some necessitated the use of a portable fan which rested on top of one of the Butterworth lid holes and was once again propelled by high water pressure.

Some of the tanks would also need sweeping out as rust and scale would have been knocked down from the tank's bulkheads during the Butterworth wash.

Half of the ship's tanks were coated in epoxy paint that quite regularly blistered especially after carrying a heated cargo such as Molasses. The rest were zinc coated and tended to need less sweeping although for some reason some of the heating coils on these tanks must have been turned up too high in transit and the Molasses had baked onto the underside of the coils. These ran about three inches off the deck along the bottom of the tanks and it was a case of go down on your hands and knees with a scraper and scrape it all off, sweeping up as you went.

I had to admit that the last few days had worn me out considerably.

The physical side of the work was still something I was coming to terms with but there were enough people on board prepared to make allowances for my slender build and help me out until my muscles developed a bit.

'We'll get you in the ship's gymnasium once we leave Rotterdam, Lar.' Bob Dewhurst had threatened.

Howard and Mel in the galley also said they would 'beef' me up although I needed little encouragement to eat three meals a day.

I was called at six o'clock the following morning. We had 'weighed' anchor half an hour ago and were now approaching the entrance to Rotterdam harbour.

Forward and after berthing stations would be in half an hour's time.

I made Myself a quick cup of coffee and went out onto the poop deck to watch as we slowly glided past several fully laden coal barges and a couple of small coastal tankers.

Dawn was just beginning to break although the murkiness of the atmosphere with its limited visibility confirmed that there was unlikely to be any sun this morning. It was also damn cold and I went back inside to put my parker jacket on before proceeding forward to take the tugs that would assist us alongside.

We made fast two tugs on the fo'c'stle head as we passed four giant BP holding tanks on our port side belonging to their massive refinery positioned at the harbour entrance.

We stood back from the tugs as they began to pull us round to starboard, the tug wires singing and cracking at the strain they were put under almost causing them to snap.

'They'll have you in two if they go, Jasper.' The Bosun offered as a word of caution.

I had no intention of finding out and stood behind the foremast looking back down the maindeck as the darkness slowly turned into a mizzly grey.

Once around the first corner and with the strain now taken off the tugs we could prepare our ropes for berthing.

Vlaardingen East's three wooden jetties jutted out slightly from the causeway that accommodated the small refinery and group of tanks that made up the complex. A Stolt tanker, roughly the same size as our ship, occupied the first jetty and we slowly cruised by a coastal tanker before coming to rest some hundred feet out from the third jetty.

As we were to go alongside the jetty 'port side to' the port tug was released and it shot round our bows to our starboard side to assist the other tug, plus the two from the after end, in pushing us alongside.

As we came close enough to the jetty Mr. Kelly threw a heaving line onto the quay, almost taking one of the dock worker's head off in the process. Two ropes, one head rope and a spring, were sent out from different fairleads on the heaving line and as soon as they were placed over their respective bollards on the jetty we began to pick up the slack. Together with the tug's pushing and our own heaving on the ropes we were soon alongside.

The heaving line was thrown back on board and we sent the remainder of our ropes ashore to secure the ship in position for the duration.

By the time we had rigged and sent the accommodation ladder ashore and topped the port derrick to lift the shore cargo hoses on board I was more than ready for my breakfast. It was gone half past eight.

The rest of the morning was spent following the tank inspectors around and mopping up any last remnants of water or scale that they may have found down the tanks that were to be loaded here.

With all the tanks passed we could begin to take on board our 26,000 tons of toluene (did somebody say it was explosive?)

We would be on this berth for at least 36 hours before hopping across to another terminal a bit nearer central Rotterdam to load the caustic.

Mail did arrive at lunchtime courtesy of the ship's Agent and via the Chief Steward. I received two letters from my Mother with all the up-to-date Evening Telegraph clippings about how well the Poppies weren't doing. Wimbledon were surprisingly storming the league this season and we were just above mid-table amid speculation that our manager, Ron Atkinson, was about to move into the football league without Kettering Town.

I also received a postcard from Herne Bay from Jackie.

'Dear John. Have taken a late summer holiday in Herne Bay for a week with my parents. A bit cold but sunny nevertheless. Hope you are getting on ok. Love Jack xxx.'

No letter then, I thought. Ah well, never mind, I'm sure she will write once she gets mine if she already hasn't done so.

Ray had been to Vlaardingen before and knew of a good disco in town just a short journey away on the local train service.

Peanut

That evening Geoff, Danny, Keith, Willy and I accompanied him up the road to check it out.

I had ordered myself £25 worth of Dutch Guilders from the Chief Steward. It wasn't worth getting any more as we were not going to be staying that long but Ray had warned that the drinks were expensive and a pint of Stella could work out around £1.50 (And to think we were mortified by a pound a pint in London not so long ago).

Ray was an excellent mover on the dance floor and put the rest of us, with the exception of Danny, well to shame. He was brazenly able to walk over to the local Dutch girls and join in with them as they responded and spoke to him in pigeon English.

Geoff and I just hogged the bar and could only watch on in envy.

'Come on, Jasp. Get up here and get moving.' Ray, having the time of his life, beckoned.

I did venture onto the dance floor but had improved very little since my Windmill days whilst still at school.

We left at one in the morning, Ray snogging every single female he had boogied with and the rest of us just offering a pathetic wave to the locals that had endeared themselves to us during the evening as we left.

Once on the train station platform just a few hundred yards away Ray flashed a packet of Peter Stuyvesant cigarettes. Geoff took one and thanked him.

'Geoff?' I queried. 'You don't smoke. Come to that neither do you, Ray.'

'I do when I'm having a drink.' Ray admitted. 'I haven't had one since the Dominion, but then again I've not had a drink since then. I just bought these tonight.'

Geoff was the same, only he reckoned he hadn't had a cigarette for over six months.

'Try one, Jasp.' Ray urged. 'One's not going to harm you. You must have had a sneaky drag at one stage in your life.'

I had to admit that I hadn't, although it wasn't for the lack of opportunity.

Malc had smoked for the past couple of years with his parents' blessing and many of the other lads I hung about with had dabbled with the 'weed'.

I am sure that subconsciously listening to my Father cough up half a lung and then depositing a bowl full of phlegm down the toilet pan every morning from as long ago as I can care to remember had put me off in the past but here I was relatively pissed and for some reason finding Myself accepting the stick.

Ray lit it and I immediately breathed out before I had even attempted to breathe anything in.

I still spluttered at that!

'Inhale it then.' Ray laughed as Goff and Danny looked on and demonstrated by inhaling deep for a good five seconds and letting the smoke pour out of his mouth and nose.

I took another drag and this time felt the smoke hit the back of my throat.

I spluttered again but immediately felt light-headed as the nicotine rush took immediate effect.

I took two more puffs before our train arrived and we had to extinguish them.

'It compliments the alcohol, don't you think?' Ray asked as I flopped down in my carriage seat and we sped off on the five-minute journey back to the Vlaardingen East train station.

My head was now buzzing.

'They're OK as long as you don't become addicted.' Ray summarised.

I cannot remember climbing the accommodation ladder back on board but do remember the eerie silence of the ship with only it's generators now running as opposed to the constant noise of the engine at sea as I made a not-too-successful attempt to brush my teeth before falling into my bunk.

My head span again as it hit the pillow but thankfully sleep came before the nausea took over.

The ship remained alongside for the next evening as well but we chose not to go back ashore.

The next berth that we were to go to would not become available until after mid-night and was almost an hour away so, with the ship's bar not being open whilst alongside, I decided that as I had spent most of the day recovering from the exploits of the previous evening I would tuck Myself up in bed nice and early.

It proved a wise decision as we were called at one o'clock in the morning to 'let go' the ship at one thirty.

The engine room crowd and the catering staff had all been ashore but none of the deck crowd had bothered, a fact that obviously pleased the Bosun as he had a sober crew to work with.

The 'let go' was completed on the fo'c'stle head under a bright spotlight beaming down upon us from the fore mast. Once the ropes were back on board and the tug made fast we were plunged into darkness as the light was extinguished, without warning, from the bridge deck.

We slipped silently through the black water with just the occasional turning over of the ship's engine to provide any sort of clue that we were progressing under our own steam, passing several cargo jetties and refineries along the way aglow with lights and flames.

Our forward tug accompanied us for the duration of our 'shift ship' procedure therefore we were required to stay on the fo'c'stle head for the entire time with no respite from the elements, unlike those stationed aft that could nip in to the Messroom for a quick cup of coffee or a fag.

It was decidedly chilly to say the least at this godforsaken hour of the morning and by the time we had tied up at our 'town' berth in Rotterdam it was almost four o'clock.

We had berthed starboard side alongside at this jetty, which meant switching the accommodation ladder over from the port side. It is not the easiest of things in the World to handle at the best of times but at four o'clock in the morning and with all hands tired it became a serious test of patience and required no small amount of luck.

Other than lifting the beast up onto the flying bridge by the use of the ship's derricks there was only one possible place that it could be manhandled and passed through all the pipes and obstacles which ran along the middle of the main deck to feed it from one side of the ship to the other.

The Bosun chose this option to many of the older hands annoyance and I could see why.

Once halfway between sides the operation became much less co-ordinated especially in the semi darkness with only the main deck lights to work under.

The front end of the ladder needed to be lifted up to clear number seven centre tank lids but this didn't stop those at the other end of the ladder giving it a shove and jamming Willy's hand in the process.

Willy let out an almighty 'Bastard!' as he flung his glove to the deck and grabbed his wrist, shaking the injured hand.

'Don't fucking push until I tell you.' The Bosun screamed from the starboard side as he tried to get everyone lifting and pulling in unison.

Once clear of the underneath of the flying bridge it was a piece of cake to run the ladder over the ship's side and control it's descent to the jetty with the aid of the two guide ropes. I was brave and this time descended the unrigged ladder with Bob to put the stanchions in and pass the manropes through.

Willy's hand had come up like a balloon and the Chief Steward had to be called from his bed to attend to it (the Chief Steward also doubling as the ship's doctor, although I personally wouldn't want to place too much confidence in Bill Merry, a sixty year old, red faced, doddering alcoholic, in any time of personal discomfort).

I had witnessed my first shipboard accident and Willy returned from the doctors in Rotterdam the next day with his arm in a sling and fourteen days light duties.

The Chaplain from the 'Flying Angel' in Rotterdam came on board in the afternoon to exchange a box of books for the ship's Library. As Geoff and I had a few Guilders left between us we decided to go along and visit the club in the evening. I thought it would be a bit of a novelty in that we could get a beer in this one and not be under the constraints that were bestowed upon us at the Gravesend version of the club.

Ray came along as well and I quite enjoyed the evening playing table tennis, snooker and table football, drinking beer and for some inexplicable reason finishing off Ray's packet of Peter Stuyvessant.

The club closed at eleven and we took a slow ten-minute walk back to the ship after using up the remainder of our loose change on chocolate bars and sweets for the ten-day trip across to Montreal.

Once again my night's sleep was disturbed as we were called at five thirty in the morning for a six o'clock departure, now fully loaded, from Rotterdam.

This time the weather was not kind for us and it was pouring with rain as we let go from our berth.

At least I was becoming more familiar with proceedings on the fo'c'stle head and now tended to work with both Ray and Mr. Kelly when bringing in the ropes rather than running around like a headless chicken trying to be as helpful as possible but more often than not getting in people's way.

Once again I went down below to stow the ropes for our voyage and we arrived back into the Messroom, all tugs gone and ropes stowed and heading out of the harbour breakwater just in time for breakfast.

Boy was I looking forward to it.

We spent the rest of the day on deck stowing every piece of loose equipment that could be found in case of bad weather during the crossing. If it couldn't be stowed it was severely lashed down on top of the pumprooms or along the aisles of the poop deck running alongside the accommodation block.

All the Butterworth machines were stripped from their hoses. The hoses stowed in the top of the after pumproom and the machines stowed in the midship deck locker for greasing and overhauling whilst we made our passage.

Any work on deck after today, once we had cleared the English Channel, was at the mercy of the elements although the immediate forecast had not been too bad and we wouldn't exactly be heading any further North, the Bay of St.Lawrence being virtually on the same line of latitude as the English Channel.

The Chief Steward bought the ship's bond book down to the Messroom at lunchtime.

The ship's bond being like its supermarket where we could all purchase our individual requirements from shaving foam to cigarettes. The Bosun had left strict instructions, however, that no bottles of wines or spirits were to be purchased through the bond and that alcohol could only be bought through him via the crew bar.

Understandable I suppose, as a bottle of 'Four Bells' Navy rum was only 85p. and the Bosun assumed, quite logically I suppose, that cabin drinking would be encouraged at that price but not so easy for him to monitor.

The Bosun also tried to justify this state of affairs by saying that any profit made through the bar would go to free booze during the Christmas period and to that end nobody argued.

I ordered some toothpaste, writing paper and envelopes, a bottle each of Schweppes orange, blackcurrant and lime cordial, a tin of boiled sweets and 200 Embassy . . . . . I was hooked.

The crew bar was full that evening with everybody seemingly celebrating the fact that we had left the Coast of Europe and were now heading off on our trip in earnest.

The Bosun had filled the five optics behind the bar with Four Bells Rum, Vodka, Bacardi, Gordons Gin and Grouse Whisky. All at 10p a double shot.

James was delighted that the Gin had appeared and joined the growing throng at about eight thirty, going to great lengths to add half a bucket of ice to his double gin in a tall glass, topping it up with tonic water and then disappearing into the galley for well over five minutes before returning with a plate full of delicately sliced fresh lemon. He added a slice to his drink before putting the rest away in the fridge, touching the Bosun's leg as he gluided past.

'I didn't think you cared, James.' The Bosun smirked as James brushed past him again (well, he was rather in the way as there was hardly enough room for more than one person behind the bar).

'You should be so lucky!' James tutted as he made his way over to a spare seat right between Myself and Tony Hunt, mixing his drink with a plastic swizzle stick as he came over.

'Mind if I join you girls?' He asked as he placed the drink down next to me.

'Eh, do you want an umbrella in that concoction, James or what?' Tony bellowed as James brushed fag ash from where he was about to park himself.

'Fucking hell it'll be closing time before you get to drink it, it's only a bevvy not a work of fucking art.'

James just smiled at him and sipped his gin, letting out a huge sigh of pure pleasure as it hit his taste buds.

'Goood evening, Jasper.' He turned to me, totally ignoring Tony, smiled, and in his soft, broad effeminate Scottish Brogue added, 'So coarse isn't he?'

I laughed.

The bar heaved for the rest of the evening and it was standing room only by nine o'clock.

Of the 27-crew members only Willy, who was on watch, Ray, who was on the twelve to four watch and asleep and the two Guyanese lads Des and Wayvell were not in the bar.

As well as the Bosun that remained teatotal, Bill Griggs from the engine room crowd nursed a large mug of tea for his hour in the bar and John McClean only had one glass of beer before departing early to his cabin.

Billy Griggs seemed a weird sort of character. He had been ashore in Rotterdam but not with the rest of the crowd, always preferring to go alone. He was married to a Philippine girl half his age and had a six-year-old son. Although hailing from Manchester he now lived in Manila. He was also totally obsessed with the SS.

Strange bloke, I thought, despite the fact that he was very humorous and didn't need any alcohol to come out of his shell.

Plenty was arranged during the evening for the coming week and although the bar was full with different sections talking at the same time Tony could still make himself heard over and above everybody else and seemed to have proclaimed himself as the crew bar's entertainment's Officer.

'Shall we have a movie tomorrow night, eh?' He had shouted across at the Bosun.

Apparently we had a projector on board with a choice of six films.

Tony said he would find out what night the Officers wanted their movie night to be on and that we would arrange ours accordingly. Tomorrow night if possible.

'I don't want you interfering with me either, James, when the lights go down, eh?'

Tony suggestively cautioned James to the delight of his fellow engine room crowd.

James looked up at the ceiling in disgust and adjusted his wig.

'I don't think so, dear.' He shrugged back.

As the evening wore on Mick Avery, the Carpenter, disappeared to his cabin for five minutes and returned, to a rapturous cheer, with a small piano accordion.

The next hour was just a complete hoot and a cacophony of tuneless noise as we were subjected to various renditions of 'Oh! Maggie Maggie May they have taken her away and I'll never walk down Lime Street anymore (Anymore!), It's not the leaving of Liverpool that grieves me, but my darling when I think of you'.

'In my Liverpool home' (something about a couple of cathedrals!), and so many others that I had never heard of before but all sung with a passion.

To break the Liverpool theme that Tony, Albert, Bob, Howard the Cook and several others were monopolising David Dean, one of the other middle-aged Donkey Greasers weighed in with a couple of chirpy Cockney ditties, 'The Lambeth walk' and 'There's an old mill by the stream, Dixie Dean' (he had insisted on being known as 'Dixie' from day one on board).

Even the Bosun was smiling from behind the bar as we all attempted to join in the sing-a-long and clapped our hands in time to the singing and the music.

The Bosun must have been enjoying himself, as it was five to eleven before he called last orders at the bar.

Such a shame as I had never felt better in my entire life and could have carried on partying for hours to come yet. And so, judging by the looks of contentment on the faces around me, could everybody else.

'I know, I know.' The Bosun apologised. 'But we've all got a job to do tomorrow.'

We all took another can of Tennents out of the fridge and many of the older hands ordered themselves a neat double chaser as well in an attempt to drag the evening out.

The Bosun seemed happy to do this before firmly snapping the padlock shut on the fridge door and removing the bottles from the optics (the Rum and Whisky had been emptied anyway).

Danny had attempted to get a Vodka out of the Bosun before he closed the bar but had been bluntly refused.

'You're not even old enough to be drinking fucking beer.' The Bosun had curtly answered him. Me and Geoff decided not to even bother asking.

With the Bosun out of the way along with several of the other 'lightweights' in drinking terms as Tony had put it, Mick announced that he would play his accordion on a 'one singer, one song' basis.

The younger ones amongst us reneged but we sat and endured more re-runs of what had gone before plus a heart wrenching duet from Mr. Kelly and Paddy Powell of 'Danny Boy' made all the more hilarious by the fact that neither could hardly stand up with just the slightest rocking motion from the ship sending them both wobbling towards the Messroom with their arms around each others shoulders as they crooned.

As midnight drew ever closer Mick ended the session and sent us to bed with the classic 'Lobster Song' ringing in our ears.

'Right, all join in with the chorus. You'll know it after the first time of hearing it.' He announced as he primed the accordion into the key of 'D.'

'Oh, Please Mr. Fisherman, Fisherman please,

Have you a lobster you can sell to me? Singing.

Ro-tiddley-oh. Shit or bust. Never let your bollocks dangle in the dust.

Yes, Says the fisherman, I've got two,
And the biggest of the bastards I will sell to you, singing.'
(To a man we all join in).
'*Ro-tiddley-oh, Shit or bust,*
Never let your bollocks dangle in the dust.

Well I took the lobster home, and I couldn't find a dish,
So I put it in the place where the missus used to piss, singing.
Ro-tiddley-oh, shit or bust,
Never let your bollocks dangle in the dust.

Early next morning, the missus gave a grunt,
She was running round the room with a lobster up her cunt, singing.
Ro-tiddley-oh, shit or bust,
Never let your bollocks dangle in the dust.

The missus grabbed a brush, I grabbed a broom,
And we chased the fucking lobster all around the room singing.
Ro-tiddley-oh, shit or bust,
Never let your bollocks dangle in the dust.

Well we hit it on the head and we hit it on the side,
We hit the fucking lobster till the bastard died singing.
Ro-tiddley-oh, shit or bust,
Never let your bollocks dangle in the dust.

There's a moral to my story. And it is this;
Always have a shufty before you have a piss, singing.
Ro-tiddley-oh, shit or bust,
Never let your bollocks dangle in the dust.

That's the end of my story, there isn't any more,
There's an apple up me arse and you can have the core, singing.
Ro-tiddley-oh, shit or bust,
(And to a slow, rising crescendo),
Never let your bollocks . . dangle . . . innn . . . theeee . . . duuuuuust!!'

Mick rounded off with a loud burst of notes as everyone applauded their own efforts to keep up with the chorus.

It was now well gone midnight but despite the amount of beer I had consumed I still found it hard to fall asleep, the adrenaline still pumping from a fantastic evening.

Sleep obviously had taken over me eventually because after what had once again only seemed like twenty minutes later my light was being switched on and a ginger bearded, red faced Irishman was peering into my face.

'Ro-tiddley fucking-oh, Jasper. It's seven o'clock.' George announced (how on Earth had he managed to do the 4-8 watch considering the state he was in at mid-night)?

Oh! My frigging head!

I coughed and spluttered as I tried to arouse myself. Only becoming aware now that I must have smoked about twenty cigarettes last night.

I crossed the alleyway in my underpants, had a piss for about five minutes solid, coughing and swaying as I went, flopped back onto my bunk and sat there with my head in my hands.

I lit my first fag of the day.

I couldn't face a full breakfast, much to the delight of Tony, electing for just a slice of toast and marmalade to go with my coffee.

It was grey and misty outside and although not raining as such the air and the sea combined to give the effect of drizzle. Visibility was poor and due to the rough weather that had got up overnight we were confined to the areas around the accommodation block for our work today.

The Bosun had detailed all hands to scrub and wash the ship's housing from the Bridge deck down, a task commonly known as 'sugiing' (sugi-mugi being the technical, nautical term for any type of shipboard detergent).

Eight of us made our way gingerly up to the bridge deck (I was not the only one suffering by a long way), four either side of the housing block with each member of each team armed with a deck scrubber, a bucket of watered down caustic soda, and a can of teepol (industrial mild green fairy liquid or sugi-mugi).

I was on the starboard side of the ship, unfortunately the weather side hence the coldest and the wettest, with Mr Kelly, Des and Wayvell. Ray, the twelve to four watchkeeper joined us on overtime at nine o'clock.

The watered down Caustic Soda had an amazing effect on the rust streaks that ran down the various parts of the accommodation block especially around scupper downpipes from the deck above and around portholes, lifting it almost immediately upon application and a little bit of persuasion with the deck scrubber. We had to wear goggles and plastic gloves as well to protect our eyes and skin from the Caustic. Even watered down to a weak 5% of Soda content it still gave the skin a nasty sting (as I found out when some suds blew off the top of my mixture and hit me full in the face making my cheeks burn).

'I'll soon sort that.' Ray shouted at me as I rubbed my cheek with my glove, thus making the situation and the pain even worse.

He picked the wash-down hose up off the deck which was connected to the high-powered fire line that ran around the housing, turned it on and proceeded to aim the jet of water straight at me. Up and down my oilskins at first and then full in the face and at an acute enough angle to lift my sou'wester off my head and completely drench me in salt water.

'You bastard.' I screamed as the sting of the salt added to the discomfort of the mild Caustic Soda solution.

Smoko duly arrived at ten o'clock and we all scurried back into the comfort of the Messroom soaking wet, kicking our squelching wellies off in the small decontamination area and generally soaking the tea and coffee making area that Arthur, the Messman, had just lovingly cleaned.

'You shower of dirty bastards.' He remonstrated as the engine room crowd joined us as equally covered in oil as we were wet to add to the sullying of the room.

I chain smoked for the entire thirty minute break as I drank my coffee and joined Ray, Bob and Albert in a foursome at Cribbage.

It was obvious that Ray and Bob were beginners at the game and they couldn't understand how well I could play until I explained that my Grandfather had taught me to play at the age of eight.

I agreed to give Bob more intensive lessons in our cabins later on.

My hangover had completely gone by now and there was definitely something to be said about this sea air being good for you.

We steadily progressed down the four decks to poop deck level and by the time afternoon smoko came around the whole of the accommodation block was sparkling.

This being our first full day at sea there was to be a lifeboat muster and drill at four o'clock in the afternoon.

By all accounts our Captain, Terry Lord, was a stickler for his 'Board of Trade Sports', a weekly event out at sea which generally consisted of either a fire somewhere within the accommodation block, the rescue of a man gassed in a pumproom or cargo tank plus the lowering of a lifeboat.

As the fire alarms sounded at terrifying volume at the stroke of four o'clock the ship's tannoy announced 'Fire in the galley. Emergency stations. Fire in the galley.'

At such an event fifteen of the ship's Officers and crew were detailed in an emergency party to tackle the 'fire' in the galley, under the supervision of the first mate who reported to the Captain on the bridge via walkie-talkie.

The rest of us stood by our lifeboats. I was in the starboard lifeboat, number one boat, and stood around frozen waiting for them to put the pretend fire out. Once everything was under control the rest of the crew were ordered to lifeboat stations, this order being announced by the 'abandon ship' signal from the ship's whistle of seven short blasts followed by a long one. I made sure I recognised the sound just in case for future reference.

Although the sea was still fairly rough the Captain insisted on a lifeboat being lowered to its embarkation deck but fortunately he chose the port side lifeboat on the leeward side of the ship.

I missed seeing the lowering of the boat but went round to the port side after the muster to assist in it being 'brought back in' by means of a small air motor which eventually spluttered into life but packed up with the boat half-way back up the track-way. A small handle was fitted to the drum barrel and we spent the next twenty minutes sweating buckets struggling to turn the handle to pull the boat back in and attempting to re-secure the rusting gripes which held the boat in position.

After the emergency drill we just had enough time to tidy our buckets and hoses up and take them down to the after pumproom where we would be spending our overtime this evening and the rest of the week cleaning the bilges.

We were entitled to three hours overtime a day during the week, which the Bosun frowned upon if we refused. It wasn't too bad a deal. We knocked off at ten to five for dinner and turned too again at ten to six working straight through until twenty past seven. Three hours at time and a half for one and a half hours work. As long as the hour was broke, i.e. starting at ten to six broke the hour from 5 to 6, then that constituted an hour's work.

It worked out roughly to be fifty pence an hour for me and would be necessary if I was to continue the drinking and smoking habits that I was so far indulging in.

What greeted me down the pumproom bilges after dinner that evening confirmed that there were going to be less glamorous times ahead for me during this voyage.

All the crap and gunge, which had leaked out through the cargo lines and spillages that had occurred during the Liverpool discharge and subsequent tank clean, were still slopping around under the deck plates at the bottom of the pumproom bilges (and if the truth be known, along with the pungent aroma, probably several discharges previous as well).

In the far corner by one of the four massive steam driven cargo pumps was a squelchy thick mixture of Molasses, mud and God only knows what that the Bosun announced would have to be shovelled out and lifted the forty feet up to the top of the pumproom and thrown over the side.

'We'll get everything rigged up and get buckets and shovels down here to begin tomorrow morning.' The Bosun said to Me, Geoff and Mr. Kelly as we assessed the task ahead.

'Can't wait.' I enthused at the Bosun.

'Ever heard of a fucking bilge rat, Jasper?' The Bosun asked me.

"Cause you're going to be one tomorrow, my son.'

Mr. Kelly laughed as I surveyed the area that I would be digging out tomorrow. The bottom of the bilges were about three feet below the bilge deck plates which lifted up surprisingly easily. That was to prove the easy part, for as I jumped down for a closer inspection I felt my wellies stick in the thick goo and the stale stench hit my nostrils once disturbed making me almost reach and bring my dinner back up.

I sure didn't fancy being down here with a hangover in the morning.

I did not stand on ceremony once we knocked off at twenty past seven and headed, both soaked and stinking from the bilge, straight into the shower taking my boiler suit in with me to tread in with my feet as I showered as somebody else had already beaten me to the 'dhobi' machine.

The shower freshened me up superbly and I was back up to the bar for eight o'clock for a well deserved beer with Mr. Kelly and Paddy before settling down to watch our movie, 'Le Mans' with Steve McQueen starring which Mel had set up and was to start showing at half past eight.

'Le Mans' appeared to be the best film in the two boxes sent to us (we had a choice of six, but nobody had heard of any of the others).

'You generally get a couple of decent films in a batch.' Tony explained as I sat down after examining the projector and the three spools that the film came on.

'A Western, if you're lucky, as well but the rest are usually a pile of shite, eh! Never mind it passes the time.'

I agreed with him, quite looking forward to the show.

I almost died with laughter as the movie began because before the main event Walport, the distributors of the movies, always added a safety at sea film and I couldn't help casting my mind back to Gravesend as the hammy acting was once again played out before my eyes and tomato sauce was plastered everywhere as the Second Chef lopped his finger off in the bacon slicer.

'Dozy bastard.' Mel shouted out as howls of derision came from the room.

'That'll go in the stew tomorrow, that will. Eh!' Tony shouted before the all too familiar scary music built up to a crescendo whilst homing in on the Second Chef dancing around the galley holding his three fingered hand.

Steve McQueen duly won the Le Mans race and bagged the bird and I gracefully departed for bed as soon as it finished at just gone half past ten, although in theory it was only half past nine as the clocks were to be retarded by one hour tonight due to our travelling West and thus falling behind G.M.T. (four hours in total before we reached Montreal).

The delights of the after pumproom bilge awaited me the next morning, as well as the following morning and the morning after that as it took an age to dig out the shit that had collected in there over the period of time since it had last been dug out, if at all ever.

In all honesty, despite the smell, I probably had the better of the deal along with Geoff and another of the A.B's who took it in turns down the bottom of the pumproom loading the 5 gallon drums of crap that we had dug out onto the hook at the end of the line which then had to be hoisted to the top and taken out onto the maindeck before being dumped over the side.

Geoff and I reflected, on more than one occasion, that the Sea School had been very purposeful in skirting around information given to us about days like these.

Over the course of the next few evenings, after Geoff and I had scrubbed ourselves clean, we took an hour on the ship's wheel each. We would need to spend a total of ten hours steering time deep sea before we could obtain our steering certificate from the Captain.

It was quite monotonous for the hour I went on the wheel between eight o'clock and nine with the ship heading on a constant course of 290 degrees and even downright depressing to go back the next evening and find it exactly the same.

Whilst at sea the ship generally steers in 'Auto-Pilot'. That is that as soon as the ship veers off from it's pre-set course the helm will automatically be put on to counteract the movement of the ship's head away from it's intended course.

This all appears quite simple as minor adjustments are automatically made and the ship never really ventures much beyond two degrees either side of its target, despite the inclement weather conditions and size of swell.

Once the Auto-Pilot is taken off, however, and the helm placed in manual it is a different story.

I immediately put too much starboard wheel on to compensate for the ship drifting off to port and as a consequence the ship's head began lurching to starboard and I was unable to stop it before the head had swung round to 355 degrees, almost due North, and without some pretty swift intervention from the third Officer in charge of the bridge watch.

We eventually brought the head back round to the desired 290 degrees and Willy, who was on the wing of the bridge as lookout, came and stood by me for the next ten minutes until satisfied that I was in control.

It was certainly a bit different to Jolly Jackson's simulator at Gravesend and although bored rigid stood at the wheel steering the same course for an hour I could now appreciate the need for getting the feel of it deep sea before being let loose on the helm in the English Channel or even the St. Lawrence Seaway.

On my third night at the wheel the Captain came up onto the bridge. I hadn't realised he was there as the bridge was in complete darkness except for the dim glow of the two radar screens, one either side of the bridge itself.

'Port easy.' The Captain ordered from the screen on my starboard side.

'Port easy!' I immediately replied turning the large wheel just over five degrees to port.

'Steer 280.'

'280, Captain.' I replied, now that I realised who had given the order.

I brought the heading round to 280 and managed to keep it steady for a good thirty seconds before confirming my new course.

'Steady on 280, Captain.'

I was thanked and the Captain went behind me into the chartroom to plot the new course with the third mate.

I was quite taken aback by the whole matter of factness of the situation. I at least would have expected a 'What the fuck is he doing at the wheel of my ship' attitude upon seeing that I was in total control of millions of pounds worth of ship, not to mention forty plus Officers and crew.

It left me with a rather satisfied opinion of myself.

Hey, these people really are trusting little old me, the thick, scrawny, form S tosser from Kettering.

I didn't touch the bar that evening. I needed to put aside a couple of hours for letter writing and I simply had to do some dhobying. My socks were beginning to crust up a little and I made a mental note that I must buy some more at the earliest opportunity.

I told both my Mum and Jackie about my exploits on the wheel to date and the fact that I had actually altered the ship's course by a whole ten degrees this evening under the instructions of none other than the Captain.

I didn't dare tell either that I had quickly become a twenty cigarette a day man, my Mother would be mortified.

The weather outside had shown no signs of improvement as the weekend approached and as a result our workload continued to concentrate around the pumproom bilges right through until Saturday lunchtime when the Bosun declared a half-day. Far better to have the Saturday afternoon off than the Sunday which was paid at double time.

With the engine room crowd knocked off for the afternoon as well the Bosun relaxed his strict bar hours and declared that it would remain open right through until eleven in the evening.

I had a shower immediately after lunch and joined everybody else in the bar by one o'clock for a feast of cribbage, dominoes, darts and anything else we could lay our hands on that had been stashed in the small gymnasium such as scrabble and monopoly.

I was hopeless at darts, a fact compounded even more so by the dart board being positioned, once swung open and secured, right where the curtain segregating the bar from the Messroom was with the 'oche' positioned slightly off centre to the board as the bar itself was in the way. It was difficult enough merely standing up at the bar with the constant pitching and rolling of the vessel but to attempt to hit a double twenty at the same time was nigh on impossible.

Also at risk was anybody returning from the Messroom with a sandwich or a cup of tea. Not only did they have the hefty curtain to contend with but they also ran the risk of bashing into the board, or even worse receiving a wayward arrow to the leg.

I decided that I had had all the excitement I could take by half past four after attempting to master five's and three's and went down to my cabin to write another letter to Jackie and take an afternoon nap.

I resurfaced just before eight o'clock in the evening to find that, although most had followed suit and taken a break from the session, Mr Kelly and Paddy were still going strong and pretty much the worse for wear.

The evening then soon degenerated as Mick brought his accordion back into the bar and we were treated to a repeat of every song that we had heard on Monday night, the lobster song this time being greeted by a rapturous round of applause with even James joining in with the chorus despite turning red when he sang the word 'bollocks.' Some new songs were also thrown in for good measure.

The Chief Steward had joined the rest of his staff in the bar. He had initially sat down wearing his epaulettes on his uniform shoulders but had received an almighty rollicking from Tony.

'Eh! This is the crew bar, you know. You're quite welcome to sit in here and have a beer but you can take those fucking stripes off before you do.'

He was deadly serious (as well as pissed). It was the first time I had witnessed any animosity directly towards the Officers from one of the crew.

Bill apologised and took them straight off. He quite obviously wanted to have a drink tonight and my guess, as the evening wore on, was that judging by the amount of rum he was actually throwing down his neck it may have been frowned upon had he been consuming this much in the Officer's bar.

He more than made up for his indiscretion by treating us to a moving rendition of Frank Sinatra's "My Way" and "Mack the Knife".

I had slowed my drinking down by half nine, making a can last me the best part of an hour and just soaked up the atmosphere for the rest of the evening whilst everyone attempted to make fools of themselves.

Despite the noise Dixie Dean had managed to fall asleep right in the middle of a conversation and Paddy Powell took five minutes to get up out of his seat and stagger to the toilet. A search party had to be sent out for him thirty minutes later as he too had fallen asleep, slumped over the cistern, with everything still hanging out.

The Bosun called last orders bang on eleven and this time I braved a double rum and coke which, surprisingly, he allowed me to have.

It went down a treat as one by one everybody staggered down to bed.

Sunday morning was a lay in. We didn't have to turn to until nine o'clock and if all Saturday nights were to be like this one it was just as well.

By the middle of the following week we had reached the Gulf of St.Lawrence, it had taken us nine days to cross the Atlantic and it would still be another 36 hours at least before we reached our destination in Montreal.

The watches were doubled up as we passed through the Honguedo Passage and into the St.Lawrence River itself with the automatic Pilot taken off and manual steering re-engaged.

Geoff and I had only managed five hours each on the wheel during the Atlantic crossing so we would have to wait a while longer yet before being allowed to take the helm under a Pilot's instructions.

It was mid-night when we crept past Quebec City but by the time we awoke the next morning the river had narrowed considerably from nightfall yesterday evening to leave us staring up at banks of forests either side of the ship in breathtaking autumn colours of evergreen, yellow, gold and rustic brown.

There had been a slight snowfall a couple of days ago high up in the forest hills and this all added to the wondrous sight before my eyes that I could only ever have imagined before, but never with such astounding beauty. Small townships appeared from out of nowhere hidden amongst the half naked trees, all contributing to the effect with their bright blue, red and cream painted log exteriors.

I leant against the starboard side maindeck handrails with the Bosun and Mr. Kelly as we took a break from undoing all the Butterworth lids and generally preparing the deck for berthing.

'Sure is a sight to behold, so it is.' Mr.Kelly gasped as if still overcome with the sheer magnificence of the area despite having seen it all countless times before.

To my surprise the Bosun revealed that he hadn't been here before, which may have explained his leniency towards allowing us to break off from our work to take in the scenery surrounding us.

We berthed in the dark again, just an hour short of midnight, thus giving us little chance to appreciate the beauty of the city.

We passed what were now becoming the finishing touches to the Olympic City and basin being built for the 1976 Olympic games due to commence the summer after next and berthed in the old Montreal side of town but at the refinery berth some considerable distance from the City centre itself.

'Better get used to being parked a long way from town on this fucking heap.' Mr.Kelly advised me, the cold air quite visibly coming out of his mouth under the bright fo'c'stle light as he spoke.

We would be alongside here in Montreal for a maximum of eighteen hours and I was hugely disappointed, as I would at least have liked to have got off the ship for just a brief walkabout if nothing else. The drinking age is 21 in Canada anyway so there was no way I could have gone ashore for a beer.

'Not only are we miles from anywhere, we couldn't even get up the road if we wanted to.' Mr.Kelly groaned the next morning as we began to break the Butterworth hoses out of storage in preparation for more tank cleaning after we departed.

George and Bob, who had been on the 4 to 8 watch, and Simon, one of the Stewards, managed to get a taxi into town after breakfast for the morning but for the rest of the dayworkers we had to contend ourselves looking out through the damp mist at the skyscrapers which dominated the skyline beyond the near completed giant Ferris Wheel of the Olympic Village.

They returned shortly after mid-day proclaiming it was 'crap' anyway. I guess the idea of a taxi ashore to the shops and very little else didn't appeal too much after the 'Dominion' or when there was Brazil just around the corner to look forward to.

We slipped out of Montreal almost as un-noticed as we had entered, under darkness, and with just a couple of token blasts on the ship's whistle.

I had been further disappointed by the fact that we had received no mail in Montreal, it had apparently all been sent to Peekskill, so it would be at least another three days before I heard from home. Not that I was missing home that much but I was still hopeful of hearing from Jackie.

The view up the St.Lawrwnce compensated some way as to how I was feeling at the minute and as I gazed again the next morning on our way out of the river I knew that the picture of the forests would live with me forever even if I never came back this way again.

The scenes were not dissimilar when we awoke on Monday morning to find ourselves in New York harbour before turning up the Hudson River and onwards towards Peekskill.

Now these really were what you called skyscrapers and once again I was left feeling very privileged as I looked up in awe at the Statue of Liberty, the Empire State Building, the Twin Towers of the World Trade Centre and the Manhattan Skyline in general.

The murky weather that had accompanied us for so long from Rotterdam through to Montreal had all of a sudden given way to fresh, crisp, glorious sunshine and we tied the vessel up, starboard side to, at a rickety old wooden jetty which jutted out into the river some hundred or so yards away from the riverbank where we could just about make out a couple of shore tanks hidden amongst the dense woodland.

It took us well over an hour to tie the ship securely alongside. The main reason being that once we were within touching distance of the pier we had to lower two of our headropes into a small rowing boat that the two occupants then had to row over to near the bank to secure the eyes of the ropes over a bollard, on top of a single pontoon rising out of the river, accessible only by means of a fairly unstable ladder running up it's side.

The whole task being made all the harder by the fact that they were attempting to row against the six knot current that was presently running down the river as well as pull our mooring rope which was gathering in the water underneath our bow and being swept down river as we fed it out.

We gave them what I thought to be a quite friendly round of applause as, twenty minutes later, the head ropes were thrown over the bollards only to be given a shake of the fist and a rather menacing 'fuck you' from the two worn out boatmen.

The process was then repeated twice more for the two deck springs, although this was marginally easier as they were tied up to the main jetty itself and they received some shore-side assistance, and then back out to the pontoon with two further head-ropes.

Despite being a dodgy, rotten looking old jetty it did possess the luxury of its own accommodation ladder much to our delight. We stayed out on deck to assist in bringing the shore hoses on board by means of the ship's derrick, despite it being lunchtime, and by the time we finished the Bosun declared that the dayworkers could have a half-day off.

Peanut

It may have been a Tuesday afternoon but I cared not. Geoff and Myself went straight up to see the Chief Steward for a $100 sub each (around £25), and came back down to the Messroom with two big parcels of mail that the ship's Agent had just bought onboard. We all gathered round excitedly as Mel sifted through all the letters putting them into individual piles.

Danny must have had the most, at least 20 letters. His girlfriend must have written to him every single day.

My pile was very small in comparison. Three from my Mum, quite thick so I gathered they must contain newspaper cuttings about The Poppies, one from my Sister, Cath, one from Malc and Barry (a commendable joint effort of half a page each and amazingly scented with vodka), and one from Dave at Lewis's.

Nothing from Jackie.

I tried to hide my disappointment but it didn't help when, as well as Danny receiving bucket loads of mail, Ray received eight letters from his girlfriend and Keith got about the same amount from his as did several of the others.

I tried to convince myself that probably she had lost the address or that maybe she hadn't received any of mine yet. After all I had posted them from Rotterdam. They may not have found their way to the UK yet.

Who was I trying to kid?

I quickly read the letters that I had received after I had showered and decided that I would leave the newspaper cuttings for later.

Within the hour I was ready to go ashore.

The outskirts of the town of Peekskill were only a brisk thirty-minute walk away and seeing as we were still basking in glorious autumn sunshine myself, Geoff, Ray and Bob decided to take the opportunity to stretch our legs.

The exercise would do us good, as it had been three weeks now since we had left Rotterdam.

We reached a Seven-Eleven Drug Store a mile or so down the road from the oil terminal. It was very much an American version of our Spar chain of supermarkets back home.

I topped up on sweets, or candy as the irritating young shop assistant insisted on calling my jelly beans and wine gums.

'Where you guys all from?' She asked as she loaded two big brown carrier bags of goodies up for me.

'England.' I proudly replied.

'You sure like your chips over in England, don't you?' She continued as she checked my eight bags of cheese crisps into the till.

'Chips?' I argued. 'They're crisps.'

'Nat over here they aint, Mister.'

I cringed as she continued her loud interrogation of me.

'I just lurve your accent. You from anywhere near London?'

I spotted my chance of escape and pointed Geoff out at another checkout.

'No. But he is. He's from London.'

'Oh hi there.' She screeched and waved across at Geoff.

Geoff turned several shades of crimson as my girl announced to Geoff's checkout girl and everyone else in the vicinity; 'Hey, these guys are all from London, England.'

She smiled dopily at me as I paid her for my groceries.

'Have a nice day, y'all.'

We were until we encountered you.

'They love us over here, these yank birds.' Ray explained as we headed into town looking out for any clues as to the whereabouts of a bar.

'It's our accents. They can't get enough of it.'

'I should think so, Lar, if they all talk like she did.' Bob added.

'Hardly the Queen's English that you come out with though, Bob. Is it?' I observed.

We continued a further half a mile or so down the road before coming across a row of shops, garages, warehouses and, right at the end of the row, a saloon bar with a McDonald's restaurant conveniently next door, all set back from the biggest car park I had ever seen in my life.

The whole layout seemed so weird and different to me. There was absolutely nothing on the other side of the road except for a couple of run down wooden houses with tin roofs and miles upon miles of open fields.

'Everybody owns a car out here.' Ray explained. 'The actual town is still just over three miles away but the shopping malls are all littered about in the suburbs. You don't just hop on a bus and go into the town centre to do your shopping like we do back home. You get into your car or truck whenever you feel the need for a pint of milk or loaf of bread or whatever.'

'Or a burger.' I added drooling at the prospect of calling in and having a McDonalds.

Ray had been to one on his previous trip and had told me all about them on our way over from Rotterdam.

The first thing that astounded me as we entered the restaurant was the cleanliness of the place and the fact that my order was in front of me within seconds rather than the statutory fifteen Wimpy minutes that I was accustomed to.

I had ordered up a 'Big Mac' with fries and was treated to the most different, succulent burger I had ever tasted in my life, loaded with lettuce and onions and dripping with a kind of Thousand Island Dressing in a sesame seed bun.

Pure taste bud heaven.

I had tried to order chips but was told that they didn't have any, just French Fries.

'What are these if they're not chips then?' I asked Ray as I tucked into them after devouring my Big Mac.

'Chips are crisps over here. French fries are chips.'

'Eh? What are crisps then?'

I could see that I was going to have trouble speaking American.

The whole meal cost me $1.29c. which included a coke and five hundred ice-cubes. A measly burnt burger and chips without the extras would set me back nearly £2 at Wimpy's back in Kettering.

'Have we got any McDonalds in England?' I asked.

'I think there's one or two in Central London somewhere.' Geoff added. 'Not sure if it'll take off at home though. Most people prefer Fish and Chips.'

Ray agreed. 'There's all kinds of different places out here. Burger King and Wendy's are two other big burger chains and there's also a pizza chain, Pizza Hut.'

'Aren't Pizza's Italian?' I questioned.

'Yeah, but it's all easy-to-mass-produce processed crap that goes into making them and then sold off cheap because so many of the Yanks guzzle the stuff. You have a look at how many fat fuckers we come across out here. All because they're addicted to this shite.'

'Tasted good to me. I'd have another one.'

'It's OK in moderation, but you can hardly call it a healthy diet.'

We walked in to 'Happy Larry's' jeans warehouse as Ray concluded our healthy eating lecture for the day and flashed the fags.

I bought a bag of twelve pairs of black work socks for just $6.99c; what a bargain, and Bob bought two pairs of jeans at $10 a pair.

This was all getting thirsty work by now and we decided to quit the shopping and head back to the bar next to McDonalds.

A massive neon lighted sign proclaiming 'BUDWEISER' hung above the entrance to the bar as we climbed the four wooden steps up to the double saloon swing doors.

How very Wild West I smiled to myself.

Still, it did seem a novelty to be going into a bar at four in the afternoon for a beer.

The bar was dimly lit as we entered, with a few wooden chairs and tables scattered around the creaking, wooden floor. All that was missing was the sawdust and a couple of horses tied up outside.

Over to our right was a stage area with a couple of microphone stands and loud speakers. Two guys in full cowboy outfits sat tuning their guitars.

A jukebox was very aptly playing Jim Reeves' 'Welcome to my World' and further over in the corner was an American pool table.

There were only four other people in the room. All sat well apart from each other at the bar and all in their own personal cloud of smoke.

Their eyes were firmly trained on us as we made our approach to the counter.

One of the chaps stood up, he must have been nigh on seven foot, and made his way behind the bar.

'You guys wanna beer?' He mumbled purposely making no eye contact with any of us.

'Four Buds please there, Lar.' Bob immediately replied his face beaming as if to send out a friendly signal.

The guy looked Bob up and down; tipped his Stetson slightly, scowled and spat something revolting out of the corner of his mouth and onto the floor.

He drew four cold bottles of Budweiser out of the fridge in one hand, slammed four small paper doilies (definitely not in keeping with the tone of the place) in front of us, and bashed each bottle down on top of a doily whilst removing the bottle top with a bottle opener all in one swift manoeuvre.

'Aint never seen you guys in here before.' He quite menacingly remarked as he took Bob's five-dollar bill from him.

'We're off the ship, the Anco Empress, which came in this morning just up the road.' Ray declared.

'That big orange heap up at the Chevron Terminal?' A voice from behind us butted in.

We all turned as one to look at the scruffy, unshaven individual nursing his whisky and slightly worse for wear that had made the remark.

'Yeah, I see ya coming in this morning.' He unenthusiastically continued.

'Enjoy your beer, fella's. There's a group on a bit later. Gets a little lively.'

I raised my bottle to him and the approval seemed to put the guy behind the bar a bit more at ease.

We walked off with our beers towards the pool table and the jukebox being careful to take our doilies with us. The jukebox only offered Country and Western but between them Bob and Ray seemed able to find enough Dolly Parton, Johnny Cash and Tammy Wynette to satisfy ourselves and the growing number of locals that were slowly filling the place up as Geoff and I made arses of ourselves on the pool table.

I had never played pool before but seemed to be able to adapt slightly better to it than snooker mainly due to the smaller size of the table and the larger size of the pockets.

What we didn't have a clue with was the rules but at least we amused some of the locals with our interpretation before we gave up, politely declining their offer to play us for twenty bucks a frame.

It was also the first time I had sampled the American Beer and although it tasted OK ice cold straight out of the fridge it soon became quite sickly as it warmed up.

Before we knew it the place was jam-packed and the group were about to come on to begin their set.

We had managed to find a table to ourselves in the middle of the room to keep our shopping bags under and had long since given up on the beers and gone onto Bacardi and Cokes.

All hell broke loose as the as the group, Billy J. and the Tomahawks, consisting of six geezers and two cowgirls, launched in to 'Proud Mary.'

Country hit after hit was then belted out relentlessly for the next two hours as we joined in with the clapping, Yee-haring and Yaa-hooing at all the right times so as not to look out of place (we already did as we were the only ones not in full cowboy gear).

We lasted until half past ten when we all agreed that we could take no more.

We picked up our shopping and shook hands with more people than I can care to remember as we staggered out to the waiting taxis.

Geoff was barely able to stand as the cold evening air hit us outside and as I got out of the cab back at the terminal less than five minutes drive away I ran over to the bushes and threw my cocktail of McDonalds, Bud and Bacardi back up all over the place.

'Must've been a dodgy burger, Jasp.' Ray laughed as I somehow managed to negotiate the accommodation ladder still clutching my bags of shopping.

I woke the next morning with the Mother of all hangovers but just one look at Geoff, nursing his coffee at the breakfast table, made me feel ten times better.

In his defence Geoff had drank very little since we had joined the ship so wasn't properly trained for the session we had endured yesterday afternoon and evening.

I couldn't possibly have faced another night of the same however but I had to marvel at the eagerness of the likes of Howard and Mel and the other Stewards, that had looked like death warmed up all day, to get straight back up the road again this evening. Especially Arthur, the Messman, who had been so comatose this morning that he couldn't be roused until morning smoko.

I had a quiet night on board. Geoff had gone straight to bed as soon as we had knocked off but Bob and I were able to force ourselves up to the bar for a can after our regular game of crib in my cabin.

Only James, nursing his private bottle of Gin, and the Bosun with his mug of tea were in the bar.

'Not going up the road for a bit of a knees-up, James?' I asked.

'No dear. I'm afraid fat Americans do nothing for me. I'll wait until I can get myself a nice young boy in Brazil.'

We sat and listened as James recalled his years on Cunard passenger ships and his reasoning behind signing a contract with Athel Line for the next twelve months.

'I love Brazil and these ships run down there a lot. I have plenty of friends down there and I can always guarantee finding a nice young cock to suck on whenever I'm down that way.'

The Bosun spluttered in his tea.

'For fuck's sake, Jimmy.' He tutted.

Bob and I laughed as James blew the Bosun a kiss and adjusted his wig.

The Bosun tried to change the subject by telling us that the orders had come through this afternoon that in between here and Bayport we would now be calling in at New Orleans to pick up a cargo of Soya Bean Oil for Rio de Janeiro.

'God, they're even worse in New Orleans.' James declared. 'All drag artists and drama queens.'

'And you're not a drama queen then, James.' The Bosun laughed.

'No dear. I just suck.'

With that nauseating thought in my head I decided it was time for some toast and a relatively early night.

We departed from Peekskill mid afternoon and by the time we were passing the New York skyline again dusk was falling and the clear blue sky of the afternoon was giving way to unbelievable shades of red, purple, yellow and gold as the sun set over the Statue of Liberty.

The weather then took a turn, dramatically, for the better as we headed a thousand miles South around the Florida Keys and then headed back Northwards towards the Mississippi delta.

New Orleans lay a further hundred miles up the Southwest Passage and we spent the whole working day the following Monday preparing our tanks for loading against the backdrop of the Mississippi mud flats.

I amused Myself watching the many river barges passing us, or being passed, along the way as well as various other river boats by half expecting Wicksteed Park's 'Mississippi Queen' to limp past us and be consumed in our wake.

Arriving in New Orleans late afternoon and seeing real Mississippi ferries just made the image all the more laughable.

We tied up alongside, with the minimum amount of fuss, at a cargo ship terminal in the Jefferson area of the City. The shore tanks that we would be loading from were hidden out of site behind the massive warehouses that ran for miles along the waterfront. We were all conveniently tied up, knocked off, fed and ready to hit the town by six thirty in the evening.

It was the only chance we would get, as we were only to be alongside for twenty-four hours.

I jumped into a taxi with Geoff, Alan and Simon who had both been let off early and who wanted to see a bit of Bourbon Street, like ourselves, instead of heading for the nearest boozer.

I couldn't believe as we rode downtown, that the Christmas decorations were already adorning the streets and shop windows as we passed.

'Unless it's Mardi Gras season.' I pointed out.

'Nope, they sure as hell are getting ready for Christmas over here, God damn it.' Our rather large mini cab driver confirmed.

'Gets earlier every year. Shit I only just took ma tree down from last year.' He chortled.

We laughed with him. It was the first time that I had realised that the Yanks had a sense of humour.

It did have its plus points however in that we were able to get our Christmas cards in now for posting when we arrived in Brazil. I toyed with the idea of getting a soppy one for Jackie but decided to wait and give it one last chance of receiving a letter from her in Bayport.

It seemed quite unimaginable that here we were, at the end of October, still dressed in shirtsleeves doing our Christmas shopping.

I had even treated myself to a pair of shorts for our run down to Brazil. We then decided, after we'd completed our shopping and before we went for a beer, to take a ride in one of New Orleans' famous horse drawn carriages around the French quarters.

I felt quite the little tourist as we waved regally to the passers by. I'm not too sure that the locals were too impressed at having horses hooves clomping around their small cobbled streets with bells jangling at all times of the evening but I guessed they must have got used to it by now.

We rounded the evening off with four beers in four different bars/cafes taking in the atmosphere of the tremendous live jazz musicians before heading back to the ship just after eleven.

We departed New Orleans the next day and within no time had left the Mississippi Delta behind and were in Galveston Bay surrounded by a thousand oilrigs.

Our berth in Bayport was at a large BP terminal where we would be discharging our Caustic Soda from Rotterdam.

No letters from Jackie materialised and as if that wasn't bad enough to pour salt into the wound the news on the Poppies' front was even more devastating. Big Ron Atkinson had overseen his last game in charge of us, a 3-1 F.A.Cup replay victory over Swansea, and had moved down the road to Cambridge United in the fourth division.

How could he?

I tried to put the snub from Jackie, as it obviously was by now, and the bitter pill of Big Ron's departure out of my mind and walked up to the small bar just up the road that several of the lads knew of from a previous visit called the Apache Bar.

I went up the road with Danny, the only person other than Ray that I had confided in that I actually had a girlfriend of sorts.

'What's up, Jasper?' He asked as I tried to explain to him what little I had picked up in terms of the game of American Pool that we were trying to play. 'Get a Dear John?'

'That's just it, Dan. I wish I had. At least that way I would know one way or the other.

It's all right for you, mate. How many letters was it today?'

'Just the ten.' Danny replied a touch embarrassingly considering my predicament. Ray had joined us in the bar along with Keith and Willy, whose sprained hand had now been given the all clear by the doctor.

'We'll soon get you over it, Jasper.' Ray insisted. 'We've just heard that we're calling in at Curacao for fuel bunkers on the way down to Rio. We'll take you down to the Happy Valley for a bag off.'

Willy laughed. I was not sure what he was on about and neither were the rest of the first-trippers.

'What's the Happy Valley then?' I asked.

'Loads of birds, Jasp me old mate, that's what. And all fighting over you. That's why it's called Happy Valley.'

'You'll have to count me out then.' Dan insisted.

Keith seemed quite interested though.

When we got back to the ship later that evening Billy Griggs along with the Bosun, alone in the crew bar, confirmed the goings on at Happy Valley.

'It'll be a nice, steady introduction for you before you hit the real thing in Rio.' Billy said in his slow, Mancunian drawl.

'Just make sure you don't get a dose of the fucking clap, though.' The Bosun warned.

I saw the funny side of it. Not ever having seen such a place I tried to picture a situation where hundreds of beautiful birds were falling over themselves to get at me.

No. My imagination wasn't that fertile.

We set sail for the Dutch Antilles two days later on the Sunday evening after spending a relaxing half day Saturday afternoon back up at the Apache Bar (there was very little else to do in the area of Bayport that we were in).

The Bosun had actually joined us and to my surprise let what very little hair that he had down whilst at one stage pushing himself to the very limits of humanity and generosity that we thought were beyond him by offering to buy Geoff and Me a beer.

We gratefully accepted safe in the knowledge that this would be a one off.

We awoke Monday morning to glorious sunshine and, with all the tank preparations out of the way for at least a couple of weeks, we could embark on a programme of chipping and painting areas of the main deck that were covered in rust and where previously painted metal had rusted over in sheets almost two inches thick.

Armed with 'needle guns', or windy hammers to use their correct nautical term, we set about removing the rust from the decks. After afternoon smoko the areas that had been chipped down to the bare metal was then hosed down with fresh water, allowed to dry whilst we had our dinner, and then primed with 'Red Lead' anti-corrosive paint on overtime in the evening as the sun set.

By the third day, just before reaching Curacao and now well into the Caribbean, I was parading around on deck in just my shorts such was the immense heat.

Boy was this ever the life.

Ray, whose suntan hadn't faded over the past few weeks, just went from brown to browner. I had turned a healthy shade of reddish brown but Geoff, being fair-haired, was already beginning to peel like mad on his back, which had turned a mighty fine shade of lobster pink.

Most of the older deck hands just appeared to stay permanently tanned from their years of exposure to the tropical rays but I kept sensible about things for the time being and put a shirt on in the afternoons when the sun was at its most powerful.

We arrived at the port of Willemstad on the Island of Curacao, just a hundred miles off the Northern coast of Venezuela, mid afternoon on the Thursday. A small road bridge lifted up to allow us through into the docks and after we had passed it was just as if we were literally sailing up the high street with a market place to our right hand side and a main road with shops and cafes away to our left.

People of all ages and sizes waved enthusiastically to us as we passed by and we responded likewise from our vantage point on the fo'c'stle head.

Although we were only taking on a couple of hundred tons of bunkers we still would not be able to depart until the next high tide tomorrow morning.

A shame as that meant that I would now have to pay a visit to the World famous Happy Valley this evening along with almost everybody else from the ship's company.

A whole fleet of taxis left the ship for the Happy Valley not long after dinner time and I shared with Mr.Kelly, Paddy and Ray on the short journey to the complex which was only a couple of miles away from the town and a mile inland.

A mile was just about as far inland as you could get on Curacao as the island itself was only about forty miles long by three miles wide.

It appeared to be a primitive sort of holiday camp when we arrived, and if I hadn't already known otherwise I would have sworn that I was in a tropical Butlins.

In fact the taxi driver had referred to it as the 'Campo' when we told him where we wanted to go (not that he needed much prompting, there was very little in the way of an alternative for visiting ship's crews in downtown Willemstad).

The cab driver dropped us outside the entrance to the camp, set in lush thick grassland on a small hill with small shingle pathways meandering in and out leading to various small chalet type buildings. There was a feeble rickety old fence running around the perimeter but an effort had been made with the entrance, which bore a huge sign above the large wooden gates that announced 'Welcome to Happy Valley.'

We made our way over to the focal point of the camp; a Large wooden hut, obviously the main bar, half of which was enclosed (where the bar area was) with the other half exposed at the sides although still under cover, presumably for some kind of protection from any tropical storms that may be likely.

There must have been over fifty tables neatly set out all with seating for eight people and a big dance floor away to the right of the bar where, already at this early stage of the evening, twenty or more local girls were dancing to some kind of samba rhythm with some other white men, possibly from the Norwegian ship that was also docked in the town.

Paddy soon came back to our table with the beers. A much more palatable local brew than the Yank rubbish (in my opinion) that we had got used to over the past couple of weeks and that we were now being subjected to on board.

It wasn't long though before the bar really began to fill up and we went onto our favourite concoction of Bacardi and Cokes, on ice, with a segment of fresh lime hugging the rim of the glass or 'Cuba Libres' as I was now informed that they were called by the locals.

'Going for a bag off tonight then, Mr. Kelly?' Ray laughed at Mick and Paddy.

'Jeesus, No.' Paddy replied for both of them. 'We're just grateful to be getting away from that fuckin' Bosun for a couple of hours. We'll leave that fuckin' malarkey to you youngsters.' He gestured around at Ray and me and at Danny, Keith, Willy and Geoff who had now joined us along with a couple of the young Officer Cadets, Stewart and Pete.

Danny held his hands up in terror. 'I'm with you coffin dodgers on this one.' He protested. 'A couple of beers and a bit of a boogie will do me nicely, thank you. I'm a good, faithful boy, Me.'

'Bollocks.' Ray laughed.

The bar filled up with more local girls as the evening wore on until I swear we men folk were outnumbered by at least four to one.

Ray, Keith and Danny braved it onto the dance floor. I figured they could cope well enough without my two left feet and within minutes they were heading back to our table with a posse of gorgeous, giggling beauties none of which were wearing all that much clothing in the oppressive evening heat.

One of them, a tall, long-haired brunette, wearing a slender red silky boob tube and black hot pants with red rubber boots up to her knees plonked herself down on my lap, threw her arms around my neck and planted a massive kiss on my cheek.

'Fucking hell.' I yelled out as Mick, Paddy and the rest burst out in hysterics.

'Hello baby.' My temptress seductively whispered in my ear. 'I'm Fifi. Do you like me?'

It was hard to say no considering the position I was in with her ample breasts muffling any kind of response I could utter.

A waiter had followed the group back from the bar and stood patiently waiting for Fifi's next question to me.

'Do you want to buy me a drink?' She purred into my ear.

The other girls were all employing the same tactics around our table and receiving positive responses, all except the golden Goddess that had perched herself down on Paddy's lap.

'I'm only wantin' a fuckin' beer, bejayzus.' He scowled as he tipped her off him.

The waiter went away content that he had doubled the order of Cuba Libres as the girls continued to work their charm.

Fifi was certainly managing to keep my attention and Mr. Kelly showed none of Paddy's reservations as he bounced his little beauty up and down on his knees much to Paddy's disgust.

'Are you up for a bit of the old sausage smoking then, darling?' Mr. Kelly, to my astonishment, asked her.

'A bit of what?' She screamed slapping his unshaven face.

'Okay. A bit of what will do instead.'

I wouldn't have put any of the girls older than twenty-three. Fifi took umbrage with me when I asked her how old she was (well I could hardly discuss who she thought might be keen to take over from Ron Atkinson), although I guessed she would be around twenty-one.

Danny certainly had the youngest crawling all over him and I had my doubts that he would be able to keep his vow of celibacy.

'He is Cherry boy, No?' Fifi pouted in pigeon English, pointing to Danny.

I laughed with her. Not entirely sure what she was going on about.

Ray's girl had also picked up on the line of enquiry and pointed to Danny.

'Cherry boy?' She asked Ray.

'He cherry boy, He cherry boy, He cherry boy.' Ray pointed out as he picked Myself, Geoff and Danny off one by one. 'We're all cherry boys, even Mr. Kelly.'

'No, no, no. He's no cherry boy.' She protested at Mick who was now well into the throws of negotiations with his girl.

'Go on, Mick. Go for it.' Ray urged as loud as he could.

With that a loud cheer went up as Mr. Kelly rose to his feet, stuck two fingers firmly up at Ray, put his arm around his young girl's waist and walked off in the direction of the chalets.

'See you in five minutes, you dirty old bastard.' Paddy called after him to which Mr. Kelly grinned and politely waved back.

'As long as that?' Ray questioned.

With Mr. Kelly gone Fifi whispered in my ear again.

'You want a short time, darling?'

Too bloody right I did. I was not going to hear from Jackie now; I was convinced of that, besides . . . . who would know?

Ray and Keith and several of the others all had girlfriends back at home but I seriously doubted that they would not be bagging off within the next half-hour or so whilst they were still capable and before the drink took over.

I wouldn't take bets against Danny either, judging by the way his girl had her head in his lap.

Before I had the chance to even answer Fifi's question another cheer rang round our tables as Geoff, of all people, stood up with the girl that had been fondling his crotch for the past twenty minutes.

His face turned as red as his arms as he quickly followed her down the steps and onto the dimly lit shingle path towards the chalets.

With my cuba libre now finished I rose to the bait.

'Come on then, Feefs.' I boldly ordered as I shot up out of the chair scooping her into the air as I got to my feet.

Another cheer and round of applause went up as she playfully screamed and kicked her legs high into the air as I swung her around, very nearly bloody dropping her.

'You be careful with Fido, now.' Paddy glanced up at me and advised.

Fifi gave him a glare that would turn milk as she took hold of my hand and led me away from the bar.

It was completely dark by now and only the dim light being emitted from the small lamps above the chalet doors lit our way.

We walked for less than a minute before Fifi stopped at chalet number 14 and quickly turned the key in the lock.

We entered a single room that comprised of a double bed, a set of drawers and a chair.

Fifi flicked the light switch on as she entered and a dull 20-watt table light, positioned on the floor in the far corner flickered on.

It's a good job we hadn't come here for a game of crib, I thought, but at least we could just about see what we were doing.

'It's twenty dollars for a short time.' Fifi said as she began to unzip her boots to reveal that she was, in fact, slightly smaller than me and not the six inches taller that she was with them on.

I paid her and slowly, quite nervously, began to take my clothes off.

I wanted to savour the moment.

Peanut

Fifi, however, had other ideas. She had already whipped off her pants and boob tube, to reveal a firm, small set of breasts, and was now whisking off my jeans and tugging at my underpants before I had time to realise what was going on.

She definitely had a mission to fulfil and I must have seemed like a rabbit caught in a car's headlights as I fixed my gaze on her lovely body as she threw herself onto the bed pulling me down on top of her in one, skilful movement.

She kissed me passionately on the lips as she guided me inside her and I felt a short sharp moment of pain as I began to thrust away as if my life depended upon it.

It was over in seconds as the pain gave way to pleasure and I climaxed a few thrusts later inside her and lay, motionless and totally spent, on top of her for a while after I had finished before she pushed me off.

Fifi then let out a shriek as she pulled herself backwards along the bed and away from where the action had just taken place to reveal a small pool of blood on the bed sheet.

'What have you done?' She screamed at me. 'You cherry boy?'

'Er! No.' I lied.

'Well it isn't me.' She argued pointing at the offending patch.

'Quick. I have to change sheet.'

She hastily removed the sheet, screwing it up and bundling it under the bed.

Fortunately nothing had seeped through onto the mattress.

'You should have told me.' She continued to bollock me.

'I didn't realise.' I continued to innocently protest, by now any sense of enjoyment well and truly gone from the moment.

'Never mind.' She sighed, calming down a bit. 'No harm done. Only to your pride, maybe. No?'

'You won't tell them back at the bar will you?' I pleaded.

She said that she wouldn't as we hurriedly dressed again and made our way back to the bar.

We had been gone just twenty five minutes but already Mr. Kelly was back and Geoff followed me inside two minutes.

Ray and Willy, along with the two Cadets, were nowhere to be seen but Keith and Danny had still not succumbed to temptation along with Paddy whom all the girls were avoiding now anyway.

Not surprisingly Fifi didn't hang around too long after our return to the bar. No doubt the night was still young in the girls' eyes and as our party was now either pissed or had already indulged themselves in their delights then there was little point in their staying with us unless they couldn't find another punter to ply them with what I can only assume to have been watered down drinks sold to us at extortionate prices.

Ray returned not long after Geoff and me, beaming from ear to ear as was his girl.

'Such a big boy.' She exclaimed, patting Ray's crotch.

She and Fifi exchanged whispers at the bar and both kept looking at Ray and Me and laughing.

Ray's girl returned, sat on his lap and whispered into his ear. Ray then let out a loud guffaw.

'She says you're a cherry boy, Jasp.' He announced much too loudly for my liking.

I threw Fifi a none too pleasing glance but she just carried on smirking with the rest of her mates.

I gave Ray a pathetic laugh and tried to deflect the attention away from myself.

I wasn't prepared to reveal, at this moment in time, that my previous best before tonight had been a quick vodka induced grope of Lorraine's tits at the back of the Rugby Club sometime last winter.

'Enjoy your bag off, Michael? You dirty old man.' I asked Mr.Kelly.

'Jeesus, I just talked to the girl and asked her what she wanted for Christmas.' He replied.

Mr.Kelly's girl laughed and stroked his grey whiskers and rubbed his belly.

'Father Christmas.' She just about managed to say as she kissed him on the cheek.

With it fast approaching half past ten and with the realisation that neither Danny nor Keith were interested the girls, much to my relief, began drifting back onto the dance floor although Danny and Ray did follow them for a bit more boogying.

Where Ray gets his energy from I just do not know.

Although I had no regrets about what I had got up to during the evening I felt pleased that Danny had kept to his word and only looked (and touched and snogged) but not shagged.

Fair play to him.

We left the bar with the time approaching midnight. The last hour or so had passed so quickly as the Cuba Libres flowed freely. Some of the girls kept popping back to the table from time to time but Fifi didn't show again to heighten my embarrassment.

Ray's girl returned just before half eleven and whispered once more into his ear.

'I'll be back in ten minutes, lads.' He announced grinning like a Cheshire cat as he staggered to his feet and accompanied her back to the chalets.

'Again, Ray?' I asked in shock.

'Ten minutes.' He waved back at me.

'I can't believe you went back for sloppy seconds, you dirty bastard.' I told him during our brief journey back to the ship in the taxi.

'She asked me, Jasper me old mate. I didn't even pay for it second time around. She asked me.'

'Dirty, lucky bastard.' Willy chuckled from the front seat.

The softly spoken John McClean from Stornoway was the four to eight watchkeeper now so I barely heard him calling me at five thirty for a six o'clock turn to to let go the ship the next morning.

In fact I had turned over and was rudely bought back to life by the Bosun at dead on six.

'C'mon, Jasper. Stations fore and aft. Get your dirty fucking arse into gear.'

I shot out of bed and buried my head under the cold tap before lighting a ciggy. I wasn't alone in being late for stations as I heard the Bosun continue along the alleyway calling other stragglers, Ray included.

I got up to the Messroom in double quick time and headed straight up onto the fo'c'stle, having to forego my life-saving coffee, to make the tug fast and let the headropes go.

I struggled through it and leant over the ship's side with Mr.Kelly and the Bosun as we made our way back through the High Street and past the raised road bridge and out into the already warming Caribbean.

'Get your bag off last night then, Jasper?' The Bosun enquired of me, knowing full well the answer.

'Sure did.' I admitted. 'Along with Mr.Kelly.'

'Fuck off.' The Bosun took a step back. 'You didn't did you, Michael?'

Mr.Kelly shrugged his shoulders. 'What can I say?'

'What kind of a fucking example are you to set to the young impressionable hands.'

The Bosun continued to mumble and shake his head as we made our way aft for breakfast.

We had an hour to try and sober ourselves up before turning to again to stow the mooring ropes.

Geoff actually returned to his bed for the hour but I stayed to listen to the various other stories that the rest of the lads had to tell about their night at the Happy Valley.

'I had a fucking little beauty.' Steve from the engine room announced. 'Red boots right up to her arse with gorgeous tits. Shagged it for well over an hour.'

'Not Fifi?' Ray exploded with laughter.

'Yeah, why?' Steve asked.

'She popped Jasper's cherry earlier. You had sloppy seconds.'

'Aha! So you're the Cherry Boy.' Steve mocked at me. 'She did tell me.'

I didn't know where to put my face but Tony managed to seize the moment.

'You didn't pay for it did you, Jasper, Eh?'

'Er. Yes, of course I did.'

'Fucking Cherry Boys get it for nothing around here, you should have told her, you dozy little twat.'

So that was what she meant when she said I should have told her.

'So now you've paid for a bag off that you didn't need to and you've probably gone and got yourself a dose into the bargain, eh!'

He shook his head as I searched for a response.

'If I do get a dose then he'll get one as well.' I countered pointing at Steve.

Steve gulped.

'It'll only be my fourth if I do. No big deal.' He shrugged.

'You need seven doses to qualify for your AB's ticket, Lar.' Bob weighed in with as he scoffed his full breakfast.

And here was me thinking it was down to my wire splicing and General Ship Knowledge.

'Don't worry about having sloppy seconds, Steve.' Paul the Second Steward piped up through bloodshot eyes.

'Simon and me both fancied the same bird last night so we both went to the chalet with her and shagged her one after the other.'

'It's fuck all to worry about.' Simon added. 'I was too pissed to argue and I wanted a bag off, so what?'

Tony shook his head in disgust. 'Well I'm just pleased that my two boys here didn't let the side down.'

He looked across at Keith and Danny, who were both slumped over the Messroom table.

'Only because I was too rat-arsed to be bothered.' Keith admitted.

'Roll on Rio.' Simon sighed.

We were soon back out on deck needle gunning for all we were worth in the searing heat of the day with our windy hammers. Just the cure that was needed for an almighty hangover; the sound of needle guns and chipping hammers pounding away at your head.

Still, it was Friday and we could hopefully enjoy a half-day at sea tomorrow prior to our crossing the Equator on Sunday evening.

The topic of conversation in the bar later on in the evening soon shifted from Happy Valley to the crossing the line ceremony that everyone was gearing themselves up for.

It had been mentioned briefly since our departure from Bayport but I never really knew how serious to take these people some of the time with their various descriptions of the many rituals and God only knows what that goes with crossing the Equator and entering into the Southern Hemisphere.

'We'll only take a small chunk of your hair off, Jasp.' Mel reassured me. 'I know how much you're trying to groom it back.'

'Ocht! Don't tease the poor boy.' James berated Mel, trying to defend me.

'He's already had one nasty experience this week. He doesn't need another.'

'What nasty experience is that then, James?' I asked. Already knowing the answer.

He flung his head dramatically away from my gaze. 'I heard you've been with a woman.' He spat.

'And very nice it was too.' I added.

'And he was a Cherry Boy as well, James. Eh!' Tony added.

'Ocht! Even worse.' James tutted. 'You'll be needing to check your bell end every day for the next fortnight now.' He warned, looking down at my nether region.

'I hope you gave it a good wash in the shower this evening.'

'Eh, what do you reckon, James? Big Stevie was up there seconds after Jasper last night. Sloppy seconds eh!'

James looked absolutely mortified by the revelation.

'How could you, dear?' James asked Steve.

'You'll be all right in Rio in a week's time, Jimmy.' Steve joked, trying to cheer James up.

'And so I will.' James smirked, tossing his head back and touching his wig.

'So what does go on at these crossing the line ceremonies then?' I innocently asked.

I didn't get much of a reply but Mel kept grabbing little bits of my ever growing locks and making snipping gestures with his fingers.

'I'm in the galley every morning sharpening my scissors.' He taunted.

'The water in the sink goes down the plug hole in the opposite direction once we cross into the Southern Hemisphere.' Billy Griggs confidently announced.

'You what?' Keith laughed.

'It's true. It's all down to magnetic fields.'

'Fuck off.'

'Honestly. You have a look after we've crossed tomorrow night.'

'And how am I supposed to know?' Keith argued. 'I've lived in the Northern Hemisphere for nearly seventeen years and I can't tell you which way it drains now for fuck's sake so how am I going to know if it's different on Monday?'

'Have a look tonight and then see if it's different on Monday, you Nob Head.'

'Yeah, right. What exactly is it you've got in that tea, Billy?'

James turned to me to answer my original question.

'On the passenger ships I was on there was always a big pompous ceremony with every Queen or bitch on board trying to outdo each other in the costume department.' He revealed.

I laughed at the mental image he portrayed.

'I can tell you dear, I've seen some right un-pleasantries when certain people have been overlooked in the casting of Neptune's Queen Amphitrite.' He continued.

'Bloody Nora, James.' Tony piped up. 'It's only a crossing the line ceremony, a snip off the old barnet and a dunking in the pool and let's get back to the bar for a bevvy, Eh!'

'I can assure you it's not seen like that on the passenger ships, dear.'

'Well what if there's about two hundred people onboard that haven't crossed the line before?' I asked. 'Do you have to wait all day so that they can all be rounded up, hiding anywhere in the ship, and then dunked in the pool before King Neptune and his faggot court?'

'No, Jasper.' James tutted at my use of the f. word. 'They are all just given a certificate, maybe one or two of the more gamely passengers used as sacrifices if there are no crew members that have never crossed before, but basically they just watch as the Captain and the crew make fools of themselves.'

'Can I just watch on Sunday?' Danny asked.

'No!' came Mel's curt response.

I still didn't know whether the rest were winding us up but James said that because there was such a high number of 'first trippers' on board, (as well as Myself, Geoff, Danny, Keith and Alan in the crew there were two Cadets and an Engine Room Cadet), the Captain had deemed the event worthwhile.

'Bloody decent of him.' Keith had remarked.

The weather had now become so unbelievably hot as we headed South for Rio. Not surprising, I suppose, bearing in mind our proximity to the Equator.

We would officially be crossing the line at around two o'clock on the Monday morning but knocked off at afternoon smoko on the Sunday to allow the rest of the crew to have their bit of fun at our expense.

I saw no point in hiding from Bob and George plus two of the engineers that had been appointed as 'Policemen.' Danny and Keith thought it might be fun to hide on the bottom plates in the engine room but they were soon flushed out and unceremoniously manhandled out onto the poop deck with the rest of us.

We were tied together with a heaving line to ensure no further attempts were made to escape and frog-marched up to the swimming pool on the bridge deck behind the funnel.

There, quite amusingly, sat Mr.Kelly in a chair by the side of the pool dressed in a yellow cloak, quite obviously sewn together from a couple of pieces of cloth from the engine room's rag bag and tied around the waist with a rope belt, a small white peak-less hat (again from the rag bag) and wellies.

He sat holding a Trident in one hand, made up from a broom handle with cardboard cut out forks.

Sat next to him was Steve from the engine room, his long hair making him the ideal candidate for Neptune's Queen, his stately dress being knocked up out of net curtain material and white table cloth again from the rag bag. A yellow paper hat from out of a Christmas cracker served as his tiara. He looked less than impressed about the whole carry on.

Next to them was Mel, holding a galvanized bucket full of some gruesome looking white foamy substance and wielding a frighteningly large pair of scissors, the Chief Steward with a stethoscope of all things round his neck, the cook, holding a cardboard spear and Paul the Second Steward.

Wayvell and Des, dressed only in swimming trunks, stood menacingly the other side of Mr.Kelly.

Bob and George led us around the swimming pool perimeter as the rest of the entire ship's complement (with the exception of the Officer of the watch) looked on from around the sides of the pool.

People were clicking away merrily with their cameras as the Captain approached Mr.Kelly, sorry . . . King Neptune, and a hush descended upon the gathering.

The Captain addressed Neptune, reading from a sheet of paper.

'The *Anco Empress* greets you, King.' He began.

'We sail from Liverpool and we bring many brave sons to be baptised in your royal waters.'

He bowed before the King and Queen before slowly, but deliberately, walking backwards away from the royal party.

He then handed a list to Bob who in turn presented the list to Neptune.

Mr.Kelly looked at the list, looked at us tied together by the side of the pool and began to read from a scroll.

'Gallant Captain. My Lords, Ladies and Gentlemen.' He began, winking at Steve by his side as he emphasised 'Ladies.'

He turned to Mel and the others beside him.

'It gives me great pleasure, once again, to see you all assembled before me.'

Turning his attention back to the Captain he continued.

'Here's to the *Anco Empress,* Captain and Crew,
Every man jack of you.
I, Neptune rule the deep below,
And guard all sailors wherever they go.
I guard all ships when far from home,
Wherever they may happen to roam.
I hold my court in tropical clime,
On favoured ships which cross the line.
If there be any among you who
Have done what they ought not to do.
Let them be brought before these chairs
To be shaved, cleansed, purged and thrown to the bears.'

Upon the signal Wayvell and Des leapt into the pool.

'Dear Captain this is our decree:
Police search out immediately.'

We didn't, of course, need much searching out but as Mr.Kelly rolled up the scroll he was reading from he was licking his lips and rubbing his hands in anticipation of what was to follow.

The Cook and the Second Steward worked their way down the line of us plastering our faces, bodies and hair in the gooey substance that Mel had concocted in his bucket before, one by one, Bob called out our names to be presented to the Barber (Mel), known unimaginatively as Sweny Todd.

'Geoffrey Allen' Bob announced, untying Geoff from the heaving line before thrusting him in front of Mel, Mr.Kelly and Steve.

Mel rubbed the lather more into Geoff's head and gathered up a chunk of his blond locks snipping quite enthusiastically away at what he had pulled up in his hand.

'Throw him to the Bears.' Mel ordered and Bob pushed Geoff into the pool where Wayvell and Des continued the ducking amid cheers and applause from the audience.

Geoff scrambled out of the pool where the Captain was waiting to shake his hand and present him with a scroll neatly rolled up and tucked inside a cardboard tube tied up in yellow ribbon.

'Dan Harvey.' George shouted at the court.

I hoped there had been a previous arrangement because Mel went for Dan's hair like there was no tomorrow cutting chunks and chunks of it out.

'Nice dress.' Dan remarked to Steve as Mel was chopping away.

'Are you taking the Queen's name in vain?' Mr.Kelly shouted as everyone within earshot burst out laughing.

'Two extra duckings for this man.' He ordered the Bears as George deposited him into the pool.

'Jasper Caswell' Bob announced as I was untied.

'Do you want to cast aspersions on my charming Wife as well, young man?' Mr.Kelly enquired as Mel sized my hair up and rubbed more gunk into my face.

'No Sir.' I sternly replied.

'I think Her Majesties Dress is lovely in a net curtainy kind of way. Go easy on the locks, Sweny old bean.'

'Mr Todd to you, you cheeky little runt.' He took two relatively small chunks off, one from either side and cast me aside with a wave of the hand.

'Be gone with you.'

Bob scooped me up in the air and I took an almighty deep breath as he threw me into the pool. I surfaced with just enough time to gulp once more before both Wayvell and Des descended upon me together to send me plunging back to the bottom.

My eyes absolutely stung to high heaven with the salt as I emerged dripping from the pool to be guided over to the Captain who presented me with my scroll.

The other four soon got their initiation and as we all stood with our scrolls Mr.Kelly rose to his feet and read from another sheet of paper.

'We will now return to our royal quarters,
For restful peace beneath the waters.
We now hand over to your care
Our loyal subjects baptised here.
We bid you all a very good day
And may your voyage be bright and gay.'f

There was a huge round of applause.
'Can I go to the bar now?' Mr. Kelly cried.
With that Bob, George, the two Engineers that had also acted as Policemen, Mel and the Cook all grabbed Steve, still draped in his curtains and threw him into the pool.

I went back to the bar with Geoff and Ray feeling quite privileged to have taken part in the event.

Ray got the beers in (we were now on the American 'Papst Blue Ribbon' which wasn't that bad if ice cold), and I unravelled my certificate which had been drawn up surprisingly neatly and in ink.

I, Neptune,
Being the true and rightful Monarch of all the Oceans
And of all the creatures that dwell therein,
Hereby bestow
THE FREEDOM of the SEVEN SEAS
Upon that noble and gallant Mariner
JOHN CASWELL.
Who has crossed that line known as the equator,
Which divides our hemispheres.
Let all who owe me allegiance
Allow the above named to pass without let or hindrance
In pursuit of that which is truly pleasing.
This tenth day of November
In the year of Grace 1974.

It was signed by Neptune, although I doubted it was by Mr.Kelly's own hand due to its neatness.

The rest of the 'court' of King Neptune quickly followed into the bar all dripping wet from their plunge into the pool and for the first time this trip both Des and Wayvell joined everybody else in a beer.

'I like that last bit, James, Eh!' Tony shouted as James entered the bar.

'May your voyage be bright and gay, Eh!'

James totally ignored the remark and continued through the bar to change into his Steward's outfit for dinner.

Mel took Danny through to his cabin to use the clippers on him and take his hair 'down to the wood' after the random snipping he had carried out on him during the ceremony.

I went for a shower straight after my beer and was glad that Mel had taken two chunks of equal proportion from either side of my head that would soon grow and wouldn't require any immediate attention.

I was pleased that my hair was growing back quite quickly now after my horrendous sea school style and although nowhere near it's former glory at least it was starting to cover my ears again. I still vowed that it would be another eighteen months at least before I let any barber of any description near it again.

Over the next four evenings as we travelled further South down passed the Equator and beyond Geoff and Myself completed our steering tickets and received the necessary certificate from Captain Lord. How many certificates could a man handle in such a short space of time?

As we approached Rio we received the frustrating news that they would not be ready to accept our cargo for another six days and we were to remain at anchor four miles off the mainland until such time as they could accommodate us.

It was already going to be a long discharge. We would be discharging our cargo of Soya Bean Oil into road tankers and that was expected to take at least five days. It was frustrating in that we were anchored in the 'outer' limits and no shore-side craft or liberty boat would be making it's way this far out to enable us to go ashore or even for the mail to be brought out to us.

Frustrating also for James, who was so near and yet so far away from his 'smally boy' encounter as Tony was calling it, and for the rest of us that, having had a warm up in Curacao, were now itching to get into central Rio for another bag off.

From a deck maintenance point of view the six days 'on the hook' were a Godsend and all the preparation work we had carried out since the weather had turned for the better could now be followed up by coats and coats of red lead paint being applied to the metalwork before the finishing coat of Battleship Grey.

The Samson Posts were chipped, red leaded, undercoated and finished in a superb gloss white as well as many other of the superstructures.

The Bosun wouldn't allow Geoff or myself to work aloft in a Bosun's chair which miffed me a little.

I had argued that we needed the experience and that the other AB's such as Bob, Albert, George and Brian were all available to make sure we did things correctly.

'You're not going aloft until you're 18.' He barked at me.

'Fuck me, Boas! I'll be 18 before we get to Durban.'

'Then you can fuck off aloft in Durban. Until then you tend the others and watch and learn from them.'

It wasn't worth arguing so I just contented myself to needle gunning more of the maindeck around the area of the starboard Samson Post but within earshot of Bob and Albert who were working aloft. At the end of each day I could feel my back burning and it was no great surprise that after three days at anchor my back began to peel. My arms and legs had also turned a healthy shade of brown, I had cut the legs off my two pairs of sea school jeans to make shorts for myself and my chest had also turned a nice shade of red.

Ray now advised me to wear a T-shirt for the next couple of days to protect the new skin and then I could concentrate on getting a decent 'bronzy.'

We finally moved into the inner anchorage late in the evening on the following Thursday and the ship's Agent was immediately on board with the mail that had been waiting for us since last week.

I had given up all hope of hearing from Jackie and so was not disappointed when the only correspondence came from my Mum and my Sister (it would have been nice to have received some sort of explanation, but it was obviously not to be).

'Not to worry, Jasper me old mate.' Ray had consoled. 'There'll be plenty of 'Dear John' letters for you over the course of the next few years. At least you can get yourself a bag off tomorrow night.'

'Yeah, what the fuck. I didn't think much of her anyway,' I lied.

We were too late to go ashore this evening, a launch was laid on for ten o'clock but nobody took the offer up.

We would be alongside until at least the middle of next week. Plenty of time, especially with the weekend upon us, to do enough sightseeing and whatever else was necessary.

The following morning, Friday, we picked up the anchor at seven o'clock and cruised effortlessly alongside in the early morning mist that had greeted us every single day since we had arrived.

The sea was like a sheet of glass; motionless except for the wake we were creating as our bow cut through the shining water.

Our berth was at a Shell Refinery on a small island to the North of the town and although linked to the mainland by a road bridge our means of getting ashore would be by launch.

We tied up without any problems in the already blistering heat. At least four miles out at sea and at anchor there was a slight offshore breeze to cool things down a bit but now alongside there were no such luxuries and the sweat literally poured off me as we made our way from the fo'c'stle head along the maindeck to secure the accommodation ladder before breakfast.

With the cargo taking so long to discharge the Bosun successfully managed to negotiate, with the Chief Mate, a half day today as well as all day off tomorrow for those that wanted it.

All that was required was that two men volunteer for night watchman duties and Wayvell and Des quickly obliged.

'I always said that Bosun was a fucking splendid fellow.' Paddy muffled into his hand at morning smoko as the Bosun revealed the deal.

'Salt of the Earth and always willing to do anything he can for the morale of the crew.' He sarcastically continued.

'Thank you, Bosun, kind sir.' He then shouted as we all excitedly cheered the news.

'Fancy going up the hill to see the real J.C. this afternoon, Jasp?' Ray asked.

'Too fucking right I do.'

The statue of J.C., or Christ the Redeemer as the locals would have it, had been looking down over us at anchor for the past week, arms outstretched, atop the Corcovado Mountain. Even from four miles away the figure was distinctive; even more so at night when it was lit up by floodlights.

Apparently it was looking directly over the Atlantic Ocean at a similar statue in Lisbon Harbour. A symbol linking the Catholic faith and strong bond between the two countries.

By twelve o'clock, after pottering aimlessly around on deck for the rest of the morning, Myself, Geoff, Ray, Willy, Bob and George were all showered, changed and ready to catch the twelve thirty launch ashore.

I had been up to the Chief Steward and got my £50 sub, and at 350 Cruzeiros to the pound I left his office feeling like a millionaire.

'You'll do well to spend all of that here, lad.' Bill remarked to me as he counted my wedge out in denominations of 10,000, 5,000 and 1,000 Cruzeiro notes. 'A beer is only about 50 Cruzeiros.'

'Don't worry, Bill. I'll have a bloody good go'. I enthusiastically replied.

We caught the launch at the end of the jetty and twenty minutes later were coming alongside the Centro pier just five minutes walk away from Central downtown Rio.

We went in search of a taxi, not too difficult as almost every second car was a yellow taxi, but all were occupied and driving seemingly randomly around the big roundabout slap bang in the middle of the town with streets leading off everywhere and totally oblivious to any other traffic or traffic lights in the vicinity.

Both motor and pedal cyclists added to the confusion and general mayhem of the area as horns tooted and pedestrians ran for their lives to get across the road.

'Fucking Jesus.' George exclaimed. 'How the fuck are we supposed to get to the taxi rank?'

We managed it, just, and I looked around for future reference at all the shops and bars in the area.

I climbed in the front seat of the first taxi with Ray and Geoff.

'Can you take us up to see the Statue?' I shouted at our driver, pointing skywards and then stretching my arms out in a J.C. pose.

'Ahh! Cristo Redentor, Si! Si!' He laughed and pulled out straight in front of a school bus.

'Other car, wait for other car.' Ray ordered him from the back seat.

'Si! Si!' he replied and indicated that they were following.

'What's with all the cars?' I motioned around us at the noise and he prattled on in Portuguese, gesturing and cursing. We were obviously on the same wavelength, just didn't understand a word each other was saying.

It took surprisingly very little time to wade through the bedlam of the Centro traffic and we were soon out in the sticks amongst the tin shacks and houses, for want of a better description, made up of cardboard and corrugated sheeting.

It appeared that all life revolved around the sea front here in Rio and although the city covered such a vast area and had a population well in excess of ten million only a small percentage resided in anything that could be remotely described as luxury.

As we were travelling the main tourist route through the shanty towns the sight of a yellow taxi prompted scores of children to run out towards us, some as young as four, with nothing on except a ragged pair of shorts, holding their hands out towards us in the vain hope that we may part with some of our loose change.

'No give, No give.' Our driver, whom we had christened Pedro, animatedly insisted.

As the taxi slowed down through necessity, not only because we were beginning our climb up the Corcovado mountain but also through the sheer volume of child beggars lining the route, Pedro instructed us to wind up our windows as young hands were thrust into the cab, tapping us on the head and shoulders.

'Please Mister, Please Mister.' they cried in better English than Pedro's.

'You want my Sister?' A boy no older than ten beckoned towards Ray. 'Come. Come.'

It was hard not to sympathise but I could understand that if we gave to one it could create more problems than it actually solved.

Pedro put his foot down as best as possible in an attempt to shake them off and they were soon left in our wake to turn their attentions onto Bob's cab that was still a fair distance behind us.

It took a good, slow, twenty minutes of weaving in and out of the mountain on the dirt track to reach the summit but when we did boy was it worth it.

Pedro and the other driver had agreed to wait forty-five minutes for us to take in the breath taking views before taking us on to Copacabana Beach.

We joined the hundreds of holiday makers, sight seers, and day trippers in climbing the steps from the car park up to the base of the statue and I could not help but feel overcome by the mighty presence of this figure standing so proudly and magnificently before me.

The sun was high in the sky and right behind J.C.'s head and, as we craned our necks and shielded the light from our eyes to look up, the slight mist gave the impression of a halo above the statue's head.

'Fucking amazing.' George whispered, 'Fucking amazing.'

'In the mood for repenting, George?' I asked.

'Not yet,' he laughed, 'might need to come back tomorrow though.'

We moved slowly around the base of the statue taking in the awesome panoramic view of the City and its outskirts. To the North the Maracana Stadium could just be made out through the thin haze. All but one of Brazil's 1950 World Cup campaign was staged in this marvellous arena culminating in almost 200,000 people cramming into it to witness Brazil lose their final pool game and thus the Jules Rimet Trophy 2-1 to arch rivals Uruguay.

The International Airport on Ilha Governador seemed surreal as we watched planes land and take off down below us steadily monitoring their progress to the same height that we were standing at.

The Sugar Loaf Mountain stood directly in J.C.'s eyeline, rising from its base and stopping short giving the appearance of a stump. It was a strange looking thing but we made a mental note that if we were here long enough and got the opportunity we would ride the cable car to its summit.

We could also make out a race-track beneath us and a couple of Rio's golden beeches before gazing out at the miles and miles of crystal blue ocean that had brought us here.

The ships at the anchorage four miles out where we had lain for a week were mere dots on the horizon and everything seemed so serene and tranquil from our vantage point.

I hadn't believed in God or had much to do with religion since I was about eight but I certainly felt the hairs standing up on the back of my neck and a cold shiver running down my spine despite the immense mid afternoon heat as I took one last look at the statue before returning to our taxis.

'Fucking amazing.' George enthused again.

And I couldn't help but agree with him.

The descent of the mountain was somewhat quicker than the ascent and Pedro needed to pull on all his years of experience to avoid us clattering into the tourist buses that we seemed to encounter on almost every blind corner that we turned.

By half past three Pedro was dropping us off at Copacabana beach. We had hired him for almost two hours and he charged us 2,000 Cruzeiro's (less than £6).

We gave him 1,000 Cruzeiros each, shook his hand, and he departed one very happy taxi driver.

Copacabana was everything we had been expecting. A three mile long stretch of beach with waves crashing ashore all the way along its length.

It was very densely populated with hotels and other high rise buildings set back in the steep hills, which gave the beach its backdrop.

The locals were obviously taking a siesta at the moment as it was nowhere near as crowded as I had anticipated but as we had been dropped off fairly central we figured that the best way to become acclimatised to our new surroundings and feast our eyes on the activities taking place would be to sit outside the bar we were next to and order a Cuba Libre.

It was quite amusing as we sat down at our table across the main road from the bar on the patio leading down to the beach watching the waiter trying to negotiate the road, our six Cuba Libres balanced precariously on his tray as he made a determined mad dash for it, bobbing and shimmying between the uncaring, speeding vehicles.

We decided to run up a tab and watch the several games of topless beach volleyball that was going on in our immediate vicinity.

After my second drink I couldn't resist the temptation any longer and along with Ray and Geoff rolled my trousers up above my knees, discarded my shirt and made a beeline for the breaking waves.

The sea was so warm it was unbelievable. It was impossible to paddle too far out though due to the size of the swell but I had seen enough to know that I would need to invest in a pair of swimming trunks for tomorrow afternoon.

We ordered sandwiches as the rush hour traffic came and went with our waiter becoming more and more agitated that none of us could bother our arses and cross the road ourselves to get our drinks, preferring the snapped finger approach.

Before we knew it the sun was setting and we had been sat there for four hours.

As the volleyball finished the football started as hundreds of kids descended upon the beach, throwing shirts down anywhere to mark the goalposts and displaying skills far superior to anything I had ever witnessed at Rockingham Road, Kettering before (or Filbert Street for that matter).

That glorious offshore breeze that we had enjoyed at anchor for the past week had returned as the light faded and although I could gladly have remained on the beach front for another couple of hours we contemplated returning to the 'Centro' for a bit of action and where we knew the rest of the crew would be gathering by now.

Our bar tab was ridiculously low and worked out about £4 per head.

We flagged two taxis down with ease and just over five minutes later was back at the 'Centro' which by now, under darkness, had transformed itself from the dowdy, shabby appearance of the daytime to a splendid array of lights and sound that was impossible not to be lured into.

Souvenir shops and cheap clothes shops lined the main drag off to the left of the roundabout and straight over from the taxi rank was the 'Florida' Bar, closely followed by the 'Cowboy' Bar with the 'Pussycat' Club just across the road.

'This'll do for starters, Lar's.' Bob proclaimed, rubbing his hands together in anticipation.

We opted for the Cowboy Bar. Mel and Howard had mentioned it from their previous exploits and sure enough they were sat at a table quite close to the bar as we paid our 500 cruzeiro entrance fee and entered the massive, smoke filled darkened room.

Flamenco and Samba music belted out of the loudspeakers and the huge dance area was illuminated with a state of the art revolving disco globe. At one end of the square dance floor was a stage with three poles, each occupied by girls in bikinis writhing and gyrating up against them.

Mel and Howard were already in the company of two beauties as we joined them on the next table.

'Haven't they got any Slade or Status Quo?' I shouted at Mel at the top of my voice.

'This is sexy music, Jasp.' He screamed back. 'Meant to get you in the mood, boy.'

He leant over to the girl beside him and gave her a sloppy French kiss.

'This is Mimi' Mel introduced me.

'Charmed I'm sure.' I yelled as I waved at her.

'I was with Mimi last trip and came looking for her again tonight.'

'Wow, a proper girlfriend.' I mocked.

'They don't like it if you go with another girl here.' He said, quite seriously.

'They call you a butterfly.' Mimi's gaze hardened at the mere mention of the word butterfly.

'Him butterfly?' She asked Mel, gesturing towards me.

He managed to persuade her that I wasn't. Bloody hell I'd only just sat down.

The drinks soon arrived, beer for the time being as I had consumed enough Cuba Libres on the beach. It was a local brew 'Brahma Chopp', which I deduced must have translated as 'good beer' but probably didn't.

In what was now becoming time honoured tradition no sooner had we sat down than six young lasses descended upon us from out of the shadows, stroking our hair, touching our legs, knees, bodies, groins and smothering us with kisses and thrusting their breasts into our faces.

Absolutely disgusting.

'Remember what I said now, Jasp.' Mel shouted at me again, 'Make sure you get the best one as you can't change your mind.'

I nodded.

'And you can't get this one for fucking free either as you're no longer a Cherry Boy, you dopey sod!'

I turned round swiftly. I hadn't seen Tony and Steve behind me at the next table.

'You dirty old man. I hope you've had a shave.'

Tony had the most gorgeous half-Chinese, half-Brazilian looking brunette bouncing on his lap. She could not have been over 18.

'When are you going to grow up? A man of your age.' I asked in a disgusted tone.

'Never.' He laughed and buried his head into her ample bosom.

The first group of girls had left us although one had stayed with George after he had shown signs of interest and bought her a drink.

Ray had gone on to the dance floor with a couple of the Cadets and I was on my third drink before I spotted the most gorgeous short-haired blonde dancing close to him.

I had seen Ray look her up and down but in my now half drunken state I told myself: 'Fuck you, Ray. This one's mine.'

I joined Ray on the dance floor and positioned Myself between him and my target before lifting my arms in the air and waggling my legs about to the rhythm (well that's all everybody else was doing).

'Fucking hell, Jasper's dancing.' Ray shouted at the top of his voice.

'I told you I couldn't dance so I've come up here to prove it.' I laughed.

With that I spun round and danced frantically almost face to face with the girl I had set my sights on. She was even more fantastic close up. She wore very little make up, which pleased me, was wearing a very thin pink cardigan with nothing underneath and a short black skirt with the obligatory thigh length PVC boots.

She looked very European but still had that hint of Latin in her eyes as well as in her voice.

'Hi.' I drooled.

'Hello.' She replied with a sweet smile.

'Oi!' Ray nudged me in the back. 'I was going to chat her up.'

'Tough.' I retorted.

'Can I get you a drink?' I asked her.

'Sure.'

I led her back to our table and ordered Myself a Cuba Libre. She insisted on a Gin and Lemonade, presumably so that she would just get a small glass of Lemonade and I would be charged for a Gin.

Whatever.

As soon as we sat back down she nuzzled herself up against me. Her smell was absolutely stunning and I could feel myself becoming aroused as she brushed herself against my crotch.

'Do you want a short time or all night?' She asked.

I didn't even realise there was an option.

Mel explained that there were motels off the back streets that hired rooms by the hour or apartments by the night.

I suppose I hadn't really thought about it as my only previous experience had been with the chalets at Happy Valley.

'What did you think she was going to do? Invite you home?'

It was 3,000 Cruzeiros for a short time and although all night was tempting (I was extremely tired now), most of the others were planning to catch the half past midnight launch back to the ship. It was ten o'clock now so I had ample time.

She led me out of the bar as soon as I had told her of my preference and, after only a few yards away from the place, turned up a dark side street and into a shabby doorway where she rang the bell.

A foreign voice spoke through an intercom system.

'Laura.' She announced and the door immediately clicked open.

'You pay the lady,' she said to me as we passed a hatch at the bottom of a flight of stairs. Behind the hatch was a seventy-ish year old woman, her Nan for all I knew but doubted it.

I paid her my 3000c's and followed Laura up the first flight of stairs and along a small dingy corridor to an unlocked room.

Laura turned the dim light on and bolted the door. As I looked around I could have been back in Happy Valley.

Despite the surroundings it didn't detract from the fact that Laura was, in my drunken opinion, by far the best girl on the market this evening and it felt so good when she expertly slipped out of her clothes and started to undress me whilst kissing my body all over.

As she peeled off my trousers and underpants she took me into her mouth and I felt that I was going to explode there and then.

'Jesus Christ.' I exclaimed. Remembering how close I had been to him not too many hours ago.

Laura laughed and lay back on the bed guiding me into her. She really was gorgeous.

'We've got just under an hour. You can come twice if you like.'

I thought she was being optimistic considering the amount of alcohol I had inside me but my first effort was over so quickly that I was able to manage a second attempt some twenty minutes later.

I lit us both a cigarette, stumbled naked to the filthy toilet in the corner of the room behind a curtain to relieve myself, splashed myself in cold water from the equally filthy sink and dressed in silence as Laura quickly re-dressed in her skimpy outfit.

I got back to the bar at just after eleven to discover that Mel and Tony had departed for an all-nighter.

Laura asked me if I would be back again tomorrow evening and I promised that I would. She then left me in no doubt whatsoever as to my fate with quite a graphic cut-throat signal to me should I dare to turn butterfly.

I took a slow walk back to the jetty with Ray, Geoff, Howard and Steve. All of whom had disappeared and then reappeared at around the same time as I had. The two Cadets along with Bob and George were waiting at the jetty when we arrived there.

The launch back was superb. A sobering breeze cut through the air and onto our faces as we discussed the night's events.

Neither the two Cadets nor Bob and George had bagged off. They tried out the other two clubs after we had left but said that the 'Cowboy' was the best.

'I thought you were well in with yours, George.' I remarked.

'Nah. I couldn't be bothered.' He shrugged. 'When we went over to the Pussycat Club she was fucking in there and then accused me of being a fucking butterfly.' He laughed in his thick Irish Brogue.

'They take it that seriously that you can be accused of being a butterfly without even going with one of them.'

'Yes', I agreed. 'I had my fortune told on the way out this evening.'

'At least you got the best one of the lot, you jammy bastard.' Ray pointed out.

'I know, I know. And I'm going back for more tonight.'

'Even though she's on an all-nighter right at this very minute with some Swede stuck seven blocks up her.' Steve intervened.

'Cheers for that thought, Steve. So I can't go with any other girl for fear of getting my neck slit but she can have as many blokes as she likes.'

'That's just about how it works.' Steve sadly summed up.

We fell up the accommodation ladder, there was very little sign of any cargo activity, waved to Des, who was overseeing our safe arrival back on board, and went straight to bed. It had been a long day.

I still struggled to get to sleep. The room was spinning round and I could still taste the Bacardi at the back of my throat despite a rigorous teeth-cleaning session before I placed myself delicately on my bunk.

Laura was still fresh in my thoughts. She WAS the best girl in the club this evening and as I looked up at the deck head, afraid to move a muscle, I promised myself I would not get so drunk tomorrow evening so that I could enjoy it all the more.

I just about made it to my sink in time. I chundered up the entire contents of my stomach until there was nothing left to bring up, except that I kept on heaving and retching with nothing happening.

It was eleven o'clock before I awoke the next morning. Thank Christ it was a day off.

What the fuck is that God-awful smell coming from my sink?

I glanced over at the sight of breadcrumbs and sweetcorn blocking up my sink and wondered how on Earth it had managed to come out an orange colour.

I lit a cigarette, wrapped a towel around my waist and staggered to the ice water fountain at the end of the alleyway to pour myself a pint of diluted blackcurrant cordial.

Two paracetamols and a shower later and I could just about attempt to unblock it without suffering repercussions.

Mel and Howard looked no better as I made it up to the Messroom just before lunch-time and if it wasn't for the Officers and the few crew that had bothered to turn to I suspect lunch today would have been cancelled.

'Omelette, chips and beans is all you're getting out of us today.' Mel announced.

'That'll do for me.' I replied. 'How was the all-nighter?'

'Fucking brilliant. I missed breakfast and got back at nine o'clock this morning.'

Ray and Geoff surfaced shortly after me and we planned to do a bit of shopping this afternoon before going back to the Cowboy later on. The launches ran fairly regularly from ship to shore and bearing in mind that we didn't want to lose any of our souvenirs decided to catch the half one boat ashore, do our shopping and come back at five for dinner before going back again in the evening.

We didn't stray far from the Centro on our return and, ignoring the temptation of a swift livener in the Cowboy, headed straight down the *Rua Buenos Aires* and into the curios shops.

I had been quite taken by the wonderful assortment of Butterfly Trays and wall mountings containing the pressed creatures that the craft shops were full of. Some were massive and in glorious shades of deep blue, yellow and brown.

I bought three of various sizes as well as a glass dinner tray with a hand painting of the Corcovado Mountain with the statue on top overlooking the Sugar Loaf Mountain at sunset for my Mum.

They were all wrapped up carefully in paper by the continually smiling shop assistant and taped up in such a way with a handle that I could carry them with ease. The whole lot costing me just over a tenner.

Ray and Geoff bought very similar souvenirs and we sat outside a small café opposite the Cowboy bar and had a couple of Brahma Chopp's each before catching the launch back to the ship.

I was still feeling a little delicate so decided to take a couple of hours nap before catching the eight o'clock launch back ashore.

Geoff decided that he couldn't take another night like last night and stayed on board but I was determined to partake in round two with Laura.

Danny and Keith came along with Myself, Ray and Mel who was well up for it again having shaken off his hangover with a couple of hours kip in the afternoon.

Mimi was waiting for Mel in the Cowboy as soon as we arrived but there was no sign of Laura or the girl that Ray had been with last night as we ordered our beers and waited for the hordes to descend upon us.

I don't know what it is about Danny but once again, as soon as we had sat down, the most gorgeous young bird came over and plonked herself down on his lap smothering him with kisses and professing her undying love for him. She was an absolute stunner and I could sense Danny beginning to crack as the evening wore on.

I had shown no interest in the girl that was all over me which was probably just as well as Laura came into the bar at half nine and headed straight for me. She gave the girls that had been sitting with me and Ray a right ear bashing in Portuguese and locked her arms around me, kissing me fully on the lips as she sat down.

'You no butterfly?' She demanded as she sat back, waving her arms frantically at the now departing two girls.

'Of course not.' I protested. 'You're the only girl for me.' I assured her slipping my hand down her top and fondling a lovely piece of breast.

She giggled and slapped the offending hand playfully.

At precisely ten o'clock she began muttering sweet nothings in my ear again and stroking my balls. I was powerless to resist and without saying another word she got up out of her seat and led me back to the same apartment block as last night.

Events took on a very similar nature to last nights only this time we entered a room further down the corridor after I had paid the same lady my money.

I wasn't as drunk as last night having only just gone onto the Cuba Libres in the last half hour or so thus my stamina was slightly better tonight and I lasted all of three minutes before spending myself.

'Mmmm! That was so good.' Laura sighed as I stayed inside her.

I leapt off and lit us both a cigarette which we smoked whilst she tried to put some life back into me.

I worked my way all over her body with my tongue until I was ready again, surpassing all previous records by lasting a creditable five minutes this time.

Danny and Keith were nowhere to be seen when I returned to the bar, Ray said that they had gone over to the Florida Bar. I think to get away from the temptation of the girl that had attached herself to Danny in here although she may have followed him over there.

We intended catching the half past midnight launch back again. Ray's girl from last night had not turned up but he had been contented to flaunt himself on the dance floor.

Laura had asked if I would be back again tomorrow night but I was well aware that I had already made a large dent in my sub and only had about fifteen pounds left.

I moved my hand in a 'maybe, maybe not' motion and shrugged my shoulders. I was once again treated to the knife across my throat signal as I cuddled up to her in an embrace of reassurance.

'I look for you tonight. If you are not here you had better not be with anybody else.' She threatened, far too menacingly for my liking.

'If I am not here I will still be onboard my ship.' I confirmed.

With that Ray and I walked back to the launch.

At least tonight, I knew, I would be able to get to bed without throwing up.

Mel returned again at nine o'clock the next morning just as we were turning to. It had seemed ages since we had last worked but we were soon brought down to earth with a bump by the Bosun who was rubbing his hands with glee at getting his workforce back again.

'Right, you horrible shower of dirty bastards. I hope you're ready for a different kind of humping because there's all kinds of stores arriving later on this morning as well as Butterworth hoses to get ready for when we leave on Tuesday.'

We all groaned as we lifted our weary limbs from off the comfort of the Messroom chairs and out into the searing heat of the morning.

'It's Sunday, Boas.' Ray argued. 'Can we not go and pray?'

'You'd better fucking pray that these stores aren't fucking heavy, Raymond.' He mocked.

There was still no sign of Danny or Keith by morning smoko. The Engine Room Staff had worked yesterday and were on their day off today.

'Danny definitely went with that bird.' Mel confirmed. 'If they're not down below in their cabin then they must have stayed for an all-nighter.'

George shook his head in disgust. 'Danny, Danny, Danny.' He tutted.

The day had been tiring and by five o'clock the activities and over indulgence of the last two days were catching up on us, so Ray and I decided on a quiet night onboard this evening.

As we sat in the bar having a thirst-quenching pint of shandy before our evening meal James strutted through the bar.

'James!' I shouted holding my arms out as if greeting a long lost brother. 'Where have you been? I haven't seen you since we docked.'

'No, and if I had my way I wouldn't be here now.' He sighed.

'How's the arse cheeks, James?' Tony bellowed from the corner, causing the Bosun to choke on his cup of tea. 'Get a good reaming did they?'

'Honestly!' James blushed, and then added: 'Yes thank you, my young man was gorgeous.' He strutted, almost penguin like, through the bar before stopping at the Messroom curtain and, turning round to me, winking and adding in a devilish tone; 'And so was his Father.'

Tony howled out with laughter.

'Did you see the way he was walking? He looks as if he's been riding a fucking horse for two days solid, eh!.'

'Somebody's been riding him all right.' Billy Griggs observed.

I had my early night. Going down to my cabin at half past eight after everyone else except Ray, Geoff, the Bosun and I had gone ashore on the launch.

It seemed eerily silent but I took advantage of the time to write home to my Mum and Sister telling them all about my trip up to the statue. I reserved the other details for Barry and Malc.

The Soya Bean Oil was still constantly discharging all the time we were alongside but only very slowly. Because of the nature of the cargo, once nearing the end of the discharge sediment can be found at the bottom of the tanks. Usually only about two inches deep below the heating coils which ran along the bottom of each tank.

On some cargo's such as Palm Oil or Tallow the sediment could become very thick and would require a bit of persuading once there was only about a foot of cargo left in the tank.

The Soya Bean Oil we were discharging was of a lighter consistency than both Palm Oil and Tallow but there was still a risk of sediment forming at the bottom of the tanks so we would still be required to go down the tanks near completion of discharge and mix the sediment up with the remaining foot or so of cargo. This process was known as 'Puddling.'

Several of the tanks were ready for Puddling throughout Monday with the lion's share becoming ready on Tuesday to hopefully complete the discharge by sunset that day.

One good thing about the deal was that the crew received $200 per tank that required puddling.

An even better deal considering we had 19 tanks that would require attention with all monies split between the deck crew.

Again Geoff and Myself were left feeling a bit frustrated by the pedantic Bosun who would not allow us to go down the tanks as we were still only classed as 'boys'.

The rest of the lads, however, led by Mr Kelly argued our case for a share of the money as we would tend the tanks whilst they were down there puddling and it was agreed that we would receive a share between us (it worked out at $237 per man so Geoff and me would receive $118 each, around £30).

Seven tanks were indeed puddled during Monday and it was quite a sight to behold.

George was still a complete wreck from the night before as he entered the first tank at ten in the morning along with Bob, Mr. Kelly, and Willie who were not much better, followed by Brian, Ray and the Bosun.

It was quite a precarious operation climbing the thirty five feet down to the bottom of the tank on a very slippery, almost vertical, ladder split into two with a platform half way down, in waders that reached up to their knees and carrying a wooden squeegee or puddling stick.

Beginning in the bay furthest from the cargo pump the lads then proceeded to work the sediment in with their feet as the pump painstakingly slowly continued its discharge.

Slowly we began to see the clear bottom of the tank from our observation point on the main deck, peering down a Butterworth hole. The lads then started to push the last of the oil towards the pump with their squeegees.

It was over in less than forty minutes and despite us having rigged a fan on one of the lids for ventilation purposes they all emerged sweating buckets, and in George's case close to collapse.

We handed each a bottle of by now luke-warm water as they flaked out on the deck searching for air. There was none of course as it was only marginally less uncomfortable out on deck as it was down the tank.

'One down, eighteen to go.' The Bosun gleefully remarked.

George groaned.

He was spared the next tank as the AB's took turns in resting depending of the size of the tank. Some of the smaller tanks only required four or five men otherwise they would be tripping over themselves, others required all hands.

Amazingly, despite not finishing the last tank of the day until half past six, George was ready and raring to go along with the rest of us for the eight o'clock launch ashore.

I had decided to sub another fifteen pounds worth of Cruzeiros and forced myself to go and find Laura again for another bag off.

Danny had succumbed to temptation on Saturday night and he and Keith had not only spent two nights with their girls but also all day Sunday on Copocobana beach with them.

Despite the remorse Danny was on the launch along with Keith and the rest of us.

'Fuck it.' Had been his response to George's playful disgust with him, and I tended to agree with him.

I was having the time of my life.

I hadn't been sat down in the Cowboy Bar for more than five minutes or made any headway through my first bottle of Brahma Chopp when I received the most almighty thump on my right arm. I spun round to see Laura staring daggers at me.

Peanut

'Where you last night?' She scowled, thumping me again in exactly the same spot.

'Owwww!' I protested rubbing my arm. 'I stayed on board the ship.'

'You butterfly.' She said sternly, shaping to thump me again.

'No.' I argued, covering my tender upper arm. 'I didn't have any money.'

'Ahh! No money no honey.' One of the girls that had already congregated around us smirked.

Ray then intervened confirming that we had both, along with Geoff, stayed onboard last night as we had tried to explain to her on Saturday and the penny must have finally sunk that she hadn't seen either of the three of us last night.

'Oh, my baby.' She purred throwing her arms around me. 'I think you butterfly. I'm sorry.'

I responded to the lip lock that she had gripped me in and all of a sudden my painful arm had been overtaken by the sheer embarrassment of what was going on inside my trousers.

'Finish your drink, darling and let's go.'

I wasted no time.

Once back inside the dingy apartment I explained that I only had enough money for a couple of drinks last night and that I had only subbed more today.

She pressed her fingers against my lips.

'You should still have come to see me.' She said softly. 'Only 1,000 Cruzeiro's tonight. It's your last night.'

I made the most of it. Enjoying and savouring every second I spent stroking, feeling and touching her delicious body.

I was going to miss this kind of attention when we set sail across the Atlantic for Durban in South Africa (our orders having come through this afternoon).

Such had been my eagerness to enjoy the delights of Laura that I was back in the Cowboy Bar by just after ten o'clock.

Laura sat on my lap and we enjoyed a Cuba Libre each as we watched all the others in turn disappear for an hour and return beaming from ear to ear.

I still maintained that Laura was the best of the bunch and with not having to worry about Jackie my conscience was clear. Danny's conquest was an absolute beauty and it was amusing to watch him down in the dumps during the day full of remorse and yet so eager for more come the evening time.

We all bid a playful, tearful farewell at midnight before taking the short walk back to the jetty to catch the launch.

I gave Laura a long, tender kiss flinching as she squeezed the arm that she had previously battered.

She lifted my shirt-sleeve up to reveal a purple bruise. 'You will remember me for a couple of days, No?'

She giggled.

I most certainly would.

We climbed back on board determined to get a good sleep ahead of the busy puddling schedule the next day.

The twelve remaining tanks loomed ahead of us and even George had come back relatively sober this evening.

That was more than can be said of Tony and Arthur the Messman who, much to our amusement, got halfway down the stairs from the Messroom to the alleyway below arm in arm before tripping over and falling the final ten steps to land in a snotty, still singing heap at the bottom.

My last recollection was watching the pair of them bouncing off the bulkheads singing 'Kung-Fu Fucking Fighting' before I crashed onto my bunk.

By mid-day the next day it was fairly obvious that we were not going to complete the twelve tanks by eight o'clock this evening (the latest we could sail; otherwise it was the following evening).

We had only puddled two tanks and the three large centre tanks still had no end of cargo in them.

'How many Cruzeiros have you got left, Jasp?' Ray excitedly asked at lunchtime. 'I reckon we can get another bag off out of this.'

Just then Arthur appeared in the Messroom doorway, his arm in a sling. He had been to the doctors this morning.

'Fucked.' He looked up at us and remarked, his thick black hair still all over the place and his eyes bloodshot. As he shuffled past our table he stopped beside where Tony was sitting.

'Arm's fucked.' He laughed. 'You've broke me fucking arm you drunken scouse twat.'

'I'm OK.' Tony smirked.

'You fucking should be. You landed on top of me.' Arthur continued as they both fell about laughing.

'So what happens now then?' I innocently enquired.

Arthur turned to face me. Flung his good arm horizontal, made an aeroplane noise and shouted. 'I'm going home in time for Crimbo, Jasper me old mucker. I'm fucking going home.'

'You lucky bastard.' Steve exclaimed. 'Hey, Tone! Any chance of you following me down the stairs tonight?'

By six o'clock Arthur was gone. Suitcases packed, the Agent on board to collect him and escorted away in a taxi for a two night stop-over in Santos before flying back to the UK

Ray and I mustered 5,000 Cruzeiros between us and decided that we would join George and Bob up the road again for yet another final night at the Cowboy Bar.

We still had the three large centre tanks to complete the next day and I thought it would be a good idea to surprise Laura as well as satisfy my almost now animalistic lust.

It was me that got the surprise. Laura was not in the Cowboy Bar and neither was Ray's girl or Danny's or anybody that we particularly recognised.

I went over to the Florida Bar with Ray on the off chance and there she was. On the dance floor, wearing a see-through black vest, white shorts and her knee length boots, looking as sexy as ever, dancing with a bloke more than likely in his forties.

I stood there catching flies as she danced around him, smooching with him and showering him with all the passion she had given me not twenty-four hours earlier.

'Ah, you've found her then.' Ray shouted in my ear as he returned from the bar.

'We were supposed to have left today, you know.'

'I know' I conceded.

We returned to Bob and George in the Cowboy Bar and lo and behold at just gone eleven in walks Laura on her own. She seemed embarrassed to see us and remonstrated with me that we had said we were leaving today.

'You butterfly?' I sarcastically asked.

'You leave. Fuck you.' She spat and thumped me on my arm again.

'Probably not a good idea to have come back tonight.' I said to Ray as she stormed out of the bar.

It was quite obvious that she had seen it as deceit on my part although naiveté may have been a better phrase.

I realised that she was a working girl and as much as I had been taken in by her charm and beauty as well as the attention she was offering me I had probably mistakenly misunderstood that for something else.

No. We shouldn't have come back tonight.

I'd learn, I thought. And fast.

We completed the cargo mid-afternoon the next day and set sail, without any cargo onboard, bound for South Africa just as the sun was setting over J.C. still standing proudly atop the Corcovado Mountain.

We had been in or around Rio for almost two weeks.

I was surprised that we had been sent across the Southern Atlantic Ocean with no cargo on board but apparently it was not uncommon. We now had definite orders of another cargo of Molasses from a combination of Durban and Lorenco Marques, which we would be taking back to Rotterdam.

The down side was that the cargo would not be ready until mid December in Durban and we were ordered to slow steam across the ocean making a ten day voyage last fifteen.

Very few people stayed in the bar after we had stowed the ropes and been stood down from our fore and aft stations.

I had stood out on the poop deck with Ray and Geoff watching Rio fade further and further into the distance as the light deteriorated until it was just a row of lights in our wake.

'Until the next time, then.' Ray had pondered as we delighted in the much-welcomed cool sea breeze that we had been deprived of over the past two weeks.

'That was a fucking brilliant run ashore.' I offered as a general summing up of the past few days alongside. I quickly showered and returned to the bar where only the Bosun, Tony, Mel and the Chief Steward sat deep in discussion.

'I'm glad you've come back up Jasper.' The Bosun began. 'We were just talking about you.'

'You were?' I asked suspiciously.

'Well you know we've lost the Messman until a replacement joins in Durban, don't you?'

'Ye-e-e-s.' I curiously agreed.

'Bill's just come down to ask if we can help out, and I've volunteered your services over to the catering staff until Durban.'

'You have?'

'You've only got to keep the Messroom clean, mop a couple of alleyways, lay the tables out at mealtimes and help serve the food in the galley.' He argued forcefully, but with a grin.

'At one time not so long ago,' Tony pointed out, 'there was no such thing as a Messman. It's only a luxury that the crew have been given in the last couple of years or so.'

'Quite.' The Bosun agreed. 'Before that it was always the runty little deck boy that cleaned the crew accommodation and served them their grub anyway.'

'What about Geoff doing it?'

'I've volunteered you. At least give it a go for a week. See how you get on and if you don't come up to scratch then we'll give Geoff a shot.'

I agreed somewhat reluctantly.

I was swayed when the Bosun had said that he would give me four hours a day overtime for working from six in the morning until one in the afternoon and then again from four until seven in the evening. I would be knocked off an hour earlier than the dayworkers and get three hours kip in the afternoons.

Bill thanked me with a can of Brahma Chopp (we had exhausted our supply of Yank beer, thank God, and now had the recently familiar Brazilian brew on board).

Des was now on the 4-8 watch and he bounced into my cabin, much too cheerfully for my liking, at six o'clock the next morning.

'Rise and shine, Mr. Messman' He joyously called to me in his deep, Guyanayan voice, his smile lighting up his dark face.

'What the fuck's the time?'

'It's six o'clock, Jasper. Time to get that Bacon sizzling. Hee! Hee! Hee!'

I groaned as he left my cabin still chuckling to himself. How the hell can somebody that never drinks be that annoyingly cheerful?

I got up to the Messroom for a quarter past six, made Myself a coffee and sat down for a fag before starting work at half six with Howard, Mel, Paul, Simon and Alan the Galley Boy.

'No James?' I enquired.

'He won't come in here.' Paul said matter of factly without lifting his head from his coffee. 'He gets withdrawal symptoms after we've left places like this. He probably won't be able to walk properly for a couple of days yet anyway.'

I laughed.

'What do you want me to do then, Chef?' I asked Howard.

'Wash up any plates or cutlery left in the sink in the night pantry area, empty the gash bin over the side, set the tables for breakfast, make sure none of the cereals have run out, fill the hot water geyser and then come and help us in the galley with the eggs and bacon.'

'I can't cook eggs.' I protested. 'I struggle with toast.'

'You will by the end of the week, Jasp. me old mate, you will.'

He bounced up out of his chair and headed for the galley, 'After breakfast come into the galley and help Alan strap up (wash up) and by the time all the lads have turned to you can have your own breakfast with us.'

He looked back at me for some sort of signal that I had understood so far. I nodded.

'And after breakfast?'

'Sweep and mop the Messroom through; tidy up and hoover the carpet in the bar, washing the glasses and polishing the tables. Make sure the geyser is full for morning smoko. We'll just take it up till then for now.'

'Ok.' I agreed putting my fag out and going straight over to the geyser that we had just about emptied.

'From empty it takes a good twenty minutes to boil up once filled with cold water.' Mel began to explain.

'The secret is to keep topping it up at regular intervals so as it never gives luke-warm water when people are trying to get a cup of tea. It isn't appreciated.'

I could understand that.

Des came down from the bridge at seven o'clock to call the dayworkers. 'Morning Messy! Hee! Hee!'

'Hello again Des.'

'I is going to be telling everybody we got ourselves a fine, young Messman when I call them.' He said slapping me on the back.

'Thanks Des.'

The Bosun and Billy Griggs shuffled sleepily through at five past seven and made themselves a large cup of tea each.

'Morning Jasper.'

'Morning Boas, Bill' I replied. 'I got woke up in the middle of the bloody night to get up for work.'

The Bosun just smirked as they sat down at their respective places in the Messroom.

I went back into the galley to help get the plates ready for breakfast but could overhear the Messroom banter as the lads began to surface for their breakfast.

'Hey. There's no fucking ash tray on this table.' Tony's voice shrieked through at me.

'Aven't we got a fucking Messman, or what?'

'Any tomato sauce knocking about, Lar.' Bob's Scouse accent boomed. 'Come on Jasper, buck your fucking ideas up.'

'Where's me favourite cup?' Mick the Chippy moaned.

Most thought it was hilarious but I just kept a low profile until the hatch opened up at seven thirty.

They all converged on the hatch at once; Steve piped up first. 'Fried egg breakfast, Jasp.'

Keith. 'Same here.'

Sid. 'Two four and a half minute boiled, Messman Sir. No snot.'

The Bosun. 'Two poached with tomatoes, please Messy' (at least he had the decency to say please).

Bob. 'Doubly egg brekkie, Lar. Sunny side up and don't break the yolks otherwise I'll fucking burst you, you little twat.'

Dixie piped up amongst the crowd. 'Usual please, Jasp.'

'How the fuck do I know what the usual is?'

'Come on, Jasper. Sort yourself out.' Ray shouted from the back of the queue.

'Mind your back' Mel warned as he zoomed over from the hot plates balancing three breakfasts on one arm.

'Full house.' He shouted offering one of the breakfasts to Steve.

'No black pudding.' Offering the next to Tony.

'There's yours, Boas.' Giving the two poached and tomatoes across the hatch to the Bosun. 'Right, Jasp. Come and get Bob's, Keith's and Dixie's.'

My head was spinning but within five minutes the Messroom hatch was clear. Mel was in his element and quite clearly had breakfast down to a fine art. Howard kept out of his way preparing pasties for lunchtime as he continued to deal with the stragglers in the Messroom and the demands of Simon and James who were serving in the Officer's Lounge.

I caught sight of a flustered James and gave him a little wave. He smiled but was obviously not having a good time of things as he dropped and smashed a coffee cup in his state of disarray.

The deck and engine room crowd turned to at eight and I sat down, lit a fag and breathed a huge sigh of relief.

Mel called me into the galley and made me prepare my own breakfast.

It wasn't that difficult. I managed to fry two eggs without breaking them, add two rashers of bacon and two sausages from the tray in the oven without burning myself and easily rounded the whole thing off with a ladle full of plum tomatoes.

'Nothing to it is there Jasp.' Mel smiled as he sat opposite me with his own breakfast.

'Can't understand why they need so long at sea school to learn it.' I said sarcastically. 'Piece of cake.'

The rest of the morning flew by as I cleaned the Bar and Messroom before the lads returned at morning smoko and then was detailed to mop the alleyway leading off from the bar where the Bosun and the rest of the Petty Officers had their cabins.

Serving dinner was a lot easier as it was just a set menu of soup, entrée, main course and sweet.

Only a handful ever had soup and very few bothered with the entrée unless it was something like spare ribs.

'It's only on there to pamper the bloody Officers.' Howard had explained, and from the menu's I had seen since being on board they very rarely consisted of anything appetising. Avocado with Vinaigrette Dressing today.

'What the fuck's that shite?' Tony had earlier enquired.

By ten to one I had strapped up, had my own lunch, wiped the Messroom tables down and was in the bar having a quick can of beer with Mel before going down to my cabin, changing into my shorts and heading up to the Monkey Island with a blanket and a book for three hours serious bronzying.

Maybe this Messman lark isn't such a bad thing after all.

I was quickly in to the routine and although I did miss not doing the deck maintenance jobs (the tank cleaning would start next week as the weather deteriorated slightly as we headed South) decided that I would see it through and gain the experience.

I took more note of people's preferences the next morning and by Saturday was able to have most breakfasts ready as soon as the individuals came to the hatch. Even to the extent of taking charge of a pan of twelve eggs frying at the same time.

'Get that fucking heat distributed over them, Messy.' Tony screamed at me as I tentatively flicked the fat over the top of the heating eggs with my egg slice.

Now that we were back at sea the Captain would be round at eleven o'clock for his inspection of the accommodation area. Until now I had only needed to be particular with my own cabin for cleanliness on such occasions but as the Bar and Messroom were public areas I set about freshening the whole place up straight after breakfast.

As soon as the lads had departed from morning smoko I gave the Messroom Bulkheads a quick suji to leave the whole place gleaming.

At twenty past eleven the white-gloved Captain appeared, torch in hand, through the galley with the Chief Engineer and the Chief Steward. My mind was cast back to the inspection of our dormitory at Gravesend and the fussiness of Captain Spearing running his hands above the lockers.

Captain Lord did exactly the same with my Messroom window ledges.

'Bad luck.' I thought to myself. 'I've just washed them, Buddy.'

'Very good.' The Captain noted to the Chief Steward. 'Better than when Arthur was here.' He said with a smile in my direction.

'You should see the After Pumproom Bilges, Sir.' I joked back knowing full well that he had watched us climb out of them all the way across from Rotterdam to Montreal earlier in the trip from the safe distance of the Bridge.

He laughed and Bill gave me a wink as they proceeded out through the Crew Bar giving it the third degree as they went.

As it was Saturday it was a half day for the deck and engine room crowd but I decided to take it easy drink-wise during the afternoon as I still had to serve them dinner and thought better of being half cut in the galley amongst all the hot plates and ovens (something that had never deterred Howard and Mel in the past).

Mick, Paddy, George and Tony had done their level best to drink us dry of Brahma Chopp by the time I decided to go up to the bar later in the evening.

Just ten minutes after I had arrived James made his dramatic entrance to cheers all round. Totally oblivious to the attention (or just plain contempt) he lifted his glass to the optic on the Gin bottle, poured a double, grabbed a can of tonic from the fridge and unceremoniously plonked two slices of previously prepared lemon into the overflowing glass.

He sat down, still in silence between me and Steve, as everybody continued to watch his every move.

'What's wrong with you fucking lot?' He asked after his first mouthful.

It was the first time I'd heard him swear.

'Evening James.' Tony mocked. 'How was Rio?'

'Better than this fucking shite-hole, dear.'

'Woooooaah!' The cry went round the bar.

Despite working in the galley for the past three days it was the first time I had seen James properly since we left and as the novelty of James' arrival to the bar died down I asked him. 'Well, how was Rio then James?'

'Oh! It was absolutely wonderful, Jasper. I got fucked senseless.'

The image was just repulsive as I shook my head and laughed at his statement.

James was in his late fifties now, couldn't have weighed any more than seven stone, his face was full of wrinkles and he wore a different wig for every day of the week I was sure of it. Even if I was to ever contemplate turning fruit I would be hard pushed to find him attractive, as nice a bloke as I did find him personally.

'I met a nice girl, Laura, in the Cowboy Bar.' I told him.

'Twenty years old, slender legs right up to her armpits, and the most gorgeous, firm set of tits you could ever imagine.'

'Yeuch!' James screwed his face up as if he was sucking on his slice of lemon. 'Sounds disgusting.'

The evening turned into another sing-song, the likes of which we hadn't had since our earlier westbound Atlantic crossing, as Mick's piano accordion and Mr. Kelly's harmonica made a quite welcome, if tuneless, reappearance to the bar.

I sure knew I had downed a few by the time Des called me at six the next morning. I had been used to getting an hours extra sleep on a Sunday morning after the night before but there were to be no such luxuries for a Messman.

I sat up in bed and lit my first cigarette of the day, my lifesaver, and with a thick head stumbled across the alleyway for a piss.

I struggled to pass anything at first despite the knowledge that my bladder was full and when I did it stung to high heaven. So much so that I had to sit down on the toilet to complete the job.

'Jesus Christ, that hurt.' I said to myself as I dressed for work.

It was quiet for breakfast as most hands were on a lie-in and I nursed my sore head with a cup of coffee with Ray who was now up and about preparing for his 8-12 morning watch.

Howard came through the Messroom door with Ray's breakfast (I was too ill to do it myself and Mel was late up as well).

'Morning Raymond. Anybody pissing broken bottles yet?'

'Cheers, Chef.' Ray replied receiving his breakfast. 'Not that I know of just yet. He paused for a second 'Plenty of time though.'

'What does he mean by pissing broken bottles?' I worryingly asked bearing in mind my lavatorial discomfort upon waking this morning.

'That's what it feels as if you're pissing when you've got a dose, mate. A sticky helmet and pissing broken bottles.'

I wondered if the look of horror on my face may have been a give away but just in case I waited for Ray to go back down to his cabin after his breakfast and legged it back to the toilet.

I was hoping that the pain experienced this morning had just been a chemical reaction in my body to the amount of beer I had consumed last night but my initial fears were compounded when I sat down on the toilet seat and lowered my underpants. A white, gooey patch in the gusset was staring straight up at me where my old man had been nestling and I could not produce any more pee for the life of me without one hell of a strain despite the three cups of coffee I had already drank this morning.

I spurted a tiny dribble into the pan and as I did a bolt of pain shot through my entire body from my dick down to my feet and right up to the top of my head as if I'd been struck by lightening.

I sat on the toilet with my head buried deep into my hands.

Bollocks!

There was nothing to do but go and see the Chief Steward.

I waited until after morning smoko when I wouldn't be missed and knocked on his cabin door.

'Morning Bill.' I said in a dull, serious tone.

'Morning Jasper, lad.' He replied looking up from his typewriter. 'What can I do for you?'

'Er! It's a bit personal.'

'Come in and shut the door then, lad.'

I did.

'I think I may have a dose, Bill.'

'You think? Have you or haven't you?'

'Don't really know, Bill. It hurts like hell when I go for a piss.'

'Are you blobbing up?'

I looked puzzled.

'Any discharge, Jasper? Any discharge from your bell end?'

'Er! Yes, I think so.'

'In that case you have. Don't worry lad. You're not the first and you will no doubt not be the last.'

He rose from his office desk, locking his cabin door, and beckoned me into his cabin.

'Should only be Gonorrhoea.' He casually announced as he dug around his medical locker.

'Syphilis doesn't usually rear its ugly head until after nine or ten days. I take it you bagged off in Rio?'

'Curacao as well Bill. That was well over ten days ago.'

'Chances are it's not Syph. If a shot of Penicillin doesn't shift it in a week then we'll look at the Curacao theory.'

I dropped my trousers as Bill purged the syringe.

'This is going to hurt you a lot more than it's going to hurt me.' He laughed.

'You're so considerate.'

'Try to relax.' He ordered as he dampened the flesh of my arse and I felt the needle enter me. He pressed on the syringe and I could feel my backside filling up with the stuff until he withdrew the needle and wiped again.

'There you go, lad. No alcohol for seven days. Change your underpants twice a day and wash your hands thoroughly after every visit to the toilet.'

'Am I OK to still work in the galley?' I asked worryingly. I don't know how but I maybe thought that I could keep this a secret.

'Messmen get doses, Jasper. So do Cooks, Second Cooks, Chief Stewards and even some Captains. Don't worry about it, lad, it goes with the job.'

I'm not sure whether that consoled me at the moment or not but I thanked him all the same as I left his office.

There is no way I could keep this a secret. The minute I refused a drink in the bar this evening I would be suspected.

'YOU'VE WHAT?' Ray howled with laughter at dinner time. 'Jasper's blobbing up.' He joyfully announced to the Messroom and bar all at once. 'I was going to go with her.' He gleefully remembered. 'You saved me from getting a dose.' He laughed even louder. 'Laura! I was going to fucking go with her. You told me she was the best of the lot. Cheers Jasp. Let me buy you a beer . . . Oh! No! You can't can you, Hahahaha!'

I sat at the table; just smirking pathetically and taking it all on the chin, making out I couldn't care less.

I had to. What else could I do?

'I said she was a fucking minger all along, eh!' Tony added as his penny's worth.

'You bagged off, Tone.' I reminded him. 'Could happen to you yet.'

'Not fucking likely, eh! I had a sock on, matey.'

The Bosun sat at the bar with a devilish grin on his face.

'You dirty fucking little bastard, Jasper.' He offered by way of sympathy for me. 'You can keep your dirty, grubby little mitts off my fucking eggs tomorrow.'

'Yeah, Jasp. Make sure you wash your hands properly.' Bob added.

'Never mind, Lar' he said slapping me on the back as he passed me. 'Only another six to catch before you can call yourself an AB.'

I stayed in my cabin that evening. I had taken just about as much ridicule as I could bear during the evening meal although I realised it was all good humoured it still did not detract from my feeling of shame.

There was a knock on my cabin door and Danny walked in with two cans of coke.

'You as well then Jasper, eh!' He sighed as he sat on my daybed and took a swig from his can.

'What? No, not you too, Danny.'

'Yep.' He nodded. 'Fucking charming isn't it. I even went back to her house this time last week and met her Mother.'

I know I shouldn't have done but all of a sudden I felt remarkably better.

'It'll be cleared up in seven days, Dan. Nobody at home need know.'

'Sure.' He agreed. 'Doesn't make me feel good about it though.'

'Does Tony know?' I laughed trying to cheer him up at the thought of how he would react.

'Yes he knows and has taken the piss un-mercilessly.'

At that precise moment George walked past my still open cabin door.

'Ding, Ding. Unclean, unclean.'

'Fuck off, George.'

Simon the Steward was the next to 'blob up' on the Monday morning so at least I wasn't facing my embarrassment alone.

I preferred to look on the positive side of things and as I had barely let a day go past since arriving onboard without touching an alcoholic drink decided that I now had a good excuse to go on the wagon for a couple of days and 'flush all the impurities out of my body' as Bill the Chief Steward had suggested, encouraging me to drink plenty of lime juice as well.

'There's enough Penicillin in there to cure you of all kinds of diseases.' He had charmingly explained as I was laying the table for lunch mid-way through the week.

'Scurvy, Dysentery, Botulism you name it we'll cure it.'

'I thought I only had a dose of the pox!'

I had to concede that I was feeling much livelier at six in the mornings of late without having to drag a thick head around with me until well after breakfast.

The weather was cooling now and although the sun was still fairly powerful it was accompanied by a strong Westerly breeze the more South Easterly we travelled towards the Cape of Good Hope.

This particular afternoon we were in for a treat as the Captain, aware of his orders to only slow steam across the Atlantic, had taken an eighty mile detour from our plotted course to pass within two miles of the Worlds undisputed remotest inhabited Island, Tristan da Cunha.

The ship was slowed right down as we passed the small settlement of Edinburgh, about seventy odd dwellings that had to be evacuated by the 250 or so inhabitants thirteen years ago in 1961 after a violent volcanic eruption.

All but two had elected to return two years later to continue their life of total isolation amongst the sheep.

'All interbred them.' Billy Griggs asserted, joining me by the starboard side poop deck handrails.

'Six toes each and club footed. It's either shag each other or get the wellies on and bother the sheep up in the mountains.'

'Not much of an existence.' I added. 'And bloody cold as well.' I noted as the wind whipped up around the Island.

It was no sooner right off our starboard bow than a fading blot in our wake and the excitement of seeing land over for another few days.

By Friday I was clear and so was Danny. The sensation of pissing broken bottles had left me after a couple of days as the Penicillin worked its magic and I had also thankfully now stopped sticking to my underpants.

I celebrated in the bar Saturday lunchtime and continued through until the Bosun shut the bar just before midnight despite the Chief Steward's warning that I may suffer a relapse by not giving the drug the full seven days to work.

'I'm clear.' I had shouted as if scoring the winning goal in an F.A.Cup Final.

'I should think so as well, dear.' James had scoffed. 'Fancy going with a slut in the first place.'

'Best turn fruit instead, James eh!' Tony had remarked.

James frowned. 'I think you're a closet Queen anyway, dear.'

Tony howled with laughter.

'I don't think so. Not at my age. No point turning queer halfway through your life is there? eh! Best to start off fruit from an early age and get the whole lifetimes benefits from it, eh, James.'

'If you say so, dear.'

We passed Capetown's Table Top Mountain six days later and I encountered my very first experience of the 'Cape Rollers', the term for the pitching and rolling motion that the vessel experiences around the Southern tip of Africa where the Western currents of the South Atlantic meet with those from the Indian Ocean.

We took quite a buffeting for a couple of days and everything had to be suitably battened down both on deck and in and around the accommodation block.

I had to dampen the tablecloths down prior to laying the Messroom tables and all the pots and pans in use on the galley stoves were cleverly held into position with removable bars to avoid spilling over.

There were inevitably accidents and cups, saucers, plates and pint glasses galore would come hurtling down smashing onto the deck into a thousand pieces if left unattended for a second.

'Don't worry. The Messman will see to that.' Was becoming a familiar cry.

It was difficult getting to sleep as the ship would be tossing and turning throughout the night and I wondered if, at any stage, I would be sick or not.

I think the fact that I had been introduced to the rough weather gradually helped and although feeling a bit queasy and light headed on a number of occasions during the couple of days around the cape I managed to keep everything down.

We were due to go alongside in Durban on December the fourteenth, just three days before my 18th birthday.

I knew very little of the turbulent history behind South Africa and to be quite honest wasn't really that much interested.

Billy Griggs, who knew absolutely everything there was to know about absolutely everything, had bored us rigid in the bar the other evening trying to explain the class system in the country.

I took on board enough to make out that the Blacks were at the bottom of the pile and that the Whites ruled supreme. There was very little in between.

It all sounded a bit unfair to me but Billy seemed to agree wholeheartedly with the system before going on to explain to us why Adolph Hitler had the right idea.

What a strange and disturbed man Billy was, I thought.

We entered the lengthy Durban harbour entrance in glorious sunshine and, although the sea breeze carried a bit of a chill, as South Africa's main seaside resort the beach away to our right could still be made out to be heavily populated with sun worshipers although unfortunately we would not be able to sample its delights this time around as we were only due to spend twenty four hours alongside.

The bulk of our Molasses cargo bound for Europe would be from Lorenco Marques just up the coast in war torn Mozambique.

Despite being Messman the Bosun did not spare me fore and aft berthing station duties and I did smile to Myself thinking of Billy Griggs' perception of the lifestyle here when I watched our head ropes being pulled ashore by a gang of about fifteen Black Africans under the guidance of a uniformed White Officer who paced along with them casually pointing to the bollard on the quayside that they were to throw the eye of the rope over.

Heaven forbid he should ever get his hands dirty.

Another crazy notion from this ridiculous situation was that we could not go ashore with Des or Wayvell. In fact both were advised not to go ashore at all by the Agent when he came onboard.

Apparently it wouldn't be seen in a good light that the two of them should be seen to have decent clothes and a bit of money to spend.

Besides they would have to walk on the other side of the road to us.

How ludicrous. Wayvell and Des didn't seem to mind as I suppose this wasn't the first time that they had experienced such problems but I felt quite acutely embarrassed for them and uneasy about a situation that I didn't quite fully understand.

True I had not been brought up in the company of any Black people and until I went to work in Wellingborough had never really encountered them on a day to day basis but I had grown to think very highly of my two Guyanese shipmates and they had certainly helped me and Geoff whenever we had required it.

All the same it was a shock to witness the way the Black Riggers were spoken to by their peers when connecting the shore side hoses to the ship's manifold.

Des helped one of them, struggling under extreme provocation to connect a hose by taking the weight with his shoulder whilst he connected the two flanges and received a warm but sad acknowledgement.

'Thank you, brother.'

Des patted him on the shoulder almost out of sympathy and the guy looked on in possible envy as me and Des carried on with our work together with a laugh and a joke.

As I was having my lunch the telephone in the Messroom rang and Tony answered it.

'OK, Chief. I'll tell the dirty bastards.'

He replaced the receiver.

'Danny, Jasper. Get showered you've got to pay a visit to the pox doctor this afternoon, eh!'

The Agent would be sending a taxi down at half one for the two of us plus Simon and Stuart, the deck Cadet, who unbeknown to me had also caught a dose in Rio.

I told the Bosun who seemed none to pleased with me for having an unscheduled half-day.

'If you think sticking a needle up your arse and filling you with Penicillin was painful you just wait until they stick an umbrella up your Jap's eye. He seriously warned.

'My what?' I naively inquired.

'Well they've got to find out if you're all clear or not, haven't they? Eh!' Tony interrupted. 'And the only way they can do that is by taking a blood sample and by collecting a swab from inside your bell end.'

'Still looking forward to your run ashore?' The Bosun taunted.

I concluded that it was just another wind up on Tony's behalf and that surely the blood test would suffice but wasn't so sure as Simon confirmed the methods to us rather disbelieving first trippers in the taxi to the Doctors.

I shifted uneasily in my seat as he explained, from experience, that the doctor would insert a small implement up through our Jap's eye which would then open out to reveal a couple of tiny hooks that would scrape the insides of our helmets as he withdrew it.

I began to take on a distinct loathing towards Laura (the fact that I had got myself into this situation had nothing to do with it).

Sure enough after we had each seen the Nurse in turn to give a blood sample we were summonsed one by one to see the doctor.

The embarrassment was heightened by the pure fact that everybody on the staff at the surgery knew exactly why we were there.

'Mr. Caswell?' The Doc. asked, knowingly, peering over the top of his glasses.

'Behind the curtain and pull your trousers and underpants down please.'

I duly obliged and watched in horror as he came round the side of the screen armed with his small medical bowl containing some cotton wool, a couple of plastic slides and an eight inch long thin surgical tool that could only possibly be the umbrella.

He ordered me to sit down and pull my foreskin back.

I did not like the look of this.

As if performing keyhole surgery he squeezed my Jap's eye expertly open with his gloved thumb and forefinger and inserted the umbrella a good inch inside.

I am not even going to attempt to describe the sensation as the hooks were engaged and scraped back down against my urethra wall. Suffice to say that broken bottles doesn't even come anywhere close.

My sample duly submitted I could breathe easily again and hastily pulled my trousers back up.

'Not very pleasant is it son?'

Fucking understatement of the year.

We could laugh about it as we refused the taxi back to the ship that the Agent had laid on for us, electing instead to walk the short distance to the bars along the sea-front to sample the local beer.

It was gone four o'clock anyway and I had a few dollars on me from my puddling money to see me OK for a couple of hours.

Two pubs were worth a visit and we sampled the 'Cockney Pride' first for a beer and a massive plate of fresh prawns for four before moving on to the unique 'London Town' pub.

Unique in that inside the Palm Beach Hotel is a red, double decker London Bus. Straight out of Cliff Richard's 'Summer Holiday', a novelty if ever I saw one and more than a good enough venue to consume lots of the local Castle Beer.

The more we drank the more we needed to visit the toilet hence soothing the damage that had been done in the Doctor's Surgery earlier in the afternoon.

'Never, never ever again.' Danny quite categorically insisted as we sat upstairs on the upholstered bus seats, the overwhelming urge to jump over to the sides and occasionally press the bell getting the better of us at regular intervals.

'I will remain faithful now for as long as I live.'

'Jesus, would you look at the tits on that, Dan.' Simon shouted.

'Where? Where?'

Once back on board I learnt that I had been relieved of my Messman duties.

George Reily, yet another Irish Scouser, had joined the ship as a replacement for Arthur whilst we had been ashore.

He was small, fat and greasy and at 61 good company for the rest of the sad old gits in the crew bar.

We left Durban the next morning, Sunday, and were frustrated to learn that although our next port of call, Lorenco Marques, was only just over twenty four hours steaming time away our berth would not be available until Boxing Day in eleven days time.

Another bloody week at anchor but at least the weather was still decent enough to continue deck fabric maintenance work if not all together suitable bronzy weather.

Billy Griggs treated us to a potted history of Lorenco Marques and the region of Portuguese East Africa in the bar that evening.

'Used to be just as good as Rio here.' He began. 'But the commies are still trying to get the fucking fascists out as we speak. They'd never be able to do it without the Russian's backing but the Portuguese are pulling out quicker than Jasper should have done with that bird in Rio when he discovered she was poxed up to the eyeballs.'

I resented the comparison.

'Lorenco's bombed to smithereens now. The whole infrastructure's bolloxed and the Portuguese have even tipped cement down the sewage system as a parting gesture. I find it hard to believe we've even got a cargo to pick up from here.'

'Shouldn't we be getting danger money?' Steve asked.

'Only if you're daft enough to go ashore when we get alongside. Get mistaken for being Portuguese and you'll be shot at dawn.'

By the time Billy began airing his beliefs as to why the revolution was justified we had all had enough and I think he sensed it as he just stood at the bar continuing his waffle but with everybody else engaging in their own conversations.

We anchored off Lorenco the following evening and the next day, Tuesday December 17th heralded my 18th birthday.

The Bosun refused my request not to work overtime that evening and then insisted that I 'fuck off straight down to get a shower' once we did eventually knock off.

Upon my return to the bar just after half past eight the place was heaving.

The bar had been decorated out with streamers plus a 'Happy 18th Birthday Jasper' banner as well as Christmas decorations that had also been hastily erected in my short absence.

I felt choked as the Bosun, repeat the Bosun, bought me my first can of beer of the evening.

I had been trying desperately not to think too much about being away from home for my birthday and for Christmas but as my Mother always ensured that our living room at home was decorated for my birthday and seeing the bar festooned as it was for my benefit it brought a lump to my throat.

The bar was packed as James came in from the galley delicately balancing a tray with a gigantic birthday cake with 18 lit candles on it that Mel had made especially for me.

James puckered his lips at me as I was treated to a rendition of 'Happy birthday to you. Happy birthday to you. Happy birthday dear Jasper. Happy birthday to yoooou.'

'Oi! I'm not that grateful.' I protested, side stepping James' advancing face.

I blew the candles out amid huge cheers and was encouraged to make a wish.

'I wish I hadn't fuckin' bagged off in Rio.'

Tony then reached down to the side of his chair and presented me with a large box wrapped up in green crepe paper.

'Sorry there's no proper wrapping paper, eh!' He apologised as he offered me his hand.

'Happy birthday, son. We've had a bit of a whip round.'

I was totally gobsmacked as I opened the box to reveal all kinds of goodies from the ship's bond.

1,000 Rothmans King Size (bang goes my hopes of packing up as a New Year's Resolution before I got home), six tins of boiled sweets, four bottles of cordial, toothpaste, writing paper and envelopes, a Gillette Razor (still not required) and two 'Fruit of the Loom' vests.

'I don't know what to say.'

For once in my life I was, literally, speechless.

'Thanks.' I blushed. 'You really are a bunch of pricks.'

I got absolutely wasted for the rest of the evening. I wasn't allowed to buy Myself or anyone else a drink and for the first time in the trip not only was the Chief Steward in the crew bar but Frank, the Chief Mate, also came down for a drink with me and to wish me a happy birthday as did the Fourth Mate, the two Cadets and a couple of the Engineers.

Later in the evening there was a knock at the bar door and in walked Captain Lord.

Interestingly Tony didn't shout at him to remove his epaulettes.

He asked for a small whisky and water, came over to me and shook my hand wishing me all the best, spoke to the Bosun for five minutes and then left.

I felt extremely honoured.

The next week at anchor waiting for Christmas and to go alongside dragged.

The daily routine changed very little.

Get up and have breakfast. Needle gun an area of maindeck. Have smoko, needle gun an area of maindeck. Have lunch and a can of beer, needle gun an area of maindeck. Have afternoon smoko, fresh water the needle-gunned area of maindeck. Red lead said areas. Have dinner and then potter about on overtime tidying the various deck lockers. Get a shower, go to the bar, get pissed and go to bed.

It was the first time I had become a little bit bored with things.

We had a couple of movie nights thrown in but there are only a certain amount of times you can watch 'The Graduate', and you can only watch 'Red Ridge Valley' once (or give up halfway through the second reel as I did).

Geoff and I did take it in turns for a day each to help Bob and Brian in the making of a new Pilot Ladder which gave us a bit of practical experience but other than that we had to contend ourselves with making up rope lashings with an eye splice in one end and a back splice in the other.

Any wire splicing or mooring rope splicing was given to Albert, Bob, George or Brian if the Bosun didn't do it himself.

It was nice that Christmas Day was falling mid-week as the tedium was broken up nicely. None of the galley staff, with the exception of the new Messman came up to the bar on Christmas Eve.

Their day would be extremely busy catering for all our needs and even though there weren't too many in the crew that could drink as much as Howard and Mel I got the impression that personal pride played a big part in the presentation of Christmas Dinner and that both wanted to approach it with a clear head.

I got up at ten on Christmas Morning to find Mr. Kelly, Paddy, Tony and Dixie already on the beer.

The Bosun somewhat reluctantly agreeing to open the bar all day as well as offer free beer out of the bar profits.

It didn't feel like Christmas Day at all. Sure we had decorated the bar and had a sad looking tree balancing precariously in the corner but outside the sun was shining and there was warmth in the sea breeze.

I made myself a coffee and sat down in the bar with the old codgers.

'What's the matter with you, Jasper eh!' Tony scoffed. 'Dose come back has it? For fuck sake it's Christmas. Get a beer down you lad.'

He was right of course. I tipped my coffee down the sink and went behind the bar to the fridge just as the Bosun walked through.

'You're becoming a fucking alki, Jasper.' The Bosun said disapprovingly.

'Lighten up, Boas. It's Christmas.'

'It's just another day, son. Just another day.'

It wasn't, of course, just another day as far as Howard and Mel were concerned and they didn't disappoint as we left the now almost full crew bar for our Christmas Dinner at midday.

I had the Turkey, which almost melted in my mouth it was that tender, with all the trimmings. A luxury I had never before experienced in the past on Christmas Day as our meagre resources at home only ever extended to a flimsy, rather anaemic looking Chicken with roast potatoes.

Tournedos of Beef was also available. A round, succulent three-inch thick wedge of beefsteak, and a popular choice for a lot of the older hands. The sight of the blood pouring out of Tony's and dribbling down his unshaven chin slightly putting me off.

It was all washed down with a choice of either 'Blue Nun' white wine or a gorgeous sparkling South African Red called 'Cold Duck.'

Now I'm no connoisseur of wines, I only just about knew that they came in three different varieties of dry, medium and, er! whatever the other option is.

This little number that the Chief Steward had purposely ordered two cases of whilst in Durban just for the occasion tasted very much to me like the 'Corona' Cherry Pop that I used to buy from Bailey's every week with my pocket money, and went down just as easily with the accompanying bubbles shooting up my nostrils as I guzzled it back.

I struggled through my home made Christmas Pudding with Brandy Sauce and sat at the table, bloated, with my favourite post meal ciggy pulling crackers and donning silly paper hats with the rest of the lads, slowly finishing off the wine.

We retired back to the bar just in time for the galley staff to sit down to their Christmas Dinner. The Chief Steward insisting that they all take their places with their bottles of wine as none other than Captain Lord, The Chief and Second Engineers, the Radio Officer and the Chief Mate waited the table for them.

The gesture was well appreciated by them all but pushed to the boundaries when Simon clicked his fingers and addressed the Captain as 'garcon' when he wanted another glass of wine.

Whilst having their dinner and whilst we continued to veg. out in the bar the junior Officers and Cadets were in the galley strapping up and tidying the saloon ready for the evening cold buffet to be set out.

The galley staff finally joined us in the bar around mid afternoon and it wasn't until later on in the evening when I traipsed round to the saloon for more food that I fully appreciated the magnitude of their task today.

The top table in the saloon was set out more banquet style than buffet and in the centre of the table, looking decidedly sorry for itself, sat a roasted suckling pig with an apple ceremoniously wedged in its mouth.

'Shouldn't the apple be up its arse?' Tony asked Mel.

No expense had been spared by Athel Line to ensure that we were well and truly pampered and we rounded the day off with complimentary bottles of Drambuie, Cognac and Harvey's Bristol Cream, which I obviously tested but, apart from the Harvey's which I had tried before, found very sickly and didn't enjoy one bit.

Paddy and Mr. Kelly consumed a whole bottle of Drambuie between them leading to the conformation of the fact that they would indeed drink any old shite.

'I'm surprised you've got any fucking liver left, Paddy.' The Bosun had commented.

Paddy just raised his glass in return and offered the Bosun the permanent grin that had been etched on his face since the free booze had begun to flow this morning.

I didn't last much past eight in the evening and when I did decide to turn in only the catering staff remained in the bar. Geoff and I helped Mr. Kelly take

Paddy down to his cabin despite his incoherent protests that; 'I'm all right, I'm all right. Where's that fucking Bosun? I'm gonna thump the bastard.'

Boxing Day seemed such an anti-climax and it was as if yesterday had never occurred.

The only difference being that as it was a bank holiday we were being paid double time and we didn't turn to until nine o'clock.

We would be going alongside at mid-day and we spent the morning topping the Starboard derrick, moving the accommodation ladder across and bringing the mooring ropes up onto the fo'c'stle and poop deck respectively.

When we did get alongside our misery was compounded by the Agent confirming that there was no shore leave for us as the tanks were still thundering along the main drag seeking out the last pockets of Portuguese resistance and besides there was a seven o'clock evening curfew in place.

The loading of the cargo would be a slow process to boot with only two eight-inch shore side hoses connected up to the manifold.

It was heartbreaking from the Bosun's point of view to see sticky, gooey Molasses being dropped and trampled all over our newly painted sparkling grey maindeck.

Things went from decidedly bad to worse when we were told that we would be alongside for at least an extra two days making it five instead of three. The Bosun had only stocked enough beer for the three days and although he had attempted to ration it during the third day we ran out early evening on the fourth.

A stand up battle had begun between Paddy and the Bosun during afternoon smoko on the fifth day 'Is there any chance of a case of beer off the Chief Steward for knocking off time, Boas?' Paddy had asked.

'Look, Paddy. If I've told you once I've told you a thousand times.' The Bosun calmly replied. 'We'll be sailing tomorrow morning. The Chief isn't allowed to open the bond or beer locker until then. Another day without won't harm you' (I had my doubts by the way Paddy was shaking).

'Can you not ask the Officer's bar to lend us a case?'

What happened next took me, and I'm sure everybody else in the Messroom, completely by surprise.

The Bosun shot up out of his chair and within a split second had dived over towards Paddy, gripping him by the throat and pinning him up against the wall.

'There's no beer until tomorrow you little cunt.' He screamed and before Tony could get out of his chair to restrain him he had slapped Paddy so hard around the face that it had turned beetroot instantly and sent him crashing back down into the seat that he had just been manhandled out of, breaking the backrest off completely such was the force.

'Hey, there's no need for that.' Mr. Kelly protested dashing over to attempt to comfort his friend.

'Want some, Kelly?' The now fuming and heavily breathing Bosun demanded clenching his fists this time.

Kelly held his hands up. 'No, Boas. Enough, come on enough.'

'Enough, Boas, eh?' Bob Dewhurst sprang to his feet. At only 25 and a good eighteen inches taller proving a worthy mediator.

The Bosun sat back down catching his breath but still struggling for air in his rage.

'Little cunt.' He spat back in Paddy's direction.

'Fuck off to your cabin, Paddy.' Bob wisely advised.

He did as he was told and calm was restored.

It had upset me quite a bit as I admitted to Bob later on that evening as he came round to my cabin for a game of crib.

I suppose I had seen us as one big happy family and as I had tried to get along with everybody I guess I was struggling to come to terms with the fact that there were going to be differences of opinion and personality clashes somewhere along the line.

'I'm surprised the Bosun hasn't twatted him long ago, Lar.' He confessed.

'Don't let it worry you, kid. You worry when people start chasing each other around with meat cleavers and fire axes.' He laughed as I gulped and looked at him for some kind of sign that he was joking.

He raised his eyebrows at me to suggest that he wasn't.

We departed soon after breakfast the next day, New Years Eve, much to everyone's relief.

The thought of seeing the New Year in without a beer far too traumatic for any of us to imagine.

For a supposedly war ravaged city we had seen or heard very little evidence. Police Car sirens wailing through the City Centre some two miles away as near as we came to even a hint of the troubles surrounding us.

In all it had been a fairly depressing few days since Christmas and I hoped that seeing the New Year in might improve the mood amongst the crew a bit who had been dry for the last forty eight hours.

The situation between the Bosun and Paddy had eased as Paddy was now on the 8-12 watch for the duration of the eighteen day passage back up the West Coast of Africa and on through the Bay of Biscay and back up to Rotterdam.

The mood did indeed return to normal as we all partook in the seeing in of 1975 with some considerable style. It was the first time in my life that I had ever indulged in these festivities, never before having grasped the significance of celebrating the dawn of a New Year.

I was therefore just a silent contributor in the events at midnight as we gathered round the foremast, linking hands and singing some song called 'Old Langsine' or something. Sounded German to me although I was assured that it was Scottish.

We rang the ship's bell up on the fo'c'stle head twelve times and the Captain gave several blasts on the ship's whistle (hopefully we were clear of any shipping by now), and then returned to the bar.

In a rare display of generosity the Bosun kept the bar open until one o'clock and almost begrudgingly watched as Paddy took four cans from the fridge for himself now that he had been relieved of his watchkeeping duties. We could have taken the next day off if we wished but I personally saw no reason to as did any of the others and we turned to at nine to begin smartening up the maindeck for our arrival back to the European Continent.

We expected a couple of rough days going back round the Cape but we would then experience a week to ten days of brilliant bronzy weather as we headed back up to the equator.

My monthly pay slip, or Kalamazoo as it was known as, revealed that I had earned a staggering £22 for the month of December. However this was an improvement on my November total of £6.23p after all my Cruzeiros had been deducted from my salary.

My bar bill had been horrendous for the last two months also and I had a total of £68.40p on board the ship to my name.

'Ah well, you've saved a little.' Ray noted, trying to sound encouraging that I had, at least, not spent all of my wages.

'I bet the likes of Mr.Kelly and Paddy haven't got much more than that in the ship and they're on three times your wages.'

I nodded an agreement but decided that I must cut the drinking down a bit between now and Rotterdam.

I would be getting at least 32 days paid leave at the end of the voyage (8 days per month), even if we paid off before the end of January, and I wanted something to show for my efforts other than a butterfly tray and a note to visit my Doctor when I got back home to Kettering.

The Cape Rollers whipped the ship around a bit as we passed through them again but a combination of the fact that we were more heading into the current this time and the fact that we were fully laden contributed to an altogether much smoother experience for the twenty four hours or so that we were at their mercy.

Emerging out the other side and with each day now becoming hotter and hotter it was a case of roll the shorts up as far as they could go and roll the socks down so that as much skin as possible could be exposed to the sun's rays.

I was determined to go back home in the depths of winter with as dark a tan as I could possibly achieve.

The deck programme for the week was just paint, paint and more paint. The areas of the maindeck that had blistered with the Molasses being spilt upon it were scraped by me and Geoff using a long handled deck scraper and red leaded again each evening.

Two paint spray guns had been acquired in Durban and Brian and John took one side of the ship each spraying the tank lids and Butterworth lids and any other fixture that didn't move.

'Don't lean on that fucking scraper too long, Jasper,' the Bosun had warned, 'you'll end up fucking grey.'

The ship was transformed and by the time the weather looked as if it was about to deteriorate, now North of the Equator, we rolled the entire maindeck again in grey (for the third time this trip).

'A waste of fucking time.' Mr.Kelly had lamented. 'As soon as we hit the Bay of Biscay it'll all peel off again and be full of fucking rust streaks by the time we even get to Rotterdam.'

As we arrived off the Southern tip of Portugal, thirteen days after leaving Lorenco and five days from Rotterdam we received our final orders for discharge.

One berth in Rotterdam and then across the North Sea to Wallsend, much to the delight of our two Pumpmen.

The four that had joined three weeks previous to me in Durban; Ray, Willy, Wayvell and Des were advised that they would be paying off in Rotterdam, the rest of us a few days later in Wallsend, possibly around the 25th of January.

That would give me four months to the day on board. Not bad considering I had been forewarned to expect trips of between five to seven months.

In all honesty I began to feel a little sad as the gathering tempest slowed us down to a crawl entering the Bay of Biscay having by now left the warmer climes well and truly behind.

The sheer greyness and dampness of the day matching my mood as we began sujiing the housing down from top to bottom in an attempt to brighten the ship up.

I wanted to go home. I wanted to show everybody at home what I had achieved, where I had been, my bronzy, how much of a great time I had had and how much I had grown up, but at the same time I didn't want the trip to end.

What would happen to me next? I would surely not be with such a great crew next time around. I wouldn't be a first tripper anymore.

'I don't know if I'll do another trip.' Geoff confided in me in my cabin that evening as the Bay continued to toss us around.

'What?' I couldn't believe my ears.

'I don't know, John. I've enjoyed myself but I'm not entirely sure that it's me.'

Geoff confessed to having the same fears as me regarding how we would be treated next trip. I tried to convince him otherwise but I sensed that he was being serious.

'The fight between Paddy and the Bosun made me think again.' He added. 'Although I was already beginning to have second thoughts it really scared me.'

I tried to snap him out of it. 'Look, Geoff. The Captain's giving us both a shot on the wheel coming in and out of Rotterdam. It's what we spent all that time at sea school learning.'

'I didn't pass my E.D.H., remember?' He countered.

'What about the bagging off in Curacao and Rio? Surely you fancy some more of that?'

'I did enjoy myself, yes. Just haven't enjoyed the being onboard the ship part of things that's all.' He paused for a thoughtful second before adding, 'Don't tell anyone will you?'

'No.' I sighed. 'But I hope you'll change your mind.'

'I'll think about it.'

I doubted he would.

I felt quite sorry for him. He was a quiet and shy lad despite his size and although he had his moments in the bar and ashore they were all very few and far between. I had got the impression from very early on in the trip that you were more likely to be accepted if you had a good social side to yourself. I don't in any way class that as justification for the fact that, apart from the one week, I have more or less had a good drink nearly every night since I joined. Just that it seemed the acceptable thing to do. Despite the Bosun not always approving I had never given him cause for concern through not getting up to work through my drinking habits.

Maybe it was the fact that I was a bit older than Geoff and the same could also be said of Danny and Keith whereby Keith, being the elder, was in the bar more than Danny.

What was worrying Danny, however, was the fact that despite having been given the all clear at the Doctors in Durban he was beginning to show signs that his problem had re-occurred. It left me frantically checking myself every time I went to the toilet although it wasn't that much of a significance to me bearing in mind my lack of sexual activity back home compared to Danny's.

'It's just a strain, lad.' The Chief Steward tried to convince him.

'Have you been pulling yourself at nights?'

Danny didn't answer but continued to appear worried.

Late on the Thursday evening, long after we had left the Bay of Biscay and Ouessent Lighthouse behind we arrived in the sheltered Brixham Harbour to pick up our Channel Pilot.

The Captain had ordered three men on a watch due to the poor visibility and I took up my position on the 4 to 8 watch with Brian and Ray as Geoff was handed third man on the 8 to 12 with Paddy and Bob.

It was a shock to the system as Albert called me at half past three in the morning.

'The Pilot has been onboard for two hours,' Albert informed us as we had a quick cup of coffee in the Messroom.

We were to do a half an hour about between the three of us. The first man, Brian, would do half an hour on the wheel, Ray would do half an hour as lookout on the leeward starboard bridge wing, and I would be half an hour in the Messroom. At half past four we would all move around one.

At five minutes to four Brian and Ray departed for the bridge to relieve Willie and John McClean.

'I could murder a fucking beer.' Albert confessed as we awaited their return from the bridge.

The thought of it turned my stomach as I lit another cigarette.

'Make sure you're well wrapped up when you go up there, Jasper.' John said to me as he made himself a cup of tea before going to his cabin.

I was taking no chances. I had a vest, T-shirt, sea school shirt and a hand knitted jumper from my Mother on as well as Long Johns under my jeans.

I put my duffel coat on as I made my way, outside the accommodation block, up towards the wing of the bridge at twenty five past four to allow Ray to relieve Brian on the wheel.

Ray pointed out three ships off our port bow that had been reported and two to our starboard side, both heading in the opposite direction to us.

Brian came out of the wheelhouse and stood with me.

'It's your coffee break, Brian.' I urged.

'You're all right, Jasper.' He replied. 'I'll stand with you for your first half an hour.'

'Thanks mate.' I replied although I was feeling fairly confident.

Visibility was no more than four miles but I was able to keep a good eye on the ships to my port side, two of which we were overtaking, and the other two passed us on our starboard side within a couple of minutes.

I squinted through the freezing dark haze and spotted my first ship two points off my starboard bow.

'Go in and tell the Second Mate, then.' Brian encouraged.

'Vessel two points to starboard, Dave.' I reported to David Graham, the Second Officer, who was already plotting its course along with all the other vessels in view on the large radar screen on the starboard side of the wheelhouse.

'Thank you, John.' He replied. 'That one is five miles away which means the visibility is improving.'

I felt suitably chuffed with myself as I joined Brian back on the wing of the bridge.

It was soon five to five and I stepped up to the wheel, behind Ray, to relieve him of his quartermaster's duties. I felt both nervous and excited at my first stint at the wheel under Pilot's orders.

'All steady on zero eight eight degrees, Jasper.' Ray whispered in the darkness.

'She's taking the occasional bit of port wheel, but no more than five degrees at a time to keep her steady.'

'Aye, Aye.' I replied.

'Okay, Jasp?'

I took the helm. 'Okay.'

'Wheel relieved on zero eight eight, Pilot.' Ray shouted at the silhouette seated by the bridge windows high up in the Pilot's chair.

'Zero eight eight. Thank you, Sir.' He replied.

The ship remained steady for a good five minutes before I heard the dreaded click in front of me and the card indicated that the heading was slowly drifting off to starboard.

I applied my five degrees of port rudder and took it off again as the head slowly but satisfyingly eased its way back to zero eight eight and stayed there.

I could see the Second Mate and the Captain out of the corner of my eye at the radar screen and after a brief consultation the Captain went over to the Pilot and spoke softly to him, pointing out my ship to starboard that I had reported earlier.

'Starboard Five.' The Pilot ordered, almost taking me by surprise.

'Starboard Five, Pilot.'

'Steer One zero two.'

What? What happened to Jackson's 'Meet the helm?' Or 'steady as she goes, Mr. Quartermaster?'

Shit. We were already hurtling to one zero two. The ship on our starboard bow now having been transferred to our port bow.

I threw caution to the wind and applied twenty degrees port wheel to steady the ship.

It stopped on one zero four, I was well chuffed.

I slowly eased the head back to the ordered course.

'One zero two, Pilot.'

'Steer one zero four.'

Bastard. I've just come from there.

With the ship already drifting to starboard I just left the wheel amidships and applied port wheel once it started to naturally drift to starboard.

'Steering one zero four, Pilot.' I confirmed not even a minute after he had ordered it.

'Thank you, Sonny.'

Brian relieved me after half an hour.

'Well done, Jasper.' He whispered as I handed over to him.

'Thank you, Sonny.' The Pilot acknowledged as I informed him of the change at the helm.

'Well done, Jasper.' The Captain called from the radar.

I felt bloody great as I made my way back to the Messroom for a well deserved coffee and ciggy and by the time I had completed another hour's stint as both lookout and helmsman considered it a walk in the park.

The Bosun was delighted with me as I assured him that I had encountered no problems at all, which was confirmed by Brian.

I hoped that Geoff was coping just as well and that the pure excitement of actually steering the ship in heavy traffic may persuade him to change his mind about his future.

There was very little to do on deck because of the inclement weather and the Bosun didn't call us to work overtime in the morning so I had a massive breakfast and showered before climbing into bed at half nine.

It seemed a strange time to be sleeping and I could sense the daylight creeping through my cabin porthole despite the fact that I had dropped my 'deadlight' down over it.

I must have slept well because no sooner had my head hit the pillow than Albert was calling me again at three thirty in the afternoon.

'We're well passed Dover now, and will be up at Rotterdam about two in the morning. Not sure yet if we'll be going straight alongside.'

This was far too much information for me to take in as I struggled out of bed, still trying to work out why I had been asleep in the daytime.

I survived a much more hectic evening watch as we altered course virtually every minute in the congested sea-lanes of the North Sea.

I took the chance at eight o'clock in the evening that we would anchor off for the night and had a deserved couple of beers, proud of my achievements over the past few hours.

Geoff had done well in his stints at the wheel but was still nowhere near as enthusiastic as I was about the whole thing.

Ray went straight down and showered after our watch to commence some serious packing. The bastard was going home tomorrow.

I stood in Ray's cabin doorway as he packed contemplating whether to get a shower or not.

I couldn't believe he was going home tomorrow. It only seemed five minutes since we had first met.

'It's been a good trip, hasn't it Ray.' He stopped loading his suitcase and turned round to look at me, unaware that I had been watching.

'Brilliant.' He replied. 'Even better than my first trip.'

'Yeah, it's been good.' I confirmed.

'Are you going to come back with the company?' He asked.

'I think so. I've got used to it and know the layout of everything on deck now. It'll certainly be easier if I do come back on another ship like this.'

'That's why me and Willy came back.'

He paused.

'Geoff?'

'I don't know, Ray. Probably not.' I shrugged.

'I don't think he's cut out for it. You'll be all right next trip. You never know, I might even be there with you.'

'I hope so, mate.' I admitted.

He smiled up at me and I burst out laughing as he packed his hair drier.

'You've got a fucking hair drier, you tart.'

'It's not just my sun-kissed body that attracts the girls, you know.'

I stifled a snigger as he flexed his arm muscles.

'Do you fancy a weekend in Sheerness when you get home, Jasp?' He asked as he continued to pack. 'I'm sure there's more going on there than there is in Kettering. We could even have a night out in London if you like.'

The idea did sound quite good and I took his home phone number, promising to give him a call when I got home.

I bid him goodnight and went straight to my bunk, still unsure as to whether I would be called for the four to eight watch in the morning but this time I just lay there tossing and turning.

For one I had slept all day so didn't feel particularly tired but most of all I couldn't sleep due to a combination of excitement for myself at the prospect of being at home soon and depression that I was losing my best friend from the trip in the morning. From the moment I set foot on the ship in late September Ray had never been far away from me.

Although never in the bar as much as I was, partly due to his watchkeeping duties and partly through choice, we had shared some memorable times ashore as well as just being someone to sit in the cabin and have a chat with.

I was going to miss him.

It seemed a totally different kind of friendship that I had realised with Ray compared to the likes of Phil, Barry and Malc at home.

It didn't bother me in the slightest turning my back on them and going away to sea. People I had known all my life and yet here I was lying awake wondering if I would ever see Ray again and worrying that maybe I wouldn't.

I must have eventually dozed off but I certainly felt as if I had been deprived of sleep when Albert called me at five o' clock the next morning.

'We're lifting anchor in half an hour, Jasper.' He announced fairly quietly.

'It's only an hour to the berth and the Captain has asked if you would like to take the helm for berthing.'

'Yeah, sure.' I yawned, rubbing my eyes.

Ray took the wheel for the first half an hour as the anchor was lifted and the Pilot boarded and then handed over to me as the crew turned to for stations fore and aft and the tugs were made fast.

We were berthing again in Vlaardingen, where we had been earlier in the trip, only at a different jetty this time.

There really was nothing to it. The combination of the tugs and the ship's engines doing most of the work as we inched alongside with just an occasional 'hard a port' or 'hard a starboard' thrown in as a small contribution.

Not that the minimum of involvement from the helmsman could take away my immense feeling of pride and achievement in the fact that I had actually steered the ship alongside.

I was stood down from the helm by the Captain once the headropes were ashore and by the time I reached the fo'c'stle head we were just tightening the last of our springs.

With us being fully loaded the accommodation ladder just slid outboard and onto the jetty that our maindeck was more or less level with.

Ray let out an almighty 'yeeha!' as a mini-bus pulled up and four people with suitcases got out together with John Lawson, the Athel Line Personnel Officer that I had met with prior to joining the ship.

I picked at my breakfast as Ray, Willy, Wayvell and Des quickly scurried down to their cabins for a shower and a last minute tidy.

Within fifteen minutes Ray was back in the Messroom, fully booted and spurred and ready to go.

The Bosun turned us to again at nine o'clock and I shook hands with the four of them that were leaving. I flung my arms around Des and thanked him for all he had done for me during the past four months.

Ray and Willy I may see again as they were contracted to Athel Line. Wayvell and Des, I was absolutely certain, I would never see again in my entire life.

'Bye, mate, take care.' I bade to Des. I was feeling quite emotional but was soon bought back to reality.

'No such thing as mates, here.' Tony butted in. 'Just Board of Trade Acquaintances.'

He was right. There was no real point in striking up good friendships with shipmates when at the end of the day it would all end in a brief handshake, a couple of token well wishes then never to be seen again.

Still, there was no harm in showing my appreciation towards someone that had done me no harm at all and had helped me immensely through the trip. I'm sure that as life progressed and I matured I wouldn't become so attached to these people in the future.

By half nine they were out on the maindeck with their suitcases and off down the gangway to the taxi that had bought their reliefs out, the flight from Schiphol to Gatwick departing at one.

'Back home before you knock off tonight, Jasper.' Ray shouted at me from the jetty.

'Keep in touch.'

I stuck two fingers up at him.

'Will do.'

With a fleeting wave and a toot on the mini-bus horn they were gone.

'Lucky bastards.' Mr. Kelly moaned at me.

'Never mind, Mick. It'll be us next week.'

Mr. Lawson was holding session in the Messroom after lunchtime talking to all of the company personnel as well as any others that wanted to see him on matters concerning the voyage.

He called me through to see him just as we were preparing to turn to for the afternoon.

'How's it going, John?' He asked as he gestured to the Messroom seat opposite him. I was surprised he had recognised me as I had changed beyond all recognition from the nerd in the Sea School uniform that had confronted him in the Mark Lane offices in September to the scruff in the boiler suit, starched with red lead and battleship grey paint, with hair that was beginning to curl again around my ears that I was presenting myself as now.

'Fine.' I replied shaking his hand.

He had obviously done his homework as he studied a file on me that he had opened out before me.

'You've got your steering ticket, turned eighteen and shown a lot of enthusiasm, it says here.' He tapped the file with his pen and smiled, bringing the pen back up to his lips.

'I have?'

'Both the Bosun and the Chief Mate have said some very encouraging things about you.'

'And Messman.' I added. 'Does it mention that I've also been Messman?'

He laughed. 'Yes, we were aware of it at the time back at the office. It proves your flexibility as well, which is always appreciated.'

He paused. 'Will you be coming back with us for another trip, John?' He asked, 'Now that you are over 18 and have served more than three months at sea and have your steering ticket we can offer you your next appointment as Junior Ordinary Seaman.

You can sign a twelve month contract with the company here and now and when you leave the vessel you will be on paid leave until the minute you join your next ship.'

I had to admit that the idea appealed. It would save all the hassle of going back to the Prescott Street Pool as soon as my leave expired and having to go through the whole process of taking pot luck as to what ship to join next time around.

Plus I felt a little sense of loyalty already. Athel Line had been good enough to encourage me to go to sea school and had then kept their promise to take me on at the end of my course.

I looked up at him and eagerly smiled. 'Where do I sign?'

'Good man.' He enthused. 'Just sign here.'

He pointed to the bottom of a two-page document ALREADY made out in my name with the title J.O.S. in the 'Capacity' column.

Now there was confidence for you.

I got up and shook his hand again. He had told me that I had twenty-eight days leave as from when I paid off the ship and that I would need to contact the company again on February 20th for my next appointment (bloody hell, I thought, I haven't even finished this one yet).

'You've signed a fucking contract?' Bob shouted at me back on deck. 'Well, you dozy bastard.'

'How do you work that out?' I argued.

'That's you fucked now. You'll always be on fucking chemical tankers. You'll never get on a proper ship now. You'll get too used to the easy life.'

'Easy life? Humping 90 feet of Butterworth hose around a deck all day in freezing cold fucking temperatures, humping ten-ton flexible cargo hoses around a deck all day, humping this, humping that. Fucking easy?'

'Yeah, but there's no proper seamanship work like wire splicing cargo runners every day like there is on a cargo ship.'

Just as well, I thought.

'No working the derricks and hatches every day, now that's hard work compared to lugging a few little hoses around.' He continued to labour the point.

'You not on contract then, Bob?' Albert asked.

'Me? Course I am, Lar. But only for a year. I signed a contract for a rest.'

'Bollocks.' I laughed.

I spoke to Geoff later that evening and he told me that he had spoke to Mr. Lawson and although he had been offered a contract as well he hadn't signed it.

'I'll wait and see how I feel at the end of my leave.' He told me although I sensed, especially with Ray and Willy now gone, that he had already made up his mind about it.

Danny had also spoken to Mr. Lawson and had asked to stay on board for another trip or a 'double-header' as it was termed. Danny's dose of the clap had returned as confirmed by the Doctor in Rotterdam this afternoon and he had now been put on a seven-day course of Streptomycin.

'Penicillin with knobs on.' Tony had reassured him.

'If that doesn't cure it then you'll be best having it fucking chopped off, eh!'

Danny was distraught and tearfully pleaded with Mr. Lawson that he couldn't possibly go home in the state he was in.

He had received eighteen letters from his girlfriend today upon our arrival back on the continent all explaining quite graphically what she was going to do in bed with him as soon as he got home.

'Tell her not to pull on it too hard, Danny boy.' Billy Griggs had advised. 'It might come off in her hand.'

Although sympathetic Mr. Lawson could only offer that Danny stays on board until the end of the coast, which could give him up to ten more days' breathing space after we arrived in Wallsend.

'The tablets should have had the desired effect by then.' Mr. Lawson surmised with all the authority of a personnel manager that has more than likely encountered this type of request and for the very same reason countless times before.

I felt really sorry for him and just kept my fingers crossed that the same fate did not befall me. I also realised that here was another scenario that I was getting involved in that I would more than likely never get to know the outcome of. I really did hope for Danny's sake that this course of action would work and felt quite upset for him.

It did make me realise that if I did ever get into a serious relationship back home (as if), that these could be the consequences for myself in the future if I continued to bag off with the same amount of enthusiasm as I had this trip.

We departed from Rotterdam harbour late on Monday evening for the short hop across to Wallsend, but instead were ordered to anchor outside Rotterdam for two days due to our berth on Tyneside not being available until Thursday.

Just our luck. Everybody was now just desperate to get off the ship even though, for some, it had been one of the shortest trips in their entire sea going career.

We had plenty of bar profits to turn into liquid so the Bosun put free beer on in the crew bar for both the Tuesday and Wednesday nights sat at anchor.

The two new AB's that had relieved Des and Wayvell took the anchor watches between them and I joined the rest of the crew on both nights reminiscing on some of the finer points of the last four months.

Both Mr. Kelly and Paddy left us in no doubt as to what they had thought of Athel Line, The Anco Empress and, in particular, the Bosun.

'If every ship in this company is run by a Little Hitler like that then good fucking riddance.' Paddy politely summed up his own feelings.

'You can stick this company right up the little fat fucker's arse.'

'You won't be signing a contract then, Lar?' Bob enquired.

'No, I fucking wont. You can stick your fucking contract up his arse as well.'

Apart from John McClean and Mick the Carpenter all the rest of the deck crowd were on a company contract as well as the entire engine room staff and all except Simon from the galley staff.

Nobody seemed to mind Paddy's outburst though.

'I told you, Paddy. I'm only here for a rest.' Bob continued.

'Rest my fucking arse.' Paddy continued, biting now at everything Bob and the likes of Tony could throw at him.

'You'll be straight on the phone when you get home asking to sail with your favourite Bosun again next trip, I bet eh!'

Paddy almost choked on his beer.

'I don't think so.'

I shared a final drink with James on the Wednesday evening before we lifted anchor the next morning.

James had given me great entertainment this trip with his effeminate mannerisms but underneath the charade I had managed to tap in to a very likeable old man.

Despite his liking for all things young and male he had never once tried anything odd with the likes of Myself, Geoff, Keith or Danny and I would imagine that by conducting himself in that manner he had managed to survive at sea all these years with that particular interest lurking under the surface.

It was always amusing to see Tony pucker up to him on any given night and request that James 'Give us a kiss,' and to watch James' disgusted reaction as Tony drunkenly slobbered all over him.

'Eucht. I want thrilling not killing, dear.' He would remonstrate.

These were more likely to be the memories that I would take back with me rather than the tank cleaning and the turning to for stations in the middle of the night, in sub-zero temperatures.

We set off for the UK in the early hours of Thursday morning. Thankfully, although still absolutely freezing cold outside, I wasn't required as a third man to a watch as the visibility had improved considerably out in the North Sea.

I spent Thursday evening packing and mopping my cabin out as well as completing all the formalities of picking my money up off the Chief Steward. I was paying off the ship with a staggering £265. 84p.

It was more money than I had ever seen in my life before and although it included my 28 days leave pay it would still leave me with more than enough after I had offered my Mum the 84p. for my board.

I could go down to the town and have a field day in 'Roadnights,' buy as many LP's as I wanted and drink Myself stupid in the Peacock every single day of the week if I felt like it.

And boy did I feel like it. I was fucking rich!

I tried to get some sleep as I was fully aware that we would be called early for stations but as well as the excitement knotting up in my stomach I found it very hard to drop off.

Peanut

'You've got the channels, Lar.' Bob had explained as we had one last game of crib in his cabin earlier that evening for the all time Crib Championship of the World, which the bastard won after me teaching him how to play it.

'Channels?' I questioned.

'You're excited at going home. It's called the channels when your stomach tightens up at the thought of going home.'

'Don't you get them?' I asked.

'Fuck, no. Only soft-shites like yourself get the channels.'

It was pitch black and bloody freezing as we made our way for'ad at half past midnight to get the ropes up and stand by for the tugs.

Apart from a couple of the jumpers I was wearing all the rest of my working gear, jeans, duffel coat, boiler suit and shoes were being dumped as soon as we tied up.

They would not be required for a month or so.

Tying up was no easy achievement. Despite the dock being quite well sheltered we were still being blown off the jetty by the gale force winds and the tugs had to put in an almighty thrust to help us alongside.

We made it for four in the morning. Three and a half bloody hours freezing on the fo'c'stle head for my departing act.

The next morning just seemed surreal.

Mr.Lawson was back on board right on breakfast time. He had stayed in a hotel overnight.

The bar was full of suitcases. People were unrecognisable.

Billy Griggs had a suit and tie on. I had only ever seen him in a blue boiler suit with a rag tied round his forehead by day and a pair of grubby grey trousers and an equally grubby white vest by night.

He went up to sign off in the Chief Steward's cabin at eight and by nine was gone.

The rest of the engine room staff weren't far behind. Obviously they hadn't been up half the night on stations so were able to make a quick exit (all except Danny).

'See you, Jasper.' Tony shouted through the Messroom as I had a quick ciggy after my breakfast before going up to sign off and organise my own taxi.

I got up and firmly shook his hand. Tony had also kept me amused during the trip as well as re-christening me.

Keith and Steve were with him as well as they were all travelling to Liverpool together.

I shook hands with them as well as they did a tour of the Messroom and shouted their farewells through the galley hatch to Howard and Mel, who would not be getting away until tomorrow.

I had a couple of options as to my travel arrangements.

I could catch the Newcastle to London train and keep Geoff company until Peterborough and then get a bus or taxi from Peterborough to Kettering (roughly 22 miles). Or I could take a more direct route changing somewhere stupid like Leeds and then Sheffield before joining up with the Inter City Service to St. Pancras calling at Kettering.

I didn't much fancy humping my suitcases around too much today in the wind and the rain so decided to catch the train with Geoff. A taxi to Kettering would only be about a tenner, surely. I could afford that.

Me and Geoff went up to sign off mid morning. I thanked Bill for his help earlier in the trip with my little problem and he smiled as he wished me luck and to be more careful in the future.

I was given my discharge book back, now stamped with my first appointment, signed by Captain Lord and endorsed with the official Athel line stamp.

My steering certificate was also inserted at the back of the book.

I took one last look around the four walls of my cabin that had been my home for the past four months, gave one last check that I had left nothing behind and locked the door.

I rapped Geoff's door and we lugged our heavy suitcases up the small stairs and up to the bar. The Bosun, who would not be leaving until tomorrow, was in his usual perch at the end of the bar with his mug of tea and we handed our cabin keys over to him.

He offered me his hand.

'Cheerio, Jasper my son.' He said as I thanked him for his help during the trip.

'Maybe see you again sometime?'

He turned to Geoff.

'Thank you, Geoff. Will we be seeing you again?'

Geoff didn't answer but just smiled and thanked the Bosun as I had.

I was determined to say cheerio to all of the deck crowd before I left and went back down below to make sure I saw everyone even going to great lengths to wake Paddy up.

'I'm going now, you lazy bastard. Get out here now.' I shouted through his locked cabin door.

'Fuck off.' Came a muffled response.

I banged again and heard the key turn in the lock.

'What the fuck do you want now?' He asked bleary eyed.

'Aren't you paying off today, Paddy?'

'Sure, but we don't fly over to Belfast until tomorrow, for fuck's sake. Fuck off home and leave me in peace.' He smiled.

At that point Mr. Kelly came out of his cabin next door. I had obviously roused him as well.

'What the fuck's all the racket?'

'I've come to say goodbye you pair of miserable bastards.'

'What time is it?' Mick asked.

'Half past ten.' Paddy replied. 'Pubs open in half an hour.'

With that Mick sprang to life, offered me his hand and wished me all the best.

'Don't stay too long on these poxy Chemical Tankers, now. Will you?' He advised as a parting warning.

'I'll try not to. Take care.'

I said my goodbyes to John, Brian, Albert and George. All of whom were in the last throws of packing.

Again the casualness of it all surprised me.

'Yeah, cheers mucker, all the best.' Was all that I got from George accompanied by a short handshake.

'Bye.' And a half-hearted attempt at a wave from John.

Miserable bastards. Anybody would think they didn't want to go home.

Back up in the Messroom Bob had arranged a taxi to Newcastle Central for eleven and I managed to catch Danny before he went back down to the engine room after morning smoko.

I followed him out onto the poop deck and stood in the pouring rain with him before he disappeared down the engine room hatch and out of my life forever.

'Hope you'll be OK, Dan.' I said in my best-concerned voice.

'It seems to have gone away again.' He replied. 'I'll be fine. You have a good leave and find yourself a girl.'

I laughed and patted him on his shoulder in recognition of the friendship we had forged during the trip, being careful to avoid any grease on his boilersuit.

That just left the catering staff to bid farewell to.

'Cheerio, James, you old tart.' I shouted through to the saloon pantry where James was scurrying around preparing the Saloon for lunch for the last time.

'Ocht! Come here my dear; let me give you a big kiss.'
Not bloody likely.
I offered my hand instead and he shook it, weekly.
'I was only kidding, have a good leave, Jasper.'
I smiled and ruffled his wig as I about turned. Something I had been itching to do all trip but had never dared.

'See you lads.' I shouted as I passed back through the galley at Howard, Mel and Alan still busy faithfully peeling spuds at the sink 'til the last.

'Have a good 'un, Lar!' Howard shouted back.

Mel wiped his hands on a cloth and offered me one of them.

'See you again, mate.' He said, wishing me luck. I genuinely did hope that I would see him again.

I hadn't got to know George, the new Messman, that well in the brief time he had been onboard but I tapped him on the back as I passed through the Messroom back to the bar where Bob and Geoff were waiting for me, suitcases at the ready.

'Come on Lar, the taxi will be waiting' Bob hurried me along.

The Bosun grabbed my suitcase, which weighed a tonne.

'Fuck sake, what have you got in here? A couple of fucking Butterworth machines?'

'Make him carry it himself, Boas.' Bob urged.

'Fuck off. I want to make sure he fucking goes.'

'Thanks for that, Boas. I'll miss you too.'

The Bosun dropped the case at the bottom of the gangway and with a quick wave he was back on board.

I looked up at my cabin porthole as we passed along the jetty to the gate where our taxi was parked outside.

My deadlight was down and I had forgot to take the 'Poppies Power to Victory' headline down that I had cut out of a newspaper clipping that my Mother had sent me and stuck on with sellotape.

We jumped into the taxi and twenty minutes later were pulling in at Newcastle Central Station. We had kept the taxi driver amused along the way with our reminiscing from the Happy Valley and from Rio. Bob taking great delight in announcing the consequences that I had suffered.

It was eleven thirty and Bob dashed to the ticket office to exchange his rail pass for a ticket to Liverpool, Lime Street, on the train now standing at platform four which departed in ten minutes.

Geoff and I had a bit longer to exchange our passes as our train to London departed at twelve.

We got our tickets and lugged our suitcases over the bridge to the other side opposite where Bob's train was just departing from. As it slowly moved out I heard an unmistakable scream.

'Oi, Jasper!'

I looked along the train and from two carriages forward I could see Bob's head sticking out of a door window.

'Fuck off!' He screamed at the top of his voice as all heads along our platform awaiting the London train turned towards him.

The train eased itself out of Newcastle on time and Geoff and I made our way into the buffet car just two carriages away on the announcement, five minutes later, that it was open for snacks and hot and cold beverages.

As the train picked up speed we tucked into an extortionately priced egg and cress sarnie washed down with a can of Carling Special Brew, a treat after getting fed up with Castle Beer for the past five weeks.

We returned to our seats with another can but said very little.

I was content to sit and look out of the window as a soggy Yorkshire passed me by followed by an even soggier Lincolnshire and before I had realised where we were the train was slowing down on its approach to Peterborough.

'Fuck me we're here.' I shot up out of my seat and started to manoeuvre my suitcase out of the inadequately sized left luggage compartment behind our seat.

'Cheers then Geoff, take care.'

We shook hands. I hoped he decided to return for another trip. It had been the best part of nine months since I had first met Geoff at Gravesend and saying goodbye to him now seemed to be closing the chapter on that part of my life for me.

All the torment and uncertainty that had filled me on the day I left Kettering to go to sea school had all been erased now that I had completed my first trip and I was heading back home to rest and contemplate on the events of the past four months.

'Cheers John. See you around.'

I waved the train off and struggled to the taxi rank.

'Kettering, please.' I ordered the taxi driver as he took my bag for me.

'It'll cost you, son. A good twelve quid, I'll bet.'

'Done. Just take me please.'

Done I probably was but he left the meter off and I enjoyed recounting the events of the last four months to him on the forty five minute drive back to Kettering.

We came back into Kettering along the Barton Road and I chuckled to myself as we passed the Wicksteed Park Lake and the playground, deserted but for some mad fool walking his dog in the freezing, biting wind that had followed the rain.

'Looks like you might get snow later.' The taxi driver observed as he helped me up the steps outside my house.

'I don't care.' I replied. 'All the better for going down town in a short-sleeved white shirt and showing off my bronzy.'

I sat down in the living room on a threadbare chair and struggled to light the gas fire that my Mum had upgraded to since I had departed. The house was empty, as she wouldn't be home from work until after five. It was absolutely freezing. I gazed out at the grass in our massive back garden, at least three feet high and flapping about in the icy wind. I went upstairs and into my bedroom, which was even colder than the living room. I would approach my Mother about buying a small electric fire for the room, I thought.

It was twenty past three. I was bored already.

I unlocked my suitcase and pulled out the remainder of the money I had from the ship, shoved £50 into my back pocket and caught the half past three bus down to the town. I still had just over an hour for a mad shopping binge.

First stop: Roadnight's. A three-quarter length black imitation leather coat £25. A pair of Wrangler Jeans and a white shirt (£7.50p . . . . . rip off). Then off to Timpson's for a smart pair of black shoes, £6, then into boots for the double Yes album 'Tales from Topographic Oceans' that I had wanted for ages but never been able to afford.

I rounded it all off with a box of Black Magic Chocolates for my Mum and was back home before she was.

She knew I was in as the lights were on, I had written to her from Rotterdam telling her to expect me either today or tomorrow.

I met her as she put the key in the front door and embraced her in an emotional clinch.

'Hi, Mum. I've bought you some prezzies. What's for dinner? I'm starving.'

She held me at arms length, looking me up and down, admiring my suntan and the fact that my hair was rapidly growing.

'You've put weight on.' She noticed. 'Not much, but a bit.'

'Er! I have got something to admit to though, Mother.' I began tentatively.

'Oh!'

'Yeah, er you're not going to be too pleased but I've started smoking.'

'Is that all. I'm not surprised. I would have thought you'd have started ages ago.'

I relaxed again. She was obviously that pleased to see me that I guess I could have told her anything.

'It's not as if you've caught some disease from anyone, is it?'

Oops.

I sat in the living room watching telly as Mum made me a much missed dinner of mince and potatoes and decided then that I couldn't be bothered to go back out this evening. Malc and Barry could wait for another day. Neither knew I would be home this early so I let Mum heat a copper full of water up and transfer it to the bath for me after dinner. It had been fully four months since I had wallowed in my own filth and although admitting to liking the quickness of a shower I felt much cleaner after I had let my body soak for twenty minutes in the boiling water enhanced with lavender scented Radox Bath Salts.

'You don't mind if I don't come back down do you, Mum?' I pleaded.

She gave me a smile that only a Mother can give. 'Of course not, Dear. See you in the Morning.'

I was shattered. Not forgetting that I had been up half the night in the freezing cold tying the bloody ship up in Wallsend and then all the travelling involved in the rest of the day plus the sheer shock to the system that actually being back home brings.

I had forgotten how cold my bedroom was but warmed slightly as I quickly put my pyjamas on (how strange they felt after spending the last four plus months sleeping naked) and clambered into my bed covered in the obligatory ten blankets for this time of the year.

I stuck track four, my favourite, of my newly acquired LP on and let Jon Anderson's haunting vocals and Steve Howe's exquisite guitar send me into another World.

The track finished and I heard my record player click noisily off.

I was too tired to even get up to switch it off.

Jon Anderson's words kept going through my head 'nous sommes du soleil, we love when we play.' but they were soon pushed to one side as tiredness overcame me and I drifted . . . . and drifted . . . .

'Oh, Please Mister fisherman, fisherman please.
Have you a lobster you can sell to me?
Singing Ro-tiddly-o, Shit or bust,
Never let your bollocks dangle in the dust.'

To be continued . . . .

Resources

Shipwrecked Fishermen and Mariners' Royal Benevolent Society.
1 North Pallant
Chichester
West Sussex
PO19 1TL
Shipwreckedmariners.org.uk

The Mission To Seafarers
St Michael Paternoster Royal,
College Hill
London
EC4R 2RL
Missiontoseafarers.org

Royal National Lifeboat Institution
West Quay Road
Poole
BH15 1HZ
Rnli.org.uk

The National Sea Training School/College Gravesend Association
Mr J.D. Meadowcroft (President) c/o 15, Springbrook Cottages,
Alford,
Surrey
GU6 8HT

Other websites

Merchant-navy.net
Shipsnostalgia.com
Allatsea.cx
Merchant-mariners.co.uk
Shipspotting.com
Balmaha.net
http://myweb.tiscali.co.uk/navysong/homepage.htm
http://rnli.org/findmynearest/station/Pages/Burnham-on-Sea-Lifeboat-Station.aspx
http://www.burnham-on-sea.com/barb/
http://www.sarbot.co.uk/
http://www.facebook.com/RipDylanCecil

http://patgodonline.blogspot.co.uk/
http://www.facebook.com/oldkettering
http://www.wicksteedpark.co.uk/

Printed in Great Britain
by Amazon